Anne Francis

Anne Francis

The Life and Career

LAURA WAGNER

McFarland & Company, Inc., Publishers
Jefferson, North Carolina, and London

LIBRARY OF CONGRESS CATALOGUING-IN-PUBLICATION DATA

Wagner, Laura, 1970–
Anne Francis : the life and career / Laura Wagner.
p. cm.
Includes bibliographical references and index.

ISBN 978-0-7864-6365-7
softcover : 50# alkaline paper ∞

1. Francis, Anne, 1930–2011. 2. Motion picture actors and
actresses — United States — Biography. 3. Television actors
and actresses — United States — Biography. I. Title.
PN2287.F66W36 2011 791.4302'8092 — dc23 [B] 2011021151

BRITISH LIBRARY CATALOGUING DATA ARE AVAILABLE

Front cover: Anne Francis in a publicity photo, ca. 1950s;
background © 2011 Shutterstock

Manufactured in the United States of America

*McFarland & Company, Inc., Publishers
Box 611, Jefferson, North Carolina 28640
www.mcfarlandpub.com*

To Jackie Jones,
A kindred spirit, a friend unparalleled

TABLE OF
CONTENTS

Preface and Acknowledgments   1

Introduction   3

Biography   5

Filmography   123

A. The Films   123

B. Television   156

C. *Honey West* Episode Guide   228

Bibliography   245

Index   249

PREFACE AND ACKNOWLEDGMENTS

A beautiful blonde stands in a darkened room, rifling through a suitcase. Suddenly, out of the shadows, a large, menacing man with a gun surprises her. Unfazed, the blonde keeps nonchalantly searching until — in a flash — she hurls the suitcase at him, knocking the gun from his hand. Just as swiftly, she leaps on him, landing a well-placed knee to his body and forearming his face with a bone-crunching thud. Leaving the wounded man a crumpled heap on the floor, Honey West exits the room.

I sat in stunned silence. I was but nine years old when I witnessed this on television. At this early age, tough women weren't new to me; I was a regular viewer of *Wonder Woman, The Bionic Woman, Charlie's Angels,* and *Police Woman.* This was the late 1970s, the heyday of strong women battling crime. But, here it was the summer of 1979 and I was watching a television series that premiered fourteen years before, enjoying it far more than the newer network shows. I had no idea at the time that *Honey West* paved the way for these newer shows.

It's hard to describe the impact *Honey West* (1965–66) and especially Anne Francis, with her distinctive trademark mole to the right of her bottom lip, had on me at that impressionable age.

Anne Francis. I knew the name even then. I had previously seen her in episodes of *Wonder Woman* ("Beauty on Parade," 1976) and *Charlie's Angels* ("Pom Pom Angels," 1978), her latter performance so potent it had given me nightmares. Playing a prostitute-turned-murderous religious fanatic with a scary deadpan expression and short dark wig, an unblinking Anne proved to me even then what a versatile, flexible actress she was. I had also seen her in *A Lion Is in the Streets* (1953) and *Forbidden Planet* (1956), two movies that sailed right over my head at the time. *Honey West,* however, I could relate to. There was something empowering about a karate-chopping female private eye who could duke it out with the big boys and win.

It wouldn't be until it aired on cable in the mid–1990s that I was able to watch the show in its entirety. The years had not dulled my love and enjoyment, even though I was now an adult.

Anne Francis still rocked as Honey, but now I was better able to appreciate her subtle comedy moments, her ability to make simple or potentially trite lines gems. She was totally perfect for the role — an absolutely gorgeous blonde with a down-to-earth flair for comedy, but a blonde woman who didn't look helpless. You could honestly believe that Anne, standing a formidable 5'8", could take care of herself. There was nothing weak about Anne, nothing of the damsel in distress in her. And, unlike the detached aloofness I felt from Diana Rigg's

1

Emma Peel and Stefanie Powers' April Dancer, Anne radiated a warm, identifiable likeability. It was the ideal mating of actress and character.

Now, years later, I am still a fan, and I become an even stronger one with each viewing of a TV appearance or movie. Anne Francis was more than Honey West and there was more to her than *Forbidden Planet*, her best-known movie role.

This book came about when I decided enough was enough: Anne Francis was a much more versatile actress than people realize; if they were exposed to more of her obscure work, they would see this. This is the reason this book covers not only her easily accessible motion picture credits, but also her television appearances, which are harder to find. Difficult though they may be to locate, they are hidden gems worth seeking out because they reveal one of our best actresses. This book is an attempt to enlighten casual fans, get a nod of agreement from her fellow diehard admirers, and, I hope, inspire others. Anne Francis was a damn fine actress.

*   *   *

If, as Friedrich Nietzsche said, "A good writer possesses not only his own spirit but also the spirit of his friends," then I must thank the following pals, all of whom helped me in my quest to give Anne further recognition. Some contributed material, others just gave of their love, support, and friendship; either way, I am appreciative of: Matthew R. Bradley, Gloria Fickling, John C. Fredriksen, Jeff Gordon, Bob King (my editor at the magazines *Classic Images* and *Films of the Golden Age*), Mike Hawks (at Larry Edmunds Bookshop), Frances Ingram, Gary Kent, Marvin of the Movies, the late Doug McClelland, Milton T. Moore, Jr., James Robert Parish, Carol Peterson, Charlotte Rainey, Christina Rice, Jake Vichnis, Luke Vichnis, and Archie Waugh.

I extend a special thank you to my brother, Tom, who is always there to help me when I need him. And I cannot thank my terrific mother, Frances, enough. She encouraged me to follow my dreams when I was a young movie fan.

Lisa Burks, a wiz at research, as well as a terrific writer in her own right, was a huge help with research early on. Lisa is one of my dearest friends and she never tired of listening to me rant about Anne's brilliance. Anne Francis' friend, writer Tom Weaver, was key in the creation of this manuscript, giving me advice and graciously sharing interviews.

A big "thank you" to bashful TDW, who, again, prefers to remain anonymous. He did some valuable proofreading on my manuscript and saved me from some very embarrassing errors. He also supplied me with many welcome laughs during the writing of this book. He's quite a guy, one whom I love very much.

How could I ever adequately thank Jackie Jones, this book's dedicatee? She has encouraged me, prodded me to finish this, talked movies with me, made me laugh, put up with me, and has been a dear, dear friend during some tough times. You can't ask for much more, but she always seems to go that extra mile for me. Jackie is a special lady, and I'm very proud to call her my friend. This book could not have been completed without her.

And, finally, I must thank Anne Francis herself. A strong, determined lady, a versatile actress, she found herself typecast in Hollywood and did much of her best work on television. Through personal and career setbacks, she plugged on and never let it get her down. I thank her for sharing her acting gifts and remaining true to herself. When I was a young girl, she captured my imagination and motivated me.

INTRODUCTION

"There is something new in Hollywood and 20th Century–Fox has her — a blonde Mona Lisa who never allows her strikingly beautiful face to reveal her thoughts and feelings. Her name is Anne Francis and she is a tall, self-assured youngster who in repose is a perfect prototype of the classical Leonardo da Vinci portrait."

It's apparent from this 20th Century–Fox press release how the studio saw their new contractee, Anne Francis, in 1951—how all of Hollywood saw her after the actress was plucked out of radio and television and signed to a major motion picture contract. Anne was treated, simply, as a beautiful young thing who would pose sexily for the movie cameras and crank out cheesecake photos for the studio publicity machine.

Even in the beginning, there was a glimpse of range and acting sureness that few young actresses have. She tried to combat her image, in countless interviews, telling everyone how she actually laughed at her sexy photo shoots. But, as she once said, "I can't fight my face." Although she's a gorgeous blonde with blue eyes and a distinctive mole, she was also a very down-to-earth person who always took her craft seriously. (She revealed to writer John Stanley years later that she went to a doctor about her mole. "I told him I wanted it removed. He said, 'Anne, I wouldn't touch it.' I asked why. He said, 'That mole — it's part of who you are.'")

By the late '50s, and just off another studio contract, with MGM, she had tired of the Hollywood rat race and, in a bold move, decided to transplant her talents back to television. Going from movies into TV in the '50s and '60s was considered a comedown, but Anne Francis survived and, in fact, thrived in the new medium.

Today, because of this move to TV, she is somewhat taken for granted. We live in a media world that measures a player's worth in Oscar nods and big-budget movie roles, paying tiresome tribute to the same handful of actresses such as Bette Davis and Katharine Hepburn. Dozens of equally talented actresses are forgotten in the process.

Anne Francis belongs to a select group of underrated players who solidly worked through movies and television roles for many years, never giving a bad or even mediocre performance. Even when the roles were mediocre, she never was. She did, indeed, give Oscar-worthy (*Girl of the Night, Brainstorm*) and Emmy-caliber (*Twilight Zone, Police Woman, Ben Casey, Hardcastle & McCormick*) performances, but, in fact, what she is better known for today are her cult roles in the sci-fi classic *Forbidden Planet* (1956) and the television series *Honey West* (1965–66), not to mention her exceptional good looks.

"I've been fortunate enough to be in three true cinema classics," she said about *Bad Day at Black Rock* (1955), *Blackboard Jungle* (1955) and *Forbidden Planet* (1956). "Each one is a riveting, tight piece of entertainment and I'm proud to have been involved in each of them." But although they were good exposure for a young actress, and have assured her place in cinema history today, they did not stretch her acting talents much.

Uninformed "film historians" do not help matters. One such author wrote about Anne's performance in *Forbidden Planet*, "[She is] beautiful and charming. Her range and conviction are not great, but she's adequate in the film, and unlike some actresses of her age ... she is capable of seeming quite intelligent. It was her best performance until her underrated *Honey West* TV series of several years later." Because of misinformation like this, from someone who obviously has not seen more than a small fraction of Anne's work, it is definitely time for a fresh evaluation.

BIOGRAPHY

Anne Lloyd Francis was born on September 16, 1930, in Ossining, New York, near Sing Sing prison. In fact, because the family doctor was unavailable, it was a doctor from the correctional institution who delivered Phillip and Edith Francis' only child. She remembered her early years in the New York countryside as "relatively quiet ones." Her grandmother, who lived with them, took Anne on nature walks. "Mine was a barefoot life," Anne recalled in her book *Voices from Home*, "family dog at my side, and whenever I was hungry, vegetables from Mom's carefully tended garden."

Of her father, Phillip, she remembered a quality about him that "all who met him respected. Though he was a gentle man, his physical strength was most impressive and I never knew anyone to bully him. He did not flaunt that strength. One just knew not to cross him. Two actors with whom I have worked had that same quality — they were James Cagney and Robert Ryan."

Her idyllic life changed abruptly. Seeing that six-year-old Anne was a naturally beautiful child, a friend suggested to her mother that she would make a good child model. "We went to the Robert Powers modeling agency," Anne continued in *Voices from Home*. "While we were waiting in the lobby, Mr. Powers stuck his head out of his office door, pointed to me and said, 'I'll take that one!'" The family moved to Manhattan and, noted Anne, "As simple as that, the barefoot girl became a child model. With black patent leather shoes, hair in ribboned braids, I joined the ranks of the other professional children in an adult's world of the marketplace.... The bewilderment of working in a competitive market was not easy for me, as I was an uncompetitive person."

"Earning a few dollars a week was important in those days to help put food on the table," she told author Marty Baumann in his *The Astounding B Monster Book*. "My dad lost his business as an aftermath of the Depression, which is why we moved from the country to the city. He took a job as a salesman in Macy's basement, and my working helped with the finances. Families pulled together in whatever way they could to make ends meet."

Things happened fast after that, and Anne was soon modeling in national publications. She also soon found herself involved in radio. "A friend of my folks was a radio actor and he suggested that I audition for Madge Tucker, whom he knew, for *Coast to Coast on a Bus*," Anne told *Nostalgia Digest's* Cary O'Dell in 1996. With the rest of the ensemble of child actors, she "sang, did little fun stories each week." Soon, she was appearing on such radio programs as *Let's Pretend*, *Rosemary*, *Aunt Jenny's True Life Stories*, *Ellery Queen*, *Big Town*, and, she estimated, about 3,000 other broadcasts. So many, that she was soon tagged the "Little Queen of Soap Operas." ("The 'little queen' of anything sounds so silly," she remarked later.) She also remembered to *Nostalgia Digest* a show featuring First Lady Eleanor Roosevelt. "She really loved kids. And I was one of a small group who performed on a radio show that was built around her, where she was being interviewed. I did a scene with her talking about charity programs."

This was a lot of work for a young girl to handle. "I learned by hard knocks," Anne told Marty Baumann. "If you didn't perform the way they wanted, your lines were given to another kid."

A nine-year-old Anne made her television debut on an NBC Christmas show, *Christmas Bells*, in 1939. "I was part of a group of kids of Madge Tucker's who performed," she explained to Cary O'Dell. "It was another little fairy story with princes and princesses. We sang and danced. I remember I wore a red satin off-the-shoulder dress, though I had nothing to hold it up with!"

She nabbed a small, but plum, part in the 1941 Broadway production of *Lady in the Dark*, playing a younger version of Gertrude Lawrence's Liza. It was her stage debut.

On July 1, 1941, Anne made television history when she appeared on CBS's first day of television programming, at 3:25 P.M. Produced, directed and written by Phillip Booth,

"Little Queen of Soap Operas." A portrait of Anne when she was working regularly on radio in the 1940s.

the show featured Lydia Perera as a mother reading "Jack and the Beanstalk" to her young child, ten-year-old Anne, while artist John Rupe drew pictures explaining the story. Each episode featuring a different story, the program aired each afternoon for about six months. She also took part in the station's first color tests. Anne told reporter Bill Byers in 1965, "I think we had about 100 viewers, and I earned $25 a week. We did our last program December 7, 1941. Then all TV production stopped until after the war." Adding an interesting postscript, Anne stated, "After we were done with our show, a man in a buffalo plaid shirt, with moccasins with his toes sticking out, would come over. He came on after us [on the station], singing songs. And that's how Burl Ives got his start."*

Anne attended New York's Professional Children's School, which she remembered as "strict. If you didn't keep your grades high, the child welfare board pulled you out of working." When work became just too much, particularly during her three-year stint (1944–46) as Kathy Cameron on radio's *When a Girl Marries*, she had a tutor three days a week. She recalled in *Voices from Home* not being happy, and "though I loved my parents and grandmother with whom I shared a three-room flat on the West Side, I was an only, lonely child. I really didn't understand the business and felt quite alien to all that was going on around me. Many of the children in the professional school I attended seemed to take to it like a

*On April 23, 2006, the Academy of Television Arts and Sciences inaugurated the Gold Circle Award. Anne was one of the first five inductees, alongside Merv Griffin and Jane Wyman, of this prestigious honor, which is "reserved for professionals who have spent over 50 years serving the television industry."

duck to water. I suffered stomach cramps when faced with pressure. I lived in a dream world a large part of the time. Perhaps it was my way of coping with worldly behavior, but I consider it a saving grace now that I look back."

It was with *When a Girl Marries* that Anne really began to get noticed and featured in radio magazines. Eleanor Harris, in March 1946's *Radio Mirror*, informed her readers that the "wistfully lovely" fifteen-year-old "loves cake, Van Johnson, and a boogie beat," calling her "pretty enough at fifteen to knock over a stag line without lifting an eyebrow." It is no surprise, then, that in May of '46 MGM became interested in Anne. "She signed a seven-year movie contract and is on her way to Hollywood," reported AP. "Even at 15 she looks like a movie star, with great big blue eyes and long blonde wavy hair."

Typically, once MGM had her, they didn't know what to do with her. Anne's first film was *Summer Holiday*, starring Mickey Rooney and Walter Huston, filmed from June to October 1946. Playing Elsie Rand, Arthur Miller's (Michael Kirby) girlfriend, Anne's wordless role (shot in two days) amounted to two flashes on screen — watching Richard Miller's (Rooney) graduation and later sitting in a horse-drawn buggy. She does get her first screen credit, twelfth billed, as "Ann Francis." She told a reporter in 1951, "My first motion picture was the big disappointment of my entire career. I can joke about it now, but there was a time I just couldn't discuss it. I was 15 at the time and thought of myself as an experienced actress. I was brought to Hollywood by MGM and sat around for a year waiting for the big first part. When it came, it was a walk-on in a Mickey Rooney comedy. I went back to New York vowing some day I'd beat the Hollywood jinx and I studied pictures in my spare time because I knew I'd get a second chance, or make one."

The movie credited as Anne's film debut, because it was released before *Summer Holiday* (which was held up until 1948 due to production problems), was the Esther Williams vehicle *This Time for Keeps* (1947). The AFI and IMDb both list Anne's uncredited part as "Bob-bysoxer," but there's no such role in the film, nor is Anne visible among the many women in the cast. March 1947's *Radio Mirror* claimed her bit was "a brief scene with Jimmy Durante."

"I was for one year — good Lord Almighty, I look back, hah!— at MGM," Anne laughed to Matthew R. Bradley in *Filmfax* about her first tenure at the studio. "I was just a kid then, and I was going to the MGM schoolhouse with Liz Taylor. Natalie Wood was there when I was there, and Margaret O'Brien and Janie Powell and Dean Stockwell, a whole bunch of kids." And that's mostly all she did.

Her option was then dropped. "It was an economy wave, they told me. Things really must have been tough, because my salary wasn't that high," she told Hal Humphrey in 1960.

A relieved Anne left Hollywood. "I couldn't wait to get back to New York," she added to Humphrey. She found it tough going as she tried resuming modeling work. "I was a has-been. Everybody wanted to know why I didn't make it in Hollywood. There's nothing lower in New York than a Hollywood cast-off."

She was still pursuing film work, but in New York. For David O. Selznick, Anne appeared as one of three teenagers (another is Nancy Olson) in the Sepiatone finale of *Portrait of Jennie*, a movie that had begun filming in New York in March of 1947, only to be widely released in 1949. "I was still a kid when I did *Portrait of Jennie*, very obviously," Anne told Tom Weaver in 1994. "It was just one quick scene, but I am glad that I shared the scene with Ethel Barrymore in a very minute way. She was very charming, very nice.

And I remember [director] William Dieterle wore white cotton editor's gloves — but I'm not certain why!" (The German-born director wore gloves because he had a germ phobia.) The short part did give Anne her first movie line. Looking up starry-eyed at Joseph Cotten's portrait of Jennifer Jones, Anne sighs, "I wonder if she was real."

Newspapers were reporting that Anne was testing at various studios in 1948, but nothing stuck. She did more modeling and was making the rounds looking for acting work. "One day I walked into a Broadway office to see if there was a role for me in a film that was in casting preliminaries," Anne recalled in *Voices from Home*. "As I stepped out of the elevator, I realized I had already been there a month or so before and left [some of my] pictures. I was turning to leave when Paul Henreid, the star of the film, peered around the door and beckoned me in. He and the director [Bernard Vorhaus] asked me to read a scene for them. They liked me, screen-tested me that afternoon, and I was cast in the plum role of the teenage prostitute with a baby in a movie called *So Young So Bad*. It was the first film break for Rita Moreno and Anne Jackson, as well as for me."

Billed as a film that "Reveals how girls go bad," its realism and rawness is a bit startling today. It's a movie, however, that has not been given proper credit. *The New York Times'* Bosley Crowther, who called the film a "miserably inept little item," faulted the production for lack of "intelligent understanding, devotion to authenticity and restraint."

It was Crowther, in his review, who started the now–universal criticism of this movie: that it was a rip-off of Warner Bros.' now-classic *Caged* (1950), which starred Eleanor Parker. "As a matter of fact, several incidents in this picture very closely correspond to incidents in the latter," he wrote, "such as the cutting of a sensitive inmate's hair by a sadistic guard, the former's suicide as a consequence of chagrin and a retaliatory insurrection by

Working as a model and seeking movie roles in the late '40s in New York City.

Anne in New York City, late 1940s.

the brutally enslaved and terrified girls." Of course, he thought *Caged* "was pretty awful, but this film is so much worse — so clumsily made and acted — that it is downright embarrassing to watch. It looks as though all of the performers, even Paul Henreid in the leading role — that of the kindly psychiatrist — are rank and unencourageable amateurs. And the sloppy direction of Bernard Vorhaus is so lacking in professional quality that one might think he would be requested to turn in his card by the Screen Directors Guild. With all due desire to look brightly upon the efforts of new producing groups, we can only commend the Danzigers for titling their film appropriately."

Ouch. And truly off-target.

So Young So Bad's script was written by Vorhaus and former actress Jean Rouverol, with an uncredited assist from Joseph Than, and was based on real-life incidents in an unnamed home for girls in Upstate New York. A Jewish home for the blind and the elderly in Upstate New York was the shooting location for the institution, here in the movie known as the fictional Elmview Corrections School for Girls. Even though *So Young*'s story was based on events not related to those in *Caged*, one contemporary author, Richard Barrios, calling this a "blatant clone," defended the rip-off claim by absurdly stating that "it's more

In her first featured film role, Anne played Loretta, a troubled 16-year-old busted for prostitution, in *So Young So Bad* (1950). Paul Henreid (right) starred (and co-produced) as a psychiatrist at the Elmview Corrections School for Girls who tries to help her.

likely that the *Caged* script was leaked out at some point than that their resemblance is totally coincidental."

Filming began on *So Young So Bad* (1950) in July of 1949 under the title *Runaway*, at Paramount's Astoria, Queens, studio. Henreid co-produced (under his banner Monica Productions) as well as starred. It was the second solo production of the Danziger Bros., Edward J. and Harry Lee, the first being *Jigsaw* (1949). The brothers formerly did location shooting, process shots and sound dubbing for scenes used in other producers' Hollywood productions, but they decided that there was money to be made doing their own films on the cheap in New York. Both *So Young So Bad* and *Jigsaw* were shot almost entirely on the streets of Manhattan, in apartments and in Wall Street offices, often favors from friends and relatives for a few hours of shooting. For *So Young,* they shot in and around such familiar places as Rupert's Brewery, on 92nd Street, the Carousel in Central Park and in the laundry of the Vanderbilt Hotel on Park Avenue.

"One problem we have in filming among Manhattan's natural settings," Harry Lee Danziger said in the film's pressbook, "is we have to do more cutting on real-life scenes made in the east. Too many New Yorkers are enthusiastic 'sidewalk superintendents' who like to shoulder their way into scenes. Sometimes we stage phony noisy and theatrical shooting of scenes several blocks from the actual shooting to lure away the onlooking crowds When they run to the phony 'shooting,' then we can quietly do the actual shooting on the place they have deserted."

"We really earned our scale pay," Anne remarked in *Voices from Home,* remembering the location shooting "all over New York City in the sweltering heat with few amenities. There were rough dramatic scenes that often became improvisations on the run, realistic tussles and water hosings, with a slapping scene with Catherine McLeod that left me unable to lift my head from the pillow the next day. The director was intent upon realism. One part of that 'realism' I detested. He insisted that I wear falsies, and made the wardrobe woman sew buttons on the tips so I would look sexy when the water hosing took place and drenched me from head to toe. That was my first taste of some of the indignities of the world of filmmaking."

Nowhere is the brutality more evident than in the scene where the girls are punished with the fire hose. The scene goes on far too long; it is apparent that the girls, being brutally pelted by a steady stream of water, are not being stunt doubled as they slip, slide and get caught under the water.

Considering her limited screen experience and the rough shooting conditions, Anne, as the trampish, beautiful Loretta, shows a striking range of conflicting and progressing emotions as a 16-year-old, busted for prostitution, with a baby she wants to give up and forget. "Men like me," Loretta grins to psychiatrist Dr. John H. Jason (Henreid). "Women don't," she adds dismissively to Ruth Levering (Catherine McLeod). Just "bumming around" after her short-lived marriage, she seductively tells an uncomfortable Dr. Jason that "I like a lot of guys — for a little while." The doctor sees her as "a child who's had to use sex as a defense, as a weapon, to get what she needs," while she eventually develops a crush on him. It's a complex, demanding part, requiring much from the then–18-year-old. Loretta is at turns defiant, seductive, and violent, and, in a remarkable scene revealing her feelings for Dr. Jason, she switches from optimism and tenderness to hurt bitterness. The moment where she wrestles with her own conscience, torn over putting her baby up for adoption,

Top and above: Publicity shots of Anne as the defiant and sexy teen in *So Young So Bad* (1950).

is nicely done, with just the right amount of awkwardness to make it believable. Perhaps because of her early training in radio, Anne, as she would in later roles, uses her speaking voice to good effect; raising and lowering it, often within the same line reading, to emphasize her character's shifting feelings.

After filming wrapped, she promptly embarked upon live television in New York. "Live TV was very challenging," Anne remarked to Matthew R. Bradley in *Filmfax* years later. "On top of the fact that you were doing a live show, you did not have the feel of a warm-bodied audience there participating with you as you moved through the show, so you didn't have any instinctive knowledge of how your audience was responding. You had only that little red light on the camera looking back at you, and a lens, you know, and a lot of darkness beyond the camera, so it was, I think, a more frightening experience [than stage work], because all the way through a live television show, you were dealing completely with the unknown, as far as the audience was concerned."

Anne appeared on *Studio One*, *Suspense*, *Kraft Television Theatre*, *Believe It or Not*, and *Lights Out*. She also hosted a weekly TV series called *Versatile Varieties*, doing commercials for the floor-covering company that sponsored the show. "I did the commercials for Bonny Maid Linoleum," Anne explained to *Nostalgia Digest*. "I was Bonny Maid. I wore the Scot plaid outfit and the tam and I was pursued by two evil characters named Wear and Tear and every week I outwitted them with my skid-resistant tile linoleum. We did these little skits and, at the end of the show, I and two other Bonny Maids sang." Two of the Maids were future Oscar winner Eva Marie Saint (*On the Waterfront*) and Carol Ohmart (later of *House on Haunted Hill*). Beverly Phillips was also a Maid for a spell. The gals each earned $75 a week.

In June 1950 Anne joined the cast of the Robert Siodmak–directed *The Whistle at Eaton Falls* (1951), produced by noted documentarian Louis de Rochemont, famous for his earlier work on the *March of Time* newsreels. Like his previous film, *Lost Boundaries* (1949), *The Whistle at Eaton Falls* was lensed on location in New Hampshire, this time in the Seacoast region, encompassing Portsmouth, Exeter, Dover and Rochester. It starred Lloyd Bridges, Diana Douglas, Dorothy Gish and Carleton Carpenter. Anne has a small part as Carpenter's girlfriend who models for his paintings.

Taken from a case history in the files of a Harvard professor, the story dealt with a blue-collar labor leader who is suddenly appointed president of a failing New England factory. He is forced to close the plant in order to save it, but takes a beating from the residents of the factory town who don't understand.

Bit parts were played by Seacoast residents, that and the location give the film a realism it certainly wouldn't have had in a Hollywood studio. "Historically, the film is a valuable celluloid record of life in this New Hampshire region, wedged between the Great War and the Cold War," explained historian J. Dennis Robinson. "The Cocheco Mill, where much of the filming took place, today is an office building. The factory owner's home, the once

Behind the scenes on the early television program *Versatile Varieties* (1949). Anne (left), Dorothy Phillips (standing center) and Carol Ohmart (right) surround an unidentified guest. The three played the Bonny Maids who sang the commercials for Bonny Maid Linoleum and appeared in skits.

grand Sawyer Mansion, was long ago replaced by a Howard Johnson's, which has since given way to a Burger King."

Whistle, released through Columbia, was well regarded at the time for its semi-documentary feel and conviction, but today it plays rather dryly. It's well-meaning and earnest in its look at two-faced politics, labor talks and American ideals, and the acting is stellar, but at 96 minutes, it's too long and talky. Siodmak, best suited to *noir*ish entries such as *Phantom Lady* (1944), *The Suspect* (1944), *The Spiral Staircase* (1945), *The Killers* (1946), *The Dark Mirror* (1946), and *Criss Cross* (1949), seems out of his element here and the film's pace suffers for it.

Anne sang for the first time in *The Whistle at Eaton Falls*, a duet with Carleton Carpenter, "Ev'ry Other Day," which was also composed by him. Anne's singing talent would be exploited several more times on television (*Adventures in Paradise, Hong Kong, Banjo Hackett, Barnaby Jones, Home Improvement, Jake and the Fatman, Murder, She Wrote*). It was reported in 1960 that she would sing the title song over the credits to her upcoming *Girl of the Night*, but it never happened.

Back in 1947, Anne told

Anne and Carleton Carpenter in *The Whistle at Eaton Falls* (1951).

Radio Mirror that she was interested in becoming a "fine dramatic actress." In 1950, she decided to take some steps in that direction. In *Voices from Home* she wrote,

> Anne Jackson and others with whom I had worked were going to the Actors Studio. My interest was aroused and I felt that I might be ready for the discipline that had trained so many fine performers in the theatre. I had done well in live TV [productions] of those days. I had done some summer stock [*My Sister Eileen*], but nothing on Broadway since I was a child, and theatre was considered the actor's greatest challenge.
>
> I applied for an audition with the Actors Studio at the same time [*So Young So Bad*] was released [in April of 1950]. I never got to that audition. Darryl Zanuck, who was head of 20th Century–Fox, ran the picture and offered me a contract with that studio. As strange as it may sound, I didn't want to go to Hollywood. New York and Hollywood actors were then more than the logistical miles apart in work attitude. Hollywood was frightening and alien to me.... Family and the pressures of "business heads" worked against my wishes and off I went to Beverly Hills, a victim of my own success.

It's interesting that Zanuck, initially attracted to the young actress because of her showy bad girl in *So Young So Bad*, brought her to 20th Century–Fox for a totally different type of part.

Her first — and, as it would turn out, best — role at Fox was as the lead in *Lydia Bailey* (filmed in 1951, released in '52). While the film followed much of the structure of Kenneth Roberts' sweeping, romantic 1947 novel, Michael Blankfort and Philip Dunne's screenplay freely condensed, rearranged and downright changed many of the incidents and characters. Roberts' historical novel chronicled the battle of the island of Haiti to free itself, and keep itself free, from the French who had occupied it under Napoleon. Even though much of the novel revolves around a man's obsession and search for Lydia, she is a mere supporting player in the book. The film version puts Lydia front and center. The adaptation takes liberties with the classic story, but many are for the better.

Early publicity photograph of Anne, just before she signed her 20th Century–Fox contract.

"I was completely wrong for the part in *Lydia Bailey*," Anne short-changed herself to Cork Millner in 1983. "It should have been a flashy, dark-haired actress like Linda Darnell. I was much too blonde and much too young for the character. But it was quite an experience for the first time out, and I learned what Hollywood was all about. I didn't like everything I saw and did, but that's what Hollywood and the studios wanted of me."

In actuality, Fox made the right decision when they chose the newcomer over such actresses as Micheline Prelle, Jean Simmons, Linda Darnell and Susan Hayward, all of whom were announced for the role, because Anne was perfectly suited for the Lydia Bailey of the novel and the film. At the time, the role was deemed "the plum acting assignment of the year." At the same time Anne was being tested for *Bailey*, she was also considered for the lead in *Anne of the Indies* (1951), to be directed by Jacques Tourneur. Jean Peters nabbed the part of the lady pirate instead, which was for the best because Anne was a much better fit for Kenneth Roberts' heroine.

In the novel, Lydia possessed a "quality of unquenchable youth," a gentle young lady, like Anne herself, in her early twenties, with "perpetual sunniness and good sense" and a constant store of sweetness. Truth be told, this version of Lydia is just too perfect, lacking any kind of personality other than a romantic view of a ladylike, even-tempered woman.

The title role in *Lydia Bailey* (1952) was called "the plum acting assignment of the year"; Anne beat out established actresses Micheline Prelle, Jean Simmons, Linda Darnell and Susan Hayward for it. It was her first film for Fox, but was released as her second.

The film's interpretation of the title character was much different, much more appealing, instilling the story with an inspiring sense of one's own country. The movie Lydia is bitter, living in Haiti, having renounced her loyalty to America and her inherited lands there; she is not interested in political matters, not caring one way or the other about anything. Engaged to the older D'autremont (Charles Korvin), she meets Albion Hamlin (Dale Robertson), a dashing lawyer from America sent by her father's estate. It is her growing attraction and love for Albion that ignites a spark in Lydia, slowly changing her outlook as she fights these new emotions within her.

Lydia Bailey has much to recommend it including first-rate performances by Anne and Robertson, an attractive twosome, who work exceedingly well together. Contrary to her concerns, an absolutely gorgeous Anne makes her character's transformation both believable and affecting. The silent looks she gives Robertson are filled with longing and bewilderment, as she tries to comprehend her contradictory feelings.

Anne's dissatisfaction with the movie might have had to do with the difficult nature of the shooting and her unhappiness over her new surroundings. "Dale was an easygoing country boy who seemed to take the Hollywood scene completely in his stride," Anne said in *Voices from Home*. "I was unbearably homesick and was frightened by the prospect of a seven-year stretch during which I would have no say in my career. I felt no great confidence in the 'experts.' One's physical attributes were of prime importance and once more falsies and/or padded bras were attached to my young body. I was in an emotional and physical tailspin throughout the whole film. I lost my balance and any confidence I had begun to acquire as a young adult."

Problems started immediately. She fell off a horse practicing for a scene, badly bruising her knee when the animal rolled over on her. "I used a cane when not in front of the cameras. I developed makeup poisoning from the dark pancake they put on me for the escape scenes where I masqueraded as a Haitian native. To cap it off, I developed strep throat for the remainder of the film production. Once when I asked for assistance from the director [Jean Negulesco] about the intent of my character for a scene, his answer was, 'You're an actress. Act!' Lost? Yes."

The cane she used for her injury? Publicity explained: "Anne Francis, though suffering pain, was consoled by the fact that the cane she hobbled around Hollywood with once belonged to George Washington. The General presented the cane to Anne's great-great-great-grandfather." It's doubtful Anne was consoled, simply because the cane was most likely taken from the prop room.

Perhaps piling her misfortunes on a little *too* thick, the studio described for the press

Dale Robertson puckers up for this romantic publicity pose for *Lydia Bailey* (1952), but Anne doesn't look too enthusiastic. The two have no such love scene in the movie.

two other mishaps that supposedly occurred on this set, both of which are slightly amusing and worth noting. In the commissary one day she "struck a match to light a cigarette and the burning tip flew right down the inside of my dress and burned my tummy," she told a reporter, hopefully with a straight face. Even better was when she was waiting for first-aid after falling from her horse. A cat and dog were fighting in her "immediate vicinity" as she was sitting in her canvas chair. Suddenly, the "animals carried their battle right into her lap. She got scratched as a result of that." The latter story is, unbelievably, true, and was also related by Miss Francis in her book. As she observed, "That little fracas left me looking like something from a Tom and Jerry cartoon!" Madcap doings on the set of *Lydia Bailey*.

The tribulations didn't stop there. When the film finally had its world premiere at Port-au-Prince, Haiti, on May 4, 1952, Anne, Robertson, William Marshall and some other members of the production flew there for a four-day festival, just in time to celebrate Haiti's 150th year of independence. During a four-hour horseback ride in the rain to the Citadelle, the ancient fortress of the first king of Haiti, it was reported that Anne "wrenched a shapely leg and bruised an arm ... when she careened off a horse and rolled 25 yards down a jagged Haiti mountainside. The honey-haired siren jolted to a stop when her slender body struck a tree." Dorothy Kilgallen told her readers that Anne also "took a mean kick from a donkey during a sightseeing tour." It's hard to tell which of these brutal-sounding mishaps are true and which were created for publicity. Anne claimed that most of the accidents on the *Lydia Bailey* set were real, but at least one thing, the mule story, was partly press agent Leo Pillot's handiwork. His son, Judd Pillot, recalled to the Bergen County, New Jersey, newspaper *The Record* in 1995, "Anne Francis somehow fell off the mule, and he said, 'Are you all right?' and she said, 'I'm fine, Leo, I'm fine,' and he said, 'No, you're not, you hurt your ankle.' He had rescue people come up and get her, and it turned into a big story." Coming home to the States, Anne "collapsed at LaGuardia airport ... just before takeoff time, and had to be carried onto the plane." True or not, none of it exactly sounded like she had the best screen experience.

Anne's first released Fox movie was *Elopement* (1951), made near the tail end of *Lydia Bailey*'s shooting. (The company shot around her for a few days while she completed *Bailey*.) *Elopement*, a rather dumb, naïve and pointless comedy, featured her first over-the-title billing, second to Clifton Webb, who played her father Howard. Anne is Jacqueline Osborne (nicknamed Jake), a graduate student who, on the spur of the moment after her college graduation, decides to elope with one of her professors, Matt Reagan (William Lundigan). The whole film is taken up with her and Matt in a car getting on each other's nerves, and her parents and her future in-laws bickering in another car as they (wisely) rush to stop the elopement.

Richard H. Larsh, in his review in *Pacific Stars and Stripes*, efficiently

Anne coming home to the States after the world premiere of *Lydia Bailey* at Port-au-Prince, Haiti. She had hurt her ankle when she fell off a mule on a sightseeing tour.

struck the spike on the head about this bit of drippy drivel. Pointing up the film's tediousness, the never-ending scenes set in two separate cars, Larsh wryly stated, "The great Alfred Hitchcock made movie history when he gave us *Lifeboat* [1944], in which all the action took place on one small set, the limited confines of a lifeboat adrift in the sea. Henry Koster, who directed *Elopement*, has the temerity to adopt this technique in part by placing Webb and a half dozen other lesser actors and actresses in the interior of an automobile and keeping them there for a good portion of the film. Unfortunately, Tallulah Bankhead isn't in the car and the lines given to Webb are few in number and pack no power to entertain. It's the dullest auto ride we've ever been involved in. We couldn't wait to learn if the lovers ever did get married, but we rather suspect everybody lived happily ever after." Unfortunately, they do, but adding insult to injury for the viewer, the couple never does go through with the "elopement."

This was followed by a much better comedy, written and directed by Claude Binyon, the clever and hilarious satire *Dreamboat* (1952). Anne, again playing Clifton Webb's daughter, is brainy, too-serious college student Carol Sayre, with no time for boys, who meets Bill Ainslee (Jeffrey Hunter) on a trip to New York with her father and falls in love. But it's Webb's film all the way as he gives one of his best, most underrated comedy performances as respected college professor Thornton Sayre, whose past career as swashbuckling leading

"It's ANNE FRANCIS, new, starry-eyed sensation!" touted the ads for Anne's first released Fox film, *Elopement* (1951), co-starring William Lundigan (left).

man Bruce Blair in silents is revealed when his old co-star Gloria Marlowe, played by Ginger Rogers, starts hosting and showing their films on television.

Unfortunately, Anne's character is underwritten. She is supposed to be "transformed" by her meeting with gorgeous Hunter, but we never see that develop; it just happens. Plus, the film had set up in the beginning the other college students' bitchy attitude toward too-smart, no-time-for-play Carol, but the viewer never gets the expected wrap-up: Carol going back to school, with new outlook and beau in tow, to show up her detractors. But, all in all, *Dreamboat* is one of those overlooked gems that takes you by surprise and makes you laugh out loud.

Even though she had very little screen exposure up to that point, in an October 1951 *Photoplay* magazine poll, Anne came in sixth as a "Best Bet for Stardom." The winner in the female category was Mitzi Gaynor; also coming in before Anne were Janice Rule, Pier Angeli, Monica Lewis, and Joyce Holden; Polly Bergen, Marge Champion, Barbara Rush and Susan Cabot rounded out the list. All women were given scrolls and invited to a dinner at Ciro's.

Jimmy Fidler informed his readers about the up-and-comer: "Professionals rate Anne's mezzo-soprano voice as superb. She started studying piano at six, and today she can play well enough to make a living at it as a concert artist, teacher, or variety performer. She paints 'with the ease and assurance of a master,' say her friends. She prefers watercolors, but she is equally as adept with oils. She works in ceramics, too, for relaxation — and she writes poetry and short stories, but these latter more for her own amusement."

Save for *Lydia Bailey*, 20th Century–Fox wasn't really doing Anne any favors. Her roles in *Elopement* and *Dreamboat* were typical starlet roles; they were more Clifton Webb movies than her own, giving her nothing to work with. "Starlet!" Anne growled years later to Cork Millner. "How I hated that word — starlet. It sounds like something cute and snuggly, and has the connotation of a little fluff of an actress on a producer's arm; a hollow, empty-headed image in a padded bra. But that was what I was, at least in Hollywood vernacular — a starlet. I was in the business, but I wasn't of the business.

"You see," she continued, "at the studio they only groomed stars, not actresses, and I had begun to realize there is a lot more to life than being a big star. I needed to discover the real me — the inner me."

Fox announced her for all sorts of projects (*Take Care of My Little Girl, Prince*

Anne in *Dreamboat* (1952), her second film as Clifton Webb's daughter. "The character was a female Webb," Anne told the press. "Throughout most of the picture, she was the dull girl who wore glasses and lacked glamour. The picture was fun to do, but I don't think it was good for me. I think all the producers and directors on the lot considered me as sort of a character type of actress after that, I wasn't given any [glamour] roles."

Valiant, Hawk of the Desert, King of the Khyber Rifles, Woman's World, O. Henry's Full House, Eighth and Elm, Love Me, Love Me Not), none of which materialized for her. They were not keeping her particularly busy with actual work. The most intriguing project that never saw the light of day was *The Facts of Life*, to co-star Anne and Marlene Dietrich as mother and daughter, to be produced by Frank McCarthy. She was to reunite with *Lydia Bailey*'s Dale Robertson in *My Wife's Best Friend*, to co-star Gene Tierney, but when that film was ultimately made, in 1952, it toplined Macdonald Carey and Anne Baxter. *The Bright Promise*, a film in various stages of development at the studio since 1947, was announced for Anne and Richard Widmark in 1952. The film was never made. Also in 1952, came announcements of the fascinating-sounding *Cabin B-13*. "Corinne Calvet is going to get herself good and murdered — and I don't mean by you znow zwho. It's for her new movie, *Cabin B-13*, a sea-going mystery in which Calvert plays a French girl murdered on a luxury liner," Louella Parsons reported in her column. Gary

With Jeffrey Hunter in *Dreamboat* (1952).

Merrill and William Lundigan were also to be featured in the Robert Bassler–produced chiller.

So, it wasn't as if there was a dearth of projects floating around the studio for Anne. Fox could have put her into any number of films; they just chose not to.

Instead, she went on the obligatory junkets the studio planned, did publicity stunts, cut a cake at a party for the League of Women Voters of Los Angeles, and appeared at naval hospitals in variety shows with other Fox contract players. They dubbed her in '52 "The Palomino Blonde" because, said the dubious publicity, "Anne Francis has hair like a pony's mane — and the constitution of a horse...." Clearly, someone was asleep at the publicity wheel to let that go out, especially the photos of Anne whinnying alongside a horse in photos. "The one without the mole," she quipped later to *TV Guide*, "was the horse." (Very briefly, the studio considered calling her the "Translucent Blonde." Neither nickname stuck.)

Prophetically, Hedda Hopper claimed that Anne was "getting the same type of build-up 20th gave Peggy Cummins," certainly nothing to boast about. In fact, if they were, indeed, thinking of Cummins (who, years earlier, was fired by the studio during *Forever Amber*), what they did to Anne in regard to her casting in *The Snows of Kilimanjaro* (1952) makes perfect sense.

Anne was contracted to join Gregory Peck and Susan Hayward in this major adaptation of Ernest Hemingway's short story. "It was terribly painful to go through," Anne told Tom

Weaver in 2006. "All the clothes were made by Billy Travilla, and fitted on me, of course. I had the role memorized and had worked on it for weeks. Anyway, I was called on a Friday night by Lou Schreiber, Zanuck's right-hand hatchet man, and told not to bother showing up on Monday, 'cause I was not doing the role! Cute, wasn't it? Billy Travilla had known all along. Ava [Gardner] and I had the same measurements, and she stepped into 'my clothes' on Monday. To make matters worse, the press was given the story that I had been replaced, which sounded like I wasn't doing a good job, right? And worse than that, that Ava had sent me two dozen roses as a consolation! I never met the woman, and certainly never had flowers from her!" The story that circulates nowadays about Anne's false start on this film does not do her justice at all — that director Henry King didn't think she was sexy enough for the role. How this came to be the established reason for Anne's dismissal is anyone's guess, but it is entirely wrong.

On the Fox lot with Tyrone Power. The two never made a movie together, but they came close twice. He turned down the male lead in *Lydia Bailey* and she was announced for his *King of the Khyber Rifles* (1953).

Hedda Hopper's explanation after the fact was, "The part was first written for Ava, but she went on suspension for turning down a picture at Metro. Since 20th couldn't borrow her under those conditions, Anne was announced for the role. Ava's suspension was suddenly lifted, making her eligible for work at 20th; and that studio snagged her quickly." Hopper didn't clarify, however, why it was perfectly okay to treat a young contract player this way.

Ava, in her autobiography, said she heard that *Arlene* Francis was the original choice for the role, commenting that she, Ava, fit the part better than Arlene. There was and is a huge difference between Anne Francis and Arlene Francis, an older actress known mostly for her appearances on game shows in the '50s.

After knowing each other for only a few months, Anne and Bamlet Lawrence Price, Jr., a UCLA student, wed on May 19, 1952. "He was poetically fragile, darkly handsome, had a brilliant mind and seemed exceedingly self-assured," Anne explained in *Voices from Home*. "My insecurities reached out to this 'man of the world,' and I am quite sure that he considered himself a sort of Pygmalion. I was a beautiful young actress, well-bred, but without the advantage of higher education. I know now what a 'Higher Education' is, but didn't then. I romanticized him greatly and believed his flashing black eyes held some ancient wisdom locked deep within."

"Bam," as he was nicknamed, was working toward a Ph.D. and was a graduate student in the dramatic arts. Born on June 10, 1925, in Tulare County, California, he served as a B-25 pilot during the Second World War. The son of a rancher from Northern California, he had hopes of becoming a filmmaker. "He was obsessed with his film project," admitted Anne in *Voices from Home*, "for I'm sure he felt its outcome would determine his place in the industry. He seemed to have little patience with himself. I supported us, which was an unhealthy arrangement in those days when the male/female models were so sharply defined by society and our parental upbringing. I was confident that he would make his mark once his film was completed and that the industry would see his genius, but the marriage did not survive the work." As Anne prophetically put it about their wedding day, "Our hell began, and lasted three years."

The film Bam was working on was an exposé of juvenile narcotics, *One Way Ticket*, an exploitation movie with a $14,000 budget. Price got far more publicity for his student film than he should have. Because he was married to a movie star—one who supplied $4,000 of her own monies to help finish the project—he was interviewed for newspapers that ordinarily would never have given him the time of day. "I try to show that family tensions precede the dope habit in adolescents and give them a psychological tendency toward narcotics," Price told Erskine Johnson in January of '53. "It's not a popular theory. But I don't think that happy, well-adjusted youngsters with good family relations fall prey to narcotics, even when they're peddled around the high schools. The weakness starts earlier—at home." Both of Bam's parents appeared in the film and, to save money, his and Anne's Westwood home was used in some scenes.

Amid the publicity he was getting for his movie, Bamlet supplied reporters with a lot of copy during his marriage to Anne. In July 1952, all the newspapers were bizarrely reporting that Anne and "husband Sam Price [*sic*] are the rugged type. The other day they walked 16½ miles to visit friends. During the hike they traded shoes with each other to relieve their aching arches. Both wear the same size."

And if Anne was "Hard Luck Annie" during the filming of *Lydia Bailey*, Bam would eventually take up the mantle. In February 1953, it was reported that the "husband of Anne Francis suffered a severe back injury when he crashed into a tree while skiing in the Sierra Nevada Mountains. Miss Francis, who was with him at the time of the accident, had to walk two miles to summon an ambulance."

Anne was still getting some head-scratching publicity herself. She showed up at a movie premiere with a white patch over her eye because she had injured it on an outing at Ocean Park Pier. Then Anne was made Miss California Relays 1953, presiding over the California Relays on May 16. She appeared in the Parade of Songs as well as reigning at the twelfth-annual relays. Simple, right? Read this news account, from *The Modesto Bee*:

> Then for awhile everything continued nicely. It got colder and in order to keep warm Anne would periodically go into a Charleston to chase away the chill. It was a slip-up on an impromptu 23-yard dash that led to her downfall.
>
> The movie actress tripped while running second in a sprint with her attendants and injured her right ankle. A doctor was summoned and Anne had her ankle bandaged up. Most of the eyes of the spectators (male, that is) were turned to Anne at the time.
>
> Some 15 minutes later the pretty queen limped off the field aided by two junior chamber escorts...

Sheilah Graham probably said it best in her column, "Hollywood Today": "Pretty Anne Francis broke her foot watching the relay races at Modesto. Don't ask us how."

Fox loaned her out to Cagney Productions, Inc., for a supporting role as swamp siren Flamingo McManamee in *A Lion Is in the Streets* (1953) opposite James Cagney (right).

With nothing to offer her, Fox loaned her out to Cagney Productions, Inc., for a supporting role as Flamingo McManamee in *A Lion Is in the Streets* (1953), based on Adria Locke Langley's successful 1945 novel about a peddler-turned-politician, Hank Martin, loosely based on Louisiana senator Huey Long. The film has faced unfair comparisons to the classic Oscar-winner *All the King's Men* (1949), where Broderick Crawford played a senator much like Huey Long. According to *Variety*:

> The Adria Locke Langley novel was a long time coming to the screen since first purchased by the Cagneys for filming. Along the way it lost a lot of the shocker quality and emerges as just an average drama of a man's political ambitions. James Cagney plays the swamp peddler who tries to ride into the governor's mansion by making a crusade of the plight of poor sharecroppers. The portrayal has an occasional strength, but mostly is a stylized performance done with an inconsistent southern dialect that rarely holds through a complete line of dialog. Barbara Hale is sweet and charming as the schoolteacher who marries him. The fiery Flamingo of the book has been watered down considerably and doesn't give Anne Francis much opportunity.

Instead, the film presented Anne's sexy, fiery young swamp siren ("With them long legs and that long neck, she's like a wild flamingo") in a more romantic, sympathetic light, except for the still-potent scene where, jealous of Hank's wife Verity (Barbara Hale), Flamingo

A publicity portrait of Anne from 1953.

leads her to a section of alligator-infested swamp in an attempt to kill her. "It was a fun role," Anne remembered to Matthew R. Bradley. "I do remember, though, an exhausting day when I was out in the middle of this lagoon when we were shooting. I had a pole, and I was going to try to knock Barbara Hale out of the boat and tip it, and I just remember [director] Raoul [Walsh] yelling at me over and over again, 'Pole! Pole! Pole!' and the lake that we were working in was bottomless and it was almost impossible to get any traction. I was exhausted by the end of that day. But I enjoyed working with Jimmy [Cagney]. He was a delightful man. He reminded me a lot of my father in many ways. He was a gentleman — I guess that's the best way to put it — and he had a lot of inner strength to him. Nobody would ever try to pull anything on Jimmy, and yet he was a complete gentleman at the same time. A very nice man."

There was some talk after her loan-out for *Lion* that she was going to be let out of her Fox contract. The beginning of 1953, however, saw its renewal — although it was evident Fox simply had no plans except lucrative loan-outs for her.

Mid–1954 was marked by personal problems. Husband Bam got very sick, and at first it was thought that the 29-year-old had had a heart attack. It was actually a bad case of pneumonia that affected his heart muscles and lungs. He was in the hospital for three days, and it was iffy if Price would survive. It would take him months to recover, with Anne right beside him nursing him back to health.

She was given the second lead (with John Agar) in *The Rocket Man* (1954), an ordinary, passable comedy with some sci-fi elements made for Panoramic Productions, the company run by producer Leonard Goldstein that made flat-screen pictures for Fox. (It was originally called the even-more-misleading *The Kid from Outer Space*.) The *Los Angeles Times*, way off the mark, called this assignment at the time "probably the most important part" of Anne's career. Supposedly, Goldstein had seen her in *A Lion Is in the Streets* and thought of her for

With John Agar in *The Rocket Man* (1954), an ordinary comedy (co-scripted by comedian Lenny Bruce) with some sci-fi elements. The movie's nominal leads were Spring Byington and Charles Coburn.

this role. It was a comedy spruced up with the idea that an orphan's (George Winslow) toy ray gun has real powers.

The main interest *The Rocket Man* generates today is that shock-comedian Lenny Bruce had a hand in the scripting with Jack Henley. *The Hollywood Reporter* (November 3, 1953) revealed that Bruce was assigned "to strengthen comic sequences," although the viewer would be hard pressed to find said comic sequences. Bruce gives himself more credit in his autobiography: "They were working on a picture called *The Rocket Man*, and Buddy Hackett told them, 'Lenny's very good, he's funny and he can create and everything. Why don't you let him have a crack at it?'" It was supposedly Bruce who added the ray gun plot device. "That was the whole different twist I gave the picture: the magic space gun." But nothing could save this Oscar Rudolph–directed production from being the conventional comedy that it was. When asked by Marty Baumann about Bruce, Anne remarked, "I was most fond of Lenny. He was a real pussycat, and wanted me to go out with him. I told him I would be terrified to do so, and that was that!"

She was sent out for another loanout, this time to RKO, for a supporting role in *Susan Slept Here* (1954). Dick Powell is Mark Christopher, an Oscar-winning screenwriter playing nursemaid to juvenile delinquent Susan Beaurgard Landis (Debbie Reynolds) on Christmas Eve, then becoming inspired by her as a movie subject. Anne is his glamorous, much-married, and very jealous girlfriend Isabella Alexander. The Frank Tashlin–directed comedy is filled with innuendo and many funny situations, particularly featuring Glenda Farrell, as Powell's wisecracking secretary Maude, who dislikes Anne's hot-tempered socialite character.

Why couldn't Fox give her a role like this? True, Anne's third-billed role is a supporting one, but she throws herself into it with gusto. Anne seems to be having a ball as she breaks picture frames over people's heads, dresses up as an alluring spider woman in a dream sequence, and sashays around in minks and turbans with style and verve. Coming to Mark's apartment to get a good look at Susan, her possible "competition," Isabella stalks the kid like a tigress out for the kill and, in a simple piece of business handled brilliantly by Anne, takes out her black-rimmed glasses and very carefully inspects Susan up close.

One drawback is the nuisance of Reynolds' character. Her opening scenes of rebellion and screeching are fun but they, unfortunately, give way to a cheery, well-meaning, starry-eyed kid with an early maternal instinct, and, as played by the usually okay Reynolds, it gets irritating fast. Even worse is the age difference between Powell and both Reynolds and Francis. Powell clearly looks and acts his age here, but his character is supposed to be in his mid–30s, while Reynolds and Francis at the time were 22 and 24 respectively. (We're to believe that Reynolds is 17 in the film and would ever be interested in Powell. Sorry, no.)

Opposite, above and following page: **Three behind-the-scenes shots of Anne (with sailor suit-clad Dick Powell) as a spider woman in the dream sequence in** *Susan Slept Here* **(1954), which she did as a loan-out to RKO.**

With this loanout, Anne completed her 20th Century–Fox contract. "In some ways, I'm happy to be out," she said at the time. "The freelance market is pretty good these days. Studios don't mind using outside players, but they don't like to borrow from other studios, which hold them up for a lot of money. Warners had to pay three times my usual salary to borrow me for the Cagney picture. Unfortunately, I didn't participate in the profits on the deal."

She theorized that her problem at Fox was the "role I did in *Dreamboat*. I played Clifton Webb's daughter, and the character was a female Webb. Throughout most of the picture, she was the dull girl who wore glasses and lacked glamour. The picture was fun to do, but I don't think it was good for me. I think all the producers and directors on the lot considered me as sort of a character type of actress after that, I wasn't given any roles.

"If I had to do it over again, I probably would turn down the picture. It's different for

Publicity shot of Anne on a bearskin rug.

someone who is established — like Elizabeth Taylor — to do such a role. The public is familiar with what she is like ordinarily. But I was a new personality, and people figured that was the kind of girl I was."

She admitted that "at present, the studio is booming two young girls — Marilyn Monroe and Terry Moore. They have a few young girls around 17 that they are grooming. Otherwise, they're letting everyone go. The studio isn't making enough pictures to keep a big contract list working."

Anne claimed that she went to Darryl F. Zanuck in frustration, trying to figure out the studio's lack of interest in her. "Mr. Zanuck admitted that I was a good actress. But he told me frankly that I didn't come across sexy on the screen. So the studio let me go."

There was brief talk after she left Fox that she was thinking about doing a television series with her husband Bam, but these plans never went through. Instead, freelancing, she went to Warner Brothers for the World War II epic *Battle Cry* (1955), filmed in mid–'54, directed by Raoul Walsh, and starring Tab Hunter, Aldo Ray, Van Heflin, Raymond Massey, and James Whitmore. It was another supporting part, as Rae, a young woman whom soldier Marion Hotchkiss (John Lupton) meets and falls in love with on a ferry, unaware that she is a V-girl. (During World War II, a V-girl was a slang term used to refer to a woman who had a particular fondness for the boys in uniform. They often later turned to prostitution. The "V" stood for "Victory," since the girls were helping the war effort by entertaining the boys.) In Leon Uris's novel, Anne's character is a common prostitute working in a brothel. The moment in the novel where the soldier finds out the girl's true profession is much more heartbreaking and shocking than in the film, but the Production Code demanded certain changes.

It was a small part for Anne, but she was able to convey a girl-next-door sweetness that belied her party-girl image, making the soldier's growing love for her believable. However, unlike the other women in the movie (Dorothy Malone, Mona Freeman, Nancy Olson), Anne's character is never really explained; she was more of a presence in the novel, where she shared her feelings with the soldier in letters. In the novel, too, her character is ultimately sympathetic and tragic. They exchange many letters, talking of their future together, but after the soldier's death, she disappears, never to be heard from again. The movie just brushes the character aside quickly, and, we the viewer, get no satisfactory resolution to their relationship, which just abruptly ends.

Some actresses found the gruff, rough Raoul Walsh difficult, but Anne, who worked with him on *A Lion Is in the Streets* and *Battle Cry*, had nothing but praise for the director. "I loved him, absolutely adored him," she said in a *Filmfax* interview:

> I thought he was a wonderful man. There was no pretension about this man at all. He had a patch over one eye and, as I recall, he kind of wore khaki things and jackets or sweaters sort of just starting to come apart at the elbows, and he would roll his cigarettes, like a lot of men did in those days.... Raoul would go to the back of the set, while the scene was rolling, and turn his back on the scene while we were doing it. I recall the scene I did with Johnny Lupton on the ferryboat [in *Battle Cry*], he disappeared, went to the back of the set while we were doing the scene, and then after we finished the scene, I heard him call out, "Cut!" He came back and he said, "Were you both comfortable with that?," and we said yes, and he said, "Okay, print it!" He could tell from the sound of the scene, as far as he was concerned. He could hear whether it was playing the way he wanted, and I remember talking to other actors who had had the same experience with him. He just would walk away and listen.

During the making of *Battle Cry*, Anne and Aldo Ray headed a campaign in Hollywood to raise money to build a chapel in memory of Father Maguire, who originated the famous phrase "Praise the Lord and Pass the Ammunition."

Anne would remain friends with Tab Hunter, the main star of *Battle Cry*. In January 2006, just after Tab's autobiography, *Tab Hunter Confidential: The Making of a Movie Star*, was published, Anne wrote on her website, "I have just finished reading my friend Tab Hunter's book. Many people in it I knew, and it reminds me of much of the terrors of the business that I went through as well. I admire him for his integrity in not diagramming his personal life. Tab lives here in Santa Barbara, and we run into each other at the beach now and then. He often has his adorable whippet dogs with him. They are both so sweet and loving. Tab has a lovely home just up the road from me."

A bigger, meatier part came for Anne with MGM's *Rogue Cop* (1954), starring Robert Taylor and Janet Leigh, although, again, it was supporting. Anne brings much to her role that is not in the screenplay, one reviewer praising her "incisive and tragic portrayal" of hard-drinking moll Nancy Corlane. As in William P. McGivern's original novel, Anne's character is a victim of her love to the abusive Dan Beaumonte, played with steely-eyed hardiness by George Raft. Drinking too much, she's bored and stifled by her tense relation-

Freelancing after Fox, she went to Warner Bros. for ***Battle Cry*** (1955), which was filmed in mid–1954. In this World War II epic, directed by Raoul Walsh, Anne meets soldier John Lupton (right) on a ferryboat; he falls in love not realizing she is a V-girl.

ship with the gangster, who keeps threatening to throw her "back in the gutter." In a performance that contains many good moments, two, in particular, stand out as exceptional. Drunk and disoriented, Nancy laughs at Beaumonte who has just been punched in the stomach by Det. Sgt. Christopher Kelvaney (Robert Taylor). Tipsy, she giggles at him, playfully mocking him as she pours ice all over him. In an instant, Beaumonte stares up at her, hate in his eyes. Just as quickly, Nancy sobers up, lowering her voice's register as she pleads, "I didn't mean it, honey. Honestly, sweetie, I didn't, I swear it." This incredible scene ends with Beaumonte sending his stooge Johnny Stark (Alan Hale, Jr.) to deliver her to a group of guys. "I'm gonna pay you off good. Fix you up so I don't want to touch you again," Beaumonte snarls, as she clings, pleading, screaming, to be forgiven. It's a harrowing scene that leads up to her next memorable moment — going to see Kelvaney after her gang rape. "Got a drink for a cast-off?" she weakly asks as she slowly, numbly enters Kelvaney's apartment. Eyes glazed, makeup smeared, Anne's catatonic stare, then final teary, rambling breakdown when she realizes that Kelvaney has not heard about his brother's fatal shooting, should have proven to Hollywood what a fine, nuanced actress she was.

It did nab her, in 1954, a contract with MGM, definitely a step-up from Fox, in many ways. Fox, instead of keeping her busy or finding roles that suited her talents, let her stagnate. At MGM, there was no chance of her sitting idly by, and the caliber of films she received rose. The problem with this new contract was that, despite her excellent work in *Rogue Cop*, they still saw her as just a beautiful ornament for the leading man. That Anne was able to transcend this shallow treatment is a testament to her resourcefulness as an actress.

In February of 1955, news wires were stating, "She and her husband, writer and television producer Bam Price, are considered to be one of the happiest and most ideally suited of Hollywood's younger couples. They share a small hilltop home in the Brentwood Acres where the actress assists her husband in preparation of his scripts and where they have one of the largest record collections, both classical and jazz, in the film colony." (It should be noted that Bam was not getting any work in movies or television, nor would he ever. Louella Par-

Anne's performance in *Rogue Cop* (1954) as George Raft's abused, hard-drinking moll won her an MGM contract.

sons mentioned that he was set to do a TV show called *Journal of Fear* in 1956, but that project never materialized.)

The couple announced their separation in March of '55. "This split is a genuine puzzler," wrote Erskine Johnson that month. "She played nurse to him for months during an illness that almost took his life less than a year ago." When Anne was granted a divorce in April of '55, she received the $4,000 she had loaned him for his film, plus a twin bed; it was reported that Bam got the other bed. Anne testified that Price informed her that it was "important for my character" to do without a maid, even though at the time she was working a 12-hour day at MGM six days a week. "He seemed to feel all actors had a rather easy life," she added. "He seemed to feel that actors weren't worth much."

Bamlet Price's *One Way Ticket*, renamed *One Way Ticket to Hell* (and *Teenage Devil Dolls* on DVD), would eventually have its premiere in December of 1955. *The New York Times* even reviewed it, though Bam probably wished they hadn't:

> The sensationalism implicit in the title of *One-Way Ticket to Hell* is hardly evident in this depiction of drug addiction and narcotics traffic which arrived at the Globe yesterday. A case history of a young girl's descent into enslavement to the habit, this obviously serious attempt to illustrate and warn against the disastrous effects of the evil emerges largely as an unimaginative cops-and-robbers-type melodrama. Although its intentions are undoubtedly noble this latter-day parable is crude and without force.
>
> Turned out in quasi-documentary style — there is no dialogue, the story is related in "voice-of-doom" fashion by Kurt Martell, the off-screen narrator — it affords its cast little opportunity to develop character.
>
> Bamlet L. Price Jr., the independent quadruple-threat who produced, directed, wrote and plays Cholo Martinez, one of the villains who leads the heroine astray, may be listed as an ambitious and busy man. Nothing more. Barbara Marks only occasionally rises to the emotional levels called for in the role of the disturbed lass who drifts from a broken home to an eventually broken marriage, to marijuana, sleeping pills and heroin. The other members of the cast are not effective. Neither is *One-Way Ticket to Hell*.

Price's bad luck would extend into 1956. Harrison Carroll reported in his column, "In San Francisco arranging distribution for his film, *One Way Ticket to Hell*, he suffered a perforated ulcer. They rushed him to Mt. Zion hospital where he was on the operating table for two hours. Part of his stomach had to be removed." Reportedly, Bam went into teaching in his later years. He died on August 23, 1996, in Los Angeles, California.

After the divorce, Anne entered therapy. "My visits were prompted by a number of months' trying to readjust from the divorce and realizing I was about ready to flip and I didn't know in what direction," Anne told *TV Guide* in 1965. "When I went into analysis, I didn't know whether I'd come out of it quitting the business or what. I came out of it five and a half years later knowing that I love it. It was the greatest investment I ever made."

In August 1955, MGM issued a brochure entitled *Stars of the Future*. "Fulfilling the desires of theatermen and their audiences for bright new talents," it read inside, "MGM takes pleasure in presenting some of the promising young players who appear in MGM pictures." Twelve "Stars of Tomorrow" were listed, with brief descriptions and a photo alongside: Robert Dix, John Kerr, Taina Elg, Jarma Lewis, Steve Forrest, Lillian Montevecchi, Anne, Roger Moore, Vic Morrow, Russ Tamblyn, Jeff Richards, and Don Taylor. The booklet described Anne as "appealing in blue jeans as in décolleté evening dress."

For her first film under contract to MGM she did, in fact, wear blue jeans. The assign-

A glamour shot of Anne in the MGM years.

ment was an impressive one: *Bad Day at Black Rock* (1955), co-starring with acting heavyweights Spencer Tracy and Robert Ryan. Tracy "would be very moody sometimes — the black Irish moods, you know," Anne remarked to Tom Weaver. "Then at other times, he'd be extremely accessible — he'd sit and work on a scene with you, and go over and over and *over* the lines. He was both an angel and — a stinker sometimes, depending what was going on in his own personal life with his physical problems and perhaps his personal emotional problems."

Likely because of the sensitive nature of the subject matter, Howard Breslin's short story, "Bad Time at Honda" (first published in *American Magazine* in January '47), took awhile to see celluloid life. It told a powerful story of a man, Peter Macreedy, who, arriving by train in a small town, stirs up tensions, is greeted by hostility, and uncovers the murder of an elderly Japanese-American farmer. Macreedy's mere presence in town evokes conflicting emotions in the guilty-conscienced residents.

In July 1953, Joel McCrea was announced to star, with George Sidney directing from a screenplay by Don McGuire. By November, though, these plans were called off. Soon, Dore Schary, head of production at MGM, assigned Richard Brooks to direct with Millard Kaufman hired to adapt the story. Brooks caused problems, however, because he was reportedly nervous about the racist killing storyline. Brooks had already confronted intolerance head-on with his 1945 novel *The Brick Foxhole* (made into the 1947 movie *Crossfire*), but the mid–'50s were a whole different climate, generating caution because of the Blacklist and the House on UnAmerican Activities Committee. Some saw *Bad Day at Black Rock* as an indictment of the House Committee, and, quite possibly, that scared Brooks off the project. Finally, he would be replaced by John Sturges. Spencer Tracy, in his last role under his long-term MGM contract, was persuaded to star as the renamed John J. MacReedy.

Above and following page: Anne on the Lone Pine desert filming location of *Bad Day at Black Rock* (1955) with John Ericson, who played her brother in the film, and a dog that wandered onto the set.

The true hero of *Bad Day at Black Rock* was screenwriter Millard Kaufman, who took Breslin's simple story, expanded it, and added a more pervasive tension, piling on layers to the already thought-provoking narrative. Instead of a man of quick action with an Italian-made Beretta at the ready as in the story, the screen MacReedy now has a paralyzed left arm and is a man of deliberate action, only using judo during one brief, effective moment when he is threatened.

The original story's wrap-up was anti-climactic, as Lancey Horn, who is thought to have done the actual killing, reveals it to be an accident. Here, the character of Horn is changed to the bad-to-the-bone, controlling Reno Smith (Robert Ryan), and the farmer's death was no accident.

Anne plays Liz Wirth (Liz Brooks in the short story), who runs the town's garage. In Breslin's version, she had a past relationship with Horn which was broken up as a consequence of the killing. At the conclusion, it is she who gets Horn to confess to Macreedy the town's secret, to set things back to "normal." In the movie, however, Liz is very much under Smith's control, as he romantically strings her along, ultimately getting her to lure MacReedy out in the open in an attempt to kill him in the desert. Her loyalty is repaid with her life.

As the only woman in the cast, Anne's contribution has been dismissed by most critics, then as now, as irrelevant. True, it is not a significant part, except for her final scene, but she handles her role well. She told interviewer Matthew R. Bradley that she didn't feel intimated on the set at all, being the only woman in the cast. "Gosh, no! I had a heck of a good time. I went out and practiced shooting with Lee Marvin, who kind of showed me how to shoot; you know, go out in the desert with the guys and shoot."

She related the rougher aspects of the filming to Tom Weaver in 1994. "*Bad Day at Black Rock* was hard. It was a very, *very* difficult show, because we were doing it in August in a place called Lone Pine, which is next to Death Valley, in the desert. The temperature was about a hundred degrees. And in those days, they used klieg lights to offset the sun. So, *with* those lights, we were working in 115, 120 degrees. We all lost a tremendous amount of weight; I mean, at the end of the day, who was hungry? You just dragged yourself back to the hotel. Spencer Tracy had a *very* hard time. They had to coax him more than once to please, *please* see it through, because it was terribly draining for him. For everyone! I mean, I was in my early twenties, so if it was hard for me, you can imagine how some of the others must have felt."

Even though Millard Kaufman complained years later that in scene after scene, "Anne is gussied up like some kind of prairie bimbo," how do you promote a movie with no real romantic angle or sex appeal? The MGM publicity machine put their heads together and came up with this: "Anne Francis traveled all over Texas in tight jeans to promote the movie *Bad Day at Black Rock*," reported all the newspapers.

Bad Day at Black Rock was the first of three movies Anne did with John Sturges, a director she considered one of her favorites. He was "a very kind, gentle, precise, artistic, moody man," Anne told *Filmfax*. "I was very fond of John. He was a very caring, thinking person."

Continued Anne, "[John] was a quiet and thorough man, having done his camera homework on paper long before his arrival on set. He and [editor] Ferris Webster were a fine team on *Bad Day at Black Rock*. Such wonderful visuals and dramatic cuts. John had been an editor before he was a director, so he really knew what could be done in the editing room."

Her character in *Blackboard Jungle* (1955), as schoolteacher Rick Dadier's (Glenn Ford) pregnant wife Anne, who is harassed into an early labor by a malicious student's letters and phone calls, yielded more acting benefits, although it, too, was a smallish role. Anne radiates an innate sweetness and understanding, exhibiting good chemistry with leading man Ford ("Glenn was fun and loved to tease"), making her gradual frantic anxiety most effective. "[H]e remembered her sweetness above all, the sweetness of her that he had never found in another woman, the thing he loved most about her," Evan Hunter wrote about Anne's character in the source novel.

With Glenn Ford in the classic and controversial *Blackboard Jungle* (1955). Anne's role was judged by many to be unimportant, but it served as a catalyst for the teacher's eventual decision to take back his class from unruly students.

Critics were a little hard on her; in actuality, her character is important because it is through her that the teacher finally takes a stand. "I'm just going to get up there and teach," Dadier (Ford) insists in the beginning of his tenure. "Hell, I'm not looking to be a hero." It is not when he is blatantly ignored, hassled and beaten up, but when his sweet, innocent wife's health, and the safety of their unborn baby, is threatened that the instinct to fight back is finally stirred in him. Anne's innocence is in perfect contrast to the harshness and mean-spiritedness of the students, especially Vic Morrow's surly character of Artie West. It's a key portrayal, underrated because of the sheer naturalness Anne brings to it.

Director Richard Brooks, who turned down a big assignment, *Ben-Hur* (eventually released in 1959), to do *Blackboard Jungle*, nixed the studio's offer of color because he favored the starkness of black and white. He also turned down leading men Robert Taylor and Mickey Rooney for the role of teacher Rick Dadier. Glenn Ford, a popular actor with an everyman quality to his acting and looks, assumed the role, and brought with him something the character needed: audience identification.

Brooks' *Blackboard Jungle* screenplay was based on Evan Hunter's 1953 "compassionate and poignant" novel of the same name, which had promised to reveal "a crisis in the lives of thousands of American children." It was a subject, according to Dore Schary, which scared a few people in the industry and Loew's president Nicholas M. Schenck in particular, who wanted Schary to reconsider going through with the project. "I had only one argument for Schenck," Schary wrote in his autobiography. "'Nick, you're suggesting I give up on a film that might earn us nine or ten million dollars.' Nick asked me how much it would

A publicity shot of Anne during her time at MGM

cost. I had a rough estimate of $1,200,000. He said go ahead." The film would eventually gross over eight million dollars.

Although it was a hit, and is credited with ushering in the era of rock 'n' roll with the song "Rock Around the Clock" by Bill Haley and the Comets prominent on the soundtrack, *Blackboard Jungle* met with much controversy. Several schools across the country bristled over the delinquency shown on screen. The novel had boasted to be the "first novel to dramatize one of the top social problems of our day. It is shocking and frightening and based on fact," but MGM put a disclaimer at the beginning of the film: "We, in the United States, are fortunate to have a school system that is a tribute to our communities and to our faith in American youth.

Today we are concerned with juvenile delinquency — its causes — and its effects. We are especially concerned when this delinquency boils over into our schools. The scenes and incidents depicted here are fictional. However, we believe that public awareness is a first step toward a remedy for any problem. It is in this spirit and with this faith that *Blackboard Jungle* was produced."

The New York Times questioned such a disclaimer, writing, "This seems unfirm ground from which to reach for 'public awareness' of a problem of great contemporary concern." But you couldn't blame the studio for trying to protect itself. Certain theaters were even putting their own warnings onto the film, with one theater in New Jersey stating: "To our patrons, the school and situations you have just seen are NOT to be found in this area. We should all be proud of the facilities provided OUR youth by the Public School of New Brunswick." The film was banned in Memphis and Atlanta because it was judged "immoral, obscene, licentious and will adversely affect the peace, health, morals and good order of the city."

Continued the *Times*, "For this drama of juvenile delinquency in a high school ... is no temperate or restrained report on a state of affairs that is disturbing to educators and social workers today. It is a full-throated, all-out testimonial to the lurid headlines that

During the making of *Blackboard Jungle*, Glenn Ford shows Anne (left) and visitor Katy Jurado (right) several points of interest.

appear from time to time, reporting acts of terrorism and violence by uncontrolled urban youths. It gives a blood-curdling, nightmarish picture of monstrous disorder in a public school. And it leaves one wondering wildly whether such out-of-hand horrors can be."

Be that as it may, it seemed to do nothing to spur reform. Instead, the film was charged as being "anti-schools," that the conditions shown onscreen did not exist in the nation's school system. Schary, however, referencing real-life inner-city schools such as those depicted in *Blackboard Jungle*, was able to cite news accounts supporting the film's issues. Schary wrote in his autobiography, "Senator Estes Kefauver came to Hollywood to investigate movies — he meant one movie, *Blackboard Jungle*.... He called me as his first witness. He explained that he was in Hollywood to learn whether we acted responsibly when making [this] film." After providing the Senator with information on juvenile delinquency, the production chief asked Kefauver what he found objectionable about the film. "He admitted he

had not yet seen it," Schary wrote. "I suggested that there seemed to be a lack of responsibility in his investigation."

Years later, Anne was surprised by all the uproar surrounding the picture. "I actually didn't realize it was going to turn into quite a political vehicle," she told Terry Blass in 1996. "MGM was not allowed to send *Blackboard Jungle* over to Europe for the festivals, because the government felt that they didn't want Russia to see such unrest in our country. That was the main reason. They thought Dore Schary had opened up a whole political upset by showing this, and it was undermining America by showing these kids in the schools behaving badly."

Working on the film was much easier. Anne fondly recalled the young ensemble cast, including Vic Morrow, Sidney Poitier, Jamie Farr (billed as Jameel Farah), and Paul Mazursky,

Anne looks on as Roly P. Nall, past president of Optimists International, presents Glenn Ford with their "Man of the Year" award in recognition of his activities in support of the organization's slogan, "Friend of the Boy." Nall praised Ford for his performance in *Blackboard Jungle* as "pointing up the problems of juvenile delinquency facing the modern educator."

most of whom would go on to big careers. "Sidney Poitier was just fabulous," Anne remarked to Matthew R. Bradley. "He just exuded such inner strength and integrity. He has always had that and he always will have that, He's a very beautiful human being."

Screenwriter Millard Kaufman said of his past dealings with director Richard Brooks, "He was invariably mad at somebody or something. When he wasn't, he pretended to be. A colleague once said that whenever you tried to be pleasant with Richard, you'd catch him at the wrong moment. But like an interior lineman or a head-hunting pitcher, he had at times made his rage work for him." Anne was more diplomatic when referring to her *Blackboard Jungle* director: "Richard Brooks was a soft-spoken man who could suddenly, out of nowhere, yell at a crew member. He was definitely a perfectionist, with an editor's eye. I admired that talent. However, his impatience could be most unsettling. I grew up in a family that stressed (there's a key word!) perfectionism."

During this time, Anne had a chance to broaden her acting range with the lead in *Baby Doll* (1956), directed by Elia Kazan, and based on a Tennessee Williams story about a child bride in Mississippi. "I was supposed to do that, and some things went on with Mr. Kazan. I said, 'No, thank you,' and I was not in it," Anne remarked to David D. Duncan in 1997.

Instead, MGM gave her the lead opposite Cornel Wilde in the John Sturges–directed *The Scarlet Coat* (1955), a lively swashbuckler, set during the American Revolution, with an excellent supporting cast which included George Sanders, Michael Wilding and Robert Douglas. "The American Secret Service came into being with the celebrated 'Case of Gustavus,'" read the film's written prologue. "The identity of Gustavus–Benedict Arnold has been known for generations, but the story of how he was unmasked has only been revealed in recent years. This is that story." Wilde (taking over for Stewart Granger) goes undercover to discover Benedict Arnold's whereabouts and plans. Although

Anne romances spy Cornel Wilde during the American Revolution in the lively swashbuckler *The Scarlet Coat* (1955).

her role as a "hussy" involved with Wilding but conflicted by her feelings for Wilde was vaguely written, Anne plays her limited part with an appealing coolness.

Anne was announced for the female lead opposite her *Rogue Cop* cast mate Robert Taylor in *The Power and the Prize* (1956), directed by Henry Koster, but the role she got in its place would cement her place in cinema history.

"Do you ever get sick of talking about *Forbidden Planet* [1956]?" Marty Baumann asked the actress in an interview.

"Not so far, but try me!" Anne saucily replied.

Much has been written about Anne's role of Altaira Morbius, naïve daughter of Dr. Edward Morbius (Walter Pidgeon). When her name comes up anywhere, it is usually connected to this sci-fi classic. It isn't, by any stretch of the imagination, her best role or performance, but there *is* something magical about it. Anne's innocence illuminates in such a subtle, yet sexy, way that it still resonates with audiences. The character, she told Tom Weaver, required "no great preparation on my part; I wasn't that worldly-wise at that point myself."

Forbidden Planet is recognized as the *crème de la crème* of science fiction films, a classy beacon in a sea of cheap space travel and monster movies of the '50s. Its eminence does not make it more entertaining than other films of its ilk, but its literate script by Cyril Hume,

Michael Wilding, Anne and Cornel Wilde share a laugh on the set of *The Scarlet Coat* (1955).

the sleek, impressive MGM production values, the animation by Walt Disney Studios, and the dignified playing by Walter Pidgeon elevate it above all others.

The script has uncredited origins in William Shakespeare's *The Tempest*, but with several obvious modifications. The father's repressed incestuous feelings for his daughter manifest themselves into a deadly Id monster that threatens those around them, particularly the man she falls in love with. This was pretty heady stuff for a sci-fi movie in the 1950s. "I think that when I did the film, I *was* aware of its metaphysical implications," Anne remarked to Tom Weaver in 1994. "At that time, we did *not* have what is called today New Age thinking, which is very involved with metaphysical thinking. So for me, when I was doing *Forbidden Planet*, it seemed quite obvious that the Id was similar to what one in metaphysics would call the mass subconscious, and that what we put into this mass subconscious in our thinking comes back. Much as, in the Bible, it says, 'That which I have feared the most has come upon me.' So at that time it didn't seem dumb to me that the collective thinking is creating monsters — like nuclear bombs and everything else. The story made sense enough to me at the time."

The father's feelings, however, were not shown until the conclusion, and not blatantly. "His jealousy was hidden until the very end, when he was enraged, when the monster was approaching and taking over completely, but I don't think we were doing a modern day-type drama about the father-daughter emotional syndrome thing," Anne explained to *Film-fax*. "That's not what any of us were playing at the time, until they got down to the final deal of his being jealous, but he never played with sexual intent with me on the screen. So I didn't have any feeling about it when I was playing the role, other than he was my beloved father, in whom I trusted, and who certainly was a kind and gentle man who seemed to love and care for his daughter and want only the best for her, which of course is shown in the last scene as well. He's so protective of her and worried about her and fearful of what was going to happen to her, so that on the surface he was not aware of all of the anger and frustration and jealousy that was going on inside."

Anne was portraying a naïve character, one who had never seen a man before other than her father, so when the men from the rescue party on United Planets Cruiser *C-57-D*, commanded by J.J. Adams (Leslie Nielsen), arrive on the fourth planet of the red star Altair, the young girl is, of course, curious. The men, especially Lt. Farman (Jack Kelly) and

Anne as Altaira Morbius, the beautiful, naïve daughter of Dr. Edward Morbius (Walter Pidgeon), in *Forbidden Planet* (1956). Although it was not her best role or performance, the sci-fi classic remains the movie Anne is most identified with.

Adams, are attracted to the shapely blonde who has no inhibitions of any kind (she swims in the nude, runs around with a tiger and a deer), simply because she doesn't know any better. The character could have been played with an irritating, wide-eyed, cloying obviousness by another actress, but Anne plays it straight, soft-spoken, with a gentle serenity that makes Altaira appealing and genuine. This ethereal quality makes the character work.

"It was not an in-depth study of character going on," she confessed to Weaver, again not realizing the valuable quality she gave the character. "I was the ingénue. It was pretty well defined, who each of us was. It was a science fiction fairy tale and I was the sleeping princess, no more, no less. I was awakened by the prince who landed in his flying saucer. I don't think anything more could be made of it; that's what the story was and there really wasn't much else to do. Yes, it's condescending, but that's what the story was."

Contrasting with this wholesome manner is the way Altaira *looks*. At first, the censors had a fit with the costuming that Helen Rose supplied, and so a whole new wardrobe was ordered. "There were some costumes that they decided were too revealing," Anne continued

Forbidden Planet (1956) is recognized as the *crème de la crème* of science fiction films largely because of Cyril Hume's literate script, MGM's sleek, impressive production values, the animation by Walt Disney Studios, and the fine cast. Here the men from the rescue party on United Planets Cruiser C-57-D, including (on left) Commander J.J. Adams (Leslie Nielsen), Lt. "Doc" Ostrow (Warren Stevens), and (far right) Lt. Jerry Farman (Jack Kelly), arrive on the fourth planet of the red star Altair, and meet Dr. Edward Morbius (Walter Pidgeon, center) and his daughter Altaira.

to Weaver. "One was a silver lamé jumpsuit with silver boots — just absolutely gorgeous. It is rumored that Dore Schary's wife Miriam nixed it, saying that it was just too sexy, too extreme. It covered me from head to toe, along with the silver boots that matched this lamé suit. Kind of shows how far we've come since then!"

Above and following page: Two wardrobe test shots of Anne from *Forbidden Planet.*

Again, Anne was the only woman in the cast, but, she told Weaver, she had absolutely no trouble on the set:

Walter Pidgeon loved to recite dirty limericks. He was a wonderful gentleman in every way, except for his proclivity for dirty limericks, which *were* really very, very funny — they were sort of "the thing" back then, and none of the gentlemen on the show could match 'em. Walter and also George Sanders, who was on another film that I did [*The Scarlet Coat*], both loved dirty limericks. And Leslie Nielsen I was madly in love with. Les was a very gentle, kind, terrific guy, just as he is today. He had a great sense of humor; today it has become more extreme than it was when I

worked with him in those days [*laughs*]! But Les, much like Burt Reynolds — they both have a wonderful basic outlook on life and they don't take themselves terribly seriously. Or, if they *do*, it's not noticeable on the outside.

Through the years the movie gained in prestige and cult status. Richard O'Brien in the 1973 British stage play *The Rocky Horror Show* (later adapted by him for the movie, *The Rocky Horror Picture Show*, in 1975) referred to *Forbidden Planet* and Anne in his song "Science Fiction/Double Feature." Anne's reaction to this song reference is typically wry and unassuming. "Yes, I've heard it. I don't think it's momentous, but I think it's fun."

When Weaver asked her if she thought while filming it that *Forbidden Planet* would become such an enduring classic, Anne replied candidly, "At the time, I don't think that any of us really were aware of the fact that it was going to turn into a long-time cult film, *much*, much stronger today than it was then…. *Forbidden Planet* just had a life of its own, something that none of us was aware was going to happen."

Near the time of *Forbidden Planet's* premiere, MGM "gave a grand luncheon on one of their huge soundstages for MGM affiliates from all over the world who were visiting and being entertained by the 'Big Wigs,'" Anne remembered in her March 2000 website newsletter. "All of the contract players were summoned to make an appearance at this festive occasion." She continued,

> As I walked through the door onto the soundstage, I noticed far off in the left corner behind a curtain, there was an interesting activity taking place. Cameramen were busy clicking away as the affiliates were having their picture taken with the new young Leo the Lion. Leo was the logo for MGM studios. Their films would open with the magnificent Leo roaring, and then the title of the movie

Leslie Nielsen and Anne take a break on the set of *Forbidden Planet*. "Les was a very gentle, kind, terrific guy, just as he is today," Anne told author Tom Weaver in 1994.

would appear. Leo was known worldwide. The older Leo was being retired, and this youngster was making his debut at the luncheon. Quite a public relations coup. I decided I wanted to have my picture taken with him as well! I love cats. Actually, I love most animals that I can think of.

So I started over toward the corner of the stage, and as I progressed, Dore Schary happened by, and I guess he saw the gleam in my eye. He said, "Don't you dare!" I smiled, and as he disappeared in the crowd, I proceeded on my course. You see, I was young, like Leo! The photographers greeted me happily; eager to get a shot of an actress. Leo was just gorgeous up close, and I couldn't wait for my turn to be next to such a fabulous creature. He was wonderful with all the men who individually stood next to him for a picture they would proudly take home. The trainer beamed from the sidelines.

Finally, it was my turn, and I eagerly sat on the stool, introduced myself to Leo, and the cameras started to click. But strangely something happened to Leo's demeanor. He began to make little odd guttural sounds, similar to those heard at the zoo when the big cats know it's near dinner time! Quite suddenly, I was enveloped by the hot pungent smell of large cat's breath, and for some reason Leo's teeth were resting on either side of my head along my temples! I sat stone still! The cameramen stood stone still! A couple of weeks before this I had done a layout with two Bengal tigers. During that shoot, I had turned my back, and one of the cats lunged for me. The trainer interceded and then gave me a lecture. He told me never to turn my back on a large cat, and if I were ever in a situation where a cat grabbed me with his mouth or his claws, to stay perfectly still. He explained that big cats were just like domestic cats.

If you pull away, they dig in deeper. Glad he told me! Here was the test. I could hear Leo's trainer, as if in an echo chamber, in a sort of a sing-song voice crooning, "Nice boy, nice boy ... let go, let go." Leo was taking his own sweet time. I think he was trying to get the point across that he was tired of this photo sitting (or in his case, standing). He had center stage. He licked the top of my head with his rough tongue. He dawdled and grunted. Then very slowly he opened his mouth and moved his head toward my right ear, caressing my hair with his tongue and flipping it this way and that! He continued his strange sounds as his breath still invaded my nostrils. Continuing the ritual of grooming my hair, he finally reached my ear and his sandpaper tongue lapped at it. It tickled! One of the photographers couldn't resist grabbing a shot at that point. Lucky for all of us that the flash didn't upset

Leo the Lion gets up-close and personal with Anne at an MGM luncheon in 1956.

Leo! He lingered at my ear for a torturous moment, as the trainer continued to intone, "Nice boy ... nice boy." Finally, he retreated! The breath and vocalizing were gone at last, and the trainer decided, quite wisely I thought, that the photo session was over for that day!

I was amazed when I saw the picture of us later to see that I was laughing. Probably just as well, because they say that an animal can sense fear. I guess I just didn't have time for fear.

Some months later the picture was used for an ad in *Variety* magazine. A full page of Leo and me that said, "Leo tells Anne Francis about the new pictures to come at MGM." Sure! Dore Schary never said a word to me about my disobedience. I really appreciated that.

* * *

The exception to the typical parts she was getting at MGM was *The Rack* (1956), based on a Rod Serling television script. Anne's underrated performance as Paul Newman's widowed sister-in-law Aggie Hall is fascinating to watch. (A critic from the *Globe-Times* sniped, "Anne Francis is unnecessary to the plot.") She brings a quiet, simmering intensity to her sad-eyed character, erupting only a few times in anger, frustration or tears, before hastily putting up a brave, calm front for Capt. Edward W. Hall Jr. (Newman), a former American POW during the Korean War up on court-martial charges for collaborating with the enemy. Remarkable is the scene where, ostensibly trying to cure a drunken Hall's hiccups, she yells at him, motivating in him the will to fight. Aggie's strength is underscored by her own sadness for her late husband who was killed in the war. This was not the work of an empty-headed starlet — not by a long shot — but of a seasoned, effective and powerful actress.

About Newman, here in only his third film, Anne told *Filmfax*, "I thought he was terrific.... I remember saying to him, 'You know, I'm really not too thrilled because I know that they wanted Pier Angeli for this part,' which was true. I was told by the director [Arnold Laven], 'Can you act like Pier Angeli? That's really who we wanted.' Lovely. So I happened to mention that to Paul this one day, because I really was very uncomfortable with the whole situation, to be working on something that I felt nobody

Anne during the MGM years.

wanted me on, and Paul said, 'Well, don't feel too badly. They wanted Brando for my part!' So we both were working under circumstances that were a little pressed...."

From this intelligent performance, Anne was given her most frivolous assignment, co-starring with Tom Ewell in *The Great American Pastime* (1956). It was a typical wife role, nothing truly special because it was basically Ewell's movie, which was evident by the movie's working title, *Father's Little Leaguer*. Anne's real-life poodle, Walter Smidgeon, made his debut in this movie, and would be seen a lot with Anne in the coming years in publicity shots. Smidge, as he was nicknamed, had a few acting roles, including on TV's *The Thin Man* in '57 and a later appearance with Anne on *The Alfred Hitchcock Hour*.

Since her divorce from Bamlet Price, Anne had dated actors Liam Sullivan, Brad Dexter, jet pilot Lieutenant Jimmy Loew, and Bill Holmes, champion judo expert from the Los Angeles sheriff's office. But now it was Herman Hoffman, her *Great American Pastime* director, who began squiring her around town. The 47-year-old writer-director had been the associate producer on *Bad Day at Black Rock*. There were talks of another project together, *The Mystery of Misty Creek*, to co-star Robert Taylor, but plans fell through.

"Looks like blonde Anne Francis is trying to take over Barbara Stanwyck's territory," reported Louella

Top: Anne's underrated performance as Paul Newman's widowed sister-in-law Aggie Hall in *The Rack* (1956) is one of her best of the MGM years. *Right:* Anne played the subordinate role of Tom Ewell's wife in *The Great American Pastime* (1956).

Parsons in late May '57. "In *Hired Gun* agile Annie plays a typical Stanwyck role, being a Texas girl about to be hanged who escapes over the border into Mexico, only be tracked down by Rory Calhoun, a fate most girls wouldn't mind a bit."

Not exactly Stanwyck territory. Anne is framed for the murder of her husband and about to be hanged. When she escapes, it's up to Calhoun to bring her back, or prove her innocent. It was a good, action-packed Western, with great stunts and an initially combative relationship between the two leads to make it interesting. But it was hardly the type of role an actress of her caliber should have been playing. Nor was her last for MGM, *Don't Go Near the Water* (1957), a supporting part, attractive to look at and be vied over by hunky Jeff Richards and Earl Holliman, but nothing more.

But getting real acting roles in Hollywood was becoming a harder prospect for her. She had asked MGM to test her for Paddy Chayefsky's *The Catered Affair* (1956), but when the movie went before the cameras, Debbie Reynolds had the part she wanted. A glamour girl was supposed to know her place and act according to the then-set rules of Tinseltown. Columnist Patsy Dinan reported that Anne was declining to follow the path of the typical glamour girl. "Anne has indicated her distaste for the glamour business by (1) refusing to pose for cheesecake, (2) refusing to tour the nightclub circuit, and (3) refusing to discuss whether she wears undergarments," Dinan noted.

"I'm not the Marilyn Monroe type at all," Anne confessed to Vernon Scott in 1956. "I just can't loll around in bathing suits with my mouth hanging open and my eyes half-closed. Every time they ask me to get a sexy look on my face when I'm posing in the picture gallery I break up. To me that idiotic look is funny, not sexy." She added, "I'm trying to establish myself as an actress. Once a girl gets set as a cheesecake queen, it's hard for her to do anything else. Besides, I don't want to put my body on exhibition. I wouldn't want people staring at my legs any more than I'd want them hanging around my apartment. It's this way; I don't want to be categorized as someone who isn't me."

November of '56 brought a serious health scare to the young actress. A few sources say she was hospitalized for a kidney infection. Another, in December, said she was recovering from an operation for adhesions, the result of a recent

In her dressing room at MGM, Anne studies a script alongside her poodle, Walter Smidgeon.

appendectomy, and was finally able to come home for the holidays. All agreed that she was on bed rest until the beginning of 1957. Luckily, she already had a few films in the can to be shown.

Anne left MGM in 1957, confessing that she was unhappy at the studio after awhile, feeling "swamped and controlled." She revealed to Hal Humphrey in 1960, "I know it

Anne is wanted for the murder of her husband and Rory Calhoun is hired to bring her back for hanging in *Hired Gun* **(1957).**

sounds silly, but I never could convince [MGM] that I was important. When I was filming *Don't Go Near the Water*, they gave me the crummiest dressing room you ever saw. But when Eva Gabor came in, she was given a very posh dressing room. She wasn't under contract, but I was, you see.

"I couldn't bring my dog on the lot, and do you know they still remember I have a dog? *Twilight Zone* is shot at MGM, and when they heard I was coming out to do it the other day, somebody said, 'Don't let her bring her dog.' Imagine that! It's funny, really."

Anne elaborated about MGM to Tom Weaver in 1994:

Anne relaxes on location near Lone Pine during the filming of *Hired Gun.*

A lot of wonderful people, a lot of great crew people — but there was always the unfathomable hierarchy. I was never a very political individual; I was not able to play a lot of the games that were played in those days. I guess I was sort of a maverick in many ways. I had come out from New York, where the attitude was far more stressed as far as being an actor, and looks were not really as important. Then I came out here where we were admonished to not be seen with curlers in our hair at the local market, to be made up at all times. Jeans and tennis shoes and old shirts were not acceptable at the lot. So in many ways, it was kind of hard. Also, one would be taken to task for one's friends. I remember one day I was seen talking to a black actor at a restaurant quite close to the studio — it was a purely innocent meeting with other friends, but I was seen talking with him earnestly about a subject. And I was on the carpet the next day — I was not to be seen talking to any black actors, thank you very much. (Which I did not pay heed to.) So in many ways I didn't really fit what was expected, what the mold was supposed to be.

Record producer-arranger Buddy Bregman came into her life in August of 1957. He seems to be the one who planted in Anne's head the idea of trying singing, and not just on camera. That August she entered into an agreement with Safari Records for them to produce and release an LP of her singing 16 jazz standards. It isn't clear how many of the songs she did record, but the company ultimately did not follow through, did not supply her with the promised $800 advance for the recordings and did not release the album. In 1959, Anne received a $10,800 judgment against Safari for breach of contract. She brought one of her recordings, "People Cry at Stations," and played it for Superior Judge John Gee Clark in the courtroom. After listening to it, the judge supposedly quipped, "Was it a hit or a miss?" To that Anne retorted, "This sounds like the Peter Potter show," a reference to the then-popular TV show *Juke Box Jury*. Because of the failure to produce the records and due to the fact that she was kept under contract, her income dropped from $40,000 in 1957 to $17,000 in '58, she told the court. Under the ruling, Anne was released from the contract.

Eva Gabor (left), Anne, and Gia Scala flank Glenn Ford in this publicity photograph for ***Don't Go Near the Water*** (1957). It would be Anne's last film under contract to MGM.

In a risky move, Anne turned back to television after she left MGM. "I had grown up working in television and I had reached the end of my rope as a contract player at Metro-Goldwyn-Mayer," she told David D. Duncan. "They were always looking for a new face, so I thought, forget it, I want to go back and do television. In those days, that was the death knell for an actor. You worked television, you didn't do film. Of course, they cross over all the time today." She conceded to Matthew R. Bradley that "in some cases I guess it did do some harm" going into TV, but "it kept me working, and I enjoyed doing *The Twilight Zone* and a number of other television shows that I would not have had a chance to do if I'd been under contract, so I was glad to keep working in television.... They were exciting days, and challenging work, and I enjoyed that."

Syndicated columnist Mike Connolly reported in May of '58 that Terry Moore, Piper Laurie and Anne were are all "vying for the starring role in Speed Lamkin's new play, *Comes a Day*. Star spot in same is based on Speed's own myriad-career'd sister, Marguerite Lamkin, ex-wife of Harry Brown, who wrote 'The Sound of Hunting,' who is now teaching Liz Taylor how to Southern-drawl her dialogue in *Cat on a Hot Tin Roof* by Marguerite's very good friend, Tennessee Williams." Anne, Dana Wynter, and Alexander Scourby volunteered their time in 1959 to reading books at the Recording for the Blind, Inc., headquarters in the Fremont branch of the Los Angeles Public Library.

Since Anne was not under contract to a studio in the late '50s, there wasn't anyone to protect her in regard to publicity, checking on what she was handing out to the press. Under a studio contract, press agents strictly monitored what their stars said, being sure to spin positive at all times. Anne didn't have that looking-out-for-her luxury in late 1959 when she gave a rather odd interview to Vernon Scott. Scott was a syndicated columnist who obviously liked Anne and interviewed her numerous times through the years. He would always cast her in a good light, but there was little he could do with some of the material she gave him about her "lonely private life": "Living alone as I do can be a pretty lonesome existence. But there's nothing so terrible as being lonely when you are married. The public doesn't realize performers are no different from anyone else. Despite what appears to be success from the outside, we can be alone, confused and hurt as the next person."

Scott noted, "There's little glamour in Anne's life. She lives by herself in a West-

"I'm not the Marilyn Monroe type at all," Anne confessed to Vernon Scott. "I just can't loll around in bathing suits with my mouth hanging open and my eyes half-closed. Every time they ask me to get a sexy look on my face when I'm posing in the picture gallery, I break up. To me that idiotic look is funny, not sexy." She was trying to establish herself as an actress, and the TV roles she accepted in the '60s went a long way proving that.

wood duplex with a poodle named Smidgeon. When not working in movies or TV, which is about six months a year, Anne paints furniture, plays at golf and reads."

Speaking of her social life, Anne remarked, "I have dates three or four nights a week. Otherwise I stay home alone and try to write TV scripts. Sometimes I cook real wild dinners all for myself to keep from being depressed about being alone. Once in awhile I invite a date over for dinner, but I don't go out with anyone in particular."

Especially downbeat was the part where she lamented that if she did marry again, she didn't want to have children and then not have time for them because of her work. Although, she admitted, "I'm not fooling myself about quitting acting either." (Anne did eventually have problems when she had children.)

Adding to the overall pathos of the interview, Anne ended on a very sad note: "Actors aren't as important as they or the public think. You can quit right now and nobody would care. There are dozens of others waiting to take your place. In this town there are lots of pretty, talented girls. No matter what, I'm going to stick to my writing. Maybe it will be the answer for me."

Luckily, happier times were ahead.

For a time, it was thought that she would co-star in MGM's *The Subterraneans* (1960) when that project was in pre-production in 1959. Janice Rule was first considered, but when she was unable to do the assignment, Anne stepped in. Soon, however, Rule's schedule was cleared, and Anne was out.

Anne's television roles afforded her the chance to play different kinds of roles. Hal Humphrey said in mid–1960,

> You think Stella Dallas had trouble? Let me introduce you to Anne Francis whose TV and movie roles make Stella (or Helen Trent) look like playgirls in an old Mack Sennett comedy. The tall, attractive Anne has in recent weeks on TV been a psychoneurotic, spy, gun moll, beatnik and woman of easy virtue. Next Friday night (June 10) on CBS, Rod (*Twilight Zone*) Serling turns her into a mixed-up wooden mannequin in a department store. Nine days later (19) Alfie Hitchcock has Anne portraying a charming but evil murderess. Now usually this is the type of actress who will sit you down, blink her wide blue eyes at you and say, "Oh, how I'd love to be just Jane, the girl next door." Not our Annie! She goes for these unnoodled roles. "They're fun," she says. "I get a real workout as an actress. Even more important, it's a form of therapy. I get to study and probe these characters, and I learn from them, too."

Anne reappeared on the big screen in an emotionally charged role in *The Crowded Sky* (1960), an early disaster film about a commercial plane and a jet colliding in mid-air. In Hank Searls' novel of the same name, Anne's character of Kitty Foster barely existed, so screenwriter Charles Schnee, who had overcomplicated Searls' story to begin with (too many subplots, flashbacks and voiceovers), had to come up with a whole new backstory for the stewardess. And what he came up with was a doozy. "I'm an ex-tramp," she tells pilot-struggling artist Mike Rule (John Kerr) with a straight face, "and I know myself. One kiss and I blast off. Past the point of no return. So I just make it a point never to take that first kiss." It's a movie filled with people with serious emotional issues: Mike has some unresolved father problems and a combative relationship with fellow pilot Dick Barnett (Dana Andrews), and Anne, aside from her ex-tramp status, carries the memory of having an illegitimate baby taken away from her years before. Anne and Kerr, a nice, engaging couple, are dramatically sound, considering the material they had to work with. In a few scenes,

In the soapy *The Crowded Sky* (1960), Anne played "ex-tramp" Kitty Foster, a stewardess in love with pilot Mike Rule (John Kerr).

Anne, in particular, manages to lighten some of the heavy soap, getting off some wry lines.

Anne married Beverly Hills dentist Dr. Robert Abeloff ("a gentle soul") on January 31, 1960, in Las Vegas; it was the second marriage for both. Newspapers described their nuptials as a "sudden decision," although the two had been dating on-and-off since 1958. "To all outward appearances our alliance seemed a most fortuitous one," Anne noted in *Voices from Home.* "I was panicked at the thought of marriage, but we took the plunge, and soon after knew it was a mistake. He was on rocky emotional ground, as was I. That, along with financial disagreements, and the crazy male/female roles that the world assigned to us at birth were insurmountable. However, we bumped along for a psychologically bone-crushing three years."

It's interesting to note something Anne told Vernon Scott in November of 1958 when she had just started dating Abeloff:

> The social system in Hollywood keeps a girl from meeting men she'd like to know better — or go out with on dates. The only people an actress meets at parties are show business people. It's restricting and pretty darned dull. Even when you do meet a man outside the tight little circle and want to talk about his activities and interests, you end up talking about movies or Hollywood gossip. It spoils everything.
>
> The "outsider" rarely asks me for a date. Usually it's because he's overwhelmed by the magnified importance of the fact I'm an actress. It is terribly difficult to overcome that obstacle.
>
> Sometimes I'm embarrassed about being a performer. It sets a girl apart and makes you wonder what man would want to put up with an actress in the first place, especially an intelligent man who has deeper interests than the world of show business.

"Outsider" Robert Abeloff was not someone who felt comfortable in Anne's show business world, and he let her know it. Anne would say later that he would question her for hours at night about what went on during her workday. The atmosphere was unhealthy and they separated on August 24 of that same year. She filed for divorce in November; they reconciled soon after.

"An Exciting Step Forward into a New Realm of Adult Motion Pictures!" was how *Girl*

Various hair tests for Anne's character Kitty Foster in *The Crowded Sky*.

of the Night was advertised in 1960. Suggested by Dr. Harold Greenwald's "social and psychoanalytic study" *The Call Girl* (1958), it seemed an unlikely candidate for a screen adaptation, especially in the Code-run times of the early '60s. In his study, Greenwald analyzed 26 real-life call girls, learning of their childhoods, of their work, and piecing together the circumstances that made them "girls of the night." One of Greenwald's case studies, named "Sandra," is the sole, reworked inspiration for the movie.

This little-seen low-budget movie was underappreciated at the time, as it is today, but it contains Anne Francis' best film performance. Anne plays the New Jersey–born Robin "Bobbie" Williams, a young woman molested as a child, feeling worthless, told that "sex is an evil and dirty thing," and manipulated by her boyfriend Larry Taylor (John Kerr), who is also her pimp. After being beaten by a customer with a cane — a dark, brutal, but implied scene — she is open to the advice of psychologist Dr. Mitchell (Lloyd Nolan). He attempts to "make her stand on her own two feet," to understand that the suppressed memories and problems of her childhood need to be fought for her to be a productive member of society. The first step: To loosen the vise-like emotional grip Taylor has on her.

Anne gives a virtuoso, gutsy performance as a girl "beautiful enough to be a model, chic enough to be a debutante, desirable enough to be a wife — and special enough to be none of these. She has no legal occupation. But she lives on Park Avenue and drips mink." Anne is at her best in the therapy scenes with Nolan, exposing every nerve, experiencing every emotion of her character's life, as feelings, long held dormant, rise to the surface. She

"An Exciting Step Forward into a New Realm of Adult Motion Pictures!" proclaimed the ads for *Girl of the Night* (1960). Anne had the then-daring role of a call girl going under analysis to get out from under the grip of her rough profession and the control of her boyfriend-pimp, played by John Kerr (seated). The film contained Anne's best film performance and was her favorite movie.

wavers between truly wanting help, to anger, to feeling it's all a waste of time. In these scenes, Anne uses her radio-trained speaking voice brilliantly, deepening it, coloring it, to give certain lines a more persuasive meaning. "I was going through analysis at the same time," Anne revealed to Lynn Voedisch. "It was really weird to do analytical scenes on the couch. I enjoyed the role because it was challenging and filled with a great deal of emotion. I could feel myself changing from a woman into a child when I was supposed to be under hypnosis."

She totally commands attention in the lead, making this the true feature film showcase of her career, a vivid reminder of her largely untapped acting versatility on the big screen. Charles Stinson of the *Los Angeles Times* called Anne's performance a "powerful portrait" filled with "genuine sensitivity and intelligence." Reviewer Norman Rose wrote that Anne "attacks Bobbie with confidence and a tigerishness that belies her all but angelic appearance."

She explained to Liza James of the *Tucson Daily Citizen* that a transformation came over her. "No role ever got under my skin so much before. This time I really went through an emotional wringer. I felt like Robin. I was Robin. It was a frightening experience at first, until I realized the significance of what was happening to me. I was actually breathing life into Robin, making her a real person, not just a character in a play speaking lines." She credited her "probing conversations" with the author, Dr. Harold Greenwald, with helping her get a handle on her character. "You might say Dr. Greenwald psychoanalyzed the part for me. He explained how Robin's sad role in society stems from a lonely childhood, how she wears a mask of defiance which is the hallmark of every 'call girl,' how beneath that mask is a frightened child." She added that what she was doing was not Method acting. "Definitely not. I'm not talking about a technique of acting at all. It goes much deeper than that, and must precede actual rehearsals or performances. What it boils down to is living the part emotionally, feeling the joys and sorrows, the fears and frustrations, of the human being the author has created."

As her boyfriend, John Kerr (best known for his colorless second lead in the movie version of *South Pacific*) is a surprise. *Girl of the Night* reveals shadings to the actor most film fans are unaware of. Manipulating his girlfriend, coaxing her with a combination of lies, putdowns and proclamations of love, the weasely Kerr is letter-perfect. He wants money, status, and power, and sees Bobbie has the perfect vehicle for those goals. His wholesome, all–American appearance and deceptively gentle demeanor only add to the actor's effectiveness.

Shot on location in New York City, *Girl of the Night* met with a bit of resistance at first because of its touchy subject matter. But, because of the film's tasteful handling of its subject and its academic source novel, the Legion of Decency gave it a special classification. The film's director, Joseph Cates, told *Variety* at the time that his approach to the material "is devoid of any lurid, graphic details; instead [it] is a study along psychiatric lines" and that the studio had assured him that the "ad campaign would be marked by an absence of any kind of 'low exploitation sell.'"

Today, the script's frankness is still potent, but it is best summed up by the *Oakland Tribune*'s Jack Anderson: "The producers' only recourse is a sort of compromise: a little, but not too much, psychological discussion, a little sex, a little violence and lots of innuendo." While the script by Ted Berkman and Raphael Blau is, on occasion, a bit corny, especially in these more "enlightened" times, the acting is sure, steady, and earnest.

"*Girl of the Night* is special to me because it was such a demanding role," Anne com-

Anne shares a smile in between scenes of *Girl of the Night*.

mented years later. "It really was a *tour de force*, and a wonderful chance to run the gamut. The fact that it was the story of a prostitute under analysis was rather risqué, I guess, at the time, though there were no licentious scenes in the picture. I don't think there was a love scene, really. However, the studio [Warners] soft-peddled it and it opened without any fanfare, though I was pleased with what reviews we had."

One of the best scenes in the film comes early on. Dr. Mitchell, a psychologist trying to gradually and cagily help the young woman, and Bobbie, cautious but ultimately tired of her lonely, sad existence, do some slight sparring:

DR. MITCHELL: Occupation?
BOBBIE: Model.
DR. MITCHELL: Fashion or photography?
BOBBIE: All right, doctor. We don't have to play *What's My Line*. I'm not a model, doctor. I'm a call girl.

The anguish, sincerity and remorse Anne Francis puts into this revelation elevates *Girl of the Night* from other exploitation films of its ilk. It seems a pity that such an obscure gem contains her best performance (and that film fans instead remember her for her mini-skirted innocent in the sci-fi classic *Forbidden Planet*). It's a rich, brave performance well worth seeking out.

It was probably publicity, but it was alleged that Anne was turned down for an unnamed Walt Disney film at the time because she played a call girl in *Girl in the Night*. This "ban" would not stay in effect, as Anne would have a good role in two *Wonderful World of Disney* Gallagher specials in 1965.

Anne remained off movie screens for five full years after *Girl of the Night*, although she was mentioned for the leads in George Montgomery's *From Hell to Borneo* (also called *Hell of Borneo*), Robert Taylor's *The Cry of the Laughing Owls* (renamed *Johnny Tiger*), and another that she remembered to Cass Warner Sperling and Cort Millner:

My agent sent me a script, *Claudelle Inglish* [1961]. I thought the story was trite and my part a caricature of a soap-opera character. I told my agent I didn't want to do it, and immediately got a call to appear before Jack Warner. I didn't want to go. Not because I was afraid of him (at least he'd never made a pass at me), but I just didn't want to get in a hassle. Of course, I went. Jack was in his huge office, sitting behind his huge desk, a casting director by his side.

"Anne, baby," he started, "this is a good juicy part: farm girl, abandoned by her boyfriend, becomes a man-hater."

I disagreed and argued that the script was dull, the language ugly.

"Anne, do this part for me."

"'It's just not right for me.'

"Aw, Anne...." Then he pulled out his billfold and

Anne is at her best in the *Girl of the Night* therapy scenes with Lloyd Nolan (left). She uses her radio-trained speaking voice to good effect, deepening it, coloring it, to give certain lines a more persuasive meaning. It was a gutsy performance.

slowly started slipping money out of it. He kept doing this all the time I was there. I guess it was his way of bribing me to do the part. I refused. The movie was made with Diane McBain, and bombed.

A couple years later, I went to a Hollywood event and found Jack sitting opposite me at the dinner table. He leaned over and said how much he loved the movies I had made for the studio. Then he looked me deep in the eyes and said, "You know, you're a wonderful actress, Arlene."

In March 1962, Anne gave birth to a daughter, Jane Elizabeth. But the new addition did not help the faltering marriage and, on February 26, 1963, the two separated again. In July, Anne filed for divorce for a second time. This time she accused Abeloff of mental and physical cruelty, yet gave no details. She asked for a division of community property, child support, plus a temporary monthly alimony of $1,390.

In August, Abeloff fought this, claming he earned little more than $10,000 a year in 1961 and 1962, although he was presently making a gross income of $23,000 annually. Anne said she earned $10,000 in the last three weeks, but that she was not currently employed. Abeloff countered that she had made $100,000 the previous year. Superior Court Judge Arnold Praeger denied Anne's bid for alimony, stating, "It appears that this lady, Miss Francis, makes more money than her husband. Alimony and attorney fees are not a matter of right when a wife has sufficient income to pay." She would receive only $175 a month for child support (some sources say $150), no alimony, and custody of their daughter.

She told NEA in June of 1964, "I have been here [in Hollywood] ten years. I've had two husbands, two divorces, one child and five and one half years in analysis. And now I feel suddenly like a whole new world is opening up. I was ready to flip one way or another. This was just after my first marriage broke up. I was in such a state I could easily have become an alcoholic. Or even committed suicide. Fortunately, I knew I needed help, so I went to a psychiatrist.... You know; there are so many people in this town who need help and don't get it. When Marilyn Monroe killed herself [in 1962], I had a few bad days — that could easily have been me."

Anne went on to discuss what she learned from her analysis: "First, I know now there is no magic shortcut to anything. If you want to go from here to there, you have to go directly. And if there are obstacles in the way, you must conquer them. You must face up to the things which stand in your way and defeat them. Second, I've learned to forgive my own mistakes. Most of us are harder on ourselves than we are on others. We expect perfection from ourselves, but are willing to forgive the mistakes of our friends."

Admitting to her faults, Anne was candid: "I've had two broken marriages. I'm not proud of that. But I've come to realize that businessmen make mistakes, too. It's just that a mistake in marriage is such a personal mistake."

These mistakes, however, taught Anne to be self-reliant, a

As a glamorous book reviewer in "The Fraudulent Female," an episode of Tony Franciosa's TV show *Valentine's Day*.

theme that would crop up many times through the years in interviews with the actress. "Last weekend, *I* put up a swing set for my daughter, Janie, who is two. And if you've ever tried to do that, you know it isn't easy. The directions are complicated and it's a hard job. But I was able to start with Step 1 and go all the way through. A few years ago, I couldn't have done it."

In late June, after this interview, she was back in court. It was charged that estranged husband Robert Abeloff threw a brick through her window and broke into her house to see their daughter.

The mid–'60s were a very productive period for Anne, despite her hectic private life. She was seen on many different shows (*Dr. Kildare, Alfred Hitchcock Presents, The Alfred Hitchcock Hour, The New Breed, Going My Way, Ben Casey, Arrest & Trial, Burke's Law, Kraft Suspense Theatre, Temple Houston, The Man from U.N.C.L.E., The Reporter, The Virginian*), in demand as a guest star because of her ability to play any kind of role. Nowhere is this more evident than on *The Alfred Hitchcock Hour*'s "What Really Happened." When Eve Raydon's (Anne) husband is poisoned, her mother-in-law (Gladys Cooper) accuses her of his murder. Through two sets of flashbacks, the two women tell the same story, but from two different points of view. In Mrs. Raydon's version, Eve is a greedy, adulterous manipulator; in Eve's it is just the opposite. Using the same situations and dialogue, Anne is able to play both sides of the same woman — with stunning results.

With her poodle Walter Smidgeon on *The Alfred Hitchcock Hour*'s "What Really Happened." Anne is able to play two sides of the same woman as, through two sets of flashbacks, two women tell the same story, but from two different points of view. The results were stunning.

Anne's most memorable and talked-about TV roles during this period were the two she did for *The Twilight Zone*, "The After Hours" (1960) and "Jess-Belle" (1963), both examples of classic television at its best.

In January 1964, with just a day's notice, Anne replaced Joan Hackett in *The Satan Bug* (1965), starring George Maharis. It was reported that Hackett suffered a severe sun allergy on location, but Anne's assertion to Tom Weaver, that Hackett had "some sort of altercation" with the producers "about how the character should be played," makes more sense — because, in fact, there's no character for Anne to play. A very beautiful Anne just stands around, barely uttering any lines. *The Her-*

ald-Journal's Joan E. Vadeboncoeur rightly noted, "[She] was meant to be the romantic interest for Maharis but the film barely touches on that and her flip sense of humor, which could have sparked the film, goes untapped."

The film is a good suspenser, but the acting is a little rough at times. Maharis, while attractive, is stilted and his line readings sound just plain phony. Vadeboncoeur picked up on this: "Maharis doesn't show much this time around. He reads his lines in monotones for the most part and never gets excited enough about the job until the finale. Richard Basehart, one of the scientists, can also be a bad actor and is here. Best he return to his TV submarine [on *Voyage to the Bottom of the Sea*]."

"I liked the script very, very much; it was an interesting script," Anne told Tom Weaver, but she felt that the film's pace dragged. She explained to Weaver that director John Sturges and editor Ferris Webster

were having meetings at lunch every day about another movie they were going to be doing, *The Hallelujah Trail* [1965]. Unfortunately, I think that *Satan Bug* kind of suffered a bit in the editing room because of this next project that they were into. I felt that *The Satan Bug* was not Ferris Webster's best job of editing: There are *long* drive-ins, *getting* out of the car, *walking* all the way up to the house, another person *opening* the door — they did not have cuts that would have kept that movie moving, and so the pace was dragged out tremendously. And it was the kind of a movie that *had* to have fast pacing. So I was very disappointed when I saw it. And the only thing I can consider is the fact that John and Ferris were pressed for time for this other biggie, *The Hallelujah Trail*, and that *Satan Bug* suffered. But, as I said, originally the script itself was terrific.

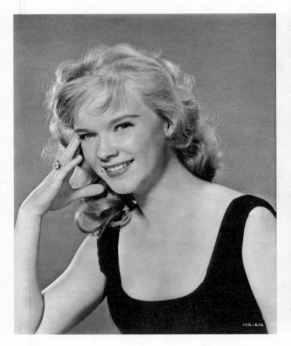

Left: An early '60s portrait showing off Anne's mixture of beauty and likeability. *Right:* Anne took a risk in the '60s, working steadily on television. "In those days, that was the death knell for an actor. You worked television, you didn't do film. Of course, they cross over all the time today," she remarked to David D. Duncan. But she conceded later that she didn't regret her decision. "They were exciting days, and challenging work, and I enjoyed that."

Much better for Anne was *Brainstorm* (1965), directed by actor William Conrad, a role that should have cinched her at least a Best Supporting Actress Oscar nomination. Although she's the lead, it is basically Jeffrey Hunter's movie, about an already-unbalanced man, Jim Grayam (Hunter), feigning insanity so he can kill Lorrie Benson's (Anne) abusive husband Cort, played with perverse coldness by Dana Andrews, so they (Jim and Lorrie) can be together. In the opening sequence, Lorrie has finally gotten up the nerve to kill herself, taking pills and lying in her car which she has placed on the railroad tracks. Jim, a stranger, unaware of her suffering, saves her. Being handed her over to her husband, Anne's look of pathetic sadness and panic are overwhelming; finally giving way to a torrent of unnerving screams and sobs. It was Anne's most intensely poignant performance, a rollercoaster of emotions that are heartbreaking to watch.

"That was directed by Bill Conrad, who is one of the brightest directors I've ever worked with in my life," Anne told Tom Weaver. "He is absolutely incredible. Before a hysterical scene that I had in that film, Bill came up to me and he said, 'Now, when you get into the sobbing, I would like it to reach a peak'—and he gave me the sound of the highest pitch that he wanted in this sobbing scene. It was very exciting to work with somebody who had that much of an insight into the sound that he wanted."

It was Conrad's third film as director in 1965, *Two on a Guillotine* and *My Blood Runs*

Stepping into Joan Hackett's role with just a day's notice, Anne co-starred with George Maharis (left) in *The Satan Bug* (1965).

Cold coming before this; he would helm only one more movie as director, *Side Show* (1981). The rest of his work as director came on TV, starting in the late '50s and ending in the early '70s. "He was a fabulous director. He never got credit for that, and he was wonderful," Anne elaborated to *Filmfax*. "[H]e just had a great eye for [the] camera, and he would walk in on the set and see something that would suddenly set it all off in his mind, and away we'd go. We go on a wonderful trip, both visually with camera, and with the scene as well. He was brilliant."

Conrad did have a good visual sense, his pacing was okay, but he was defeated by the absurd script by Mann Rubin, from a Lawrence B. Marcus story. He utilized his settings well, filming around Los Angeles, at the Bunker-Ramo plant in Canoga Park, and the Warner Bros. lot.

Brainstorm was a good movie, unfortunately marred by its descent into implausibility, when Jim Grayam is sent to an institution and tries to manipulate Dr. Elizabeth Larstadt (Viveca Lindfors). Some scenes are just laugh-out-loud funny, such as the scene where Lorrie coaches Jim with cue cards to test his ability to fight off a truth serum drug. Hunter's halting stuttering and Anne's seriously perplexed reactions are just comedy gold, but, unfortunately, not meant as such. The film's first half, detailing Jim and Lorrie's growing relationship, was a good, solid emotional drama, showing all three lead characters off to maximum effect. Even better is Anne's last scene with Hunter as she visits him in prison. Her hushed, on-the-verge of-tears but determined talk with him reveals much about her troubled character, which she called in interviews a "nympho-alcoholic," and is played masterfully by Anne.

Just before *Brainstorm* had its premiere, Anne was still battling her ex. She told Dorothy Kilgallen, "I'm still in the process of working out a property settlement with Dr. Robert Abeloff. I divorced him last year. I have the custody of my daughter, Jane Elizabeth, who is two. I haven't been steady dating with anyone. It takes a girl years to get over a wrecked marriage. At this point I want no exclusive contracts — except for acting."

After all was said and done with her ex, Anne told Hedda Hopper in the beginning of 1966, "This kind of prolonged delay builds up unnecessary bitterness and is a useless hassle. However, that's all past and there's no unpleasantness any more. Janie sees her father twice a week. It's important for her to know her father and to feel that she is loved by him — and he certainly dotes on her."

Asked if she had plans on remarrying, Anne said forcefully, "Not on your life! After two unsuccessful tries, I'm in no hurry. Right now, I doubt I'll ever marry again."

*   *   *

"The odds are really against the show," executive producer Aaron Spelling said less than a month before *Honey West*'s TV debut. "The question is whether the public will accept a girl lead in a half-hour adventure show." At the same time *Honey West* was announced on ABC's fall's schedule, CBS had touted their own variation, a show built around secret agent Selena Mead, to be played by Polly Bergen; those plans were quickly nixed.

Anne Francis did, indeed, make television history in 1965 when she became the first lead actress portraying a private eye, and a karate-chopping one at that. Co-starring John Ericson and Irene Hervey, *Honey West* ran on ABC for only thirty episodes, but remains today fresh, fun and influential. What made *Honey West* so special, explained long-time fan, *Newsday* TV reporter Diane Werts in 1999, was not the glamour and the gadgets, but "Anne

Francis' confidence. Her fierce intelligence and self-reliance illuminated the character with a special light for girls like me just beginning to see we had more options than we'd been led to believe."

The way the role came about, said Anne, "reads like a story about extrasensory perception, but it's pure fact. I had turned down numerous offers for series — no housewifery week after week for me, nor any of the kooky characters that pass for comedy. When my agent asked me what kind of character I would consider, I told him the nearest way I could describe it was a sort of female *Burke's Law*, an adventurous career gal in glamorous surroundings, with an accent on adventure. Then I added there was about as much chance of a role like that as there was of my inheriting a gold mine.

"Within two days he called back to say Aaron Spelling wanted me to star in a series, and that the best way he could describe it was a sort of female *Burke's Law*." She was also given 20 percent of the show, but, like most stars back then given this kind of arrangement, Anne did not and would not in the years ahead profit from it.

The ABC-TV show *Burke's Law* had premiered on September 20, 1963, executive-produced by Spelling for Four Star Television. Cool and debonair Gene Barry played Captain Amos Burke, Los Angeles chief of detectives — a multi-millionaire chauffeured to crime scenes in a Rolls-Royce. (Co-Four Star founder Dick Powell had played Inspector Amos Burke previously, on his 1961 TV show *The Dick Powell Show*.) *Burke's Law* was unique and before its time, said Spelling, because "it kidded murder." Anne had already

Top and above: Anne is abusive Dana Andrews' nympho-alcoholic wife in *Brainstorm* (1965), here letting loose after her suicide attempt is thwarted. "That was directed by Bill Conrad, who is one of the brightest directors I've ever worked with in my life," Anne told Tom Weaver. "He is absolutely incredible. Before a hysterical scene that I had in that film, Bill came up to me and he said, 'Now, when you get into the sobbing, I would like it to reach a peak'—and he gave me the sound of the highest pitch that he wanted in this sobbing scene. It was very exciting to work with somebody who had that much of an insight into the sound that he wanted."

guested on *Burke's Law* ("Who Killed Wade Walker?") the previous season as a murder suspect. Near the end of *Burke's Law*'s second season, on April 21, 1965, writers Gwen Bagni and Paul Dubov introduced the character of Honey West to television audiences in the episode "Who Killed the Jackpot?" Bagni and Dubov, who later developed and wrote for Honey's own show, presented a different, slicker interpretation here.

> BURKE: So you're Honey West.
> HONEY: So you're Burke.
> BURKE: I'm not sure I like the way you said that.
> HONEY: Oh, don't worry. To know me is to hate me.
> BURKE: Yes, I've heard some stories.

Gwen Bagni and Paul Dubov were signed by Four Star on September 21, 1964, to write the initial pilot script, while Anne was signed immediately after filming finished on *The Satan Bug*. On September 27, 1964, she told columnist Hal Humphrey, "I never wanted to do a series, but how

A cool-looking Anne takes a break for the camera during the making of *Brainstorm*, a film that contained one of her best performances.

many years can you go on guesting? This character Honey West is sophisticated and a swinging-type girl. I like her."

"I'm sort of a female Gene Barry — or latter-day Pearl White," Anne explained further to a reporter about Honey in mid–February '65. She also talked about the plusses and minuses of portraying TV's first female private eye. "I spend half my time sliding up and down ropes or jumping off buildings or slugging someone. But there are compensations. I drive a sleek, expensive sports car and wear Paris originals."

Making things more grueling, at the same time she was filming the one-hour pilot, she was filming her heavy, dramatic role in *Brainstorm*, and spending four hours a day taking karate and judo lessons in addition to her acting chores. "I'll appreciate doing comedy," she smiled to Vernon Scott. "I'm really tired of tearing my guts out in heavy drama. For instance, I had five hysterical scenes in my first week's work on *Brainstorm*. That takes a lot out of an actress. After a week of playing a hysterical woman, it's difficult to shake the mood, when you leave work."

Honey is an unruffled, ironic blonde, fast with the quips as well as her fists ("You're just not my type," she tells one amorous guy as she karate chops him). Ladies' man Burke is definitely interested in her, as are her employee Sam Bolt (John Ericson) and her lawyer, Chris Maitland (George Nader).

> BURKE: Isn't murder a little out of your line?
> HONEY: We aim to please.
> BURKE: You've already succeeded. May I give you a lift?

HONEY: You taking me in?
BURKE: Is that an invitation?

She is naturally faced with chauvinism ("We should never have given them the vote," remarks Sam Bolt). But Burke comes to realize her capability, though he's still attracted to the private eyeful:

BURKE: Honey, have you ever...
HONEY: Uh-uh. I fly solo.
BURKE: Don't fly too close; I'm
           liable to clip your wings.
HONEY: So you're Burke.
BURKE: And you're West.

Who was Honey West and how, where and when did she originate? The series of *Honey West* books that started it all were written between 1957 and 1971 by "G.G. Fickling"— in reality the Laguna Beach–based husband-and-wife team of Forrest "Skip" Fickling and Gloria Fickling. (The "G.G." stood for Gloria Gautraud, Gloria's maiden name.) There were eleven novels about the "nerviest, curviest P.I. in Los Angeles": *This Girl for Hire* (1957), *A Gun for Honey* (1958), *Girl on the Loose* (1958), *Honey in the Flesh* (1959), *Girl on the Prowl* (1959), *Kiss for a Killer* (1960), *Dig a Dead Doll* (1960), *Blood and Honey* (1961), *Bombshell* (1964), *Honey on Her Tail* (1971) and *Stiff as a Broad* (1971).

Anne Francis made television history in 1965 when she became the first lead actress portraying a private eye, in *Honey West.* John Ericson, who previously appeared with her in *Bad Day at Black Rock* (1955), played her partner Sam Bolt. The show lasted only thirty episodes, but remains influential today.

The idea of a female private eye — something not seen much in popular fiction up to that time — was a tough sell. "In fact, nobody would touch it," Gloria Fickling remarked to Kevin Burton Smith in *Mystery Scene* in 2004. "But I really believed in Honey, so I said to Skip, 'Know what? We're going to hock our last dollar and go back to New York City and pound the pavement until we sell Honey West.' And that's exactly what we did — we had thirty days before our budget ran out. And on the thirtieth day we sold Honey West [in 1957 to Pyramid Books].

"But even then, the editor they put in charge wasn't crazy about it. He said, 'Okay, okay, I'll go along with this, but you've really got to change that name — Honey West just ain't gonna cut it.' But we stuck to our guns, and I think we were right — it's a magic name."

The formation of the name was simple. "We thought the most used name for someone you really like is Honey. And she lives in the West, so there was her name," Skip told Dennis McLellan of the *Los Angeles Times* in 1986. As for inspiration, Gloria insists that Skip based a lot of Honey on her, but Skip explained to McLellan that, initially, "I first thought of Marilyn Monroe, and then I thought of Mike Hammer and decided to put the two together." Interestingly, *Blood and Honey* (1961), the eighth book in the series, is dedicated to Julie London, the blonde actress-turned-sultry pop singer of the '50s and '60s: "To Julie London, the symbol, the embodiment and the fire of Honey."

Anne excelled as Honey West, said reporter Diane Werts, because her "fierce intelligence and self-reliance illuminated the character with a special light for girls like me just beginning to see we had more options than we'd been led to believe."

The 28-year-old Honey had "taffy-colored hair, blue eyes and a baby-bottom complexion." Questioned in the first novel, she gave reporter Fred Sims a rundown: "38–22–36. Five feet five. One hundred and twenty pounds. Normal childhood diseases. No dimples. Small birthmark on inside of right thigh. Both parents dead. No known living relatives." (Unlike Miss Francis, Honey didn't get a mole near her lip until the ninth book, *Bombshell*.) A graduate of Long Beach City College, Honey, as per *Blood and Honey*, "likes masculine men, martinis on the rocks, fast cars, black silk stockings, water skiing, rare steaks, Hemingway, Roquefort salads, dancing, sour cream and chives, apple turnovers and baseball." She carried, in a blue (later pink) garter holster, a tiny, pearl-handled Hi-standard .22 revolver. "You got firepower from just about any angle," one witness to the garter holster marveled.

She had become a private investigator because her father, P.I. Hank West, was ambushed and killed in an alley behind the Paramount Theater in Los Angeles. It was suggested that she would eventually avenge her father's murder, but she never did — nor did she ever try. Instead, she took over his office and carried on the family business, despite too-vocal protests from the men around her. "I was in this business for a lot of reasons," Honey said early on in *This Girl for Hire*. "I was tired of being accused, insulted and pushed around for doing a job men considered wrong for a woman."

Her mother died giving birth to Honey. Mom had danced at The Casino on Catalina Island and acted in B movies. Honey describes her in *Blood and Honey* as "actress, artistic, angel."

Honey's sparring partner was handsome Lt. Mark Storm of Homicide, who, more often than not, between marriage proposals, gave her a hard time and was always warning her (yelling, mostly) to get off a particular case. Honey, "a dame who's got more dangerous curves than Indianapolis Speedway," made the exasperated, insanely jealous Storm feel "like an H-Bomb about to be triggered." She kept him at arm's length, but you couldn't blame her. Mark Storm spoke for keeping the little woman in the kitchen, away from the work force. He would get angry in book after book when Honey disregarded his "advice" to quit and stop "trying to prove you're something more than just a woman." Before their time, these books shattered the private eye genre's standards. "Damn you, Honey!" Storm roared in *Girl on the Loose*. "Damn you for being in this crummy racket, for letting yourself in for capers like this where somebody is either stripping you down or taking wacks at you with a tommy gun. You haven't got enough sense to pound a rat hole! ... Any sensible woman your age would be married by now with a couple of kids. And instead of dodging lead you'd be dodging burps from the newest baby."

In *This Girl for Hire*, Storm heatedly asks, "Honey, why don't you get out of this business? What are you trying to prove?" Honey gives it to him with both barrels, speaking for a whole generation of liberated women:

> You've got a lot of guts to tell me what I ought to do — where I ought to get off! Sure, I'm a woman! I act like a woman, think like a woman, look like a woman, but I'm mixed up in a rotten dirty business that men think they own by right of conquest! But you've never stopped to consider that half the crimes in the United States today are committed by women — and half of those committed by men are provoked by women. So where does that leave you? In a business operated seventy-five percent by females! All right, so you don't think I'm nice. What are you going to do about it?

A leather-clad Honey tooled around in a Cobra sports car (here, however, she poses with the Jaguar XK-E she drove in the *Burke's Law* episode that introduced the character). An action-oriented female lead was so ahead-of-its-time in 1965 that syndicated columnist Kay Gardella warned her readers, "Television writers and producers are chipping away at the female image. If the women in this country aren't on guard, their youngsters will be weaned on a concept of womanhood that makes Frankenstein's monster look like Alice in Wonderland."

And Honey definitely was tough. ("It was a dirty sort of a smile that I felt like wiping with the flat of my hand to see if it might come clean," she said about one man.) Her father had taught her judo, which she always used to good effect. After punching one suspect in the stomach, he complained, "You don't allow much time for questions."

"That's my policy," Honey smiled. "I always hit first. That way nobody gets hurt."

"Nobody, meaning you."

"That's what my father always said," she replied simply.

Honey of the books has been described by other writers as a "loose woman" and "sex-loaded." This is misleading. Through eight of the eleven novels, Honey was never described as having sex with anyone. ("And I hope you don't think I'm just another girl out for a good Marine," Honey tells a suspect in *A Gun for Honey*. "Call me old-fashioned if you want to, Reed, but I like things to develop slowly.") If anyone unsavory came on to her — and every male who laid eyes on her found her irresistibly attractive enough to aggressively try — Honey was sure to put them down with a karate chop or kick to the head or stomach. She was never really in any serious sexual harm, usually taking every advance with good humor ("Down, Rover!") or with some much-needed violence.

Her main problem amounted to what we'd call today "wardrobe malfunctions." In every novel, Honey West would accidentally lose her clothes. ("Can I help it if I'm always losing clothes?") There was nothing obscene about it; the Ficklings would never graphi-

A lithe Anne Francis poses for a publicity shot wearing an elegant full-length dress (opposite) while in another publicity photograph from the same period (above) it's all about the eyes.

cally describe Honey's anatomy when she shed her dress or bathing suit. It was her "thing," and it had a silly innocence about it that added to the fun of the novels. In *Blood and Honey*, she is chased in the snow, wearing just a flimsy negligee and high heels. ("A blue-eyed blonde in soaked-to-the-skin silk and high heels didn't stand much of a chance against a giant with a gun in a dark alley in the middle of the blizzard.")

The humor of the Ficklings saved the Honey West series from the often sleazy and sometimes offensive content. Nothing was truly taken seriously, except the brutal violence. "I went for my blue garter, but his gun was easier to reach than mine. His hand darted inside his coat and produced a .45. I dropped the hem of my dress, reared back and hit him in the Adam's apple. He didn't say another word. The hideous choked sound that gurgled up into his throat couldn't begin to compete with the scream that split his pained lips when he hit the ground. I added one well-placed kick, picked up his automatic and started for the black sedan."

Bombshell (1964) is the novel that changed the formula. She was now described as "Honey West, the sexsational female private eye": Honey now carried her gun between her breasts (mean trick, I guess, if you can do it) and there were unsettling, graphic scenes of torture. She meets bounty hunter Johnny Doom and, shortly thereafter, the innocence of the Honey West series comes to an end — she promptly has sex with him. Times were changing in the mid-'60s and it was thought that Honey, in the wake of James Bond, should change with them. But the series, as fans knew it, was gone, and the changes were not for the better. She was now killing her enemies instead of simply beating them up. A perversity had slipped in, which is a shame because *Bombshell* had a solid story. (Skip Fickling wrote a script based on this novel for a movie that was never produced.)

James Bond's influence effectively killed off Honey for good when the series reappeared in 1971, after a seven-year absence, in two back-to-back novels, *Honey on Her Tail* and *Stiff*

Setting and outfit — or lack thereof — are the only similarities in these two promotional photographs of Anne from the mid–1960s: Lounging by the pool (above), friendly and open, and posed in a towel (opposite) and seemingly distant.

as a Broad. "My name: Honey West. I was a full-time private detective once. Until the government got its hands on me. Now I'm known as an international eye-spy [for the CIA], which is a provocative title for a dirty business." She was exposed to LSD, an evil organization nonsensically named MAD (Mord Aterrorizer Dominar), and much more sex. In fact, in these last two novels, although Honey protested a couple of times not wanting to have sex, it happened anyway. Unlike the early novels, where she dispatched the too-amorous, Honey unbelievably simply gives in, overpowered by the male. The whole character and purpose of the stories were ruined.

The only interesting aspect about *Stiff as a Broad* is that it is the only novel to mention Anne Francis. Speaking of a young 20-something actress, a character says, "Honey, you know what it's like when you see a person who reminds you of somebody else. It was like a thorn in my side. I kept thinking of Marilyn Monroe, Elke Sommer, Anne Francis for starters..."

There were plans to update Honey again in the '80s. The "new" Honey, according to Skip in the *Los Angeles Times*, "has gone from being 25 to 45. She's still as sexy as ever but has a little bit more, shall we say, sexual maturity," although, he promptly added, that "she'll still be the same old Honey West. She's still got the same vibrant philosophies, the same drive and determination and the same wonderment for life that she always had." The Ficklings didn't go through with the overhaul. The early Honey West novels were tough, light, slam-bang fun and the so-called updated "improvements" could never recapture this.

* * *

The *Honey West* pilot was a success. The *Herald-Journal* called it one of *Burke's Law*'s "best outings this season," praising the script's abundance of "delectable, flip, mouse-and-cat play" and the "trim performances." Even before it aired, it was announced on March 8, 1965, that *Honey West* was "a definite for next season." The day after the pilot aired, columnist Bob Foster commented, "Although I felt that Honey West's role was a bit too slick, this is not going to stop it from becoming a most popular show.... In my book Miss Francis can do no wrong."

Four months before *Honey West* started production, Anne began studying with Gordon Doversola, a Hawaiian karate instructor. (Doversola appeared in the pilot practicing with Honey.) "Although Anne can practically commit mayhem with her karate," wrote *TV Guide*, "and in the pilot actually 'threw' her adversary, as a star she's much too valuable for that sort of fun. A stunt girl will do the rough stuff, and the actual throwing. But Anne has to look authentic in the close-ups. To keep the Honey West image pristine, Anne will be very ladylike in her use of karate. That is, she won't kill anyone with it." In actuality, it is easy to detect Anne doing some of her own flips and throws on the show. The close-ups of Anne flipping and karate-chopping her opponents were very well done and quite brutal. (In the beginning of 1966, *Parents* magazine named *Honey West* one the shows "unsuitable for young children.")

During production, Gene LeBell, wrestler, judo champion and stuntman, was called in. In his autobiography, *The Godfather of Grappling*, LeBell wrote, "Anne was, and still is, one of the most beautiful women to walk the Earth and I was lucky enough to be picked to train her to do the tickles and tackles and judo moves for the show. The first time I worked on *Honey West* she was all dressed up and everything and I didn't know her at the time. I was still very much an introvert. She came up to me and kissed me in front of everybody and I told her that I would never wash my face again. I washed my hands but not my face. Every man that met Anne Francis couldn't help but fall in love with her."

"The physical stuff has to be done correctly," Anne told columnist Ed Misurell on the set, "with the right leverages and balances because so many people are studying karate today. They would know immediately if we were faking it. The choreography of the fights is worked out before filming by my stunt girl, Sharon Lucas, and stunt man Buddy Van Horn. Originally, I did all my own stunt work, but now they are cutting down on it. They don't want me to injure myself." Her initial three-day, 17-hours-per-day schedule was exhausting. Finally, it was changed to a 12-hour, four-day-a-week one.

In a cute *TV Week* interview, Allen Rich asked her, "Suppose I was to, say, accost you in maybe a dark alley somewhere. How would you 'repulse my unwelcome advances,' as they used to say in grandma's time?"

"That would depend on whether I wanted to kill you or just stun you," Anne answered, tongue in cheek. "I think perhaps I'd just stun you. Maybe with a short chop, an elbow in the diaphragm, or, let us say, an easy flip."

"You can forget the flip, I already did," Rich shuddered.

Anne revealed to Tom Weaver in a *Starlog* interview that her study of karate came in handy many years later when she was doing a play at the Ahmanson Theater:

> I was going down the stairway into the bowels of the Ahmanson to get my auto — by that time, just about everyone else had cleared out — and I suddenly heard footsteps behind me. I went down one flight and I heard him; I went down the second flight and I heard him getting closer. I thought, "Oh, baby, I'd better do something now."
> About halfway down the next flight of stairs, as I heard the footsteps getting closer, I just whirled around and grabbed the banister in one hand — and there was this guy. He stopped short, I looked at him and he looked at me — it felt like we were there for about a half hour, although it was probably only about three seconds. He said, "Did I scare you?" and I said, "No." And I was just waiting for him to make a move, because I knew from karate training that, if he moved toward me, I might get hurt, but he would get hurt, too, because I would help him on down the stairs! So I just waited. Finally he turned around and went back up the stairs, and I went down and got in my car. Then I fell apart — just absolutely! But it worked, that instantaneous thing that just grips you, and you're prepared. I just knew instinctively that the best place for me to handle it was on the stairway with his being above me. On the flat, I would not have much of a chance.

Although British audiences (starting in 1962) had Honor Blackman on *The Avengers* (not yet imported to the U.S.), American TV viewers' only exposure to a strong female crime-fighting lead had been Beverly Garland as an undercover policewoman in *Decoy* (1957), although that series was low on violence. In 1965, pointing toward *Honey West*, syndicated columnist Kay Gardella warned that "television writers and producers are chipping away at the female image. If the women in this country aren't on guard, their youngsters will be weaned on a concept of womanhood that makes Frankenstein's monster look like Alice in Wonderland." Anne countered this by telling Gardella, "I don't think the role is unfeminine. True, ABC and the producers are concerned about this. After all, Honey West isn't a gal who goes around bars looking for a fight so she can practice judo. She simply protects herself."

And she would look extremely feminine doing it. "My wardrobe will be very high fashion," Anne continued to Gardella, "except for the times when I wear black leotards and high boots to sneak in and out of places. Otherwise, I'll be groomed in beaded gowns, chilla-trimmed jackets and wraps, a tiger coat, a black snake skin trench coat, a leopard-trimmed gown, slinking white beaded gowns, and so on."

Before the first episode aired, executive producer Aaron Spelling acknowledged that *Honey West* was risky. "We like to think of Honey West as just a normal, average American girl who is a karate expert, drives a custom-built sports car, has an ocelot for a pet and loves gadgets, like earrings that are really little gas bombs," Spelling told Cynthia Lowry. "No one has ever attempted [this type of show] before. The odds are really against the show. The question is whether the public will accept a girl lead in a half-hour adventure show."

Anne didn't see the risk, because, as she told Joan Vadeboncoeur, "There are eight million single career girls in this country who ought to like Honey and, while my role doesn't reflect the American housewife, I think she'll like me, too, because she never gets a change and would take a vicarious interest."

Even though ABC was taking a gamble headlining a strong woman in an action show, sexism was still evident. Sam Bolt, an assistant in the *Burke's Law* episode, would now, in the new *Honey West* show, be upped to partner in the detective agency. It was believed it wouldn't "look right" for a man to be taking orders from a woman. It would be okay, however, for her to disregard his advice!

On June 11, 1965, *The Hollywood Reporter* announced, "Anne Francis of Four Star's *Honey West* will be guest of honor at the 18th annual convention of California Association of Private Investigators at International Airport. Through arrangement with Tom McDermott, Four Star president, evening will be highlighted by a preview screening of *Honey West* pilot."

Four Star mapped out an itinerary of twelve cities where John Ericson and Anne would make personal appearances, leaving on September 9, to pre-sell the series. Ericson went to Cleveland, St. Louis, Chicago, Buffalo, Columbus, and Indianapolis; Anne to New York, Washington, Pittsburgh, San Francisco, Detroit, and Philadelphia.

Honey West, the girl who "served up judo chops instead of light suppers" (*The Daily Review*), premiered on Friday, September 17, 1965, with the episode "The Swingin' Mrs. Jones." *TV Week* found that the show was most popular with women between the ages of 35 and 40. ("There must be a lot of ladies in the audience who would like to slug their husbands," Anne laughed, "and they can get a vicarious thrill watching me chopping men— I've had fights in every show so far.") *TV Week* also called "svelte and sexy" Anne "[t]elevision's gift to the men." ("I had an appointment with Oliver Stone a couple of years ago." Anne revealed in 1997. "When I walked in, he threw his arms out with this big grin on his face and said, 'Honey West!' As he hugged me, I thought, well, I guess he was at that impressionable age when *Honey West* was being broadcast!")

The show used clever film techniques, some overlapping dialogue, and off-kilter camera angles, giving it a distinctive look. Also distinctive was the jazzy music score by the underrated Joseph Mullendore. Anne's stunning gowns were by Nolan Miller (later to find success with *Dynasty*), and the cool car that Anne tooled around in was a Cobra sports car. (Sam had the undercover Econoline surveillance truck with "H.W. Bolt & Co. TV Repairing" printed on the side.) Instead of carrying her gun in her garter like the literary Honey, Anne had to carry her rod in her less-risqué boot. The show was shot at CBS Studio City (formerly the Republic lot), featuring sets also seen in other shows produced there, including *The*

Wild Wild West and *The Big Valley*. The Barclay foyer set prominently featured in every *Big Valley* turns up regularly on *Honey West* ("In the Bag," "King of the Mountain," more). The opulent and luxurious sets were inspired by *Burke's Law*.

The show featured characters not seen in the novels. Ex-Marine Sam Bolt, Honey's assistant in crimebusting, was played by handsome Ericson, a former MGM contract player who had previously played Anne's brother in *Bad Day at Black Rock* (1955). Playing Aunt Meg was Irene Hervey, who was a beautiful leading lady of B movies in the '30s and '40s. Once married (from 1936 to 1957) to singer Allan Jones, she was the mother of singer Jack Jones. Her slightly ditzy performance on *Honey West* was definitely the highlight of her career.

Rounding out the cast was Bruce Bitabit, playing Honey's pet 28-pound ocelot, Bruce. The animal garnered much publicity and was nominated for a Patsy. "When cats get hot or tired, they start getting a little snarly," Anne told Tom Weaver in *Starlog*. "At times, it was like trying to hold a pair of cobras; each end of him was going one way or the other. From working with cats, I know that if one is happy, it bites and scratches, and if it's unhappy, it bites and scratches. So it really doesn't make too much difference [*laughs*]! I learned pretty much to keep ahead of him when he was squirming. I do love animals, so we got along quite well. But a lot of character actors who came on the show were petrified of him."

Bruce was trained by Ralph Helfer and his company. Helfer told Ken Beck and Jim Clark in their book *The Encyclopedia of TV Pets*, "We used a number of ocelots. They are not the easiest cats to work with. They're feisty and more like a domestic house cat: They refuse to take instructions. Bruce was played by two or three of our best ocelots. They're gentle animals, just sweet, but that's all they were. The ocelot is one of the most difficult, the same as training a bobcat. Smaller cats are not trainable. The bigger they get, the more trainable. The same is true of bears, cougars, and tigers. Small species are generally more difficult to work with than larger."

Even though she had to get regular tetanus shots because of Bruce's feisty nature, Anne got along great with the cats, according to Helfer. "[Anne] was a sweetheart, one of the few that didn't mind if the ocelot scratched her a little bit when it jumped out of her lap. She was a real animal lover." But, he adds, "Our cats were good as long as you didn't push them. They were a lot like a cheetah, absolute dolls to be around, sweet and lovable, but if they don't want to do anything, they won't do it." As for the name Bruce, Helfer says, "We ended up calling the key ocelot Bruce since everybody called it that. So we eventually adopted that name"—even though Bruce was a female.

Although most critics found the plots silly, they were unanimous in their praise for Anne. Terming the series "mock serious," *The Hollywood Reporter* said of Anne, "[She is] equally adept at vamping a suspect or tossing him for a loop with an adept judo flip.... The script ... concentrated more on flashy gimmicks than lines or plot.... Anne Francis, a very good actress, plays Honey, and she may get something to do in future segments that will test her talents." According to *TV Week*, "Anne Francis' personal appeal and underplaying have a good deal to do with the caliber of the show. John Ericson's 'Sam Bolt' fits in nicely with the star's work."

Right away *Honey West* went up against the inevitable comparisons to James Bond, as all shows about spies during the '60s were considered rip-offs if they used gadgets and fan-

tastic themes. One TV reporter, J.E.V., was adamant in stating that Honey West had very
few things in common with Bond:

> Tabbed as a "female James Bond," this series only rates that comparison loosely since *Honey West*
> is more like past master detectives as *Mike Hammer* than she is "007." Sure, she uses lots of gim-
> micks like a microphone lipstick and, on one I caught, her suntan lotion bottle was also a mike.
> But she goes in for more two-fisted, unglamorous action than does "Bond." She and her partner
> Sam Bolt waste little time on gourmet food and exotic women and the travels never take them
> to foreign lands.... The show's scripts are tautly-written and emphasize action, rather than double
> entendre dialogue — which is one reason it must be placed in the Mickey Spillane category, rather
> than "Bond," if one must type the series.

John Ericson got into the act, telling columnist Harold Stern, "Our show is a boy-girl
James Bond sort of thing. We're two adventurers. The detective angle is a gimmick to get
us into our story. We get involved beyond mere detecting. Our heavies are oddball. They
use strange devices, devices unknown except to Senate investigating committees. We're
trying to return to the typical hero and heroine. [Honey and Sam] are extreme individualists.
They don't conform. And there are no limits to the series. We can go anywhere. We wear
disguises. We're not really Bondish at all."

Honey West had a breezy, funny tone, its sense of humor making it stand out from other
spy shows. In the early episodes, the villains' scenes were played fairly straight. But, pretty
soon, the progression of villains went from the conventional type to robots, gorillas, Robin
Hood, etc., perhaps influenced by the premiere of the campy *Batman* series in January of 1966.

"This is a light, sophisticated show, all done with tongue and cheek," Anne explained
to reporter Ed Misurell during filming of an episode. "When Honey gets in a tough spot
she'll use her femininity first, and if that fails there's always karate or some of the assorted
weapons she uses. When she needs a man to pull her out, [Sam] will turn up."

Although the show increased the sales of their books even further, the Ficklings weren't
entirely pleased with it. "They hoked it up more than we'd like," Gloria complained to the
Los Angeles Times. "The books were a lot more sophisticated than the series." Truthfully,
though, "sophistication" isn't the word that readily comes to mind about the novels. What
the *Honey West* series did was to take the sleaze out of the books. "Honey wasn't cheap or
devious. She didn't use her body to get information," Anne said later. Gloria disagrees,
feeling the books "were never obscene. I mean, the books were provocative, but there was
also a sort of sweetness and innocence about them."

Also, in place of the unpleasant edge of Honey and Lt. Storm's relationship, the TV
show gave us the fun bantering of Honey and Sam, helped considerably by Anne Francis
and John Ericson's obvious chemistry. They argued, he worried, she wisecracked, they fought
together, and then they went out to dinner.

Gloria continued, "[T]hey changed the character, added too many gimmicks, and
insisted Honey have a running mate, Sam Bolt. In our books it was Johnny Doom, and he
wasn't her partner, he was just a, uh, suitor, I guess, and he wasn't bailing her out all the
time. We loved the ocelot, and we thought Anne Francis was lovely, but we didn't like
Auntie What's-Her-Name who was always around. That made Honey look like she couldn't
stand on her own, and they wouldn't let her live alone, so that no shenanigans would happen.
But in the books, Johnny and the police lieutenant — who was also crazy for Honey — were
there more to warn her than to rescue her. But of course she'd never listen."

It is typical that authors do not like when their literary creations are translated to the screen. However, there are some misconceptions in Gloria's comments. It is often assumed — by some people who haven't seen the show in years — that Sam Bolt always rescued Honey at the conclusion. This was not so. Sometimes she would save him, sometimes he saved her; they worked as a team. Honey was never portrayed as weak, unable to take care of herself. And she never listened to Sam — and he warned her in practically every episode to stay put. (It is odd that Fickling would mention the annoying Johnny Doom prominently; he appeared near the end of the series and was instrumental in the ruination of the Honey character.) "Auntie What's-Her-Name" (Aunt Meg) was not "always around," she never set limits on Honey or cramped her style. (Well, except in "The Abominable Snowman," where she wouldn't let Sam into the bathroom while Honey was taking a bubble bath.) There could be no shenanigans, anyway, because this was television and nothing of that sort was allowed back then, of course.

The show's shooting schedule was grueling and Anne said she underestimated what a "grind" it would be. "I had guested on enough shows to see what it did to the character who carries the series. But it's like getting married. You don't know what you're in for until after the ceremony! For awhile we worked between 14 and 17 hours a day, then it became clear that with our kind of show it was impossible to do it in three [days]. We now do it in four." Such a work load exhausted all the ideas she had about doing movies during the show's run. "Originally I thought I might do a film during the series hiatus, but now it would have to be a gilt-edged role to interest me. I plan to spend at least two months in Europe, where I've never been. I'll take Janie along, rent a small car and follow my nose."

These plans never reached fruition, because when the series went on hiatus it stayed there. Despite respectable ratings and a proposed move to color for the second season, ABC chose to cancel *Honey West* after one season. "Cancellation had nothing to do with ratings — it was doing very well," Anne revealed to Tom Weaver:

> But ABC was able to buy *The Avengers* for a lot less money than it cost to produce *Honey West*. Once they found that this genre would work, they dropped *Honey West* and brought over *The Avengers* — which did very well here. [*Honey West*'s] cancellation was a mixed blessing. I worked hard on that show — day after day, seventeen or eighteen hours a day. I had a four-year-old daughter at the time, and I had very little opportunity to spend any "quality time" at all with her. So in one way, the cancellation was a blessing in that I had that frustration behind me. And, for another thing, I think that if it had gone another season or two — who knows what direction anyone's life or career is going to take? I think that, when you have more than one interest in life, you can let certain areas lapse.

For her work, Anne was nominated for an Emmy in 1966. Up against her were Barbara Stanwyck for *The Big Valley* and Barbara Parkins for *Peyton Place*. Stanwyck, a good friend of Anne's, won. The day after the awards, Parkins gave an interview to Hal Humphrey in the *Los Angeles Times*. Far from the "Good Loser with Winning Ways," as the article called her, Parkins took out her claws. "I was hurt," she told him, "but if I had to lose I was glad it was to Barbara Stanwyck, who is a grand lady and fine actress. I would have hated to lose to Anne Francis. I don't care much for her work. A woman should be feminine, and not go around hitting people with judo chops the way she does in that *Honey West* show." Oh, please.

Anne did win a well-deserved Golden Globe for her performance. "I was so surprised," she told columnist Allen Rich, "that I didn't get a chance to thank all my co-workers over the air."

The Los Angeles Times noted that although the show was cancelled, Anne was mobbed at a department store appearance by 3,000 fans (only 300 were expected). The police had to be called in to control the unruly crowds. When she appeared at the premiere for the 1966 remake of *Stagecoach* in New York, producer Marty Rackin remarked, "She got more attention than any of us; she was mobbed, and she wasn't even in the picture."

"We were certainly on to something," Anne told Dennis D. Duncan in 1997. "When I looked at *Moonlighting* [1985–89] many years later with Cybill Shepherd and Bruce Willis, I thought, 'Oh, my gosh! There we are again!' You know, the blonde detective racing around flirting and carrying on and the recalcitrant boyfriend who was always angry with the girl for getting into trouble."

Backstage with Lucille Ball and Barbara Stanwyck as she and Stanwyck get their plaques for being Emmy-nominated for their roles on, respectively, *Honey West* and *The Big Valley*. Stanwyck would win the Emmy.

When *Burke's Law* was briefly revived in 1994 by executive producer Aaron Spelling and star Gene Barry, Anne showed up in a special episode on January 21, "Who Killed Nick Hazard?," which gathered together past sleuths, including Buddy Ebsen, Edd Byrnes, and Jameson Parker. Here she is "Honey Best," but don't let the name fool you. There has been speculation that she was reprising her character, that, as Gloria Fickling says, Spelling was "being greedy" not to call her "Honey West" because he didn't want to pay for the rights. But, in actuality, it was a homage, a wink to the audience, nothing more. Anne, who has the biggest guest star role, helps with the investigation of her murdered ex-husband (Robert Sacchi) while also being a suspect. At one point, Honey takes on three guys with judo, proving that in her mid–60s she still had the stuff.

BURKE: I'm impressed.
HONEY: Ha, ha, not bad for an old lady, huh?
BURKE: Not bad for a young lady.
HONEY: Well, a woman's gotta keep in shape.

There was talk in 2001 of a film version of *Honey West*, starring Reese Witherspoon, just off the success of *Legally Blonde* (2001). "I'm so excited about *Honey West* because I'm dying to do an action movie," Witherspoon said at the time. "I was such a fan of *Charlie's*

Angels and *Tomb Raider*, and I want to do one of those movies where well-known, recognizable women do their own stunts and do them so well." She also added that she wanted to bring Honey up to date, to "present a tough, buff and smart screen hero," which sounds as if she never saw the *Honey West* show or even had a clue to what it was all about.

According to Gloria Fickling, people as diverse as Dodi Fayed and Danny DeVito had movie options on the character, and Raquel Welch wanted to do an animated TV version. If Fickling has her way, Oscar winner Charlize Theron would play Honey, all the books would be adapted for the screen, and "Honey will never be portrayed as a lesbian, she will never use four-letter words, and there will be no explicit sex." Ah, good luck to you, Gloria.

A candid of Anne after she won the Golden Globe for her work on *Honey West.*

Anne told TV reporter Allan Rich near the end of *Honey West*'s run in 1966,

I don't know what the future holds, or even what I *want* to do. There are two things that drive a career girl. One is security; the other is a desire to reach the very top of her profession.

But how much security do you really need? And is it really worth it if you *do* reach the top? Last weekend I took my four-year-old daughter Jane Elizabeth for an outing at Ojai. We found a little creek and watched the trout lazily finning around. It was a beautiful day. The sun turned the place into a wonderland.

I sat still, very still for two hours. I thought: "There should be more time to enjoy things like this. Small pleasures, because this is what life is really all about."

*   *   *

The Intruders, a Universal World Premiere TV movie, was lensed in 1967, just before Anne went to work on *Funny Girl*. Filmed until the titles *A Fire in the Sky* and *Death Dance at Madelia*, it was not aired until 1970. Anne had some complaints about the film, which she shared with wire services: "On the last night of production, we had to work until midnight. If we had quit at six and shot those scenes the next day it would have cost them only possibly $3,000 more. But no — they rushed through these last few scenes that night. The

public is being cheated. They're told these films are feature film quality, feature film production. And they're not."

Anne claimed that when she saw the rushes, she thought they were "distressing." The lighting in one particular scene, she felt, was "odd." Then, later, she found out that the cameraman was under orders to light her strangely, "to make me look tired, because they felt I was too pretty." As ridiculous as this sounds Anne is right. In some scenes, she is shot from some very unflattering angles, while in others she looks very fresh and pretty. Why the director and cameraman didn't try to protect their star's appearance is unknown.

The telefilm starred Anne as Marshal Sam Garrison's (Don Murray) introverted, dissatisfied wife Leora. Long a fast-draw, he has lost his nerve and, consequently, his manhood. John Saxon plays his troubled half-

Lensed in 1967, the TV movie *The Intruders* was not shown on television until 1970. Despite her sensitive performance as Marshal Sam Garrison's (Don Murray) wife Leora, Anne was unhappy with the end result.

breed friend, Billy Pye, who is just out of jail. Their marital turmoil and brief love triangle play out against the backdrop of the James brothers and Cole Younger advancing toward their small town. Anne imbues her character with a simmering sadness that pervades the movie with its only true, unaffected feeling, doing more with a look than most actresses could do with dialogue. When she does confront her emasculated husband, she does so powerfully, with an emotion long held in check, finally coming to the surface to confront the long-repressed problems. Dean Riesner's screenplay is trite at times, but Anne treats each line delicately, elevating them to something much more than the film deserves.

In May 1967, Anne was signed for a role in the movie version of *Funny Girl*, a film that would begin shooting in July. The part she would be playing was not in the original Broadway production, although writer Isobel Lennart had originally intended it to be. Georgia James was a good character, but Lennart and everyone concerned felt that it got in the way, posed unneeded problems, and cluttered the storyline. This should have been a warning sign to Lennart when she adapted the play for the big screen, but, apparently, she paid little attention.

Fanny Brice (1891–1951) was a famous, well-liked singer-comedienne known for her work in the *Ziegfeld Follies*, where she introduced such standards as "Second Hand Rose" and "My Man." She was also popular on recordings and had a successful run as the character Baby Snooks on radio. Like Barbra Streisand, she was well known for her, shall we say, unconventional looks.

Brice's son-in-law Ray Stark had the idea of transferring her life to the stage in the early '60s. It was a long road to Broadway, however, and even when the project really starting moving forward in 1963, trouble was still ahead. The show was in rehearsals for four months, went through at least forty rewrites, four directors, and various re-orchestrations, and opening night was postponed five times, all to the tune of $750,000. *Funny Girl*, with a score by Jule Styne and Bob Merrill, premiered at the Winter Garden Theater on March 10, 1964, starring Streisand as Fanny and Sydney Chaplin as her gambler husband Nicky Arnstein. The cost was well worth it and the play was a huge success.

Anne was very excited about being cast in the movie version. She was promised some good scenes and a production number. "And a chance to work with Willie [director William] Wyler," Anne said. "That's really why I want to do it."

She told columnist Vernon Scott that *Honey West*'s cancellation was one of the lowest points of her career, but added, "As it is, maybe things have worked out for the best with *Funny Girl* coming along. My career has been unusual anyhow, and more often than not I've managed to come up with roses."

She continued, "The trouble with being an actress is that the highs are so high, and the lows are very low. Only now I'm not afraid of the downs any more. As of now, I'm in one of my high cycles. And I hope to stay that way for a while."

Unfortunately, *Funny Girl* proved to be the lowest point for the actress.

By 1967 Barbra Streisand had established herself as a major player in nightclubs, on records, on television and on the stage. She had yet to conquer the big screen, and many were skeptical that her unusual looks would transfer well in that medium.

UPI reported in June of '67: "BARBRA'S CO-STAR — Anne Francis will play a co-starring role as Barbra Streisand's sidekick in 'Funny Girl' for Columbia Pictures." Anne was not an unknown quantity in 1967–68; she was an established movie name, with more than twenty years invested in the business. But *co-star?* Maybe at first, but it was not to last. It seems the producers, perhaps skittish at the idea of Streisand's first outing as a motion picture star, were simply using a name — Anne Francis — moviegoers *would* know. It's easy today to say that *Funny Girl* was solely Streisand's movie; after all, she conquered Broadway in the same role. But at the time, before and during the production, the producers freely and extensively used Anne's name for publicity, playing up her addition to the cast. "You'll see plenty of Anne Francis in *Funny Girl*," publicity blurbs said in newspapers across the country.

Seeing "plenty of Anne Francis" apparently applied to her body, as well. Anne told Vernon Scott, "[Producer] Ray Stark has discovered my body, and decided to put me into some very revealing gowns for this picture. In one scene I appear in pasties, a G-string and hardly anything else. But beads and bangles and other things cover the rest of me up pretty well." Dorothy Manners wrote in August 1967,

> The bridal gown Irene Sharaff has designed for Anne Francis to wear in *Funny Girl* is to swoon over. I got a preview peek by accident — but I can tell you that after this the girls will forget all about those simple little wedding outfits and certainly those mini-skirted numbers worn by Raquel Welch and Ann-Margret for their "I do's."
>
> The briefest part of Anne's gown is the pink torso — really a torsoette of chiffon trimmed in small ropes of crystal beads over a long skirt. But the topper is the bejeweled turban that might have belonged to a Persian princess with clouds of pink tulle floating from the head to form the long train. With this Anne carries a small bouquet of white violets with long jeweled streamers — a poem of an outfit.

Of course, Streisand is a force to be reckoned with and *Funny Girl* was definitely her show — and rightfully so. When she's on screen, who cares about anyone else? Vocally, comically and dramatically, Streisand might not have been the best representative of Fanny Brice, but she is gloriously Streisand, larger than life and commanding the screen and our attention. But *Funny Girl* wasn't supposed to be a one-woman show, even though it played that way. The characters around Streisand were there to help tell the story.

Georgia James is described in the shooting script as "a fabulously beautiful showgirl" at forty-four years of age. Anne's entrance in the film promises much as she strides onstage, late for rehearsal, with a self-possessed, casual air. She has a brief couple of lines onstage with Fanny, giving her some advice about Florenz Ziegfeld (Walter Pidgeon). Her character was to befriend Fanny and then slip into alcoholic ruin. The character was supposed to show Fanny the downside to success.

We next see Georgia briefly during the "Beautiful Bride" number walking front and center onstage. After the number, when Fanny disobeys Flo Ziegfeld's orders and appears pregnant in a wedding gown as she sings, Georgia greets her offstage with, "My friend the show-stopper! You could have *told* me about it...." There is nothing between their first meeting and this scene to show them becoming friends and nothing seems to have been filmed to show any friendship forming. Fanny is then escorted away by an angry Ziegfeld to be reprimanded and we next see Georgia very quickly as her head bursts into the room to ask hurriedly, "Did he fire you?"

The shooting script has a short scene that includes Georgia, Fanny and the girls on a train, on tour with the *Ziegfeld Follies*. A nightgown-clad Georgia is sprawled out in a chair and as the train hits a bump she sighs, "And that's probably the most exciting thing that'll happen all day." I do not know if this scene was filmed.

Georgia's exit from the train is in the film's final cut as she stumbles down, wearing a huge overcoat and apparently little or nothing underneath. As she holds on to the conductor, she says, rather groggily, "Conductor, baby, what time is it and where are we?" When the conductor informs her that it's seven in the morning and they're in Baltimore, Georgia winces, "Baltimore. Baltimore?" Another short addition to this scene *was* filmed but cut. An old man is seen pushing a produce cart and frisky Georgia tells the girls, "A buck I get a rise out of him," as she, as per script instructions, "opens her coat. She's wearing only the briefest of panties." The startled man promptly drops his cart.

The most we see of Georgia is in the train station sequence where Fanny decides to leave the *Follies* and follow Nick to Europe,

Anne as Georgia James, a beautiful showgirl, in *Funny Girl* (1968). She had high hopes for the role.

a section that segues into the major musical number "Don't Rain on My Parade." Georgia's dialogue is brief, her appearance in the frame fleeting, at best.

The shooting script has just two more scenes that include Georgia, both of which were cut.

Fanny and Georgia have a reunion at a *Follies* rehearsal, having not seen each other in quite awhile. There is tension between Ziegfeld and Georgia, which Fanny eases. Before going to a wardrobe fitting to be measured, Fanny stops Georgia in the wings for a little talk:

FANNY (*low-voiced, stopping Georgia*): What *is* it with you and Flo? What's the matter?
GEORGIA: It's second act time, that's all.
FANNY: What's that supposed to mean?
GEORGIA: This is my fourth *Follies*. So it's probably my last.
FANNY: Sure—if you keep coming in late to rehearsals.
GEORGIA: It isn't that. If all you have to sell is a face and a body, it better be a fresh face and a fresh body.
FANNY: Ahh, come on, Georgia—you're good for *ten* more shows!
GEORGIA (*smiling*): Marvelous, that dream world you live in!
FANNY (*scowling*): I don't want anything to change, that's all!
GEORGIA (*gently*): But everything *does* change, honey—(*more lightly*) Even waistlines—so I'd better get mine measured.

The drunk scene that Anne called her best was filmed and was included in the roadshow version of the movie, but cut shortly thereafter. It's a shame the scene was cut because it served the story well, preparing the viewer for the later relationship change between Fanny and Nicky (Omar Sharif). The scene has Fanny and her mother (Kay Medford) at home. Georgia, very drunk, rings the doorbell and enters the living room.

FANNY: Georgia! I've called you a hundred times!
GEORGIA: Very — loyal. Nick tol' me. Hi, Rosie —
MRS. BRICE: Hello, Georgia. I was sorry to hear you quit the show —
GEORGIA (*shrugs*): Clock struck twelve — turned into a pumpkin. Saw him at the Phoenix Club 'bout an hour ago — sweating blood.
FANNY: Oh, come on — he was just on the phone, laughing!
GEORGIA (*shrugs*): Okay — he was laughing. Anyway — I wanna go to bed, Fan. Here. If it's all right with you —
FANNY: It's *great* with me —
GEORGIA: Because I wanna go to bed *alone*. For a change.
FANNY (*irritated*): Do you *have* to talk like a tramp?

Georgia James (Anne), Flo Ziegfeld (Walter Pidgeon) and Fanny Brice (Barbra Streisand) in one of Anne's several scenes cut from *Funny Girl.* Anne saw her meaty part cut every day, calling the treatment she received "humiliating." The final version of the film we see today contains only four minutes of screen time for Anne.

GEORGIA (*with drunken gentleness*): Fanny, I talk like a tramp because I *am* a tramp. Don't you
    ever look at the people you care about? Don't you ever *see* them?
FANNY: I see that I care about them! If that isn't enough — well, I'm sorry.
GEORGIA: Depressing — how big you are, ole friend. Makes the rest of us feel so small. So I
    won't thank you. And some day Nick won't either. And 'at's a *tip*, ole friend —
FANNY: What do you mean?!
MRS. BRICE (*jumping up*): Enough, Georgia! The maid will put you to bed! Hilda! But one
    word and I'll give you such a potch you won't sit down for a week!
GEORGIA: Attagirl, Rosie — bawl the hell out of me!

After Georgia leaves, Fanny asks her mother what Georgia meant about Nick. "Maybe that
when you look at him," Mrs. Brice answers, "you see only what you want to see."

"I see Nick as he is! I love him as he is!" Fanny counters.

Mrs. Brice simply states, "Fanny, love him a little less — help him a little more."

It was a mistake to delete this scene. If anything, the "Swan Lake" parody, which is
excruciatingly long, would have been a better, less damaging cut. Instead, they removed a
key scene, one that effectively sets up the Brice-Arnstein breakup.

It's uncertain what other scenes were planned for Georgia. As the movie stands, Anne
is seen very little, about four minutes total, never getting a full scene, just a few short snip-
pets, and one quick, weirdly hysterical and lit close-up at the train station. "But the role
originally written in the script was a wonderful, wonderful role — including a drunk scene
which I did play, but they took it out of the film. It just turned into a whole mess," Anne
sighed to Tom Weaver.

The "whole mess" has become legend. Anne found her character being cut every day,
with many people blaming Streisand's insecurities about her own looks for those deletions.
Quotes were attributed to Anne in *The Hollywood Reporter*, blaming Barbra. "Every day,
Barbra would see the rushes and the next day my part was cut or something else was cut.
Barbra ran the whole show," Anne was supposedly quoted as saying in part. "She had the
Ziegfeld girls' scenes changed — one day she told Wyler to move a girl standing next to her
because she was too pretty, and the girl wound up in the background. Eventually, the
Ziegfeld girls' scenes were eliminated altogether."

The piece, said James Spada, author of *Streisand: Her Life*, was "read or discussed
by almost everyone in Hollywood, cast a pall over the film and further sullied Streisand's bud-
ding stardom. That a respected actress like Anne Francis would speak out so forcibly against
Barbra, many felt, proved that Streisand must truly be the arrogant, egomaniacal ogre that
rumor had it. It is an image that Barbra hasn't been able to entirely shake to this day."

The press was on Anne's side all the way, noting that she wasn't the only one suffering
in the film. "Miss Streisand has made this her own private movie," columnist Gerald Nachman told his readers. Going through the rest of the cast, noting their brief contributions,
he added, "Anne Francis, an early pal, has seven lines and then vanishes."

However, the negative quotes in *The Hollywood Reporter* did not emanate from Anne at
all, but from her publicist, and it became an awkward situation for her. "I had no reason to
think that Barbra had anything to do with my scenes being cut," Anne told James Spada in
the '90s. "I think that was entirely Wyler's decision. He didn't like the character I was playing,
didn't think she added anything to the picture. There were a lot of scenes that were cut on the
very day I was to shoot them. I would sit in my dressing room, all ready to be called, and then
a note would be slipped under the door saying, 'Omit scene such and such.' It was very strange."

"I have no feud with Barbra," Anne remarked to Dick Kleiner in December of '68. "But doing that picture was like *Gaslight*. What infuriated me was the way they did things — never telling me, never talking to me, just cutting. I think they were afraid that if they were nice to me, Barbra would have been upset."

Isobel Lennart explained to Sheilah Graham in February 1968, "Anne's role was very good and she had a right to be upset when the best parts were cut. As always happens, the picture went over-length, and they had to cut somewhere and Anne's role was the most expendable, I suppose; but it was a shame because she was excellent." Supervising editor Robert Swink agreed. "I know the Anne Francis role was cut down terribly. But [Wyler] only did it for the sake of the picture. He had final cut. Streisand didn't."*

Many thought that, with all her scenes intact, Anne would have been a shoo-in for a Best Supporting Actress Oscar nomination. Instead, Kay Medford, billed ahead of Anne, was given the nomination for her role as Mrs. Brice. Streisand tied with Katharine Hepburn (for *The Lion in Winter*) to win the Best Actress Oscar.

Actress Marianne McAndrew had a similar experience when she appeared with Streisand in *Hello, Dolly!* (1969). "As was the case with Streisand and Anne Francis in *Funny Girl*," Vernon Scott told his readers, "Barbra has few scenes with Marianne in the new hit musical. For whatever reason, presumably the script, Barbra rarely appears in a two-shot with a stunning female." McAndrew told Scott, "Barbra and I have only two major scenes together, and both of them were easy. They went well. We were seven months on that picture and I can't say Barbra and I became friends. After our scenes we'd go our own ways. Barbra is a big star protected by the various people around her. I wasn't sure if attempting a friendship would be precarious for me. So I didn't.... Two women appearing in the same picture is somewhat difficult anyhow. It's competitive and hard to explain."

Anne's last word on the matter was an "Open Letter to Barbra Streisand," which she posted to her website in February 2002:

Dear Barbra,

It has gnawed at me for years that you have believed that I blamed you for cutting most of my scenes from *Funny Girl*. I felt the sadness of the misunderstanding all over again when I read a supposed quote of yours last year saying that you had heard me blame you on a TV talk show. The only talk show I did on the subject was on Johnny Carson, and Joey Bishop was subbing that night. I tried to make it plain that I did not blame you, and had no idea why I was cut from the film. To this day, I don't know the circumstances that caused the decision, but I am led to believe it probably had to do with the length of the film. The subplot of Georgia's histrionics with Florenz Ziegfeld was really not necessary to the story about Fanny Brice.

In all fairness, I understand that the press believed that I felt that way because my public relations person, who was also a very dear friend, did believe it, and she made the statements that were attributed to me. I was caught in the middle, and rather than point a finger at her, I did the best I could to refute the story whenever confronted by an interviewer. The whole thing was messy and painful. I had never been embroiled in that sort of ruckus before. I know you were going through a lot of flack

*Going too far and relying on rumors, the *Tucson Daily Citizen*'s Q&A column added more myth than fact to the story. A reader asked the question, "Is it true that Barbra Streisand wouldn't allow any pretty girls to appear alongside her in the movie *Funny Girl*?" The response: "The singer is very sensitive about her unusual looks and saw to it that no prettier face appeared in the same scene with her. With the result, of course, that she is seen only with men. Because of the dictatorial powers given her by the studio bosses, Miss Streisand cut most of the scenes featuring beautiful Ziegfeld Girls. Actress Anne Francis, a gorgeous blonde, demanded that her name be removed from the screen credits because all her big scenes were cut. The only time she appears together with Miss Streisand she is photographed from the rear."

Anne is seen briefly at the conclusion of the "Beautiful Brides" musical number. Dorothy Manners described this outfit for readers in 1967: "The briefest part of Anne's gown is the pink torso — really a torsoette of chiffon trimmed in small ropes of crystal beads over a long skirt. But the topper is the bejeweled turban that might have belonged to a Persian princess with clouds of pink tulle floating from the head to form the long train. With this Anne carries a small bouquet of white violets with long jeweled streamers — a poem of an outfit."

Between takes during the filming of Anne's first scene in *Funny Girl*. Barbra Streisand, as Fanny Brice, looks on bewildered.

as well during those stormy days when first you hit Hollywood (or it hit you!). I had hoped then that it would all blow over quickly, but when I saw the quote you allegedly made recently, I felt awful once more.

At the age of thirty-five (over the hill in those days!), the role of Georgia was a great gem for me, and I had high hopes (I had just come off of *Honey West*) that it would do a lot for my "career." The flashy role, along with the drunk scene (which hit the editor's floor), pretty much cinched the prospect of a supporting nomination with the Academy that year. So, you can understand the humiliation when each day a note would be slipped under my dressing room door, "omit scene so and so." The scene named would always be the one I had been called in to do that day. I am not whining, dear lady. We've all taken our lumps in this "Business." I'm just sharing with you what was going on at that time with me. You had your own problems. I marveled at how you handled yourself on your first encounter with the alien world of the film industry.

I have had the greatest respect for your talent and for what you have made of yourself, Barbra. You are a brilliant woman and I have always wished you the very best. One more time, it is important for me before I leave this planet to say, I have never accused you of having the role of Georgia cut to the quick.

God Bless.

P.S. Your direction of *Prince of Tides* was superb.

Unfortunately, then as now, Barbra probably didn't care one way or the other.

* * *

Long a rodeo fan, Anne went into a totally different direction in 1968 and started writing and directing an 18-minute film on the Mother Lode Rodeo in Sonora, California. She even formed a company with her friend Jim Moran. "Right now our production company is a weekend hobby, mainly because my acting career has kept me so busy," she explained to Florabel Muir. "But eventually I plan to write, produce and possibly even direct feature films. I think Lucille Ball and Ida Lupino have made the industry realize that women are just as gifted and creative in those areas as the men are."

Ultimately called *Gemini Rising*, the short film takes the view of the rodeo world through the eyes of a small boy. Anne called it "a sort of art film," and shot it with her own crew of two cameramen and a sound man. They shot thousands of feet of film, from dawn to dusk. She basically used her own money for this personal project. "Most young blondes in those days were not taken too seriously," she explained to David D. Duncan in 1997. "I had wanted to work on a project all my own from beginning to end for many years. Of course, in those days, I had managers who said, 'Look, you're an actress. You're not supposed to do this other business.' And now I look at all the women today who are doing it, and no one's batting an eyelash. But at that time, it was considered just a whim." Anne really had no plans to continue filmmaking, however.

The television movie *Lost Flight* (1969), co-starring Lloyd Bridges and Ralph Meeker, was meant as a pilot for a potential series, and was filmed in Hawaii. As a series it was a no-go, but probably would have played like a dramatic *Gilligan's Island* as the survivors of the plane crash try to cope with being stranded on a remote island.

Anne had a few good screen moments in *More Dead Than Alive* (1969), a tough Western starring Clint Walker as a killer, out of prison after 18 years, who wants to settle down to a quiet life but is unable to shed his past. It was an oft-told story, but elevated by good acting, especially by Vincent Price, and brutal action scenes. As in the later *Pancho Villa* (1972), Anne and Clint had nice chemistry, making the ending of *More Dead Than Alive* resonate with an unexpected sadness.

She was alternating her television appearances in the late '60s (*The Fugitive, The Invaders, The Name of the Game, Mission: Impossible*) with a new surge in bigscreen activity. The problem with these movie roles was that she too often played second fiddle, especially in the awful Jerry Lewis comedy *Hook, Line and Sinker*

As shipwreck survivor Gina Talbot in the TV movie *Lost Flight* (1969).

(1969). It was the last film for veteran director George Marshall, who continued to do television work up until his death in 1975. "Jerry pretty much was running the show when we did *Hook, Line and Sinker*," Anne told *Filmfax*. "George kind of let Jerry do what Jerry wanted to do. It was pretty much Jerry's film."

The romance between ex-con Killer Cain (Clint Walker) and artist Monica Alton (Anne) elevates *More Dead Than Alive* (1969) into more than a just a brutal Western.

Filmed under the title *Golden Bullet*, *Impasse* (1969) toplined Burt Reynolds as a man in charge of a group searching for a lost gold shipment, and Anne as the tennis champ he briefly romances. It was an okay actioner, with location shooting in the Philippines, but required little from her, although in one scene she utilized a karate chop to defend herself against a bad guy. Anne enjoyed working with a pre-stardom Reynolds, admiring his sense of humor and his ability to not take himself seriously. Burt wasn't too pleased with the assignment or the low pay-check, but he liked working with Anne, calling her a "great gal." (Anne also appeared on Reynolds' TV series *Dan August*, and they starred together, along with James Drury, on stage during the week of July 27, 1971, in *The Tender Trap*, with the Kenley Players in Warren, Ohio.)

Better was her lead with Don Knotts in one of his best, but most underrated, vehicles, *The Love God?* (1969). (Anne was taking over for Dyan Cannon, who had opted instead for a supporting role in *Bob & Carol & Ted & Alice*. Dick Van Dyke was the first choice for the part Knotts eventually played.) Abner Audubon Peacock IV (Knotts), a bird-calling champion of a small town, gets conned into becoming the Love God to sell magazines. Lisa LaMonica (Anne), "the golden girl of the magazine world," must convince him what a hot item he is with the ladies. Of course, Knotts' attempts at being a ladies' man are hilarious, with Anne right alongside him as a woman out for success, pretending to fall in love with him, yet finding herself inexplicably attracted for real. The scene where hired girls openly flirt in public with Abner, with Lisa getting increasingly irritated and jealous, frantically firing them one by one, is truly funny stuff. Unfortunately, it was not a successful movie, probably because it was not in line with Don Knotts' usual, family-friendly fare; the comedy was more adult-oriented, not something his fans were used to seeing in those days.

Having worked recently with two comedy greats, Jerry Lewis and Don Knotts, Anne was of course asked to compare the two and their styles. "Don is hysterical to work with,"

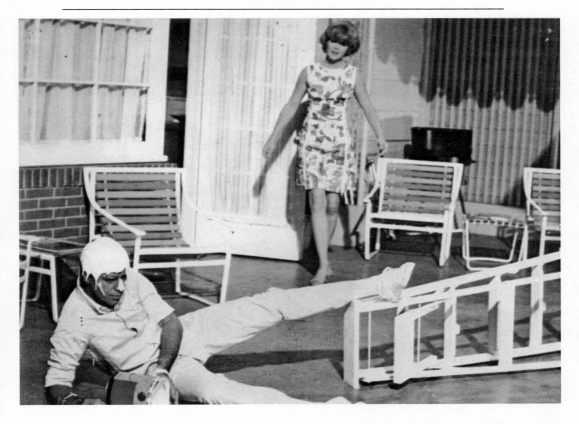

Anne plays second fiddle to Jerry Lewis' kooky shenanigans in *Hook, Line and Sinker* (1969).

Anne told Florabel Muir on the set of *The Love God?* "No ego thing with him. He's all pro. Everything is carefully worked out before he steps in front of that camera. Nothing is left to chance. Jerry is quite different. He likes to improvise; consequently working with him is more hectic than working with Don. Also, Jerry drives himself. He's always 'on.' He thrives on this business."

"It's funny in a way," Anne noted in 1969. "The best pictures I've made have all been dumped. *Girl of the Night*, which I thought was one of my best, wound up on the lower half of a double bill. And a picture I thought was a gem, *The Love God?* with Don Knotts, just wasn't exploited. Things like that can destroy you. But, like playing cards, I've been at the tables long enough to win some, lose some."

In late 1969, Anne started filming the movie *Survival*, produced and directed by Michael Campus on a budget of $100,000. The cast, which also included Barry Sullivan, Sheree North, Chuck McCann, and Suzanne Benton, worked for minimum scale plus a deferred percentage of the eventual profits. Filmed in a single room in Hollywood, with a 12-day shooting schedule, it was largely improvisational. Campus simply told his cast what personalities they would have, which one must be voted out each round, and that's all. A risky approach in the Hollywood of the time.

Campus had previously been a television director, but wanted to do an independent feature. "I had an idea for this movie," he told Dick Kleiner. "I went to a millionaire and he listened to me and gave me $100,000. So now I'm making the movie. [The premise is] different. The story, if you want to call it that, is about nine beautiful people who come to a dinner party and, together with the host and the waiter play a game." It's a game of survival: Each must convince the others they have the right to survive and not be voted out of the room. With each character's elimination, various hatreds, hang-ups and other human qualities are exposed.

The actors all went by their first names for their characters, said Campus, to help make the action more spontaneous, the action more real. Kleiner noted, "A great deal of spontaneity has developed — Chuck McCann leaped across the table at Hampton Fancher, in a bit that nobody had expected. Anne Francis broke down and wept. Dee Hartford, playing the hostess, openly ignored Otis Young, the waiter — and a black man — because she felt her character would have ignored him."

"We had two weeks of rehearsal — with videotape, so we could play it back immediately," Campus told Bob Thomas. "During that time, each of the actors had to give of himself. The script had to come from their getting to know one another. Although we followed the basic script, the cast and I literally created the dialogue and the action." For the first six days, he did the master shots of the scenes where they all played the game. At this time, he used a television system to tape the action, and then he had secretaries transcribe the dialogue so the actors could then have a script and memorize it for matching close-ups. The film saw only limited release in 1976 and remains Anne's most elusive credit.

Anne and a pre-stardom Burt Reynolds in the Philippines-made actioner *Impasse* (1969). They would team again on Burt's TV show *Dan August* and on stage in *The Tender Trap* in Ohio in 1971.

The '70s were a very busy time on television for Anne, guesting on such shows as *The F.B.I.*, *Love, American Style*, a three-part *My Three Sons*, *Columbo*, *Ironside*, *Gunsmoke*, *The Men from Shiloh*, *Barnaby Jones*, *Cannon*, *Banacek*, *Kung Fu*, *Wonder Woman*, a two-part *Baa Baa Black Sheep*, *Hawaii Five-O*, *Vega$*, and many others. What's remarkable about this work-a-day existence was its sheer variety and Anne's enthusiastic, skillful approach to all of them.

Anne is out to convince an uncomfortable Don Knotts that he's irresistible to women in *The Love God?* (1969). The film, one of Knotts' best, did poorly at the box office because it was not in line with his usual, family-friendly fare.

In May 1970, Anne adopted a daughter whom she named Margaret West. (The name "West," she said, was a family name and not a reference to *Honey West*.) The adoption was one of the first granted a single parent in the state of California. The process took about six months to finalize; "The day Maggie and Janey and I went to court was a glorious day," Anne wrote in *Voices from Home*.

A standout during this period was *Wild Women* (1970), a fun, rambunctious made-for-TV Western about women convicts posing as wives on a wagon train concealing weapons for the Army. Surprisingly, its source, the novel *The Trailmakers* by Vincent Fotre, was the exact opposite: hard, gritty, uncompromising and without any humor. Writers Richard Carr and Lou Morheim took the basic premise and somehow rolled a bouncy confection out of it.

In the novel, the character of Jean Marshek is much different from the impish, likable, headstrong lady Anne portrayed in the movie. "Her mouth was large and sensuous, her eyes mocking and challenging," Fotre wrote. Refusing to fit in, she is disliked by the other women; with her vain prejudice and overly sexual ways, she makes no friends, and doesn't care. "But Jean Marshek knew men; she knew the sweaty, dust-covered cowboys, and the rich cattle barons; she knew the oily, shifty-eyed merchants, and the thin-lipped, unsmiling gunslingers." Her casual dalliance with the scout Lecreole ultimately has tragic consequences, as her feelings for him, to her surprise, deepen but go unrequited. The novel's conclusion has her sacrificing herself to save the only man she ever loved. ("The bullet took her just above the heart. She fell over the top step; her view of the wall was obscured by the tower. She tried to drag herself forward to see if Lecreole had made it to the fort, but she was suddenly terribly tired; a heavy red fog hung over her eyes. She tried to fight it, but the fog pushed down on her, crushing out the last tiny flame of life. She closed her eyes to sleep.") It is a shame that a faithful adaptation could not be fashioned, as the multifaceted character could have proved a real acting challenge for Anne.

But, as it stands, *Wild Women* is fun all the way, one of the most underrated, enjoyable television movies of this period. Anne is all sass and wisecracks as she spars with scout Hugh O'Brian (his character renamed Killian) on the dusty trail.

"Do you want to take her along?" Killian is asked of Jean.

"Well, captain, you're picking the horses at this auction," Killian grumbles, to which Jean replies, saucily, "You have mares so far; how about a filly or two?"

She was well-matched with the virile O'Brian, and the two played off each other's strengths very well. It was a good, solid comedy role, something not often given Anne. The scene where the girls brew homemade hooch, under the dubious guidance of Lottie Clampett (Marie Windsor), and then proceed to get stinkin' drunk, is very broadly played, but still great fun.

"I had never worked with Marie Windsor and Marilyn Maxwell before," Anne told Leona Pappas. "Those two gals are great. I had lots of fun doing the film. We had a marvelous director [Don Taylor]. It is about Texas but was shot here in California."

In October 1970, Anne made another bold acting move when she accepted a role in Mart Crowley's play *Remote Asylum*, which debuted at the Ahmanson Theatre on December 1. She got the part when originally cast Dina Merrill had to bow out; her then-husband, Cliff Robertson, objected to her playing what he thought was an unsavory character. Directed by Jose Quintero, co-starring William Shatner, Nancy Kelly, and Arthur O'Connell, *Remote Asylum* centered on a group of people at a Mexican resort sorting out their troubled lives. It was not well-received, to say the least. Critic Robert C. Wylder queried his readers, "Imagine Honey West and Captain Kirk as uneasy lovers in a plush retreat in a far-away country, a sort of Mexican Shangri-La with electricity. Sound interesting? Well, it isn't, really." He did single out Anne's "stellar performance," which "revealed flashes of acting ability" whenever the play gave her a chance. If anything, the actors were not criticized as much as Crowley's writing, which was unrealistically compared to his previous success, *The Boys in the Band* (1968). "And just how are we to react to one emotional scene in particular where Miss Francis hits her bed repeatedly with a tennis racket screaming, 'I'll kill 'em, I'll kill 'em!'?" wrote Rick Talcove of the *Van Nuys News*.

"Can they find strength in their collective weakness, compassion in their selfishness, resolution in their indecision?" asked Wylder. He, nor very few critics, thought they could. *Remote Asylum* ran six weeks but did not reach its projected goal of Broadway.

"I'm having a good year. That's why I'm having so much done to my house," Anne told columnist Joan Crosby in 1971. "I consider myself very fortunate. I've had bad years. How do

Above and opposite: The late '60s briefly brought on a new, modern look for Anne.

you get through them? Pull in your belt and don't have things fixed." Crosby marveled at Anne's positive outlook. "She says that over the years, an actor can learn to handle the downs of the business. She's an optimist." Anne added that she believed that "life is filled with so many cycles. One day can make such a tremendous difference to any one of us. A year ago I had a sparse period and was living from month to month. I went through my shelves and found tilings that could be fixed and put to use."

But she had to admit that there were few roles out there for women of a certain age. "I'd really like to sink my teeth into a strong feminine role," she said to Vernon Scott in 1972. "But they aren't writing that kind of script any more unless there's nudity or vulgarity involved. Maybe the writers and producers will change their minds when they get tired of filming pornography.... Maybe some people are endurance runners. Perhaps I'm one of those. If so I hope to be playing parts without nude scenes. I haven't done any so far, and I have no intention of doing them in the future."

The early '70s were bumpy years for her and other actors of her generation. While she was still getting television guest shots and TV movie work, financially, unless you were a

Anne nabbed a choice comedy role in *Wild Women* (1970), a fun, rambunctious TV movie about women convicts posing as wives on a wagon train concealing weapons for the Army. "You have mares so far; how about a filly or two?" she saucily challenges scout Hugh O'Brian.

superstar, things were rough all over. She admitted to Mark Vasche, a reporter in Turlock, where she was making a special guest appearance at a rodeo, "Many actors have been wise enough, because of the insecurity of the field, to put enough aside for those rainy days. But we never expected this cloudburst."

She believed things were going to get better. "Independent films will bring a great change," she noted, while promoting her short rodeo film, for which she was still trying to secure exhibition venues.

In 1971 a movie such as *The Forgotten Man* was timely, but today some scenes drag and seem unintentionally funny. Erroneously reported dead, Marine Lieutenant Joe Hardy (Dennis Weaver) returns home from the Vietnam War after five years to find his life has passed him by. Added to this, he is experiencing violent mental flashbacks to the tortures he suffered while a POW. His mental state isn't helped when he finds his father has died, his business has been sold, and his wife Marie (Anne) has remarried and is pregnant. The people around him, who supposedly loved him before he went away, all now seem selfishly concerned only with their own problems, giving little thought to

A luminous publicity portrait of the actress.

the hell he has been through. In fact, knowing that he has come back with some mental issues, everyone seems oblivious that the antagonism directed toward him only makes him worse. It's this alienation element that makes this movie of interest today, one of the more realistic looks at the returning vet and his difficulties readjusting to civilian life. Filming took place around Tucson, the Marine Corps base at Camp Pendleton, and in Los Angeles.

Based on the brutal, no-holds-barred novel by Emile Richard Johnson, *Mongo's Back in Town* (1971) was pretty raw, even for a telefilm, and still packs a punch today. Johnson, an inmate at Minnesota State Prison since 1967, was the author of seven books and the recipient of the 1968 Edgar award for best first mystery novel, *Silver Street*. Johnson was serving a 40-year sentence for robbery-murder.

"Most of my books are personal experiences," Johnson told the *Tucson Daily Citizen*. "They're based on real people, changed around some. They may seem too realistic to a square John — to people on the street. But they're the way I see things. I write about unrelieved characters."

Shot in and around the San Pedro area, the movie completely captures the novel's bleak atmosphere. What couldn't be depicted because of censorship is remarkably laid out on the screen projected in Joe Don Baker's face. His scowl brings out all the significance in the mean, rotten, down-and-dirty story. Baker is perfectly cast, as is Sally Field as the

Andrew Duggan and Anne's happiness on their wedding day will soon be complicated when her thought-to-be-dead previous husband shows up alive and wants to resume their relationship in the TV movie *The Forgotten Man* (1971).

young, naïve, just-into-town girl, Vikki, who is bought by Mongo Nash and forced to succumb to his sexual demands. Anne plays Angel, his ex-mistress, the one woman who could wrap him around her finger ... but she doesn't realize, yet, that things change when a man's been in prison and has a score to settle with his double-dealing brother.

Johnson's conception of Anne's character in the novel was more sexually confident. Here, Anne takes a wry approach to the role, flippant and frankly bored in her handling of the men in her life, until her final scene where, leaning over in pain from a beating, she calls Mongo's brother and informs him that he's on his own; Mongo is coming after him.

Although she was given prominent billing, Anne had only one scene in *Fireball Forward* (1972), a neat World War II television movie that was intended as a pilot, starring Ben Gazzara, Ricardo Montalban, and Peter Falk. The movie's producer, Frank McCarthy, was a retired reserve brigadier general and during World War II was aide to General of the Army George C. Marshall. McCarthy explained, "*Fireball Forward* is not

Anne was very busy in the 1970s on television, appearing in made-for-TV movies and episodic work.

a combat film. It is a suspense story set in a military headquarters in wartime. I have wanted for a long time to depict the urgency of war without its violence and gore. There are dozens of human interest stories with World War II as a background waiting to be told." Anne played Helen Sawyer, a newspaper correspondent at the Army division headquarters. She told Vernon Scott,

> I wasn't aware of the fact that I was the only woman in the cast. When you're involved in what you're playing, the circumstances don't even occur to you.
> I love working with heavyweight actors who really dig into their work. Ben Gazzara is like that. So is Ricardo. And recently I did a *Columbo* episode with Peter Falk. They're all terrific.
> There's no question that I do a better job when I am working with real professionals. You discipline yourself to do your best work all the time, but it helps immeasurably when the actors you're working with are giving everything they've got to make it all real.

Despite the good cast, and a script co-written by Edmund North, who received an Oscar for 1970's *Patton* (also produced by McCarthy), *Fireball Forward* was not picked up as a series.

That year she was lucky enough to get an excellent supporting role in *Haunts of the Very Rich* (1972), a moody, disquieting TV movie which featured location filming at the famed Vizcaya Estate on Miami's Biscayne Bay and interiors at 20th Century–Fox. It's the old *Outward Bound*, are-we-actually-dead story, revised for the '70s. The cast, which also features Donna Mills, Ed Asner, Lloyd Bridges, and Cloris Leachman, is adequate, but their stories can't compare to those of Robert Reed as Reverend John Fellows, who has lost his faith, and Anne, portraying Annette Larrier, whose slowly unraveling psyche (and the reasons for her being there) reveals a deeply troubled woman. Annette just wants to rest and can't handle pressure, but as the tension mounts on the island, as mysterious things begin happening, she gradually starts to break mentally, finally trying to commit suicide. It's an amazing turn, subtle, progressing, and ultimately very disturbing and real. She had every right to be proud of this work.

Lillian Gallo was working as a development executive at ABC when she was given the opportunity to produce this, her first film. "Our first day was scheduled as a long day of shooting on difficult terrain in Florida," she told Mollie Gregory in *Women Who Run the Show*. "When we'd completed it, the network representative said to me, 'You did a very good job. There isn't a man who could have done it better.' Men were not accustomed to working with women. It was the nicest thing he felt he could say.

"Anne Francis wrote a letter to ABC, which was passed on to me. She said it was the first time in her career that she'd worked for a woman producer, that it was a 'wonderful experience,' that working on the set was 'different,' the crew's language was 'different,' and

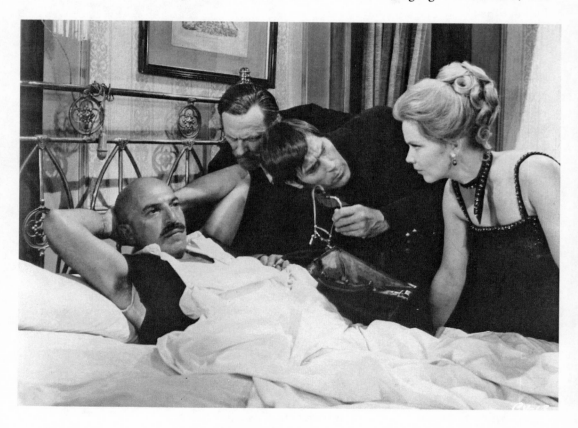

A comic scene from the satire *Pancho Villa* (1972) with Carl Rapp, Clint Walker and Anne trying to diagnose Pancho's (Telly Savalas) ailments.

that the tone I'd set as the producer was 'different.' I was touched by her sensibilities. Consciously or unconsciously, women do bring different things to the workplace. Diversity is good for all of us."

Anne reunited with her *More Dead Than Alive* co-star Clint Walker in *Pancho Villa* (1972), which was shot in Madrid, Spain. Even with a cast that also included Telly Savalas (as an improbable, not to mention bald, Pancho) and Chuck Connors, the production was fraught with money and script problems in the beginning. Producer Bernard Gordon got along well with all the principals, but in his autobiography, *Hollywood Exile or How I Learned to Love the Blacklist*, he mentions that Savalas did try to act the "star" on the movie. "Telly also made problems with his co-star, Clint Walker," Gordon wrote. "Walker had recently survived a horrifying skiing accident, when a ski pole virtually penetrated his heart. As a result of this intimation of mortality, Walker informed me on arrival that he was through with any ego trips; he only wanted a peaceful existence and friendly relations with everyone. He had gotten religion. Only too happy to take advantage of this, Telly upstaged Walker whenever he could. Walker kept to his word and swallowed Telly's tricks until the last day of shooting." When Telly wanted a two-shot changed to a solo shot of himself; Walker, according to Gordon, "exploded and refused to do the scene." Gordon was called in by director Eugenio Martin to settle the matter.

It was not all tension on the set. "Between takes, Telly wore the tiniest yellow bikini you ever saw," recalled Anne to columnist Bob Martin. "Clint thought it was outrageous."

Anne enjoyed an easygoing screen camaraderie with Walker here, as they play a married couple always fighting with each other. The part was a good one for Anne, the light comedy satire giving her some fun moments.

Pancho Villa plays as both an action-packed Western and a good-natured satire, the latter aspect going largely misunderstood and underappreciated today. Savalas in the title role turns off some viewers, who cite him as miscast, but his casting works within the framing of the satire that writer Julian Zimet, with the assistance of Gordon and Philip Yordan, created. *Pancho Villa*,

A cheerful Anne out on the town in the 1970s.

concluded Gordon, "is not a film I would nominate for any kind of award, but, despite script problems, it was finished on time and on budget, was completed ... without the endless reshooting of every other Yordan production, and it even received some favorable notices."

The John Forsythe starrer *Cry Panic* (1974), directed by James Goldstone, was a solid mystery telefeature. In the early morning hours, David Ryder (Forsythe) accidentally strikes and kills a man with his car. Confused and disheveled, he goes to a nearby house to call for help. A skeptical woman (Anne) answers the door and gives him a drink as he calls 911. When he returns to the scene of the accident, however, there is no trace of the dead man. Worse yet, when he brings the police to the house, there is no sign of the woman who let him in; another woman lives there.

Jack B. Sowards' teleplay builds up the mysterious circumstances and the hero's psychological dilemma, presenting Anne's character, the key to the whole mystery, in an ethereal

Anne presents the Miss Rodeo California 1974 belt buckle to Nani Patten. Anne was the grand marshal in the Turlock, California, roundup parade.

manner. Forsythe is fine as a man battling paranoia, unable to convince anyone what really happened. He is matched in the acting department by Ralph Meeker, Earl Holliman, and Anne, whose final scene is reminiscent of her comeuppance in *Bad Day at Black Rock*.

The F.B.I. Story: The F.B.I. Versus Alvin Karpis, Public Enemy Number One (1974) was based on a landmark FBI case. Karpis, played here by Robert Foxworthy, was one of the Depression era's most notorious criminals. His eventual capture marked the first time that J. Edgar Hoover, director of the FBI, took a personal interest in a case and brought a criminal to justice himself. This TV movie was made with the cooperation of the then-director of the FBI, Clarence M. Kelley. It boasted a first-rate cast, with Eileen Heckart a standout as a growly Ma Barker. Anne plays an Arkansas madam, Colette, who becomes Karpis' mistress while he is hiding out. Location filming took place in Grass Valley, a small town in the Mother Lode country of Northern California. It was to be the first of a series of special films produced by Quinn Martin Productions based on landmark cases of the FBI with the overall title of "The FBI Story."

In 1974, after the filming of *Karpis*, Anne was lamenting the rising inflation and the scarcity of good paying gigs. "These days TV shows, instead of paying more, are trying to get you to work for less," she told NEA. "The new residual ruling, under our new union contract, won't make itself felt for some time. And, besides, there just aren't that many jobs around now." Throughout '74 Anne appeared in print ads for Abbey carpets, proclaiming, "Abbey carpeted my home. Why not talk to Abbey about carpeting your home?"

Anne did shoot a syndicated series pilot, one she had high hopes for; it was certainly a novel idea for 1974. The premise every week would be Anne fixing things around the house (plumbing, carpentry and electricity). She thought up the title herself: *Home Improvements*. (In the 1990s, Anne guest starred on Tim Allen's *Home Improvement,* a sitcom about a man who hosts a similar show.)

She had very little chance to stand out in *The Last Survivors* (1975), a television movie based on a harrowing true story. It told of seaman Alexander William Holmes, played superbly by Martin Sheen, taking command of a lifeboat after a luxury liner sinks and the captain dies. During terrible storms, lack of food and water, he must make the decision who stays on the overcrowded boat and who goes. When they are rescued, he is tried for manslaughter. The story was filmed previously in 1957 (*Abandon Ship* with Tyrone Power); this retelling was quite good, if underrated, and didn't hold back showing the unsettling task Holmes had to perform. Anne, of course, was good, as is the rest of the capable cast, but Sheen's performance drives this riveting, unnerving ensemble piece.

A Girl Named Sooner (1975) was based on the Suzanne Clouser novel and directed by Delbert Mann (Best Director Oscar winner for *Marty*). Filmed during the summer of 1974, it told the sensitive story of an illiterate backwoods girl, Sooner (Susan Deer), taken in by veterinarian "Mac" McHenry (Richard Crenna) and his wife Elizabeth (Lee Remick). Anne plays Selma Goss, an old flame of Crenna's now involved with local sheriff Phil Rotteman (Don Murray). The movie's cost was reported to be about three times that of a normal TV film. The twenty-two-day location shoot took place in Switzerland County near Vevay, Indiana. The producers found Vevay's downtown area still conveyed the setting of the mid–1930s with its lack of parking meters and its many aging river homes.

An unnamed TV reporter from *The Transcript* summed up this movie best: "[This] is slow-moving, depressing and has a nasty scene in which kids kill a bird. It does have Susan Deer, an appealing child, as Sooner and a great characterization from Cloris Leachman. The stars are Lee Remick, Richard Crenna, Anne Francis and Don Murray, wasted in small roles." Still, Anne's few scenes were well played and understated.

She made a welcome cameo appearance as Flora Dobbs in a project that was aiming for a series run, *Banjo Hackett: Roamin' Free* (1976), and even got to sing ("My Sweetheart's the Man in the Moon"). It starred ex-football player Don Meredith but, to the *Los Angeles Times,* it was Anne's show all the way. "A number of cameo roles are laced in to beef up the pilot, played by old favorites Chuck Connors, Slim Pickens, Jeff Corey, Jennifer Warren, Jan Murray, Dan O'Herlihy and Gloria De Haven. And one is played by Anne Francis, who just may succeed before Meredith does in landing her own series as a result of being cast here."

"I play a lady of the theater," Anne told Paul Henniger, "a kind of dingy person in a cute, fun role. Banjo meets her and cons her into believing he can give her a better horse than the one she has. I'm only on screen with him about six or seven minutes." Never too keen on accepting another series since the grueling schedule of *Honey West*, Anne was nevertheless "enchanted" by the character Ken Trevey created. "Trevey, who writes with humor and has a good feeling for western lore, and I were talking about [a possible series for Flora].... My character would be a member of a traveling theatrical group in the late 19th century, their circuit being western and unique towns." Unfortunately, nothing came of the idea.

It's just astonishing to observe Anne's versatility in her TV roles, as week after week she assumed another diverse character. For instance, on October 28, 1978, she appeared on *Fantasy Island's* "Queen of the Boston Bruisers" as a likable roller derby queen, "Rowdy" Roberts, who wants to be a lady for the sake of her soon-to-wed daughter. Watching Anne, dressed in her derby uniform, talkin' trash to a derby rival, head back laughing with gusto, and then clumsily being taught social graces by Tattoo, with outstanding comic timing, has to be seen to be believed. Just days later, on November 1, Anne took it into another direction, special guesting on *Charlie's Angels'* "Pom Pom Angels." Here she's Margo, an ex-prostitute delivered to the side of God, shorn of her "ego-bleached hair" and now sporting a short black do. Wearing a brown, belted robe, rarely blinking, Anne is silently and creepily effective in her bad girl role. She raises her voice just once, snapping at upstart Kris Munroe (Cheryl Ladd), and the sudden, commanding outburst is very potent. "I think we could take care of one wicked witch," Munroe tells one of the girl hostages about Margo. The girl isn't so convinced. "She's tough and she eats regularly," she marvels. It's nice seeing Anne on the wrong side of the law for a change — being very stern, a little delusional, and, with a dagger in hand, very menacing.

The Wonderful World of Disney aired a made-for-TV movie in 1978, *The Young Runaways*. The comedy, first titled *The Snatching of Little Freddie*, was the story of two kids who get involved with bank robbers (Anne and Robert Webber). Less memorable was Anne's throwaway role in *Little Mo* (1978), the story of Maureen Connolly, who at the age of 17 became the first woman to win the "grand slam" of tennis and died young at 34. Glynnis O'Connor starred, playing Mo from ages 9 to 34. The acting by O'Connor and Michael Learned was outstanding, but the story was far too long and pointless. Reviewer Joan Hanauer called it "three hours of thwack-bonk, thwack-bonk." She incisively added, "The real life story of Miss Connolly was spectacular, but the same can't be said for the television version, despite an excellent cast ... and the best of intentions.... What went wrong? First, choice of subject matter. Off the court, Little Mo was a teenage girl whose extracurricular life was as exciting as bubblegum." Anne is underused as sportswriter Leslie Nielsen's wife, who becomes the young tennis player's chaperone on the road.

Anne had a much better role when she appeared as Patty Colson in the feature film *Born Again* (1978). The project was a labor of love for its star Dean Jones, who was himself a born-again Christian. Charles Colson was President Nixon's special counsel from 1969 to 1973, famously known as Nixon's "Hatchet Man." He was indicted on March 1, 1974, for conspiring to cover up the Watergate burglary and he was sent to prison, serving seven months of his one-to-three-year sentence in Alabama's Maxwell Prison. He converted to Christianity in 1973, writing about this life-altering event in his 1976 memoir *Born Again*.

All royalties on his multi-million-dollar book were donated by Colson to his project, the Prison Fellowship.

"This is the story of someone overcoming adversity," Anne said at the time of the film's release. "Charles Colson is controversial politically and religiously. I play a woman who loves and stands by her husband. I felt an instant rapport with Mrs. Colson when we met. I was pleased to find her honest, straightforward and a person with inner strength. Maybe most important was her sense of humor." Patty Hughes Colson became, after the Watergate

In one of her few feature films of the 1970s Anne played Patty Colson in *Born Again* (1978). Dean Jones, himself a born-again Christian, portrayed Charles Colson, President Nixon's special counsel from 1969 to 1973; known as Nixon's "Hatchet Man," Colson found God during his prison sentence.

scandal, quite private, although she helped her husband with his Christian work while he was in jail and afterwards. She declined many interviews, but was described as an "ebullient, warm, and outgoing" lady — although bearing absolutely no resemblance to Anne Francis whatsoever. She was, even at the time, gray-haired and described by many as matronly. But, no matter; Anne was able to convey other aspects of Mrs. Colson's character and her unwavering devotion to her husband.

Even though television columnist Joey Sasso reported that "Doug McClure, Tom Bosley and Anne Francis have been signed for major roles in MCA TV/Universal's four-hour two-part Operation-Prime Time presentation of John Jakes' *The Rebels*— the adventurous sequel to *The Bastard*," a major role was not what you would call Anne's minuscule part. It consisted of one scene; if you blinked, you missed her entirely. But it was a prestigious project, and she was lucky to have her name attached to it. The same could be said for *Beggarman, Thief* (1979), another mini-series, this time adapted from Irwin Shaw's follow-up to his *Rich Man, Poor Man*.

During the making of *Born Again*, Anne bought a new house, in Montecito, California, one that she planned to use, she said, as a "think tank," a meeting place for like-minded friends. She told UPI:

> I've already established the Inner Space Foundation. And my new quarters in Montecito will be dedicated to the facts and truths of illuminated ones who walk this planet.
>
> The foundation will bring together men of science and religion. There will be meetings of the

A behind-the-scenes shot of Anne with a young Don Johnson in John Jakes' *The Rebels* (1979), a "TV Event" that had her only in one fleeting scene. Anne would later guest on Johnson's television series *Nash Bridges*.

mind among people of spiritual, scientific, educational and philosophical concepts for private dialogues and public dissemination.

I don't proselytize among my friends. As president, I've provided most of the funds for the Inner Space Foundation. Last fall I received a sizable donation without solicitation. I don't believe in soliciting.

I think my board of directors is impressive. There's Dr. Jack Holland, a professor at San Jose State and an associate minister in the Unity and Science of the Mind Churches.

Also a member is the Rev. Sig Paulson of the Kansas City Unity Village which publishes *The Daily Word*. And Dr. Evarts Loomis, an M.D. and biochemist who has a clinic in Hemet, California.

There are many other scientists who will participate in seminars at the foundation beginning this summer.

At the time Anne was starting to seriously consider putting her thoughts in a book to be titled *The Inner Space*, which she hoped would shed some light on her own lifestyle and "perhaps bring some new thoughts to others." This would eventually evolve into her book *Voices from Home*.

It is a tribute to Anne's integrity and professionalism that when the big-screen roles were not forthcoming, she didn't resort to what other actresses of her age were doing: schlock horror films. She prided herself on "weathering the fickle fortunes that have done in many a Hollywood actor." She told a reporter in 1978, "I've been down so many times in my career. You have to have desire and faith in yourself and realize how much it means to really last. A lot of people nowadays think they're going to make it overnight, but it takes a lot of work and dedication."

Around 1975, Anne started delivering speeches about how her positive thinking and "acceptance of good" have contributed much to her continued success. "I still believe it's what you know, not who you know," she said at one such lecture. When asked why her career continued when some of her acting peers' careers petered out, she replied, "I am fortunate enough to have endurance with optimism. I have

The 1970s was a time of reflection for the actress. "In the past few years I've addressed many church congregations in various parts of the country. About one or two a month. My minister friends call me Reverend Anne. But I'd never think of being ordained in any of the organized religions. That wouldn't be a part of my philosophical concept. The most important thing is letting love of life move through you. I believe all things come together for good to those who believe in God."

had enough ups and downs to know that endurance wins, of course self-respect and love for what you are doing as well." She traveled to churches and other gatherings, giving her lectures.

She had been involved since her teenage years with the International New Thought Alliance. "The organization is 65 years old," Anne said in 1978. "It is really an umbrella organization for several metaphysical churches, including Science of Mind, Unity and the Church of Truth. I've been involved since I was 16. But only in the last few years have I made my own personal transition to the point where I feel born again. When a person realizes his own spiritual nature he is born again." Anne began devoting much of her spare time to studying metaphysics, religion and science.

"In the past few years I've addressed many church congregations in various parts of the country. About one or two a month. My minister friends call me Reverend Anne. But I'd never think of being ordained in any of the organized religions. That wouldn't be a part of my philosophical concept. The most important thing is letting love of life move through you. I believe all things come together for good to those who believe in God."

Only a few movie roles, big screen and television, turned up in the '80s (*Detour to Terror, Mazes and Monsters, Return, A Masterpiece of Murder, Poor Little Rich Girl: The Barbara Hutton Story, My First Love*), but these parts were smallish, not really worthy of her talents. She spent more time as a guest star on such shows as *Charlie's Angels, Trapper John, M.D.*, a four-part stint on *Dallas, Fantasy Island, Simon & Simon, Partners in Crime, Murder, She Wrote, Crazy Like a Fox, Finder of Lost Loves, CHiPs, The Love Boat, Jake and the Fatman, Matlock,* and *The Golden Girls*, among others.

There was a brief period during the mid–1980s when she changed her professional name to Anne Lloyd Francis. She had been talking about such a change since 1970. She told Dick Kleiner in 1970, "My problem is that I'm not a big name and yet I'm not a no-name. And today it seems you have to be either a big name or

In *Detour to Terror* (1980), an improbable TV movie co-produced and starring O.J. Simpson (left) a bus is terrorized by maniacs in dune buggies. Anne, as a cancer survivor, hides her bankroll, her life-savings, in her dilapidated wig.

a no-name to get along. Anyhow, I've always liked my middle name — Lloyd — better than my last name. I never really cared for the sound of Anne Francis. Isn't Anne Lloyd better?" What she would soon learn, however, is that people were confused, some not realizing this was the same actress. She soon reverted to Anne Francis.

Bob Hope made his television movie debut in *A Masterpiece of Murder* (1986). Clockwise from Hope are Don Ameche, Anne, Frank Gorshin, Jayne Meadows, and Stella Stevens.

In 1982 she penned her book *Voices from Home: An Inner Journey*. Not the typical autography, it tells of Anne's inspiring spiritual journey since childhood. It reveals an actress with all her priorities in the right place, whose philosophy was "to stand by your own beliefs and your own integrity, and just keep working, wherever you are." She told Tom Weaver in 1994,

> Through my lifetime, I have had a lot of unusual experiences that would border on psychic and spiritual and such, and I have met many people along the way who were interested in such things. That's why I wrote the book, to share my experiences, so that other people who may have been going through similar things would not think they were *crazy*. (At least, I don't think *I* am!) Unfortunately, the publishers went bankrupt within a couple of months after it was published. The wild thing was, I had a ten-minute interview with Chris Wallace on *The Today Show*—and then there were no books in bookstores [*laughs*].

She became a regular on the NBC series *Riptide*, starring Perry King and Joe Penny, in 1984. Reported Ed Berk, "Recipe for a ratings' hit: Take two quirky hunks and put them on a boat. Give them a helicopter, too. Add a lovable, wimpy computer genius. Give the two hunks plenty of barely dressed babes to look at, but make sure the babes fall for the nebbish. Sprinkle in an explosion every 20 minutes or so. Then settle back and watch viewers stampede for their sets when they hear, 'Tonight, from the producer of *The A-Team*...'"

The show, created by producer Stephen J. Cannell, focused on Cody Allen (Perry King) and Nick Ryder (Joe Penny), two "free-spirited amateur detectives" who ride around in their *Riptide* boat and fly in Cody's decrepit pink helicopter, the *Screaming Mimi*. Regulars also included Thorn Bray as geeky sidekick Murray "Boz" Bozinsky and Jack Ging as the bad-tempered Lt. Quinlan. Calling the show "crisp and fast-paced," columnist David Handler remarked, "The acting level is relatively high on *Riptide*. Penny and King have the looks and the muscles, but they aren't stiffs. They've both been around a long time and know exactly what they're supposed to do. Bray is a very funny nerd. Ging and Miss Francis are likable, crusty veterans."

The producers originally saw Anne's character Mama Jo as a Marjorie Main type—"an old, gnarled, wrinkled but feisty dame." Hardly that, Anne had a different take to the character. "Mama Jo had a lot of fun potential," she told columnist Dick Kleiner. "I had felt Mama Jo could be a fun character who could add something new to an action show. It was a gamble for me, but I had a hunch I could develop the character."

Unfortunately, after just a few episodes, Anne was dropped from the show so the producers could concentrate on the manly action. A shame, because Anne's no-nonsense approach ("You touch one of those girls, you're gonna find the imprint of my fist right in the middle of your forehead") made Mama Jo fun and likeable, adding a needed balance to the action. She was a definite asset while she lasted.

Kleiner explained the details of Anne's exit:

> On a Friday in January, NBC's executives hustled Anne Francis into a quiet room. There she did a series of 18 telephone interviews with reporters all over the country to help promote the new TV series she was on for the network, *Riptide*.
>
> Later in that day, in a small studio, she made 54 promos—brief introductions for the show that local stations could use.
>
> The following Wednesday morning, Miss Francis left a note for the executive producer of the program, Stephen Cannel [*sic*], with her thoughts and ideas on how her character could be developed for the good of the show.
>
> Later that Wednesday, Jo Swerling, the show's producer, called Miss Francis's agent and said, sorry,

Anne appeared in a handful of episodes of the TV series *Riptide* in 1984, co-starring with Perry King (left) and Joe Penny (right), as Mama Jo, salty sea captain of a touring boat with an all-girl crew.

but they had decided to drop Miss Francis's character, Mama Jo, from *Riptide*. Therefore, the actress's services would no longer be required.

The next week, Anne ran two ads, in *The Hollywood Reporter* and *Daily Variety*, which consisted of a picture of her, Perry King, Joe Penny, and Thorn Bray. Underneath, in Anne's handwriting: "Bye, boys. Stay on top! I love you. 'Mama' Anne."

Of course she was unhappy about leaving, but also realistic, Anne looked at the bigger picture, lamenting the lack of good roles for female characters on action shows. "There are none," she said. "I don't think the networks give much consideration about women on action shows. I think the networks feel that women are mindless creatures and they have no place on this kind of show."

In HBO's *Laguna Heat* (1987), "a first-rate thriller told with the style of Raymond Chandler and the grittiness of Elmore Leonard" (Daniel Ruth, *Chicago Sun–Times*), Anne is a mysterious woman who fills cop Tom Shephard (Harry Hamlin) in on a murder investigation. Her two-scene role shows her off well, as, drunk and frisky, she fears for her life, but can't stand by and do nothing. "Welcome to the last days of Pompeii," she cheers Shephard at the bar. But, underneath, there is dread.

As soon as Anne read Robert Harling's play *Steel Magnolias*, which was coming to Chicago's Royal-George Theater, she knew she had to audition for the part of M'Lynn, the mother of a soon-to-be-married diabetic woman, Shelby. The play had originally opened off-Broadway in New York, in March of '87, where Rosemary Prinz had originated the role. Pamela Berlin, who directed the off-Broadway production, directed the Chicago version as well. "It was a tremendous help to go through motherhood with two daughters," Francis told a reporter after a rehearsal. "I have a deep understanding of what this woman is about. I have the deepest respect for her."

Magnolias, Anne said, gave her a chance to "explore and examine the nature of motherly love." She explained to the *Chicago Sun–Times'* Lynn Voedisch, "You begin to get in touch with your own inner child. I remember that on Jane's fourth Christmas, I sat putting a dollhouse together. I was putting in the little curtains and furniture and all the little decorative things. Then I thought to myself, 'Do I have everything I need?' Then I laughed. I was putting myself in the place of my child. I think you begin to think like a child, because you want to give everything you didn't have. I know that's true of me."

It was an acclaimed, high-profile performance and she got much press for it. It "is one lovely treasure of a play," Voedisch wrote. "By way of saluting strong, loving women, *Steel Magnolias* touches just about every important human emotion. Pain is soothed with comedy, cynicism with spirituality, pride with vulnerability. All the actresses turn in polished performances, but Francis broke my heart as M'Lynn."

When Constance Towers took over the role from Anne in 1989, Voedisch reviewed the play again, noting, "Unlike predecessor Anne Francis, Towers plays a brittle, tense M'Lynn. Francis created a warm, unruffled character, but Towers plays her taut with anxiety. Both approaches work, but I prefer Francis' choice. Since M'Lynn is a psychologist, it would be natural for her to present a calm exterior. When her tension finally emerges from the peaceful surface, the emotion is all the more powerful. Towers is consistent in her interpretation. Her verbal ripostes with her sassy daughter are always tinged with a bit of exasperation. She wears her weariness regally, with a sense of saintly dignity. And her moment of angry denial has just the right touch of a dangerous loss of control."

The '90s saw Anne give one of her best film performances, a third-billed role as Martha in *Little Vegas* (1990). As a character, she is seen mostly in flashbacks, as she spiritually visits her younger lover Carmine de Carlo (Anthony John Denison), who is a lost soul, even more so since her death. Writer-director Perry Lang surrounds Anne's scenes with a luminous glow, one that she equally matches with her radiant, ethereal presence and sensitive, practical

Anne had a marvelous two-scene role in HBO's *Laguna Heat* (1987), a first-rate thriller told with "the style of Raymond Chandler and the grittiness of Elmore Leonard" (*Chicago Sun–Times*).

acting. Her spirit infuses Carmine, as he struggles to find a place for himself and his son, just as it does the movie, even when she is not on screen.

She turned up in *Love Can Be Murder* (1992), a pleasant mix of *noir* and romantic comedy with Jaclyn Smith as an attorney who falls in love with the ghost of murdered '40s private eye Nick Peyton (Corbin Bernsen). Anne is one of Peyton's old flames, Maggie O'Brien, involved with the mystery. "Forty years of bumpy roads," Nick marvels, "she's still looking damn good." Dan Rice of the *Daily Globe* called her performance "an example of the professional ease of a veteran. Francis still sports the beauty mark and exudes the class that has made her so memorable." That she does.

More dramatic was *Have You Seen My Son* (1996), starring Lisa Hartman Black (who also produced) as Lael Pritcher, trying to get her asthmatic son back from her estranged husband Mike (Jameson Parker). Anne is mean, possessive, and completely hardcore as Lael's mother-in-law Catherine. With steely-eyed conviction, a scary Catherine threatens to withhold her own grandchild's medication, if Lael doesn't do as they say. Black cast Anne in the role; one of her biggest thrills was the chance to work with Francis, she said. "Are you kidding? I always watched *Honey West* when it was on," Black remarked to columnist Jay Bobbin.

Anne did cameos in the straight-to-video release *The Double O Kid* (1992) and the lame *Lover's Knot* (1996), both projects a waste of her talent. She continued to act in guest spots (*Wings, Conan, Nash Bridges, The Drew Carey Show*, the new *Fantasy Island*), amazing since many of her contemporaries had fallen by the wayside years earlier.

Anne remarked in 2000, "My feeling is, if I see something that I really would love to do, then I'll go in and meet, but otherwise, I just can't see spending 10 or 12 hours a day working on something that is sad. I just think that we're dwelling so much on extreme visual violence, and I'm also kind of tired of most of the humor being bathroom and genitalia humor. It's been run into the ground. Let's get on with some situation comedy again, and some fun, you know? But that's my choice."

In mid–2000 she read for a TV pilot, *Wilder Days*, at ABC. "I had an excellent meeting with [writer-producer] Jonathan Prince," Anne reported on her website. "They settled on Marsha Mason to play the mom of a rather dysfunctional (what else is new?) family. I liked Mr.

Anne Francis in a publicity shot, taken in the 1990s.

Prince. He was quite a gentleman. You know, I'm not sure I would be happy with the series routine any more. So many hours in dressing rooms and drafty soundstages and it is dark by the time you leave to go home and dark when you arrive at the studio at 6:00 A.M. for makeup. Glamorous? I think not! But, acting. Creating a role, reflecting life's many fascinating moments. Words once grasped from the page, live in the Actor's mind as visions which are then revealed through his/her eyes and voice. Amazing things *can* happen and it is most exhilarating. *But*, that can become as addictive as any drug! Acting is like doing a freefall into the passions of the Universal Soul. (Wow! Hope you know what I mean.) It can also squeeze out any other life from the Actor's soul if he does not guard against the seduction of being a conduit for these many passions only. He must not forget he has a life of his own to be lived beyond that of the written page. I guess obsession of any sort is dangerous. But, boy, isn't it human?"

On November 2, 2001, she was honored by the Academy of Television Arts and Sciences. "[It] was quite an event," Anne wrote on her website:

An array of very talented actresses was on the stage for a moderated discussion about Women in Drama. The women on the panel were Amy Brenneman, Dixie Carter, Tyne Daly, Annie Potts, Lorraine Toussaint, Kathleen Quinlan, Sela Ward, and Melina Kanakeredes. The producers of their shows were on stage with them and it was a most lively exchange regarding the difficulties of being a woman in the industry. At the end of the gathering, Zena Bethune (*The Nurses*) and I (*Honey West*) were called up to receive framed awards. The participants on the stage were standing and applauding! What a wonderful warm experience. I was so proud to read, "The Academy of Television Arts and Sciences Honors Anne Francis for contributing to the positive image of women on television, and for breaking new ground as a lead actress in a starring role on a prime-time series. ATAS recognizes you as a Pioneer for Women in Drama."

Anne revealed in another one of her newsletters in 2001, "I went in for a reading for the new Jack Nicholson picture, *About Schmidt* [2002]. It was an excellent meeting, but the physical type may weigh against my doing it. The writer-director, Alexander Payne, was delightful and bestowed much praise, which I lapped up, of course. He is a fine writer and a pleasure to read."

It was announced in April 2002 that Anne would star in the television movie *Out of Her League*, playing the Cincinnati Reds' former owner, the rambunctious and notorious Marge

Anne Francis in a publicity shot, taken in the 1990s.

Schott. Plans for the biopic were shelved, however, after Schott's death in 2004. Typically, Anne didn't let this setback get her down. She told the *Chicago Sun–Times* that she had few regrets about her choice of careers. "I've had fun for the most part. There were some rough periods and projects that didn't turn out — and some people who didn't turn out. But that's what the maze of life is all about."

Her last acting job was in a 2004 episode of *Without a Trace*, "Shadows." It was a small, but touching, part, proving, once again, what a sensitive, effective actress she always has been.

Anne kept busy in the meantime, dedicated to helping others, supporting such organizations as Direct Relief, Angel View, the Living Desert, the Desert AIDS Project, the Unity Shoppe, the Third Age Foundation, etc. In 1992 she received the Southern California Motion Picture Council's Angel Award for lifetime achievement. Past recipients included Bette Davis, Lana Turner and Lucille Ball. Allen Reese, CEO of Palm Springs' Desert AIDS Project, told Dann Dulin in 2005, "Anne has always been there for the Desert AIDS Project. She's donated items for auctions, participated in events, and has been present for several dedications. Her enthusiasm is only surpassed by her dedication and commitment to end this epidemic."

She started reading for the Recording for the Blind and Dyslexic organization in 2001, and was asked to start off the season of the "Speaking of Stories" show at the Lobero Theater in February 2002.

Although she stopped smoking in the '80s, Anne was diagnosed with lung cancer in 2007 and underwent surgery and chemotherapy. With her typical optimism and strength, she fought the disease into remission, detailing her inspiring struggle through newsletters on her website. Between her can-do spirit and her spiritual belief in the metaphysical, Anne was able to face it all with a fortitude and a cheeriness that belied the somber nature of her illness. It was a brave fight, but Anne died from complications of pancreatic cancer at a retirement home in Santa Barbara on January 2, 2011.

Historians too often get stuck on a single, iconic role for certain actresses. In Anne's case, they seem to want to keep her forever on that *Forbidden Planet*, never bring her down to Earth. Unfortunately, they miss the dazzling performances of the rest of her career. Even though she was versatile, able to adapt to any role, most of those roles were buried on television, a medium not fully respected in the 1950s, '60s and '70s. When she was at Fox and MGM in the '50s, the idea was that she was just a pretty face, who should have taken the easy way out — forget the acting, trade on her looks. But Anne, to her credit, could never just settle for that. She was a reluctant glamour girl who wanted meaty parts, good characterizations, and a good, solid career filled with diversity. Although she never became a superstar, she got those meaty parts, and she proved she could handle them brilliantly. As bumpy as her career was, in the end she succeeded, and those of us who love fine acting are all the richer for it.

FILMOGRAPHY

A. The Films

This Time for Keeps (1947)

"Lilting Rhythms ... Lovely Mermaids ... Wacky Comedy!"

Director: Richard Thorpe. *Producer*: Joe Pasternak. *Writers*: Lorraine Fielding, Erwin S. Gelsey (story), Gladys Lehman (screenplay), Hans Wilhelm (uncredited). *Original Music*: Calvin Jackson (uncredited), George Stoll (uncredited). *Cinematography*: Karl Freund. *Editor*: John Dunning. *Art Directors*: Randall Duell, Cedric Gibbons. *Set Decorator*: Henry W. Grace. *Assistant Director*: Al Jennings. *Sound*: Douglas Shearer. *Special Effects*: A. Arnold Gillespie. *Musical Director*: Georgie Stoll. *Orchestrators*: Harold Byrns (uncredited), Ted Duncan (uncredited), Wally Heglin (uncredited). *Choreographer*: Stanley Donen. *Cast*: Esther Williams (Leonora "Nora" Cambaretti), Jimmy Durante (Ferdi Farro), Lauritz Melchior (Richard Herald), Johnnie Johnston (Dick Johnson), Xavier Cugat and His Orchestra (Themselves), Dame May Whitty (Grandmother Cambaretti), Sharon McManus (Deborah Cambaretti), Dick Simmons (Gordon), Mary Stuart (Frances Allenbury), Ludwig Stossel (Peter), Dorothy Porter (Merle), Tommy Wonder (Himself), Anne Francis, Richard Terry (Bobbysoxers, uncredited), Lina Romay (Singer with Cugat's Orchestra, uncredited), Kenneth Tobey (Soldier at Pool, uncredited). *Shooting Dates*: July 15 to October 14, 1946. *Release Date*: October 17, 1947. MGM. 105 minutes.

Summer Holiday (1948)

"You'll Laugh — You'll Sing! You'll Have the Time of Your Life!"

Director: Rouben Mamoulian. *Producer*: Arthur Freed. *Writers*: Eugene O'Neill (play, *Ah, Wilderness!*), Frances Goodrich, Albert Hackett (screenplay), Irving Brecher, Jean Holloway (adaptation). *Original Music*: Conrad Salinger. *Cinematographer:* Charles Schoenbaum. *Editor*: Albert Akst. *Art Directors*: Cedric Gibbons, Jack Martin Smith. *Set Decorator*: Edwin B. Willis. *Associate Set Decorator*: Richard Pefferle. *Costume Designer*: Walter Plunkett. *Costume Supervisor*: Irene. *Makeup*: Jack Dawn. *Hair Stylist*: Sydney Guilaroff. *Production Manager*: Hugh Boswell (uncredited). *Assistant Director*: Wallace Worsley Jr. (uncredited). *Recording Director*: Douglas Shearer. *Re-recording Designer*: Tom Gunn (uncredited). *Sound*: Frank McKenzie (uncredited). *Grip*: Herman Franzen (uncredited). *Still Photographer*: Mickey Marigold (uncredited). *Camera Operator*: John Schmitz (uncredited). *Musical Director*: Lennie Hayton. *Orchestrators*: Wally Heglin, Conrad Salinger, Albert Glasser (uncredited). *Technicolor Color Director*: Natalie Kalmus. *Associate Technicolor Color Director*: Henri Jaffa. *Dance Director*: Charles Walters. *Script Supervisor*: Leslie H. Martinson (uncredited). *Cast*: Mickey Rooney (Richard Miller), Gloria De Haven (Muriel), Walter Huston (Mr. Nat Miller), Frank Morgan (Uncle Sid), Jackie "Butch" Jenkins (Tommy), Marilyn Maxwell (Belle), Agnes Moorehead (Cousin Lily), Selena Royle (Mrs. Miller), Michael Kirby (Arthur Miller), Shirley Johns (Mildred), Hal Hackett (Wint), Anne Francis [as Ann Francis] (Elsie Rand), John Alexander (Mr. McComber), Virginia Brissac (Miss Hawley), Howard Freeman (Mr. Peabody), Alice MacKenzie (Mrs. McComber), Ruth Brady (Crystal), Terry Moore (Hatcheck Girl, uncredited). *Shooting Dates:* June 17 to mid–October 1946. *Release Date*: April 16, 1948. MGM. 93 minutes.

Notes: Although released after *This Time for Keeps*, *Summer Holiday*, a musical remake of *Ah, Wilderness!*, is technically Anne's film debut because it was filmed first.

Portrait of Jennie (1948)

Director: William Dieterle. *Producer*: David O. Selznick. *Associate Producer*: David Hempstead. *Writers*: Robert Nathan (novel), Leonardo Bercovici (adaptation), Paul Osborn, Peter Berneis (screenplay), Ben Hecht (uncredited), David O. Selznick (uncredited). *Original Music*: Dimitri Tiomkin. *Cinematographers*: Joseph H. August, Lee Garmes (uncredited). *Editor*: William Morgan. *Production Designer*: J. McMillan Johnson. *Associate Production Designer*: Joseph B. Platt. *Set Decorator*: Claude E. Carpenter. *Costume Designer*: Lucinda Ballard. *Production Manager*: Argyle Nelson. *Assistant Director*: Arthur Fellows. *Sound*: James G. Stewart (uncredited). *Sound Effects Editor*: Charles L. Freeman (uncredited). *Special Effects*: Clarence Slifer, Daniel Hays (uncredited), Russell Shearman (uncredited). *Cast*: Jennifer Jones (Jennie Appleton), Joseph Cotten (Eben Adams), Ethel Barrymore (Miss Spinney), Lillian Gish (Mother Mary of Mercy), Cecil Kellaway (Matthews), David Wayne (Gus O'Toole), Albert Sharpe (Moore), Henry Hull (Eke), Florence Bates (Mrs. Jekes), Felix Bressart (Pete), Clem Bevans (Capt. Cobb), Maude Simmons (Clara Morgan), Anne Francis, Nancy Olson (Teenagers in Art Gallery, uncredited), Robert Dudley (Old Mariner, uncredited), John Farrell (Policeman, uncredited), Brian Keith (Ice-skater, uncredited). *Shooting Dates*: Late March to mid–April 1947; mid–June to early October 1947. *Release Date*: December 25, 1948. Vanguard Films / Selznick International Pictures. 86 minutes. B/W.

Notes: Some location filming took place at RKO-Pathé Studios in Harlem, New York. Widely released to theaters in 1949.

So Young So Bad (1950)

"THEY HATE YOU! ... And Each One of Them Has a Good Reason!"

Director: Bernard Vorhaus. *Producers*: Edward J. Danziger, Harry Lee Danziger. *Writers*: Jean Rouverol, Bernard Vorhaus (story and screenplay), Joseph Than (uncredited). *Original Music*: Robert W. Stringer. *Cinematographer*: Don Malkames. *Editor*: Carl Lerner. *Makeup Artist*: Fred C. Ryle. *Assistant Directors*: James de Gangi [Jim Di Gangi], Sal J. Scoppa Jr. *Recording Director*: David M. Polak. *Wardrobe*: Edith Lutyens. *Technical Advisor*: Hon. Milton A. Gibbons. *Cast*: Paul Henreid (Dr. John H. Jason), Catherine McLeod (Ruth Levering), Grace Coppin (Mrs. Beuhler), Cecil Clovelly (Mr. Riggs), Anne Francis (Loretta Wilson), Rosita Moreno [Rita Moreno] (Dolores Guererro), Anne Jackson (Jackie Boone), Enid Pulver (Jane Fleming). *Shooting Dates*: Started on July 5, 1949. *Release Date*: May 20, 1950. Danziger Productions Ltd. / United Artists. 91 minutes. B/W.

Notes: Filmed under the title *Runaway*, and then changed to *Escape If You Can*, before the title *So Young So Bad* was settled upon. Rosita (later Rita) Moreno and Anne Jackson both made their film debuts here.

REVIEWS

"[It] appeals to the emotions because it has a warm heart as its text.... Jane, Jackie and Loretta (Enid Pulver, Anne Jackson and Anne Francis) are the three outstanding 'bad' girls in the cast.... It's an understanding story, well directed and acted." — T.N.T., *The Post-Standard* (Syracuse, New York), October 12, 1950

"FOUR BAD GIRLS LIKE FEMALE DEAD END KIDS. What the 'Dead End Kids' were for wayward boys, the *So Young So Bad* teenagers are for delinquent girls.... As Loretta, the beautiful blonde who 'went wrong,' Anne Francis turns in a remarkably moving performance...." — *The Evening Capital* (Annapolis, Maryland), September 26, 1950

Anne Francis in a publicity shot, taken in the 1990s.

The Whistle at Eaton Falls (1951)

Director: Robert Siodmak. *Writers*: Lemist Esler, Virginia Shaler. *Producer*: Louis de Rochemont. *Associate Producers*: Borden Mace, Lothar Wolff. *Original Music*: Louis Applebaum. *Cinematographer*: Joseph C. Brun. *Editor*: Angelo Ross. *Art Director*: Herbert Andrews. *Production Manager*: Carl Forcht.

Dr. John H. Jason (Paul Henreid) saves Loretta (Anne) from the water hosing punishment in *So Young So Bad* (1950).

Music Director: Jack Shaindlin. *Cast*: Lloyd Bridges (Brad Adams), Dorothy Gish (Mrs. Doubleday), Carleton Carpenter (Eddie Talbot), Murray Hamilton (Al Webster), James Westerfield (Joe London), Lenore Lonergan (Abbie), Russell Hardie (Dwight Hawkins), Helen Shields (Miss Russell), Doro Merande (Miss Pringle), Diana Douglas (Ruth Adams), Anne Francis (Jean), Anne Seymour (Mary London), Ernest Borgnine (Bill Street), Arthur O'Connell (Jim Brewster), Parker Fennelly (Issac), Donald McKee (Daniel Doubleday), Rev. Mr. Robert A. Dunn (Rev. Payson). *Release Date*: August 2, 1951. Columbia Pictures Corporation. 96 minutes. B/W.

Notes: Ernest Borgnine's film debut. Anne and Carleton Carpenter sing "Ev'ry Other Day," which was written by Carpenter.

Elopement (1951)

"It's ANNE FRANCIS, new, starry-eyed sensation!"

Director: Henry Koster. *Producer*: Fred Kohlmar. *Writer*: Bess Taffel [Bess Boyle]. *Original Music*: Cyril J. Mockridge, Alfred Newman (uncredited). *Cinematographer*: Joseph LaShelle. *Editor*: William B. Murphy. *Art Directors*: Richard Irvine, Lyle R. Wheeler. *Set Decorators*: Paul S. Fox, Thomas Little. *Costume Designer*: Charles Le Maire. *Makeup Artist*: Ben Nye. *Assistant Director*: Ad Schaumer (uncredited). *Sound*: Alfred Bruzlin, Harry M. Leonard. *Special Photographic Effects*: Fred Sersen. *Musical Director*: Lionel Newman. *Orchestrator*: Edward B. Powell. *Cast*: Clifton Webb (Howard Osborne),

Anne Francis (Jacqueline "Jake" Osborne), Charles Bickford (Tom Reagan), William Lundigan (Matt Reagan), Reginald Gardiner (Roger Evans), Evelyn Varden (Millie Reagan), Margalo Gillmore (Claire Osborne), Tommy Rettig (Daniel Reagan). *Shooting Dates:* July 16 to mid–August, 1951. *Release Date:* November 23, 1951. Twentieth Century–Fox Film Corporation. 82 minutes. B/W.

A nonsensical publicity shot from Anne's first released Fox film, *Elopement* (1951) with William Lundigan (left) and Clifton Webb (right).

Notes: Frank Morris, in his *Winnipeg Free Press* column "Here, There and Hollywood" (12/19/51), wrote, "Anne Francis, who is being starred in her very first picture, *Lydia Bailey*, is getting a chance to sing as well ... Henry Koster, who is directing her in the Clifton Webb-Bill Lundigan starrer, *Elopement*, overheard her warbling between scenes on the set.... He was so impressed he arranged with Producer Fred Kohlmar for a special sequence in which she can demonstrate her vocal prowess." Unfortunately, such a sequence was not recorded and filmed.

REVIEWS

"*Elopement* is a slight little affair.... The thing is fitfully amusing."— Gene Handsaker, *The Hammond Times*, December 7, 1951

"As the blonde, streamlined daughter, Anne Francis, a comparative newcomer, is both easy to watch and hear."— Bosley Crowther, *The New York Times*, December 21, 1951

Lydia Bailey (1952)

"Kenneth Roberts' 1000-Thrill Spectacle of Haiti's 100 Flaming Nights!"
Director: Jean Negulesco. *Producer*: Jules Schermer. *Writers*: Kenneth Roberts (novel), Michael Blankfort, Philip Dunne (screenplay). *Original Music*: Hugo Friedhofer. *Cinematographer*: Harry Jackson. *Editor*: Dorothy Spencer. *Art Directors*: J. Russell Spencer, Lyle R. Wheeler. *Set Decorators*: Paul S. Fox, Thomas Little. *Costume Designer*: Travilla. *Makeup Artist*: Ben Nye. *Sound*: Harry M. Leonard, E. Clayton Ward. *Special Photographic Effects*: Fred Sersen. *Wardrobe Director*: Charles Le Maire (uncredited). *Musical Director*: Lionel Newman. *Orchestrator*: Edward B. Powell. *Choreographer*: Jack Cole. *Technicolor Color Consultant*: Leonard Doss. *Cast*: Dale Robertson (Albion Hamlin), Anne Francis (Lydia Bailey), Charles Korvin (D'autremont), William Marshall (King Dick), Luis Van Rooten (General Charles LeClerc), Adeline De Walt Reynolds (Mme. D'Autremont), Angos Perez (Paul), Robert Evans (Soldier), Roy E. Glenn (Mirabeau), William Walker (General LaPlume), Rosalind Hayes (Aspodelle), Alvin Ailey, Carmen De Lavallade (Specialty Dancers, uncredited), Juanita Moore (Marie, uncredited). *Shooting Dates:* June 11 to late July 1951; additional sequences added from early October to mid–October 1951. *Release Date:* June 2, 1952. Twentieth Century–Fox Film Corporation. 89 minutes.

Notes: Anne's first movie for Fox, this was filmed before *Elopement*, but released after. Tyrone Power was the first choice for the male lead, but he turned it down. Film debut of William Marshall, who is best known for the title role in *Blacula* (1972).

Dreamboat (1952)

Director: Claude Binyon. *Producer*: Sol C. Siegel. *Writers*: John D. Weaver (story "The Love Man"), Claude Binyon (screenplay). *Original Music*: Cyril J. Mockridge. *Cinematographer*: Milton R. Krasner. *Editor*: James B. Clark. *Art Directors*: Maurice Ransford, Lyle R. Wheeler. *Set Decorators*: Thomas Little, Fred J. Rode. *Costume Designer*: Travilla. *Makeup Artist*: Ben Nye. *Hair Stylist*: Helen Turpin. *Assistant Director*: Ad Schaumer. *Sound Recordists*: Roger Heman Sr., E. Clayton Ward. *Special Effects*: Ray Kellogg. *Wardrobe Director*: Charles Le Maire. *Orchestrator*: Bernard Mayers. *Musical Director*: Lionel Newman. *Cast*: Clifton Webb (Thornton Sayre / Bruce Blair), Ginger Rogers (Gloria Marlowe), Anne Francis (Carol Sayre), Jeffrey Hunter (Bill Ainslee), Elsa Lanchester (Dr. Mathilda Coffey), Fred Clark (Sam Levitt), Paul Harvey (Lawyer D.W. Harrington), Ray Collins (Timothy Stone), Helene Stanley (Mimi), Richard Garrick (Judge Bowles), Richard Allan (Student, uncredited), Gwen Verdon (Girl in Television Commercial, uncredited), May Wynn (Cigarette Girl, uncredited). *Shooting Dates*: December 27, 1951 to February 15, 1952; additional sequences added in late March 1952 and early May 1952. *Release Date*: July 26, 1952. Twentieth Century–Fox Film Corporation. 83 minutes.

Notes: When Henry and Phoebe Ephron were working on the adaptation, before they were reassigned, Marlene Dietrich was considered for the part Ginger Rogers eventually played. In one sequence, Rogers wore an evening gown that was later famously worn by Marilyn Monroe in *Gentlemen Prefer Blondes* (1953). At the conclusion of the film, everyone goes to the movies to witness Bruce Blair's comeback on the screen; it is a scene from Clifton Webb's *Sitting Pretty* (1948).

"It's small wonder that Anne Francis found reason to chuckle after finishing one of her scenes in *Dreamboat*. Shot on the 'process stage,' it showed her driving, with Clifton Webb, past Sing Sing prison. And the script called for her to deliver the following line of dialogue: 'You know, I've always wondered what this place looks like.' The reason for the chuckle? Well, Miss Francis, as it happens, was born in Ossining, New York, and lived as a child in a house almost next door to the famous penitentiary!"—"Fidler in Hollywood," February 9, 1952

A Lion Is in the Streets (1953)

"THE ROARING STORY OF A GIVE-AND-TAKE GUY!
He took plenty from the chiselers ... the crooks ... and
the tin-horns ... and gave 'em nothing in return!"

Director: Raoul Walsh. *Producer*: William Cagney. *Writers*: Andria Locke Langley (novel), Luther Davis (screenplay). *Original Music*: Franz Waxman. *Cinematographer*: Harry Stradling Sr. *Editor*: George Amy. *Production Designer*: Wiard Ihnen. *Set Decorator*: Fred M. MacLean. *Makeup Artist*: Otis Malcolm. *Assistant Director*: William Kissell. *Sound*: Larry Gannon. *Sound Recordist*: John K. Kean. *Special Effects*: Roscoe Cline. *Wardrobe*: Kay Nelson. *Technicolor Color Consultant*: Monroe W. Burbank. *Story Editor*: Edward Cagney. *Cast*: James Cagney (Hank Martin), Barbara Hale (Verity Wade), Anne Francis (Flamingo McManamee), Warner Anderson (Jules Bolduc), John McIntire (Jeb Brown), Jeanne Cagney (Jennie Brown), Lon Chaney Jr. (Spurge McManamee), Frank McHugh (Frank Rector), Larry Keating (Robert L. Castleberry IV), Onslow Stevens (Guy Polli), James Millican (Samuel T. Beach), Mickey Simpson (Tim Beck), Sara Haden (Lula May McManamee), Ellen Corby (Singing Woman), Lee Aaker (Johnny Briscoe, uncredited), James Griffith (Mayor's Clerk, uncredited). *Shooting Dates*: Late November to late December 1952. *Release Date*: September 23, 1953. William Cagney Productions / Warner Bros. Pictures. 88 minutes.

Notes: Barbara Hale replaced Priscilla Gillette in the lead.

The Rocket Man (1954)

"Out-of-this-world laughter and down-to-earth charm when
the face from space turns out to be ... the kid next door!"

Director: Oscar Rudolph. *Producer*: Leonard Goldstein. *Writers*: Lenny Bruce, Jack Henley (screenplay), George W. George, George F. Slavin (story). *Original Music*: Lionel Newman. *Cinematographer*: John F. Seitz. *Editor*: Paul Weatherwax. *Art Director*: George Patrick. *Set Decorator*: Glen Daniels. *Costume Designer*: Travilla. *Makeup Artist*: Louis Hippe. *Assistant Director*: Henry Weinberger. *Sound*: Eugene Grossman. *Musical Director*: Lionel Newman. *Cast*: Charles Coburn (Mayor Ed Johnson), Spring Byington (Justice Amelia Brown), Anne Francis (June Brown), John Agar (Tom Baxter), George "Foghorn" Winslow (Timmy), Stanley Clements (Bob), Emory Parnell (Big Bill Watkins), June Clayworth (Harriet Snedley), Don Haggerty (Officer Mike O'Brien), Beverly Garland (Ludine), Lawrence Ryle (The Rocket Man, uncredited). *Shooting Dates*: November 14, 1953; late November to mid–December 1953. *Release Date*: April 1954. Panoramic Productions / Twentieth Century–Fox Film Corporation. 89 minutes.

As Flamingo McManamee in *A Lion Is in the Streets* (1953).

Notes: The working titles of this film were *Justice, Justice Brown* and *The Kid from Outer Space*. Thelma Ritter was initially set to star in this, the first in a projected series of films featuring the character of Justice Amelia Brown.

Susan Slept Here (1954)

"She slept in his bed ... wore his pajamas —
THEN SHE REALLY TOOK OVER!"

Director: Frank Tashlin. *Producer*: Harriet Parsons. *Writers*: Steve Fisher, Alex Gottlieb (play), Alex Gottlieb (screenplay). *Original Music*: Leigh Harline. *Cinematographer*: Nicholas Musuraca. *Editor*: Harry Marker. *Art Directors*: Carroll Clark, Albert S. D'Agostino. *Set Decorators*: Al Orenbach, Darrell Silvera. *Costume Designer*: Michael Woulfe. *Makeup Artist*: Mel Berns. *Hair Stylist*: Larry Germain. *Assistant Directors*: Edward Killy, Maxwell O. Henry (uncredited). *Sound*: Frank McWhorter, Clem Portman. *Musical Director*: C. Bakaleinikoff. *Technicolor Color Consultant*: James Gooch. *Associate Director*: Eddie Rubin. *Choreographer*: Robert Sidney. *Cast*: Dick Powell (Mark Christopher), Debbie Reynolds (Susan Beaurgard Landis), Anne Francis (Isabella Alexander), Alvy Moore (Virgil), Glenda Farrell (Maude Snodgrass), Horace McMahon (Sergeant Monty Maizel), Herb Vigran (Sergeant Sam Hanlon), Les Tremayne (Harvey Butterworth), Mara Lane (Marilyn), Maidie Norman (Georgette), Rita Johnson (Dr. Rawley), Ellen Corby (Coffee Shop Waitress), Ken Carpenter (Narrator, uncredited), Art Gilmore (Voice of the Oscar, uncredited), Louella Parsons (Herself, voice on telephone, uncredited), Red Skelton (Oswald, uncredited). *Shooting Dates:* Mid–December 1953 to late January 1954. *Release Date*: July 14, 1954. RKO Radio Pictures. 98 minutes.

Notes: Steve Fisher and Alex Gottlieb's play remained unpublished in 1956 and was not performed until July 11, 1961; it ran for sixteen performances. The character of Isabella has only one scene in the play, and then disappears. The role was greatly expanded for the film. Dan Dailey was the first choice for the lead, followed by Cary Grant, Mickey Rooney and Robert Mitchum. Dick Powell's acceptance of the part marked his last acting role in feature films. Jack Lawrence and Richard Myers' "Hold My Hand," sung by Don Cornell

Cool, calculating Isabella Alexander (Anne) faces her competition Susan Beaurgard Landis (Debbie Reynolds, left) in *Susan Slept Here* (1954).

on the soundtrack, was nominated for an Academy Award for Best Song. John Aalberg was Oscar-nominated for Best Sound Recording. The screenplay earned a WGA nomination for Best Written American Comedy.

Rogue Cop (1954)

Director: Roy Rowland. *Producer*: Nicholas Nayfack. *Writers*: William P. McGivern (novel), Sydney Boehm (screenplay). *Original Music*: Jeff Alexander. *Cinematographer*: John F. Seitz. *Editor*: James E. Newcom. *Art Directors*: Cedric Gibbons, Hans Peters. *Set Decorators*: F. Keogh Gleason, Edwin B. Willis. *Costume Designer*: Helen Rose. *Makeup Artist*: William Tuttle. *Hair Stylist*: Sydney Guilaroff. *Unit Manager*: William Dorfman (uncredited). *Assistant Directors*: Ridgeway Callow, Robert Saunders (uncredited). *Sound*: Finn Ulback (uncredited), Charles Wallace (uncredited). *Recording Supervisor*: Wesley C. Miller. *Special Effects*: A. Arnold Gillespie. *Stunts*: Dale Van Sickel (for Robert Taylor, uncredited). *Cast*: Robert Taylor (Det. Sgt. Christopher Kelvaney), Janet Leigh (Karen Stephanson), George Raft (Dan Beaumonte), Steve Forrest (Eddie Kelvaney), Anne Francis (Nancy Corlane), Robert Ellenstein (Det. Sidney Y. Myers), Robert F. Simon (Ackerman), Anthony Ross (Father Ahearn), Alan Hale Jr. (Johnny Stark), Peter Brocco (George "Wrinkles" Fallon), Vince Edwards (Joey Langley), Olive Carey (Selma), Roy Barcroft (Lt. Vince D. Bardeman), Dale Van Sickel (Manny), Ray Teal (Patrolman Mullins), Russell Johnson (Patrolman Carland, uncredited), Connie Marshall (Frances, uncredited), Dick Simmons (Det. Ralston, uncredited). *Shooting Dates:* April 20 to May 15, 1954. *Release Date*: September 17, 1954. MGM. 92 minutes.

Notes: The film's working title was *Kelvaney*. It was Janet Leigh's last movie under her contract with MGM. Nominated for an Academy Award for Best Cinematography (Black and White).

Bad Day at Black Rock (1955)

"MGM's SUSPENSE STORY OF THE YEAR!"

Director: John Sturges. *Producer*: Dore Schary. *Associate Producer*: Herman Hoffman. *Writers*: Howard Breslin (story "Bad Time at Honda"), Don McGuire (adaptation), Millard Kaufman (screenplay). *Original Music*: André Previn. *Cinematographer*: William C. Mellor. *Editor*: Newell P. Kimlin. *Art Directors*: Malcolm Brown, Cedric Gibbons. *Set Decorators*: Fred M. MacLean, Edwin B. Willis. *Assistant Director*: Joel Freeman. *Recording Supervisor*: Wesley C. Miller. *Stunts*: Danny Sands (uncredited). *Color Consultant*: Alvord Eiseman. *Orchestrators*: Leo Arnaud (uncredited), Alexander Courage (uncredited), Wally Heglin (uncredited), André Previn (uncredited). *Conductor*: André Previn (uncredited). *Cast*: Spencer Tracy (John J. MacReedy), Robert Ryan (Reno Smith), Anne Francis (Liz Wirth), Dean Jagger (Tim Horn), Walter Brennan (Doc Velie), John Ericson (Pete Wirth), Ernest Borgnine (Coley Trimble), Lee Marvin (Hector David), Russell Collins (Mr. Hastings), Walter Sande (Sam). *Shooting Dates*: July 20 to August 21, 1954. *Release Date*: January 7, 1955. MGM. 81 minutes.

Notes: The film's working title was *Bad Day at Honda*. Oscar nominations went to John Sturges for Best Director, Spencer Tracy for Best Actor, and Millard Kaufman for Best Adapted Screenplay. Tracy, here in his last MGM film, won a Golden Globe. MGM's *Platinum High School* (1960) was a reworking of this story.

REVIEWS

"The only female in the film is Anne Francis. She is more fetching than felicitous in this environment."— Bosley Crowther, *The New York Times*, February 2, 1955

Battle Cry (1955)

"THE SCORCHINGLY PERSONAL BEST-SELLER!"

On the set of *Rogue Cop* (1954) George Raft, Anne and Robert Taylor share a laugh and a cup of tea.

Director: Raoul Walsh. *Producer*: Jack L. Warner (uncredited). *Writer*: Leon M. Uris (novel, screenplay). *Original Music*: Max Steiner. *Cinematographer*: Sid Hickox. *Editor*: William H. Ziegler. *Art Director*: John Beckman. *Set Decorator*: William Wallace. *Makeup Artist*: Gordon Bau. *Assistant Directors*: William Kissel, Russ Saunders. *Sound*: Francis J. Scheid. *Wardrobe*: Moss Mabry. *Color Consultant*: Philip M. Jefferies [Jeffries]. *Orchestrations*: Murray Cutter. *Technical Advisor*: Col. H.P. [Jim] Crowe.

Spencer Tracy and Anne in the classic *Bad Day at Black Rock* (1955).

Cast: Van Heflin (Major Sam Huxley), Aldo Ray (Pvt. / Pfc. Andy Hookens), Mona Freeman (Kathy), Nancy Olson (Mrs. Pat Rogers), James Whitmore (MSgt. Mac / Narrator), Raymond Massey (Maj. Gen. Snipes),Tab Hunter (Pvt. / Cpl. Dan Forrester), Dorothy Malone (Mrs. Elaine Yarborough), Anne Francis (Rae), William Campbell (Pvt. "Ski" Wronski), John Lupton (Pvt. / Cpl. Marion "Sister Mary" Hotchkiss), Justus E. McQueen [L.Q. Jones] (Pvt. L.Q. Jones), Perry Lopez (Pvt. Joe Gomez), Fess Parker (Pvt. Speedy), Jonas Applegarth (Pvt. Lighttower), Tommy Cook (Cpl. Ziltch), Felix Noriego (Pvt. Crazy Horse), Susan Morrow (Susan), Carleton Young (Maj. Jim Wellman), Rhys Williams (Enoch Rogers), Allyn [Ann] McLerie (Ruby), Gregory Walcott (Sgt. Jim Beller), Frank Ferguson (Mr. Hector Walker), Sarah Selby (Mrs. Forrester), Willis Bouchey (Mr. Forrester). *Shooting Dates:* Early February to early May 1954. *Release Date.* February 2, 1955. Warner Bros. 149 minutes.

Notes: Film debuts of Perry Lopez, Don Durant, Harold Knudsen and Justus E. McQueen, who later changed his professional name to that of his character here, L.Q. Jones. Max Steiner was Oscar-nominated for Scoring of a Dramatic or Comedy Picture.

Blackboard Jungle (1955)

"A shock story of today's high school hoodlums!"

Director: Richard Brooks. *Writer*: Evan Hunter (novel *The Blackboard Jungle*), Richard Brooks (screenplay). *Producer*: Pandro S. Berman. *Original Music*: Scott Bradley (uncredited), Charles Wolcott (uncredited). *Cinematographer*: Russell Harlan. *Editor*: Ferris Webster. *Art Directors*: Randall Duell, Cedric Gibbons. *Set Decorators*: Henry Grace, Edwin B. Willis. *Makeup Artists*: William Tuttle, Dave

Grayson (uncredited). *Assistant Directors*: Joel Freeman, Hank Moonjean (uncredited). *Sound Recording Supervisor*: Wesley C. Miller. *Stunts*: Eli Bo Jack Blackfeather (uncredited). *Music Adaptor*: Charles Wolcott. *Cast*: Glenn Ford (Richard Dadier), Anne Francis (Anne Dadier), Louis Calhern (Jim Murdock), Margaret Hayes (Lois Judby Hammond), John Hoyt (Mr. Warneke), Richard Kiley (Joshua Y. Edwards), Emile Meyer (Mr. Halloran), Warner Anderson (Dr. Bradley), Basil Ruysdael (Prof. A.R. Kraal), Sidney Poitier (Gregory W. Miller), Vic Morrow (Artie West), Dan Terranova (Belazi), Rafael Campos (Pete V. Morales), Paul Mazursky (Emmanuel Stoker), Horace McMahon (Detective), Jameel Farah [Jamie Farr] (Santini), Danny Dennis (De Lica). *Shooting Dates:* November 15 to late December 1954. *Release Date*: March 25, 1955. MGM. 101 minutes.

Notes: Film debuts of Vic Morrow, Rafael Campos, and Jameel Farah (Jamie Farr). The film was nominated for Academy Awards for Best Screenplay, Best Film Editing, Best Cinematography (black and white) and Best Art Direction/Set Decoration (Black and White).

The Scarlet Coat (1955)

Director: John Sturges. *Producer*: Nicholas Nayfack. *Writer*: Karl Tunberg. *Original Music*: Conrad Salinger. *Cinematographer*: Paul C. Vogel. *Editor*: Ben Lewis. *Art Directors*: Cedric Gibbons, Merrill Pye. *Set Decorators*: Richard Pefferle, Edwin B. Willis. *Costume Designer*: Walter Plunkett. *Makeup Designer*: William Tuttle. *Hair Stylist*: Sydney Guilaroff. *Assistant Director*: Fred Frank. *Recording Supervisor*: Wesley C. Miller. *Special Effects*: Warren Newcombe. *Color Consultant*: Alvord Eiseman. *Orchestrator*: Robert Franklyn (uncredited). *Cast*: Cornel Wilde (Major John Boulton), Michael Wilding (Major John Andre), George Sanders (Dr. Jonathan Odell), Anne Francis (Sally Cameron), Robert Douglas (General Benedict Arnold), John McIntire (General Robert Howe), Rhys Williams (Peter Andre), John Dehner (Nathanael Greene), James Westerfield (Colonel Jameson), Ashley Cowan (Mr. Brown), Paul Cavanagh (Sir Henry Clinton), John Alderson (Mr. Durkin), John O'Malley (Colonel Winfield), Bobby Driscoll (Ben Potter), Tristram Coffin (Colonel Varick, uncredited), Leslie Denison (Captain Sutherland, uncredited), Robert Dix (Lt. Evans, uncredited), Michael Fox (Major Russell, uncredited), Paul Frees (Narrator, uncredited), Bruce Lester (Colonel Simcoe, uncredited). *Shooting Dates:* October 25 to mid–December 1954; additional sequences added in late January 1955. *Release Date*: July 29, 1955. MGM. 101 minutes.

Notes: Both Stewart Granger and Robert Taylor were sought for the role that Cornel Wilde eventually played. Location shooting took place in Tarrytown and along the Hudson River in New York, and, according to the credits, "We are deeply grateful to Sleepy Hollow Restorations for permitting us to photograph many scenes in their original locale at Philipse Castle in Legendary Sleepy Hollow." This was Michael Wilding's final film under contract to MGM.

Forbidden Planet (1956)

"IT'S OUT OF THIS WORLD!"

Director: Fred McLeod Wilcox. *Producer*: Nicholas Nayfack. *Writer*: William Shakespeare (play, *The Tempest*, uncredited), Irving Block (story), Allen Adler (story), Cyril Hume (screenplay). *Cinematographer*: George J. Folsey. *Editor*: Ferris Webster. *Production Designers*: Irving Block (uncredited), Mentor Huebner (uncredited). *Art Directors*: Cedric Gibbons, Arthur Lonergan. *Set Decorator*: Hugh Hunt, Edwin B. Willis. *Costume Designer* (men): Walter Plunkett. *Costume Designer* (Anne Francis): Helen Rose. *Hair Stylist*: Sydney Guilaroff. *Makeup Artist*: William Tuttle. *Assistant Director*: George Rhein. *Art Department*: A.D. Flowers (uncredited), Arthur Lonergan (uncredited), Glen Robinson (uncredited). *Recording Supervisor*: Dr. Wesley C. Miller. *Special Effects*: A. Arnold Gillespie, Joshua Meador, Warren Newcombe, Irving G. Ries, Doug Hubbard (uncredited), Robert Kinoshita (uncredited), Glen Robinson (uncredited), Franklyn Soldo (uncredited). *Visual Effects*: Bob Abrams (uncredited), Joe Alves (uncredited), Max Fabian (uncredited), Howard Fisher (uncredited), Henri Hillinck (uncredited), Bob Trochim (uncredited), Matthew Yuricich (uncredited). *Color Consultant*: Charles K. Hagedon. *Composer's of Electronic Tonalities*: Bebe Barron, Louis Barron. *Cast*: Walter Pidgeon (Dr. Edward Morbius), Anne Francis (Altaira "Alta" Morbius), Leslie Nielsen (Commander J. J. Adams), Warren Stevens (Lt. "Doc" Ostrow), Jack Kelly (Lt. Jerry Farman), Richard Anderson (Chief Quinn), Earl Holliman (Cook), George Wallace (Bosun), Robert Dix (Crewman Grey), Jimmy Thompson (Crewman Youngerford), James Drury (Crewman Strong), Harry Harvey Jr. (Crewman Randall), Roger McGee (Crewman Lindstrom), Peter Miller (Crewman Moran), Morgan Jones (Crewman Nichols), Richard Grant (Crewman Silvers), James Best (Crewman, uncredited), William Boyett (Crewman, uncredited), Frankie Darro, Frankie Carpenter (Robby the Robot, uncredited), Marvin Miller (voice of Robby the Robot, uncredited), Les Tremayne (Narrator, uncredited). *Shooting Dates*: April 18 to late May 1955. *Release Date*: March 15, 1956. MGM. 98 minutes.

Notes: Leslie Nielsen's feature film debut. Nominated for an Academy Award for Special Effects.

The Rack (1956)

"All the drama, the suspense, the power of *The Caine Mutiny!*"

Director: Arnold Laven. *Producer*: Arthur M. Loew Jr. *Writers*: Rod Serling (teleplay), Stewart Stern (screenplay). *Original Music*: Adolph Deutsch. *Cinematographer*: Paul C. Vogel. *Editors*: Harold F. Kress, Marshall Neilan Jr. *Art Directors*: Cedric Gibbons, Merrill Pye. *Set Decorators*: Fred MacLean, Edwin B. Willis. *Makeup Artist*: William Tuttle. *Assistant Director*: Robert Saunders. *Recording Supervisor*: Dr. Wesley C. Miller. *Orchestrator*: Alexander Courage (uncredited). *Musical Director*: Adolph Deutsch (uncredited). *Technical Advisor*: Colonel Charles M. Trammel Jr. *Cast*: Paul Newman (Capt. Edward W. Hall Jr.), Wendell Corey (Maj. Sam Moulton), Walter Pidgeon (Col. Edward W. Hall Sr.), Edmond O'Brien (Lt. Col. Frank Wasnick), Anne Francis (Aggie Hall), Lee Marvin (Capt. John R. Miller), Cloris Leachman (Caroline), Robert Burton (Col. Ira Hansen), Robert Simon (Law

Above and opposite: Forbidden Planet (1956)

Officer), Trevor Bardette (Court President), Adam Williams (Sgt. Otto Pahnke), James Best (Millard Chilson Cassidy), Fay Roope (Col. Dudley Smith), Barry Atwater (Maj. Byron Phillips), Dean Jones (Lieutenant, uncredited), Rod Taylor (Al, uncredited). *Shooting Dates:* Late November to mid–December 1955. *Release Date*: November 2, 1956. MGM. 100 minutes.

Notes: Rod Serling originally wrote "The Rack" as an episode of *The United States Steel Hour* (April 12, 1955). It was directed by Alex Segal and starred Marshall Thompson, Peggy

Leslie Nielsen tries to get a laugh from Anne and Paul Newman during his visit to the set of *The Rack* (1956).

McCay, and Nicholas Joy in, respectively, the roles played in the movie by Newman, Anne, and Walter Pidgeon. Wendell Corey was in both the television and movie versions. Location shooting took place in California at Travis Air Force Base, Fairfield and San Francisco and the Bay Area.

The Great American Pastime (1956)

"Star of *Seven Year Itch*—Tom Ewell is a RIOT."

Director: Herman Hoffman. *Producer*: Henry Berman. *Writer*: Nathaniel Benchley. *Original Music*: Jeff Alexander. *Cinematographer*: Arthur E. Arling. *Editor*: Gene Ruggiero. *Art Directors*: Randall Duell, William A. Horning. *Set Decorators*: Edward G. Boyle, Edwin B. Willis. *Makeup Artist*: William Tuttle. *Assistant Director*: George Rhein. *Recording Director*: Wesley C. Miller. *Special Effects*: A. Arnold Gillespie. *Orchestrator*: Arthur Morton (uncredited). *Cast*: Tom Ewell (Bruce Hallerton), Anne Francis (Betty Hallerton), Ann Miller (Doris Patterson), Dean Jones (Buck Rivers), Rudy Lee (Dennis Hallerton), Judson Pratt (Ed Ryder), Raymond Bailey (George Carruthers), Wilfred Knapp (Mr. Dawson), Bob Jellison (Mr. O'Keefe), Alexander Campbell (Judge, uncredited), Ruby Dee (Mrs. Ashlow, uncredited), Paul Engle (Forster Carruthers, uncredited), Todd Ferrell (Man Mountain O'Keefe, uncredited). *Shooting Dates*: Late June to late July 1956. *Release Date*: November 28, 1956. MGM. 90 minutes.

Notes: The working titles for the film were *Little Leaguer* and *Father's Little Leaguer*. This was writer Nathaniel Benchley's first film. The son of noted humorist and actor Robert Benchley and father of novelist Peter Benchley, Nathaniel also has a bit part in the film. Ann Miller ended her MGM contract with *The Great American Pastime*.

The Hired Gun (1957)

"Even the tough gun-slinger wasn't safe with the blonde wanted for murder!"

Director: Ray Nazarro. *Producers*: Rory Calhoun, Victor M. Orsatti. *Writers*: Buckley Angell (story), Buckley Angell, David Lang (screenplay). *Original Music*: Albert Glasser. *Cinematographer*: Harold J. Marzorati. *Editor*: Frank Santillo. *Art Directors*: William A. Horning, Urie McCleary. *Set Decorators*: Henry Grace, Hugh Hunt. *Makeup Artist*: William Tuttle. *Hair Stylist*: Sydney Guilaroff. *Assistant Director*: George Rhein. *Recording Supervisor*: Wesley C. Miller. *Special Effects*: Lee LeBlanc. *Stunts*: Regis Parton (uncredited), Chuck Roberson (uncredited). *Script Supervisor*: Richard Michaels. *Cast*: Rory Calhoun (Gil McCord), Anne Francis (Ellen Beldon), Vince Edwards (Kell Beldon), John Litel (Mace Beldon), Chuck Connors (Judd Farrow), Robert Burton (Nathan Conroy), Salvador Baguez (Domingo Ortega), Guinn "Big Boy" Williams (Elby Kirby), Regis Parton (Cliff Beldon), Dan Riss (Walt Bodie, uncredited), Edgar Dearing (Sheriff Jenner, uncredited), Nolan Leary (Judge Dwight Larson, uncredited), Chuck Roberson (Frank Cooper, uncredited), Joe Haworth (Haddon, uncredited), Pierce Lyden (Culdane, uncredited), William Tannen (Deputy-Guard, uncredited), Beulah Archuletta (Indian Squaw, uncredited), Bart Bradley (Pablo, uncredited). *Shooting Dates:* Late May to mid–June 1957. *Release Date*: September 20, 1957. Rorvic Productions / MGM. 63 minutes.

Notes: The film's original title was *Hostile Guns*. The first film produced by Rory Calhoun and Victor M. Orsatti's production company, Calhoun–Orsatti Enterprises, Inc., also called Rorvic Productions.

Don't Go Near the Water (1957)

"THE LAUGH OF YOUR LIFE-TIME!"

Director: Charles Walters. *Producer*: Lawrence Weingarten. *Writers*: William Brinkley (novel), Dorothy Kingsley, George Wells (screenplay). *Original Music*: Bronislau Kaper. *Cinematographer*: Robert Bronner. *Editor*: Adrienne Fazan. *Art Directors*: William A. Horning, Urie McCleary. *Set Decorators*: Hugh Hunt, Edwin B. Willis. *Costume Designer*: Helen Rose. *Hair Stylist*: Sydney Guilaroff. *Makeup Artist*: William Tuttle. *Assistant Director*: Al Jennings. *Recording Supervisor*: Dr. Wesley C. Miller. *Special Effects*: A. Arnold Gillespie, Lee LeBlanc. *Color Consultant*: Charles K. Hagedon. *Orchestrator*: Robert Franklyn (uncredited). *Cast*: Glenn Ford (Lt. J.G. Max Siegel), Gia Scala (Melora Alba), Earl Holliman (Adam Garrett), Anne Francis (Lt. Alice Tomlen), Keenan Wynn (Gordon Ripwell), Fred Clark (Lt. Comdr. Clinton T. Nash), Eva Gabor (Deborah Aldrich), Russ Tamblyn (Ens. Tyson), Jeff Richards (Lt. Ross Pendleton), Mickey Shaughnessy (Farragut Jones), Howard Smith (Adm. Junius Boatwright), Romney Brent (Mr. Alba), Mary Wickes (Janie), Jack Straw (Lt. Comdr. Gladstone), Robert Nichols (Lt. Comdr. Hereford), John Alderson (Lt. Comdr. Diplock), Jack Albertson (Rep. George Jansen), Charles Watts (Rep. Arthur Smithfield). *Shooting Dates*: Late February to late April 1957. *Release Date*: December 1957. Avon Productions / MGM. 107 minutes.

Notes: Anna Kashfi was replaced by Gia Scala in the lead role. Ernest Borgnine, who perfectly fit the character of Lt. J.G. Max Siegel as written by William Brinkley in his novel, was considered for the lead.

The Crowded Sky (1960)

"The most fascinating people the gods of chance
ever swept up into high adventure!"

Director: Joseph Pevney. *Producer*: Michael Garrison. *Writers*: Hank Searls (novel), Charles Schnee (screenplay). *Original Music*: Leonard Rosenman. *Cinematographer*: Harry Stradling Sr. *Editor*: Tom McAdoo. *Casting*: Alixe Gordin. *Art Director*: Eddie Imazu. *Costume Designer*: Howard Shoup. *Stunts*: Bob Harris (uncredited). *Orchestrator*: Maurice De Packh (uncredited). *Cast*: Dana Andrews (Dick Barnett), Rhonda Fleming (Cheryl "Charro" Heath), Efrem Zimbalist Jr. (Dale Heath), John Kerr (Mike Rule), Anne Francis (Kitty Foster), Keenan Wynn (Nick Hyland), Troy Donahue (McVey), Joe Mantell (Louis Capelli), Patsy Kelly (Gertrude Ross), Donald May (Norm Coster), Louis Quinn (Sidney Schreiber), Edward Kemmer (Caesar), Tom Gilson (Robert "Rob" Fermi), Hollis Irving (Beatrice Wiley), Paul Genge (Samuel N. Poole), Jean Willes (Gloria Panawek), Frieda Inescort (Mrs. Mitchell), Nan Leslie (Bev), Ken Currie (Dick Barnett Jr.). *Shooting Dates:* Mid–October to mid–November 1959. *Release Date*: September 2, 1960. Warner Bros. Pictures. 105 minutes.

Girl of the Night (1960)

> "Why They Do It... For the first time the motion picture screen
> tells the intimate, authentic personal story of girls like
> Bobbie Williams — a truth torn from New York after dark."

Director: Joseph Cates. *Producer*: Max Rosenberg. *Writers*: Dr. Harold Greenwald (book *The Call Girl*), Ted Berkman, Raphael Blau (screenplay). *Original Music*: Sol Kaplan. *Cinematographer*: Joseph C. Brun. *Editor*: Aram A. Avakian. *Art Director*: Charles Bailey. *Costume Designer*: Theoni V. Aldredge. *Makeup Artist*: Bill Herman. *Orchestrator*: Hershy Kay. *Cast*: Anne Francis (Robin "Bobbie" Williams), Lloyd Nolan (Dr. Mitchell), Kay Medford (Rowena Claiborne), John Kerr (Larry Taylor), Arthur Storch (Jason Franklin Jr.), James Broderick (Dan Bolton), Lauren Gilbert (Dan Shelton), Eileen Fulton (Lisa), Julius Monk (Swagger), Jo Anna March (Lucy Worth). *Shooting Dates:* June 12 to late July 1960. *Release Date*: November 11, 1960. Vanguard Productions / Warner Bros. Pictures. 93 minutes.

Notes: The film's working titles were *The Call Girl*, *Girl in the Night* and *Girl in the Dark*. Shot on location in New York City.

John Kerr and Anne from *Girl of the Night* (1960).

The Satan Bug (1965)

> "The price for uncovering the secret of
> the Satan bug comes high — YOUR LIFE!"

Director-Producer: John Sturges. *Writers*: Ian Stuart [Alistair MacLean] (novel), James Clavell, Edward Anhalt (screenplay). *Original Music*: Jerry Goldsmith. *Cinematographer*: Robert Surtees. *Editor*: Ferris Webster. *Art Director*: Herman Blumenthal. *Set Decorator*: Charles Vassar. *Makeup Artist*: Emile Lavigne. *Unit Manager*: J. Paul Popkin. *Production Supervisor*: Allen K. Wood. *Assistant Director*: Jack N. Reddish. *Property*: Frank Agnone. *Sound*: Harold Lewis. *Sound Effects Editor*: Gilbert D. Marchant. *Special Effects*: Paul Pollard. *Stunts*: John Moio. (uncredited). *Casting*: Lynn Stalmaster. *Wardrobe*: Wes Jeffries. *Assistant Film Editor*: Marshall Borden. *Music Editor*: Richard Carruth. *Conductor*: Jerry Goldsmith. *Musical Director*: Jerry Goldsmith (uncredited). *Orchestrator*: Arthur Morton (uncredited). *Cast*: George Maharis (Lee Barrett), Richard Basehart (Dr. Gregor Hoffman), Anne Francis (Ann Williams), Dana Andrews (Gen. Williams), John Larkin (Dr. Leonard Michaelson), Richard Bull (Eric Cavanaugh), Frank Sutton (Donald), Edward Asner (Veretti), Simon Oakland (Tasserly), John Anderson (Agent Reagan), John Clarke (Lt. Raskin), Hari Rhodes (Lt. Johnson), Martin Blaine (Henchman Posing as Henry Martin), Henry Beckman (Dr. Baxter), Harry Lauter (Fake SDI Agent), James Hong (Dr. Yang), Harold Gould (Dr. Ostrer, uncredited). *Shooting Dates*: Began shooting on January 6, 1964. *Release Date*: April 14, 1965. Mirisch Corporation / United Artists. 114 minutes.

Notes: Anne replaced Joan Hackett in the role of Ann Williams. Charlton Heston was the first choice for the male lead. Filmed in Los Angeles and Palm Springs, California. In the novel, the action is set in England.

Brainstorm (1965)

"The Most Fiendish Idea Ever Conceived by the Human Brain!"

Director-Producer: William Conrad. *Writers*: Larry Marcus (story), Mann Rubin (screenplay). *Original Music*: George Duning. *Cinematographer*: Sam Leavitt. *Editor*: William Ziegler. *Art Director*: Robert Emmet Smith. *Set Decorator*: Hoyle Barrett. *Makeup Supervisor*: Gordon Bau. *Hairstyle Supervisor*: Jean Burt Reilly. *Unit Manager*: James Vaughn. *Assistant Directors*: Howard L. Grace Jr., Monty Masters. *Production Illustrator*: Joseph Musso (uncredited). *Sound*: M.A. Merrick, Ben Sad (uncredited), William Thompson (uncredited). *Camera Operators*: Al Myers (uncredited), William John Ranaldi (uncredited). *Wardrobe*: Rose Brandi (uncredited), Ken Laurence (uncredited). *Orchestrator*: Arthur Morton. *Score Mixer*: Dan Wallin (uncredited). *Dialogue Supervisor*: James Lydon. *Cast*: Jeffrey Hunter (Jim Grayam), Anne Francis (Lorrie Benson), Dana Andrews (Cort Benson), Viveca Lindfors (Dr. Elizabeth Larstadt), Stacy Harris (Josh Reynolds), Kathie Browne (Angie DeWitt), Phillip Pine (Dr. Ames), Michael Pate (Dr. Mills), Robert McQueeney (Sgt. Dawes), Strother Martin (Mr. Clyde), Joan Swift (Clara), George Pelling (Butler), Victoria [Paige] Meyerink (Julie Benson), Stephen Roberts (Judge), Pat Cardi (Bobby), William Conrad (Mental Patient, uncredited), Biff Elliot (Detective, uncredited), Richard Kiel (Asylum Inmate, uncredited), John Mitchum (Guitar-Playing

Jeffrey Hunter feigns insanity in his plan to murder Anne's husband in *Brainstorm* (1965).

Inmate, uncredited), James Seay (Judge, uncredited). *Release Date*: May 5, 1965. William Conrad Productions / Warner Bros. Pictures. 105 minutes.

Notes: Jeffrey Hunter is billed as "Jeff Hunter" for this movie. Location shooting took place in the San Fernando Valley and at Greystone Mansion in Beverly Hills, California.

Funny Girl (1968)

"People who see *Funny Girl* are the luckiest people in the world!"

Director: William Wyler. *Producer*: Ray Stark. *Writer*: Isobel Lennart (play, screenplay). *Cinematographer*: Harry Stradling Sr. *Editor*: William Sands, Maury Winetrobe. *Production Designer*: Gene Callahan. *Art Directors*: Robert Luthardt, Linus Aaberg (uncredited). *Set Decorator*: William Kiernan. *Makeup Supervisor*: Ben Lane. *Makeup Artist*: Frank McCoy. *Hair Stylists*: Virginia Darcy, Vivienne Walker, Jan Van Uchelen (uncredited). *Unit Production Manager*: Paul Helmick. *Assistant Directors*: Ray Gosnell, Jack Roe, Michael Blum (uncredited). *Property Master*: Richard M. Rubin. *Sound*: Arthur Piantadosi, Jack Solomon. *Sound Effects Editor*: Joe Henrie. *Sound Supervisor*: Charles J. Rice. *Special Photographic Effects*: Albert Whitlock (uncredited). *Costumes (Barbra Streisand)*: Irene Sharaff. *Orchestrators*: Jack Hayes, Walter Scharf, Leo Shuken, Herbert Spencer. *Director of Musical Numbers*: Herbert Ross. *Conductor*: Walter Scharf. *Music Supervisor*: Walter Scharf. *Music Editor*: Ted Sebern. *Music Arranger*: *Dance Vocals*: Betty Walberg. *Cast*: Barbra Streisand (Fanny Brice), Omar Sharif (Nick Arnstein), Kay Medford (Rose Brice), Anne Francis (Georgia James), Walter Pidgeon (Florenz Ziegfeld), Lee Allen (Eddie Ryan), Mae Questel (Mrs. Strakosh), Gerald Mohr (Tom Branca), Frank Faylen (Keeney), Mittie Lawrence (Emma), Gertrude Flynn (Mrs. O'Malley), Penny Santon (Mrs. Meeker), John Harmon (Company Manager), Thordis Brandt, Bettina Brenna, Virginia Ann Ford, Alena Johnston, Karen Lee, Mary Jane Mangler, Inga Neilsen (Ziegfeld Girls). *Release Date*: September 19, 1968. Rastar Pictures / Columbia Pictures Corporation. 151 minutes / (roadshow version:155 minutes).

Notes: The original Broadway production opened at the Winter Garden Theater on March 26, 1964; Barbra Streisand and Kay Medford reprised their roles in the movie. This was Streisand's film debut and character actor Frank Faylen's last. Sidney Lumet was to direct but was replaced by William Wyler. Streisand won the Academy Award for Best Actress, tying with Katharine Hepburn (*The Lion in Winter*). The movie was also nominated for Best Picture, Best Supporting Actress (Kay Medford), Best Cinematography, Best Film Editing, Best Song, Best Sound, and Best Music, Score of a Musical Picture (Original or Adaptation).

Lost Flight (1969)

"They survived by chance... They lived by fear."

Director: Leonard Horn. *Producer*: Paul Donnelly. *Executive Producer*: Frank Price. *Writer*: Dean Riesner. *Original Music*: Dominic Frontiere, Stanley Wilson (uncredited). *Cinematographer*: James Crabe. *Editors*: Richard Belding, Larry Lester, Jack W. Schoengarth, Douglas Stewart. *Art Director*: Frank Arrigo. *Set Decorators*: Ruby R. Levitt, John McCarthy Jr. *Costume Designer*: Charles Waldo. *Makeup Artist*: Bud Westmore. *Hair Stylist*: Larry Germain. *Unit Manager*: Don Gold. *Assistant Director*: George Bisk. *Sound*: David H. Moriarty. *Technicolor Consultant*: Robert Brower. *Stunts*: Paul Stader, Howard Curtis (uncredited), Gil Perkins (uncredited), Carl Saxe (uncredited), Denver Mattson (uncredited). *Stunt Double*: *Lloyd Bridges*: Dick Dial (uncredited). *Cast*: Lloyd Bridges (Steve Bannerman), Anne Francis (Gina Talbot), Ralph Meeker (Glenn Walkup), Andrew Prine (Jonesey), Kasey Rogers (Mrs. Peterson), Edward Faulkner, Linden Chiles (Allen Bedecker), Bobby Van (Eddie Randolph), Billy Dee Williams (Merle Barnaby), Michael-James Wixted (Charlie Burnett), Jennifer Leak (Bee Jay Caldwell), Nobu McCarthy (Zora Lewin). Universal TV / National Broadcasting Company (NBC). 104 minutes.

Notes: A proposed pilot for a television series, it boasted location footage in Kauai, Hawaii. It was briefly shown theatrically in New York City in 1971.

REVIEWS

"[I]t is a reasonably entertaining, well-paced, technically ambitious movie that receives great assistance from its performers — notably Lloyd Bridges (the pilot) for good, Ralph Meeker (the businessman) for evil, and Anne Francis (the mistress) for marriage and the family." — Roger Greenspun, *The New York Times,* June 3, 1971

More Dead Than Alive (1969)

"Killers in pairs ... death by the dozen...
They left the west ... More Dead than Alive."

Director: Robert Sparr. *Producer*: Hal Klein. *Executive Producer*: Aubrey Schenck. *Writer*: George Schenck. *Original Music*: Philip Springer. *Cinematographer*: Jack Marquette. *Editor*: John F. Schreyer. *Art Director*: Art Loel. *Set Decorator*: William Kuehl. *Costume Designer*: Tye Osward, Joyce Rogers. *Makeup Artist*: Gary Liddiard. *Assistant Director*: Morris R. Abrams. *Sound Recordist*: Everett Hughes. *Special Effects*: Ralph Webb. *Stunts*: Charlie Picerni (uncredited), Ted Smile (uncredited). *Stunt Coordinator*: Fred Carson. *Score Mixer*: Dan Wallin (uncredited). *Cast*: Clint Walker (Cain), Vincent Price (Dan Ruffalo), Anne Francis (Monica Alton), Paul Hampton (Billy Valence), Craig Littler (Karma), Mike Henry (Luke Santee), Clarke Gordon (Carson), Beverly Powers (Sheree), William Woodson

Anne on location with Clint Walker for *More Dead Than Alive* (1969).

(Warden), Harry Lauter (Doctor), Eric Matthews (Wes Santee), Robert Foulk (Brill), Frank Baxter (Banker), Andy Albin (Fletcher), Emile Meyer (Bartender), Orville Sherman (Barber), Arvo Ojala (Mustached Man), Fred Scheiwiller (Cawley), Walt La Rue (Graber), Frank Babich (Tandy), George Sawaya (Guard Captain), Mickey Simpson (Crew Boss), Jon Ojala (Messenger Boy), Wayne Taylor (Customer), Robert Carter (Shopkeeper), Ron Heller (Townsman), Fred Carson (Outlaw at Prison, uncredited). *Release Date*: January 15, 1969. Aubrey Schenck Productions / United Artists. 101 minutes.

Hook, Line and Sinker (1969)

> "Jerry has to get away from it all! Even if it
> means a $100,000 spree on credit cards!"

Director: George Marshall. *Producer*: Jerry Lewis. *Associate Producer*: Joe E. Stabile. *Writers*: Rod Amateau, David Davis (story), Rod Amateau (screenplay). *Original Music*: Dick Stabile. *Cinematographer*: W. Wallace Kelley. *Editor*: Russel Wiles. *Art Director*: John Beckman. *Set Decorator*: Frank Tuttle. *Makeup Artist*: Jack Stone. *Makeup Supervisor*: Ben Lane. *Hair Stylist*: Virginia Jones. *Production Manager*: Herbert Wallerstein. *Assistant Director*: Hal Bell. *Properties*: Richard M. Rubin. *Sound*: Al Overton Sr., Arthur Piantadosi. *Sound Supervisor*: Charles J. Rice. *Stunts*: Jesse Wayne. *Men's Wardrober*: Guy Verhille. *Assistant Editor*: Joe Luciano. *Conductor*: Dick Stabile. *Script Supervisor*: Hazel Hall. *Cast*: Jerry Lewis (Peter J. Ingersoll / Fred Dobbs), Peter Lawford (Dr. Scott Carter), Anne Francis (Nancy Ingersoll), Pedro Gonzales Gonzales (Perfecto), Jimmy Miller (Jimmy Ingersoll), Jennifer Edwards (Jennifer Ingersoll), Eleanor Audley (Mrs. Durham), Henry Corden (Kenyon Hammercher), Sylvia Lewis (Karlotta Hammercher), Phillip Pine (Head Surgeon), Felipe Turich (Portuguese Mortician), Kathleen Freeman (Mrs. Hardtack). *Release Date*: June 6, 1969. Jerry Lewis Productions / Columbia Pictures Corporation. 91 minutes.

Impasse (1969)

Director: Richard Benedict. *Producer*: Hal Klein. *Executive Producer*: Aubrey Schenck. *Writer*: John C. Higgins. *Original Music*: Philip Springer. *Cinematographer*: Mars B. Rasca [Nonong Rasca]. *Editor*: John F. Schreyer. *Makeup Artist*: Totoy Villamin. *Hair Stylist*: Cecilia Abelardo. *Production Manager*: Vicente Nayve. *Assistant Director*: Donald Verk. *Sound Recordist*: Ben Winkler. *Stunts*: Bill Catching (uncredited). *Assistant Editor*: Linda Schlesinger. *Musical Director — Conductor*: Philip Springer. *Score Mixer*: Dan Wallin (uncredited). *Script Supervisor*: Stuart Lippman. *Cast*: Burt Reynolds (Pat Morrison), Anne Francis (Bobby Jones), Lyle Bettger (Hansen), Rodolfo Acosta (Draco), Jeff Corey (Wombat), Clarke Gordon (Trev Jones), Miko Mayama (Mariko), Joanne Dalsass (Penny), Vic Diaz (Jesus), Dely Atay-atayan (Pear Blossom), Bruno Punzalan (Nakajima), Lily Campillos (Maria Bonita), Shirley Gorospe (Sherry), Bessie Barredo (Kiling), Robert Yang (Interne), Eddie Nicart (Kuli), Richard Benedict (Owner — Bartender of Ugly American, uncredited). *Release Date*: May 7, 1969. Aubrey Schenck Productions / United Artists. 100 minutes.

Notes: Filmed on location in the Philippines in 1968, the working title of this film was *Golden Bullet.*

REVIEWS

"'Impasse' is a good one that may get away all too soon. This United Artists release, still another suspense-adventure about a gold holdup, was stuck at the bottom of a double bill yesterday only at the New Amsterdam Theater, instead of gracing local houses. Although the picture loses momentum toward the end, it has plenty going for it.... For one thing, there is the freshness of the locale in and around Manila, bright and beguiling in fine color. There is a good cast, headed by Burt Reynolds and Anne Francis.... Add to the dialogue the zip and verve of the tempo, under Richard Benedict's direction, and the blunt conviction of the characters in the lean, well-meshed script by John C. Higgins.... As the tough organizer, Mr. Reynolds is most persuasive. Almost as good are Miss Francis, as a tennis champ, and Clarke Gordon, as her father with keenly retentive memories of Corregidor." — Howard Thompson, *The New York Times*, May 8, 1969

The Love God? (1969)

"So many women... Not enough man."

Director-Writer: Nat Hiken. *Producer*: Edward J. Montagne. *Associate Producer*: Billy Sands. *Original Music*: Vic Mizzy. *Cinematographer*: William Margulies. *Editor*: Sam E. Waxman. *Art Directors*: Alexander Golitzen, George Patrick. *Set Decorators*: Marvin March, John McCarthy. *Costume Designer*: Helen Colvig. *Makeup Supervisor*: Bud Westmore. *Hair Stylist*: Larry Germain. *Unit Production Manager*: Wes Thompson. *Assistant Director*: Phil Bowles. *Second Assistant Director*: Ted Swanson (uncredited). *Sound*: Waldon O. Watson, Frank H. Wilkinson. *Stunts*: Jerry Brutsche. *Composer: Song "Summer in the Meadow"*: Lyn Murray. *Composer: Song "Mr. Peacock"*: Walter Slivinski. *Music Supervisor*: Stanley Wilson. *Choreographer*: Wilda Taylor. *Cast*: Don Knotts (Abner Audubon Peacock IV), Anne Francis (Lisa LaMonica), Edmond O'Brien (Osborn Tremaine), James Gregory (Darrell Evans Hughes), Maureen Arthur (Evelyn Tremaine), Maggie Peterson (Rose Ellen Wilkerson), Jesslyn Fax (Miss Love), Jacques Aubuchon (Carter Fenton), Marjorie Bennett (Miss Pickering), Jim Boles (Amos Peacock), Ruth McDevitt (Miss Keezy), Roy Stuart (Joe Merkel), Herb Voland (Attorney General Frederick Snow), James Westerfield (Rev. Wilkerson), Bob Hastings (Shrader), Larry McCormick (Rich), Robert P. Lieb (Rayfield), Willis Bouchey (Judge Jeremiah Claypool), Herbie Faye (Lester Timkin), Johnny

Behind the scenes on *The Love God?* (1969) with Don Knotts and Johnny Seven.

Seven (Petey), Joe Perry (Big Joe), Jim Begg (Hotchkiss), Carla Borelli (Erica Lane), Nancy Bonniwell (Toma), Shelly Davis (Ingrid), A'leshia Lee [Brevard] (Sherry), Terri Harper (Delilah), B.S. Pully (J. Charles Twilight). *Release Date*: August 1969. Universal Pictures. 101 minutes.

Wild Women (1970)

"Five Female Convicts Pose as Wives to
Mask a Military Mission into Enemy Country"

Director: Don Taylor. *Producer*: Lou Morheim. *Executive Producer*: Aaron Spelling. *Associate Producer*: Shelley Hull. *Writers*: Vincent Fotre (novel *The Trailmakers*), Richard Carr, Lou Morheim (teleplay). *Original Music*: Fred Steiner. *Cinematographer*: Fleet Southcott. *Editor*: Aaron Stell. *Art Director*: Tracy Bousman. *Music Supervisor*: George Duning. *Cast*: Hugh O'Brian (Killian), Anne Francis (Jean Marshek), Marilyn Maxwell (Maude Webber), Marie Windsor (Lottie Clampett), Sherry Jackson (Nancy Belacourt), Robert F. Simon (Col. Donahue), Richard Kelton (Lt. Charring), Cynthia Hull (Mit-O-Ne), Pepe Callahan (Lt. Santos), Ed Call (Sgt. Frame), John Neris (Sgt. Elmer Cass), Troy Melton (Cpl. Isham), Joseph Kaufmann (Pvt. Bishop), Chuck Hicks (Cpl. Hearn), Jim Boles (Warden), Michael Keep (Cadet), Loie Bridge (Margie Britt, uncredited), Kaye Elhardt (Mary Kroll, uncredited), Thomas Montgomery (Guard, uncredited), Pedro Regas (Old Indian, uncredited). *Airdate*: October 20, 1970. Aaron Spelling Productions / American Broadcasting Company (ABC). 74 minutes.

The Intruders (1970)

Director: William Graham. *Producer*: James Duff McAdams. *Executive Producer*: Bert Granet. *Writers*: William [Douglas] Lansford (story), Dean Riesner (teleplay). *Original Music*: Dave Grusin. *Cinematographer*: Ray Flin. *Editor*: J. Howard Terrill. *Art Director*: Loyd S. Papez. *Set Decorators*: John McCarthy, James S. Redd. *Makeup Artist*: Bud Westmore. *Hair Stylist*: Larry Germain. *Unit Manager*: Bud Brill. *Assistant Director*: Roger Slager. *Sound*: Frank H. Wilkinson. *Costume Supervisor*: Vincent Dee. *Editorial Supervisor*: Richard Belding. *Color Coordinator*: Robert Brower. *Music Supervisor*: Stanley Wilson. *Cast*: Don Murray (Sam Garrison), Anne Francis (Leora Garrison), Edmond O'Brien (Col. William Bodeen), John Saxon (Billy Pye), Gene Evans (Cole Younger), Edward Andrews (Elton Dykstra), Shelly Novack (Theron Pardo), Harry Dean Stanton (Whit Dykstra), Stuart Margolin (Jesse James), Zalman King (Bob Younger), Phillip Alford (Harold Gilman), Harrison Ford (Carl), John Hoyt (Appleton), Marlene Tracy (Kate Guerrera), Ken Swofford (Pomerantz), Robert Donner (Roy Kirsh), Edward Faulkner (Bill Riley), James Gammon (Chaunce Dykstra), Gavin MacLeod (Warden). *Airdate*: November 10, 1970. Universal TV / National Broadcasting Company (NBC). 100 minutes.

Notes: Filmed in 1967.

The Forgotten Man (1971)

Director–Executive Producer: Walter Grauman. *Producer*: Phillip Barry. *Writers*: Bernard Fein, Mark Rogers [Rodgers] (story), Mark Rogers [Rodgers] (teleplay). *Original Music*: Dave Grusin. *Cinematographer*: Michel Hugo. *Editor*: Frank P. Keller. *Casting*: Joe Scully. *Art Director*: Jack Senter. *Set Decorator*: Ed Parker. *Costume Designers*: Betsy Cox, Lambert Marks. *Makeup Artist*: Jerry Cash. *Hair Stylist*: Lynn Masters. *Unit Manager–Assistant Director*: Mark Evans. *Production Manager*: John W. Rogers. *Property Master*: Sam Bergman. *Sound Engineer*: Gene Cantamessa. *Sound Effects Editor*: Gene Eliot. *Key Grip*: Tom May. *Music Editor*: Rocky Moriana. *Script Continuity*: Doris Grau, Elaine Newman. *Cast*: Dennis Weaver (Lt. Joe Hardy), Lois Nettleton (Anne Wilson), Anne Francis (Marie Hardy Forrest), Andrew Duggan (William Forrest), Percy Rodrigues (Captain Jackson), Pamelyn Ferdin (Sharon Hardy), Robert Doyle (Major Everett), James Hong (Major Thon), Frank Maxwell (Colonel Thompson), Carl Reindel (Lieutenant Diamonte), John S. Ragin (Major Parkman), Vernon

Weddle (Surgeon). *Airdate*: September 14, 1971. ABC Circle Films / Grauman Productions / American Broadcasting Company (ABC). 73 minutes.

Mongo's Back in Town (1971)

Director: Marvin J. Chomsky. *Producer*: Tom Egan. *Executive Producer*: Bob Banner. *Writers*: E. Richard Johnson (novel), Herman Miller (teleplay). *Original Music*: Michael Melvoin. *Cinematographer*: Archie R. Dalzell. *Editor*: Howard A. Smith. *Art Director*: Albert Heschong. *Set Decorator*: Cheryal Kearney. *Costume Designers*: Robert Harris Sr., Dorothy Rodgers. *Makeup Artist*: Richard Cobos. *Hair Stylist*: Ruby Ford. *Production Manager*: Edward O. Denault. *Unit Production Manager*: Sam Manners. *Assistant Director*: Gordon A. Webb. *Assistant Property Master*: Thomas Gark. *Sound Mixer*: Charles M. Wilborn. *Music Supervisor*: Morton Stevens. *Cast*: Telly Savalas (Lt. Pete Tolstad), Sally Field (Vikki), Anne Francis (Angel), Charles Cioffi (Mike Nash), Martin Sheen (Gordon), Joe Don Baker (Mongo Nash), Johnny Haymer (Rocca), Harry Basch (Kanole), Howard Dayton (Blindman), Gregg Palmer (Szabo), Ned Glass (Freddie), Angelo Rossitto (Trembles). *Airdate*: December 10, 1971. Bob Banner Associates / Columbia Broadcasting System (CBS). 73 minutes.

Fireball Forward (1972)

Director: Marvin J. Chomsky. *Producer*: Frank McCarthy. *Writer*: Edmund H. North (teleplay). *Original Music*: Lionel Newman. *Cinematographer*: Robert L. Morrison. *Editors*: Harry Coswick, Charles L. Freeman, Pembroke J. Herring. *Art Directors*: Bill Malley, Jack Martin Smith. *Set Decorators*: Walter M. Scott, Jerry Wunderlich. *Unit Production Manager*: David Silver. *Post-Production Supervisor*: Samuel E. Beetley. *Assistant Director*: Jack Roe. *Assistant Property Master*: Thomas Gark (uncredited). *Composer: Song "The Longest Day"*: Paul Anka. *Cast*: Ben Gazzara (Maj. Gen. Joe Barrett), Ricardo Montalban (Jean Duval), Anne Francis (Helen Sawyer), Dana Elcar (Col. Talbot), Edward Binns (Corps Commander), Morgan Paull (Sgt. Andrew Collins), Curt Lowens (Capt. Bauer), L.Q. Jones (Maj. Larkin), Eddie Albert (Col. Douglas Graham), Robert Patten (Col. Avery), Richard Yniguez (Capt. Tony Sanchez), Kenneth Tobey (Gen. Dawson), Don Eitner (Sgt. Brock), John Gruber (Doctor), Stanley Beck (MP Sergeant), Dick Valentine (Col. Fowler), Joseph Perry (GI #1), Hank Jones (MP Private), Jerry Fogel (Signal Corpsman), Neil J. Schwartz (Cook), Henry Brown Jr. (Wounded Soldier), Klair Bybee (First Lieutenant), James Secrest (Signal Corps Sergeant), Brent Davis (Second Lieutenant), Ilse Taurins (Mme. Accard), Bob Golden (Sergeant), Buck Holland (GI #2), Daniel Keough (Supply Sergeant). *Airdate*: March 5, 1972. 20th Century–Fox Television / American Broadcasting Company (ABC). 98 minutes.

> *Notes*: Meant as a pilot for a television series.

Haunts of the Very Rich (1972)

Director: Paul Wendkos. *Producer*: Lillian Gallo. *Writers*: T.K. Brown III (story), William P. Wood (teleplay). *Original Music*: Dominic Frontiere. *Cinematographer*: Ben Colman. *Editor*: Fredric Steinkamp. *Art Director*: Eugene Lourie. *Set Decorator*: James G. Cane. *Makeup Artist*: Jerry Cash. *Hair Stylist*: Lynn Masters. *Unit Production Manager–Assistant Director*: Kurt Neumann. *Property Master*: Russell Goble. *Construction Coordinator*: Gerald B. MacDonald. *Sound Effects Editor*: William Hartman. *Production Mixer*: Harold Lewis. *Sound Re-recording Mixer*: Theodore Soderberg. *Casting*: Hoyt Bowers. *Women's Costumer*: Betsy Cox. *Men's Costumer*: Richard La Motte. *Costume Supervisor*: John Perry. *Assistant Editor*: Diane Adler. *Music Editor*: Kenneth Wannberg. *Script Supervisor*: Lily La Cava. *Cast*: Lloyd Bridges (Dave Woodrough), Cloris Leachman (Ellen Blunt), Edward Asner (Al Hunsicker), Anne Francis (Annette Larrier), Tony Bill (Lyle), Donna Mills (Laurie), Robert Reed (Reverend John Fellows), Moses Gunn (Seacrist), Beverly Gill (Miss Vick), Todd Martin (Harris), Phyllis Hill (Rita), Michael Lembeck (Delmonico), Susan Foster (Miss Upton). *Airdate*: September 20, 1972. ABC Circle Films / American Broadcasting Company (ABC). 75 minutes.

Pancho Villa (1972)

"The only man to invade the U.S.A.!"

Director: Eugenio Martín. *Producer*: Bernard Gordon. *Writers*: Gene Martin [Eugenio Martín] (story), Julian Halevy [Julian Zimet] (screenplay). *Original Music*: Antón García Abril. *Cinematographer*: Alejandro Ulloa. *Editor*: Antonio Ramírez de Loaysa. *Wardrobe Supervisor*: Charles Simminger. *Cast*: Telly Savalas (Pancho Villa), Clint Walker (Scotty), Chuck Connors (Col. Wilcox), Anne Francis (Flo), José María Prada (Luis), Ángel del Pozo (Lt. Eager), Luis Dávila (McDermott), Mónica Randall (Lupe), Antonio Casas (Gen. Goyo), Alberto Dalbés (Mendoza), Barta Barri (Alfonso), Eduardo Calvo (Banker), Lucy Tiller (Woman), Inés Oviedo (Soldadera), Dan van Husen (Bart), Adolfo Thous (Flores), F. Sanchez Polack [Fernando Sánchez Polack] (Manuel), Lola Gaos (Old Woman), Tony Ross (Photographer), Ben Tatar (Bates), Robert Hevelone (Evans), Art Larkin (Sgt. White), Gene Collins (Popowski), Dennis Vaughan (Capt. Mettle), Hal Fletcher (Major James), Lorraine Clewes (Clara), Marjorie Neville (Eudora), Nancy Baytos (Amanda), Luis Rivera (Chauffeur), Ralph Neville (Gen. Jenkins), Alberto Fernández (Priest), Bud Strait (Station Master), Luis Marín (Villista), Tony Skios [Antonio Rebollo] (Villista), Carl Rapp (Doctor), Fernando Hilbeck (Ramon), Felipe Solano (Angel), Gerardo Navarro (Mexican Diplomat), Walter Coy (Gen. Pershing). *Release Date*: October 31, 1972 (West Germany), April 16, 1973 (Sweden), January 24, 1974 (USA), August 25, 1975 (Spain). Granada Films / Scotia International / Regia-Arturo González Rodríguez. 92 minutes.

   Notes: Also called *Vendetta*.

Cry Panic (1974)

Director: James Goldstone. *Producers*: Aaron Spelling, Leonard Goldberg. *Associate Producer*: Parke Perine. *Writer*: Jack B. Sowards. *Original Music*: Ken Lauber. *Cinematographer*: Tim Southcott. *Editor*: Folmar Blangsted. *Art Director*: Tracy Bousman. *Set Decorator*: Bob Signorelli. *Costume Designer*: Robert Harris Jr., Madeline Sylos. *Makeup Artist*: Howard Smit. *Hair Stylist*: Joyce Morrison. *Production Manager*: Al Kraus. *Post-Production Manager*: Russel Wiles. *Executive Production Manager*: Norman Henry. *Assistant Director*: Bill D'Arcy. *Sound*: John Oliver. *Special Effects*: Dutch Van Derbyl. *Casting Supervisor*: Bert Remsen. *Conductor—Orchestrator*: Ken Lauber. *Music Supervisor*: Rocky Moriana. *Script Supervisor*: Doris DeHerdt. *Cast*: John Forsythe (David Ryder), Earl Holliman (Sheriff Ross Cabot), Ralph Meeker (Chuck Braswell), Norman Alden (Doc Potter), Claudia McNeil (Ethel Hanson), Anne Francis (Julie), Eddie Firestone (Dozier), Harry Basch (Jackson), Gene Tyburn (Lipscombe), Jason Wingreen (Woody), Roy Applegate (Grady), Wesley Lau (Joe Red), Jason Ledger (Stacey), Pitt Herbert (Mailman). *Airdate*: February 6, 1974. Spelling-Goldberg Productions / American Broadcasting Company (ABC). 74 minutes.

The F.B.I. Story: The FBI Versus Alvin Karpis, Public Enemy Number One (1974)

Director: Marvin J. Chomsky. *Producer*: Philip Saltzman. *Associate Producer*: Bernard R. Goodman. *Executive Producer*: Quinn Martin. *Writer*: Calvin Clements Jr. *Original Music*: Duane Tatro. *Cinematographer*: Jacques R. Marquette. *Editor*: Jerry Young. *Art Director:* James Dowell Vance. *Cast*: Robert Foxworth (Alvin Karpis), David Wayne (Maynard Richards), Kay Lenz (Shirley), Gary Lockwood (Fred Barker), Anne Francis (Colette), Chris Robinson (Earl Anderson), Harris Yulin (J. Edgar Hoover), Eileen Heckart (Ma Barker), James Gammon (Alex Denton), Robert Emhardt (Dr. Willards), Alexandra Hay (Vicky Clinton), Janice Lynde (Bernice Griffiths), Charles Cyphers (Arthur "Doc" Barker), Gerald McRaney (Smith), Fred Sadoff (Frank), Kelly Thordsen (Chief of Detectives), Whit Bissell (Sen. McKellar), Lenore Kasdorf (Rita), William Conrad (Narrator). *Airdate*: November 8, 1974. Quinn Martin Productions (QM) / Warner Bros. Television / Columbia Broadcasting System (CBS). 100 minutes.

The Last Survivors (1975)

Director: Lee H. Katzin. *Producer*: Tom Egan. *Executive Producer*: Bob Banner. *Associate Producer*: Suzy Friendly. *Writer*: Douglas Day Stewart. *Original Music*: Michael Melvoin. *Cinematographer*: Michel Hugo. *Editors*: Melvin Shapiro, George Watters. *Art Director:* Frederick P. Hope. *Set Decorator*: Bill McLaughlin. *Costume Designer*: Guy C. Verhille. *Assistant Director*: Jack Roe. *Property Master*: Terry Ballard. *Sound*: Tom Overton. *Sound Re-recordist*: Jay M. Harding. *Sound Effects*: James J. Klinger. *Dialogue Editor*: Bobbe Kurtz. *Special Effects*: Phil Cory. *Special Effects Foreman*: Charles E. Dolan. *Stunts*: Bob Herron (uncredited). *Camera Operator*: Herb Pearl. *Script Supervisor*: Marshall Schlom. *Cast*: Martin Sheen (Alexander William Holmes), Diane Baker (Marilyn West), Tom Bosley (Marcus Damian), Bruce Davison (Michael Larsen), Anne Francis (Helen Dixon), Christopher George (Duane Jeffreys), Bethel Leslie (Inez Haynes), Beulah Quo (Mrs. Peters), Eugene Roche (Prosecutor), Percy Rodrigues (Rudi Franco), Anne Seymour (Susie Mansham), Mel Stewart (Sid Douglas), Margaret Willock (Nancy Victor), William Bryant (Capt. Harris), Lonny Chapman (David Broadhead), Linda Dano (Linda Collison), Steve Franken (Don West), Leif Garrett (Billy Wright), Alex Henteloff (Francis Askin), Andrew Stevens (Checkerman), Joe E. Tata (Charley). *Airdate*: March 4, 1975. Bob Banner Associates / Columbia Pictures Television / National Broadcasting Company (NBC). 90 minutes.

A Girl Named Sooner (1975)

Director: Delbert Mann. *Producer*: James Franciscus, Fred Hamilton. *Executive Producer*: Frederick H. Brogger. *Writers*: Suzanne Clauser (novel), Suzanne Clauser, Marilyn Harris (teleplay). *Original Music*: Jerry Goldsmith. *Cinematographer*: Ralph Woolsey. *Editor*: Jack W. Holmes. *Casting*: Jack Baur. *Production Designer*: Jan Scott. *Set Decorator*: Ralph Sylos. *Unit Production Manager*: Saul Wurtzel. *Production Supervisor*: Mark Evans. *Assistant Director*: Don Roberts. *Second Assistant Director*: John M. Poer. *Sound*: John Speak. *Music Supervisor*: Lionel Newman. *Cast*: Lee Remick (Elizabeth McHenry), Richard Crenna (R.J. "Mac" McHenry), Don Murray (Sheriff Phil Rotteman), Anne Francis (Selma Goss), Cloris Leachman (Old Mam Hawes), Susan Deer (Sooner), Michael Gross (Jim Seevey), Nancy Bell (Teacher), Ken Hardin (Harvey Drummond), Tonia Scotti (Judith Ann Drumond), Ewen Bremner (Archie). *Airdate*: June 18, 1975. 20th Century–Fox Television / Frederick Brogger Associates / Omnibus Productions / National Broadcasting Company (NBC). 120 minutes.

Survival (1976)

Director-Producer: Michael Campus. *Writers*: Michael Campus (story), John D.F. Black (screenplay). *Script Supervisor*: Lynn A. Aber. *Cast*: Susanne Benton (Susanne), Barbara Blake (Barbara), Hampton Fancher (Hampton), Anne Francis (Anne), Dee Hartford (Dee), David Maure (David), Chuck McCann (Chuck), Sheree North (Sheree), Barry Sullivan (Barry), Jessie Wills (Jessie), Otis Young (Otis). Twentieth Century–Fox Film Corporation. 85 minutes.

Notes: Filmed in 1969 but not released until 1976.

Banjo Hackett: Roamin' Free (1976)

Director: Andrew V. McLaglen. *Producer*: Bruce Lansbury. *Associate Producer*: Mel Swope. *Writer*: Ken Trevey. *Original Music*: Morton Stevens. *Cinematographer*: Al Francis. *Editors*: Dann Cahn, David Wages. *Casting*: Shelley Ellison [Rachelle Farberman]. *Art Directors*: Ross Bellah, Carl Braunger. *Set Decorators*: Audrey Blasdel Goddard, Bruce Weintraub. *Costume Designers*: Mike Butler, Grady Hunt. *Makeup Artist*: Robert Mills. *Makeup Supervisor*: Ben Lane. *Assistant Director*: G.C. "Rusty" Meek. *Property Master*: Ron Chiniquy. *Sound Editor*: Jack Finlay. *Sound Mixer*: Dean Hodges. *Stunt Coordinator*: Jim Burk. *Music Editor*: Shinichi Yamazaki. *Script Supervisor*: Marilyn Giardino. *Cast*: Don Meredith (Banjo Hackett), Jeff Corey (Judge Janeway), Gloria DeHaven (Lady Jane Gray), L.Q. Jones (Sheriff Tadlock), Jan Murray (Jethro Swain), Dan O'Herlihy (Tip Conaker), Jennifer Warren

(Mollie Brannen), David Young (Elmore Mintore), Richard Young (Luke Mintore), Ike Eisenmann (Jubal Winner), Anne Francis (Flora Dobbs), Chuck Connors (Sam Ivory), Slim Pickens (Lijah Tuttle), John O'Leary (Mr. Creed), Jeff Morris (Jack O'Spades), John Alderson (Moose Matlock), Kenneth O'Brien (Wiley Pegram), Britt Leach (The Carpenter), Shirley O'Hara (Postmistress), Elizabeth Perry (Grace Nye), Doodles Weaver (Old Turkey), Ben Bates (1st Logger), Walter Wyatt (Second Logger), Albert Able (Rudolf), Faith Quabius (Ruttles), John McKee (Official), Stan Haze (Blacksmith). *Airdate*: May 3, 1976. Bruce Lansbury Productions / Columbia Pictures Television / National Broadcasting Company (NBC). 100 minutes.

Notes: A pilot for a proposed television series.

The Young Runaways (1978)

Director: Russ Mayberry. *Producer*: Jerome Courtland. *Executive Producer*: Ron Miller. *Writer*: Sy Gomberg. *Original Music*: Robert F. Brunner. *Cinematographer*: Charles F. Wheeler. *Editor*: Bob Bring. *Art Directors*: John B. Mansbridge, Jack Senter. *Set Decorator*: Sharon Thomas. *Costume Designers*: Chuck Keehne, Emily Sundby. *Makeup Artist*: Robert J. Schiffer. *Hair Stylist*: Donna Turner [Culver]. *Production Manager:* John Bloss. *Unit Production Manager–Assistant Director*: Christopher N. Seiter. *Sound Supervisor*: Herb Taylor. *Sound Mixer*: Greg Valtierra. *Stunt Coordinator*: Glenn Wilder. *Lighting Technician*: Peter McEvoy. *Orchestrator*: Walter Sheets. *Music Editor*: Jack Wadsworth. *Cast*: Anne Francis (Marian Lockhart), Robert Webber (Fred Lockhart), Gary Collins (Lt. Ray Phillips), Pat Delaney (Katherine Phillips), Alicia Fleer (Rosebud Doyle), Tommy Crebbs (Joseph T. Doyle), Richard Bakalyan (Jocko), Walter Barnes (Sgt. Abel), Lucille Benson (Grandma Hopkins), Chip Courtland (Eric), Kurt Courtland (Stanley), Sonny Shroyer (C.L. Doyle), Sharon Farrell (Mamma Doyle), Tim Pelligrino (Little Freddie Doyle), Daryn Sipes (Margaret Jean Doyle), Barbara Hale (Mrs. Ogle), Ken Jones (Mike), Jennifer Jason Leigh (Heather), Dermott Downs (Chuck), Howard T. Platt (Bubba), Dolores Sandoz (Miss Anderson), Steve Sherman (Pete), John Lupton (Benefactor), Sharon Shroyer (Mama Doyle). *Airdate*: May 28, 1978. Walt Disney Productions / National Broadcasting Company (NBC). 120 minutes.

Little Mo (1978)

Director: Daniel Haller. *Producer*: George Sherman. *Executive Producer*: Jack Webb. *Writer*: John McGreevey. *Original Music*: Carl Brandt, Billy May. *Cinematographer*: Harry L. Wolf. *Editors*: Michael Berman, Bill E. Garst, Douglas Hines, Bob Swanson. *Casting*: Lane Allan. *Art Director*: Carl Anderson. *Set Decorators*: Sam J. Jones, Ralph Sylos. *Makeup Artist*: Mike Germain. *Hair Stylist*: Christine Lee. *Unit Production Manager*: Mickey McCardle. *Executive Production Manager*: Paul Donnelly. *First Assistant Director*: Paul Helmick. *Second Assistant Director*: Gene De Ruelle. *Property Master*: Walter Wall. *Sound Effects*: Ray Alba, Bert Schoenfeld. *Sound Mixer*: Larry Hadsell. *Sound Re-recording Mixer*: Tex Rudloff. *Costumers*: Dorothy Barkley, Frank Tauss. *Assistant Film Editors*: Mike Cohn, Jim De Witt. *Supervising Editor*: Richard Greer. *Additional Orchestrator*: Carl Brandt. *Music Editor*: Ken Johnson. *Production Coordinator*: Lynne Birdt. *Technical Advisor*: Nancy Chaffee. *Cast*: Michael Learned (Eleanor "Teach" Tennant), Anne Baxter (Jessamyn Connolly), Glynnis O'Connor (Maureen Connolly), Claude Akins (Gus Berste), Anne Francis (Sophie Fisher), Mark Harmon (Norman Brinker), Martin Milner (Wilbur Folsom), Leslie Nielsen (Nelson Fisher), Tony Trabert (Himself), Ann Doran (Aunt Gert), Fred Holliday (Dr. Bruce Kimball), Len Wayland (Johnson), Justin Lord (Maxwell), Maggie Wellman (Susan), Jean Karp (Nancy Chaffee), Cindy Brinker (Susan Partridge), K.C. Kiner (Laura Lou Jahn), Tony Fretz (Doris Hart), Stacy Keach Sr. (Chamber of Commerce President), Beatrice Manley (Duchess of Kent), Jason Kincaid (Ben), Tracey Gold (Cindy Brinker), Missy Gold (Brenda Brinker), Howard Culver (Tennis Match Announcer), Ian Abercrombie (Dr. Noyes, uncredited). *Airdate*: September 5, 1978. Mark VII Ltd. / Worldvision / Spelling Entertainment / National Broadcasting Company (NBC). 150 minutes.

Notes: Based on the real-life story of tennis player Maureen Connolly (1934–69).

Born Again (1978)

"For everyone who ever wanted a chance to start over."

Director: Irving Rapper. *Producer*: Frank Capra Jr. *Associate Producer*: Paul Temple. *Executive Producer*: Robert L. Munger. *Writers*: Charles Colson (novel), Walter Bloch (screenplay). *Original Music*: Les Baxter. *Cinematographer*: Harry Stradling Jr. *Editor*: Axel Hubert Sr. *Production Designer*: Bill Kenney. *Assistant Directors*: Bob Bender, Ed Milkovich. *Supervising Sound Editor*: Richard L. Anderson. *Sound Effects Editor*: Teresa Eckton. *Assistant Cameras*: Don E. FauntLeRoy, Richard Craig Meinardus. *Camera Operator*: Ralph Gerling. *Casting*: Henry Rackin. *Score Mixer*: Dan Wallin. *Cast*: Dean Jones (Charles W. Colson), Anne Francis (Patty Colson), Jay Robinson (David Shapiro), Dana Andrews (Tom Phillips), Raymond St. Jacques (Jimmy Newsom), George Brent (Judge Gerhard Gesell), Harold Hughes (Himself), Billy Graham (Himself), Harry Spillman (President Richard M. Nixon), Scott Walker (Scanlon), Robert Gray (Paul Kramer), Arthur Roberts (Al Quie), Ned Wilson (Douglas Coe), Dean Brooks (Dick Howard), Christopher Conrad (Christian "Chris" Colson), Peter Jurasik (Henry Kissinger), Stuart Lee (Wendell Colson), Richard Caine (H.R. Haldeman), Brigid O'Brien (Holly Holm), Robert Broyles (John Erlichman), Anthony Canne (Burkhardt), Corinne Michaels [Corinne Camacho] (Raquel Ramirez), Jack Clarke (Mike Williams), Byron Morrow (Archibald Cox), William Zuckert (E. Howard Hunt), William Benedict (Leon Jaworski), Alicia Fleer (Emily Colson), Laure Adams (Gert Phillips). *Release Date*: October 1978. AVCO Embassy Pictures. 110 minutes.

The Rebels (1979)

Director: Russ Mayberry. *Producers*: Gino Grimaldi, Hannah Louise Shearer. *Associate Producer*: Bernadette Joyce. *Executive Producer*: Robert A. Cinader. *Writers*: John Jakes (novel), Sean Bain, Robert A. Cinader (teleplay). *Original Music*: Gerald Fried. *Cinematographer*: Frank Thackery. *Editors*: John Kaufman, Skip Lusk. *Art Director*: William L. Campbell. *Stunts*: Loren Janes, Neil Summers, Harold "Hal" Frizzell (uncredited). *Cast*: Andrew Stevens (Philip Kent), Don Johnson (Judson Fletcher), Doug McClure (Eph Tait), Jim Backus (John Hancock), Richard Basehart (Duke of Kentland), Joan Blondell (Mrs. Brumple), Tom Bosley (Benjamin Franklin), Macdonald Carey (Dr. Church), Rory Calhoun (Breen), Kim Cattrall (Anne Kent), John Chappell (Henry Knox), William Daniels (John Adams), Anne Francis (Mrs. Harris), Peter Graves (George Washington), Pamela Hensley (Charlotte Waverly), Gwen Humble (Peggy McLean), Wilfrid Hyde-White (Gen. Howe), Nehemiah Persoff (Baron Von Steuben), William Smith (John Waverly), Warren Stevens (Ambrose Waverly), Kevin Tighe (Thomas Jefferson), Bobby Troup (Sam Gill), Forrest Tucker (Angus Fletcher), Tanya Tucker (Rachel), Robert Vaughn (Seth McLean), William Conrad (Narrator), Guy Madison (Lieutenant Mayo, uncredited). *Airdate*: May 14, 1979. Universal TV. 240 minutes.

Beggarman, Thief (1979)

Director: Lawrence Doheny. *Producer*: Jack Laird. *Associate Producer*: Yvonne Demery. *Writers*: Irwin Shaw (novel), Mary Alice Donahue, Art Eisenson (teleplay). *Original Music*: Eddie Sauter. *Cinematographers*: Robert Caramico, Steven Poster. *Editors*: Robert Watts, Albert J.J. Zúñiga. *Art Director*: Loyd S. Papez. *Stunts*: Gregory J. Barnett. *Costumer*: Deborah Curtis. *Cast*: Jean Simmons (Gretchen Jordache Burke), Glenn Ford (David Donnelly), Lynn Redgrave (Kate Jordache), Tovah Feldshuh (Monika Wolner), Andrew Stevens (Billy Abbott), Bo Hopkins (Bunny Dwyer), Tom Nolan (Wesley Jordache), Jean-Pierre Aumont (Jean Delacroix), Dr. Joyce Brothers (Dr. Moira O'Dell), Alex Cord (Evans Kinsella), Anne Francis (Teresa Kraler), Michael V. Gazzo (Sartene), Marcel Hillaire (Magistrate), Anne Jeffreys (Honor Day), Christian Marquand (Inspector Charboneau), Cliff Osmond (Sagerac), Susan Strasberg (Ida Cohen), Robert Sterling (Colonel Day), Norbert Weisser (Egon Hubisch), Walter Brooke (American Intelligence Agent), Stefan Gierasch (Niendorf), Frank Marth (Kraler), Zitto Kazann (Ahmed), Norman Lloyd (Roland Fielding), Rob Eisenmann (Yvonne Miller), Bruce Kimmel (Richard Sanford). *Airdate*: November 26, 1979. Universal TV / National Broadcasting Company (NBC). 240 minutes.

Detour to Terror (1980)

Director: Michael O'Herlihy. *Producer*: Ron Roth. *Associate Producer*: Bert Gold. *Executive Producer*: O.J. Simpson. *Supervising Producers*: Dan Mark, Edward L. Rissien. *Writers*: Sydney A. Glass (story), Sydney A. Glass, Mark Rodgers (teleplay). *Original Music*: Morton Stevens. *Cinematographer*: John M. Nickolaus Jr. *Editors*: Jim Benson, William Mandell. *Casting*: Jerold Franks. *Production Designer*: Ross Bellah. *Set Decorator*: Sal Blydenburgh. *Costume Designer*: Grady Hunt. *Makeup Supervisor*: Ben Lane. *Unit Production Manager*: Bert Gold. *First Assistant Director*: Charles C. Coleman. *Second Assistant Director*: Hope R. Goodwin. *Property Master*: John Sexton. *Sound Editors:* Lee Chaney, Don Crosby. *Sound Mixer*: Don Matthews. *Special Effects*: Marcel Vercoutere. *Camera Operator*: Ken Richardson. *Casting Supervisor*: Al Onorato. *Music Editor*: Erma E. Levin. *Transportation Captain*: Rick Belyeu. *Location Coordinator*: Louis H. Goldstein. *Script Supervisor*: Vivian Jones. *Cast*: O.J. Simpson (Lee Hayes), Randall Carver (Neil), Anne Francis (Sheila), Richard Hill (Kurt), Kathryn Holcomb (Alicia), Arte Johnson (Harry Edwards), Lorenzo Lamas (Jamie), Gerald S. O'Loughlin (Martin Brain), Gloria Lynn Deyer (Irene Martin), Pat Keating (Joyce Landry), Chris Noel Hanks (Peggy Cameron), Phil Mead (Finch), Pat Ripley (Lenore), Thomas Rosales (Larry), Paula Victor (Sarah), Kip Allen (Charlie), Edward Blatchford (Russ), Anna Chavira (Theresa), Frederick Raymond Edwards II (Freddie), Louise Egolf (Debbie Baker), John Gill (Hillman), Freddie Hice (Tony), George Nason (Carl), Sonny Robbins (Milt), Nicole Brown Simpson (Bus Passenger, uncredited). *Airdate*: February 22, 1980. Columbia Pictures Television / Orenthal Productions / Playboy Productions / National Broadcasting Company (NBC). 120 minutes.

Mazes and Monsters (1982)

Director: Steven Hilliard Stern. *Producer*: Richard Briggs. *Associate Producer*: Rona Jaffe. *Executive Producer*: Tom McDermott. *Writers*: Rona Jaffe (novel), Tom Lazarus (teleplay). *Original Music:* Hagood Hardy. *Cinematographer*: Laszlo George. *Editor*: Bill Parker. *Casting*: David Graham. *Art Director*: Trevor Williams. *Makeup Artist*: Linda Gill. *Production Manager*: James Margellos. *Second Assistant Director*: Rocco Gismondi (uncredited). *Sound Mixer*: Owen Langevin. *Stand-in: Vera Miles and Anne Francis*: Linda Callow. *Cast*: Tom Hanks (Robbie Wheeling), Wendy Crewson (Kate Finch), David Wallace (Daniel), Chris Makepeace (Jay Jay Brockway), Lloyd Bochner (Hal), Peter Donat (Harold), Anne Francis (Ellie), Murray Hamilton (Lieutenant John Martini), Vera Miles (Cat), Louise Sorel (Julia), Susan Strasberg (Meg), Chris Wiggins (King), Clark Johnson (Perry), Tom Harvey (Hayden), James O'Regan (Paul), Kevin Fox (Punk), Angelo Rizacos (Punk), Eric Fink (Video Tech), Kevin Peter Hall (Gorvil). *Airdate*: December 28, 1982. McDermott Productions / Procter & Gamble Productions (PGP) / 905 Entertainment / Columbia Broadcasting System (CBS). 100 minutes.

     Notes: Also known as *Dungeons and Dragons*.

Return (1985)

Director: Andrew Silver. *Producers*: Yong-Hee Silver, Philip J. Spinelli. *Executive Producer*: Samuel Benedict. *Writers*: Donald Harington (novel, *Some Other Place. The Right Place*), Andrew Silver (screenplay). *Original Music*: Ragnar Grippe. *Cinematographer*: János Zsombolyai. *Editor*: Gabrielle Gilbert. *Cast*: Karlene Crockett (Diana Stoving), John Walcutt (Day Whittaker), Anne Lloyd Francis [Anne Francis] (Eileen Sedgeley), Frederic Forrest (Brian Stoving), Lee Stetson (Daniel Montross), Barbara Kerwin (Ellen Fullerton), Lisa Richards (Ann Stoving), Hanna Landy (Elizabeth Holt), Ariel Aberg-Riger (Diana at Three), Thomas Cross Rolapp (Lucky the Mechanic), Lenore Zann (Susan), Dennis Hoerter (Mechanic's Assistant). *Release Date*: January 24, 1986. Silver Pictures. 82 minutes.

REVIEWS

"Fans of Shirley MacLaine's New Age fascination with past lives should find [*Return*], a locally-produced feature film, entertaining.... This independent film has first-rate production values and excellent performances, but it lacks the necessary tension and suspense to propel it into the rank of first-rate occult movies." — Michael Blowen, *The Boston Globe*, April 2, 1989

A Masterpiece of Murder (1986)

Director: Charles S. Dubin. *Producer*: Terry Morse Jr. *Associate Producer*: Duke Fenady. *Writers*: Andrew J. Fenady, Terry Nation. *Original Music*: Richard Markowitz. *Cinematographer*: Laszlo George. *Editor*: Art Seid. *Production Designer*: Stephen Geaghan. *Set Decorator*: Dominique Fauquet-Lemaitre. *Second Assistant Director*: Karen Robyn. *Second Unit Director*: Stan Barrett. *Property Master*: Grant Swain. *Sound Mixer*: Claude Hazanavicius. *Special Effects*: David Gauthier. *Cast*: Bob Hope (Dan Dolan), Don Ameche (Frank Aherne), Jayne Meadows (Matilda Hussey), Claudia Christian (Julia Forsythe), Yvonne De Carlo (Mrs. Murphy), Anne Lloyd Francis [Anne Francis] (Ruth Beekman), Frank Gorshin (Pierre Rudin), Steven Keats (Lt. Simon Wax), Kevin McCarthy (Jonathan Hire), Anita Morris (Lola Crane), Clive Revill (Vincent Faunce), Stella Stevens (Della Vance / Deb Potts), Jamie Farr (Himself), Penny Baker (Christine Manning), Peter Palmer (Bronson), Eddie Ryder (Jerry Page), Louise Sorel (Louise), Joseph Della Sorte (Ugarti Van Meer), Richard Sargent (Maurice Beekman), Jason Wingreen (Williams). *Airdate*: January 27, 1986. 20th Century–Fox Television / Andrew J. Fenady Productions / National Broadcasting Company (NBC). 100 minutes.

Notes: First titled *A Nice, Pleasant, Deadly Weekend*, this telefilm marked Bob Hope's first TV movie and last movie *period*. Initially, the idea was to get Fred Astaire to play the former art thief who helps private eye Hope on a case; the part was eventually played by Don Ameche. "I've known him a lot of years," Hope told UPI of Ameche, "and we had a ball for three and a half weeks in Vancouver where it was filmed. We never worked together before. We had great fun. We talked about old times, laughed, reminded each other of things."

Laguna Heat (1987)

Director: Simon Langton. *Producer*: Bill Badalato. *Associate Producer*: Fred Baron. *Executive Producer*: Jay Weston. *Writers*: T. Jefferson Parker (novel), D.M. Eyre, Pete Hamill, David Burton Morris (teleplay). *Original Music*: Patrick Williams. *Cinematographer*: Fred Murphy. *Editor*: Bernard Gribble. *Casting*: Joseph D'Agosta. *Production Designer*: Joseph T. Garrity. *Art Director*: Pat Tagliaferro. *Set Decorator*: Jerie Kelter. *Costume Designer*: Karen Patch. *Special Makeup Effects*: Lance Anderson. *Unit Production Manager*: Bill Badalato. *First Assistant Director*: Sharon Mann. *Second Assistant Director*: Robert D. Nellans. *Costumer*: Denny Burt. *Music Recordist*: Hank Cicalo. *Orchestrator*: Edward Karam. *Supervising Music Editor*: Allan K. Rosen. *Cast*: Harry Hamlin (Tom Shephard), Jason Robards (Wade Shephard), Rip Torn (Joe Datilla), Catherine Hicks (Jane Algernon), Anne Francis (Helene Long), James Gammon (Grimes), Jeff Kober (Vic Harmon), Dehl Berti (Azul Mercante), Clyde Kusatsu (Coroner), Rutanya Alda (Dr. Kroyden), Gary Pagett (Pavliki), Fred Ponzlov (Ricky Hyams), Tom Pedi (Jimmy Hylkama), Peggy Doyle (Dot Hylkama), Peter Brocco (Judge Rubio), Peter Jason (Chief Hanover), Ryan McWhorter (Young Tom), Roberta Hamlen (Young Helene). *Airdate*: November 15, 1987. Home Box Office (HBO). 110 minutes.

Reviews

"*Laguna Heat* delivers a riveting detective story. There are more twists, turns, dead stops and exit ramps to nowhere ... than in the entire L. A. freeway system.... *Laguna Heat* is a first-rate thriller told with the style of Raymond Chandler and the grittiness of Elmore Leonard. Like all good detective fiction, this also is a classic morality tale of greed, fear and the search for truth and justice, no matter the cost." — Daniel Ruth, *Chicago Sun-Times*, November 13, 1987

Poor Little Rich Girl: The Barbara Hutton Story (1987)

Director: Charles Jarrott. *Producer*: Nick Gillott. *Associate Producer*: Tomlinson Dean. *Executive Producer*: Lester Persky. *Writers*: C. David Heymann (book), Dennis Turner (teleplay). *Original Music*: Richard Rodney Bennett. *Cinematographers*: Alan Hume, John Lindley. *Editor*: Bill Blunden. *Production Designers*: Eileen Diss, Bryan Ryman. *Set Decorator*: Robin Peyton. *Costume Designer*: Jane Robinson. *Key Hair Stylist (Los Angeles)*: Claudia Thompson. *Key Makeup Artist (Los Angeles)*: Ronnie Specter. *Production Manager (Los Angeles)*: Robert J. Anderson. *Executive in Charge of Production*: Dennis A. Brown. *Post-Production Supervisors*: Tim Myers, John Forrest Niss. *First Assistant Director (Los Angeles)*: Craig Beaudine. *Men's Costumer (Los Angeles)*: Armand Coutu. *Costume Coordinator (Los Angeles)*: Bernadene C. Morgan. *Cast*: Farrah Fawcett (Barbara Hutton), David Ackroyd (Graham Mattison), Stéphane Audran (Pauline de la Rochelle), Amadeus August (Count von Haugwitz-Reventlow), Nicholas Clay (Prince Alexis Mdivani), Bruce Davison (Jimmy Donahue), Carmen du Sautoy (Roussie), Anne Francis (Marjorie Post Hutton), Sascha Hehn (Baron Gottfried von Cramm), Kevin McCarthy (Franklyn Hutton), Tony Peck (James Douglas III), Zoë Wanamaker (Jean Kennerly), Clive Arrindell (Prince Troubetzkoy), Linden Ashby Lance Reventlow as an adult), Debbie Barker (Jill St John), Brenda Blethyn (Ticki Tocquet), Nigel Le Vaillant (David Herbert), Miriam Margolyes (Elsa Maxwell), Carolyn Seymour (Dorothy Difrasso), Burl Ives (F.W. Woolworth), James Read (Cary Grant), Michael J. Shannon (Morley Kennerly), Jana Shelden (Irene Hutton), Fairuza Balk (Barbara, age 12), Toria Fuller (Edna Hutton), Matilda Johansson (Barbara, age 5), Blain Fairman (James P. Donahue), Susan McDonald (Nurse), Patricia Northcott (Jessie Donahue), Liza Ross (Aunt Grace), John Lindros (Jimmy Donahue, age 11), Nancy Gair (Louise Van Alan), Julie Eccles (Doris Duke), David Gilliam (Phil Plant), Peter Scranton (Jack Pauling), John Golightly (Inspector Clair), Julie Ronnie (Sally), Ronald Leigh-Hunt (Raymond Needham), James Woolley (Clifford Turner), Vernon Dobtcheff (Jules Glassner), Nicholas Le Prevost (Sir Patrick Hastings), Tim Bannerman (Norman Birkett), Robert Holman (Lance Reventlow, ages 5–7), Jonathan Brandis (Lance Reventlow, age 11). *Airdate*: November 16, 1987. Lester Persky Productions / Incorporated Television Company (ITC) / National Broadcasting Company (NBC). 282 minutes (UK), 240 minutes (USA).

My First Love (1988)

Director: Gilbert Cates. *Producer*: Gail Mutrux. *Associate Producer*: Craig Zisk. *Executive Producer*: Jon Avnet, Jordan Kerner. *Writer*: Ed Kaplan. *Original Music*: Alf Clausen. *Cinematographers*: Tom Houghton, Mark Irwin. *Casting*: Reuben Cannon, Monica Swann. *Set Decorator*: Lisa Smithline. *Costume Designers*: Judy Evans, Evelyn Thompson. *Makeup Artist*: Ronnie Specter. *Hair Stylist*: Roxanne Yahyavi [Wightman]. *Unit Production Manager*: C. Tad Devlin. *Production Manager (New York)*: Boyce Harman. *First Assistant Director*: Stephen Lofaro. *Second Assistant Director*: Jeffrey M. Ellis. *Costume Supervisor*: Rosalie Wallace. *Cast*: Bea Arthur (Jean Miller), Richard Kiley (Sam Morrissey), Joan Van Ark (Claire Thomas), Barbara Barrie (Ruth Waxman), Anne Francis (Terry), Brett Stimely (John), Richard Herd (Chet Townsend), Kate Charleson (Barbara), Edith Fields (Marion), Julia Meade (Chris Townsend), Barbara Adside (Marie Mitchell), Lewis Arquette (Mark Grossman), Janet Brandt (Mrs. Salsky), Freddie Dawson (Inspector), Tom Fridley (Ray McDonald), Jack Heller (Marshall), Susan Johnson (Bernice), Jeannette Kerner (Annette), Jeffrey Lampert (Mr. Campbell), Larry Marco (Martin Miller), Connie Mason (Elle Lombardo), Jonathan Tisch (Concierge). *Airdate*: December 4, 1988. Avnet/Kerner Company / American Broadcasting Company (ABC). 100 minutes.

Notes: Filmed in New York City. According to an Associated Press article, when Bea Arthur was first sent the script, "I said it's too simple. [But] Gil Cates said, 'That's its charm. No one has acne, no one sweats.' He called it a fable. It's a fairy tale. It was such a pleasure to do.... People keep telling me they're surprised to see me do this kind of a role. I guess it's because I wasn't the stern Maude or Dorothy. It's refreshing to read a script like this. So much of what you see is junk."

Little Vegas (1990)

Director-Writer: Perry Lang. *Producer*: Peter Macgregor-Scott. *Original Music*: Mason Daring. *Cinematographer*: King Baggot. *Editor*: John Tintori. *Production Designer*: Michael Hartog. *Costume Designer*: Cynthia Flynt. *Construction Coordinator*: Daniel Brewer. *Sound Mixers*: Jim Hilton, Kim H. Ornitz. *Electrician*: Kyle T. MacDowell. *Wardrobe Supervisor*: Elizabeth Feldbauer. *Assistant Editors*: Jolie Gorchov, Kate Sanford. *Cast*: Anthony John Denison (Carmine de Carlo), Catherine O'Hara (Lexie), Anne Francis (Martha), Michael Nouri (Frank de Carlo), Perry Lang (Steve), P.J. Ochlan (Max de Carlo), John Sayles (Mike), Bruce McGill (Harvey), Jay Thomas (Bobby), Sam McMurray (Kreimach), Michael Talbott (Linus), Ronald G. Joseph (Cecil), Jerry Stiller (Sam), Kamie Harper (Phyllis), Jessica James (Grace), Laurie Thompson (Bethanne), A.J. Pirri (Pancho), Marit Fotland (Cecil's Girl), Carmine Zozzora (Geno), Jennifer Evans (Charity). *Release Date*: November 16, 1990. MacLang / IRS Media. 91 minutes.

The Double O Kid (1992)

> "His Weapons: A Super Soaker and a Joystick.
> His Mission: To Save the World ... Before Dinner!"

Director: Duncan McLachlan. *Producers*: Steven Paul, Gary Binkow. *Associate Producer*: Andrea Buck. *Executive Producers*: Barry L. Collier, Hank Paul. *Line Producer*: Eric M. Breiman. *Writers*: Steven Paul, Stuart Paul (story), Andrea Buck, Duncan McLachlan (screenplay). *Original Music*: Misha Segal. *Cinematographer*: Adam Kane. *Editor*: Jack Tucker. *Production Designer*: Troy Sizemore. *Art Director*: Dan Kelpinski. *Set Decorator*: Mary Patvaldnieks. *Costume Designer*: Victoria Auth. *Key Hair Stylist–Key Makeup Artist*: Suzanne Diaz. *Assistant Hair Stylist–Makeup Assistant*: Susanne Rheinschild. *Production Manager*: Michael Mandaville. *Post-Production Supervisor*: Eric M. Breiman. *Executive in Charge of Production*: Barbara Javitz. *Assistant Director*: Andrea Buck. *Second Unit Directors*: Andrea Buck, Michael R. Long. *First Assistant Director*: Steve Corzan. *Second Assistant Director*: Andre Zitcer. *Second Second Assistant Director*: Veronique Navette. *Special Effects*: Daniel Cruder. *Computer Animator*: Jay Mark Johnson. *Costume Supervisor*: Cheri Reed. *Cast*: Corey Haim (Lance Elliot), Brigitte Nielsen (Rhonda), Wallace Shawn (Cashpot), Nicole Eggert (Melinda), John Rhys-Davies (Rudi Von Kseenbaum), Basil Hoffman (Trout), Karen Black (Mrs. Elliot), Anne Francis (Maggie Lomax), Leslie Danon (French Girl), Patrick M. Wright (Banker), Bari K. Willerford (Luther), Jim Alquist (Tyler), Josh Collier (Billy), Chuck Hicks (Sam Wynberg), Seth Green (Chip), Lonnie Schuyler (Steele). Crystal Sky Worldwide / Prism Entertainment Corporation. 95 minutes.

> *Notes*: A straight-to-video release.

Love Can Be Murder (1992)

Director: Jack Bender. *Producer*: Jayne Bieber. *Executive Producers*: Rob Gilmer, Frank Konigsberg, Larry Sanitsky. *Writer*: Rob Gilmer. *Original Music*: Steven Bramson. *Cinematographer*: Paul Murphy. *Editor*: Tod Feuerman. *Production Designer*: Stephen Storer. *Set Decorator*: Kristen McGary. *Key Makeup Artist*: Melanie Hughes. *Key Hair Stylist*: Terri Hoyos. *Unit Production Manager*: Nicholas Q. Batchelor. *First Assistant Director*: Richard Schroer. *Second Assistant Director*: Steve Hirsch. *Visual Effects*: Gene Warren. *Costumer*: Scott Overgaard. *Wardrobe Supervisor*: Caroline Skakel. *Set Costumer*: Jane Lazner. *Music Editor*: Barry Moran. *Cast*: Jaclyn Smith (Elizabeth Bentley), Corbin Bernsen (Nick Peyton), Anne Francis (Maggie O'Brien), Cliff De Young (Brad Donaldson), Tom Bower (Mike Riordan), Nicholas Pryor (Philip Carlyle), Elaine Kagan (Dr. Wilde), Bruce Vilanch (Bernie), Pamela Roberts (Althea), Doug Hale (Edmund Carlyle), Scott N. Stevens (Gordon), Kimberley LaMarque (Samantha), Cameron Watson (Phil). *Airdate*: December 14, 1992. Konigsberg/Sanitsky Company/National Broadcasting Company (NBC). 100 minutes.

Have You Seen My Son (1996)

Director: Paul Schneider. *Producers*: Lisa Hartman Black, Vivienne Radkoff, Bob Finkel. *Executive Producers*: Marcy Gross, Ann Weston Begelman. *Writers*: Jack Olsen (book), Vivienne Radkoff (teleplay). *Original Music*: Misha Segal. *Cinematographer*: David Geddes. *Editor*: Judy Andreson. *Casting*: Steve Brooksbank, Mary Jo Slater. *Production Designer*: Ian D. Thomas. *Art Directors*: Douglasann Menchions, Bruce Miller. *Set Decorator*: Marti Wright. *Costume Designer*: Kate Healey. *Makeup Artist*: Dianne Pelletier. *Assistant Makeup Artist*: Debra Regnier (uncredited). *Hair Stylist*: Brenda Gibson [Turner]. *Production Manager (Canada)*: N. John Smith. *Unit Manager*: Charles Lyall. *Unit Production Manager (USA)*: John Burrows. *First Assistant Director (USA)*: Bruce A. Simon. *First Assistant Director (Canada)*: David Markowitz. *Second Assistant Director (USA)*: Conte Matal. *Second Assistant Director (Canada)*: Jason Furukawa. *Costume Consultant*: Lauren Beck. *Cast*: Lisa Hartman Black (Lael Pritcher), William Russ (Van Stein), Anne Francis (Catherine Pritcher), Scott Hylands (Solomon John), Carmen Argenziano (Chief Heman), Sergio Calderón (Temo), Jameson Parker (Mike Pritcher), Alex Doduk (Ace Pritcher), Patricia Harass (Julie), Cheryl Wilson (Joan), Terry David Mulligan (Sheriff Beck), Stephen E. Miller (Deputy Johnson), Eric Hui (Trang), Michael Northey (Officer Wilson), Jayme Knox (Mrs. McQuinn), Paul McGillion (Mr. McQuinn), Mitchell Kosterman (Officer Nye), Veena Sood (Sally). *Airdate*: January 8, 1996. Gross-Weston Productions / MGM Television / American Broadcasting Company (ABC). 120 minutes.

Lover's Knot (1996)

Director-Writer: Peter Shaner. *Producers*: Paul Rauch, Kevin Hamburger, Paul A. Kaufman. *Associate Producer*: Dan McCaffrey. *Executive Producer*: Randy Simon. *Original Music*: Laura Karpman. *Cinematography*: Garett Griffin. *Editor*: Tatiana S. Riegel. *Casting*: Victoria Burrows. *Production Designer*: David Huang. *Set Decorator*: Katterina Keith. *Costume Designer*: Cathryn Wagner. *Hair Stylist–Key Makeup Artist*: Judy Kaye Yonemoto. *Assistant Makeup Artists*: Geoff Leavitt, Tanya Milner. *Unit Production Manager*: Kevin Hamburger. *First Assistant Director*: Jay Lehrfeld. *Second Unit Directors*: Paul Alexander, Paul A. Kaufman. *Cast*: Bill Campbell (Steve Hunter), Jennifer Grey (Megan Forrester), Tim Curry (Cupid's Caseworker), Adam Baldwin (John Reed), Mark Sheppard (Nigel Bowles), Tom McTigue (Doug Meyers), Holly Fulger (Gwen Myers), Kristin Minter (Cheryl), Elaine Hendrix (Robin), Adam Ant (Marvell), Dr. Joyce Brothers (Herself), Anne Francis (Marian Hunter), Harold Gould (Alan Smithee), Byrne Piven (William Shakespeare), Sheryl Lee Ralph (Charlotte), Zelda Rubinstein (Woman in Clinic), Dawn Wells (Mary Ann), Caitlin Brown (Monique), John E. Goetz (Todd), Tiffany Salerno (Juliet), Marla Sucharetza (Erin). *Release Date*: July 12, 1996. Legacy / Republic Pictures / Two Pauls Entertainment / Astra Cinema / Cabin Fever Entertainment. 82 minutes.

REVIEW

"*Lover's Knot* is so marginal that its theatrical release is sheerest folly. It has nothing very new to say about contemporary romance, yet is in danger of talking your ears off. The video bin is surely its imminent destiny.... Lots of familiar faces pop up briefly: Adam Ant, Joyce Brothers, Anne Francis, Harold Gould, Sheryl Lee Ralph and Zelda Rubinstein among them. There are lots worse movies than *Lover's Knot*, but all the same it's a time-waster."— Kevin Thomas, *Los Angeles Times*, July 16, 1996

B. Television

Versatile Varieties (NBC, 1949–50)

Anne was a regular in skits and the commercials as one-third of a trio of Bonny Maids on this live variety show, also known as *Bonny Maid Versatile Varieties*. Eva Marie Saint,

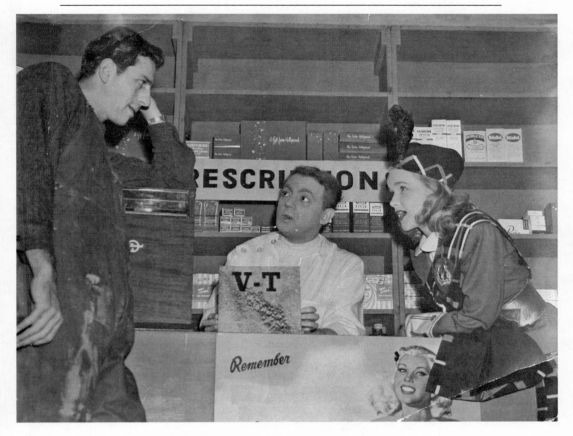

A rare candid of Anne as a Bonny Maid, with an unidentified customer and store proprietor, promoting Bonny Maid Linoleum during the time she was appearing on *Versatile Varieties* (1949–50).

Carol Ohmart and Dorothy Phillips were all Maids at some point during Anne's run on the show. The team of "Wear and Tear" also appeared in the commercials. During Anne's tenure, the hosts for this show, which was set in a nightclub, was first George Givot (1949) and then comedian Harold Barry (1949–50).

Studio One — *"The Rival Dummy"* (CBS, September 19, 1949)

Director: Franklin J. Schaffner. *Writers*: Ben Hecht (story), Worthington Miner, David Opatoshu (adaptation). *Cast*: Paul Lukas, Anne Francis, Robert H. Harris.

Plot: Gabbo the Great's (Lukas) ventriloquist dummy, Pepe, has a mind and life of its own.

Notes: Ben Hecht's 1928 *Liberty Magazine* short story "The Rival Dummy" was first made into the film *The Great Gabbo* (1929) starring Erich von Stroheim. Paul Lukas excels in this first-rate episode. The primitiveness of early live television, with its low budget and slight awkwardness, enhances this production, giving it a creepy aura, and an urgency that a more-polished adaptation might have lacked. Anne plays Wichita Jones, a young girl who works with the Great Gabbo and finds herself unwillingly enmeshed in a very peculiar and disturbing love triangle. The later scenes, with Gabbo fighting the dummy for Wichita, are outstanding, with Lukas bringing a frightening desperation to his performance. The combination of the dummy's evil laugh and Lukas' intense hysteria as he takes an axe to it is one of the most memorably disquieting moments early television ever produced. Anne gives a likable, attractive performance, but this is definitely Lukas' show.

Suspense — "Dr. Violet" (CBS, October 4, 1949)

Director: Robert Stevens. *Writer*: Halsted Welles. *Cast*: Hume Cronyn, Evelyn Varden, Anne Francis, Ray Walston, Frankie Thomas, Jr.

Plot: Cronyn plays the title, the unhinged owner of a wax museum devoted to famous murderers.

Notes: According to Anne, a young Charlton Heston was originally cast as her boyfriend in this episode, but he was replaced by Frankie Thomas. Another eerie live television production, it is helped immeasurably by Hume Cronyn's unsettling intensity in the leading role and an effective claustrophobic carnival sideshow set.

Kraft Television Theatre — "In Love with Love" (NBC, November 23, 1949)

Cast: Anne Francis, Maury Hill.

Believe It or Not — "The Man Without a Country" (NBC, February 8, 1950)

Cast: Anne Francis, John Stephen.

Notes: Based on the famous 1863 short story by Edward Everett Hale, published in *The Atlantic Monthly*, about an American Army lieutenant, Philip Nolan, who, during Aaron Burr's trial for treason, is tried as an accomplice, and renounces the United States. He is sentenced to never set foot on United States soil again.

Lights Out — "The Faithful Heart" (NBC, April 10, 1950)

Director: Kingman T. Moore. *Writer*: Douglas Parkhirst. *Cast*: Anne Francis, Liam Sullivan, James O'Neal, Dorothy Francis, John Hamilton, Riza Royce.

Plot: A wife remains faithful to the man she loves, refusing to believe he is dead.

Kraft Television Theatre — "Black Sheep" (NBC, April 26, 1950)

Cast: Anne Francis, Eileen Heckart, Richard McMurray.

Plot: "A story of romantic intrigue" said the ads about this story of a man who returns home after a long absence.

Kraft Television Theatre — "Good Housekeeping" (NBC, June 14, 1950)

Writer: William McCleery. *Cast*: Anne Francis, Nelson Olmsted, Arthur Walsh.

Plot: Wife meddles in her college professor husband's career.

Kraft Television Theatre — *"I Like It Here"* (NBC, October 4, 1950)

Writer: A.B. Shiffrin (play). *Cast*: Donald Buka, Anne Francis, Carmen Mathews, Stefan Schnabel.

Plot: A professor's houseman is a refugee who integrates himself into the lives of others.
Notes: Adapted from a play which ran on Broadway in 1946.

Lux Video Theatre — *"Waiting for Onorio"* (CBS, June 10, 1954)

Director: Richard Goode. *Writers*: Kate Phillips [Kay Linaker], Konrad Borcovici. *Cast*: J. Carrol Naish, Richard Benedict, Eleanor Fanie, Rinati Yanni, Norma Nilsson, Tito Vuolo.

Plot: A father (Naish) deserts his family after an argument about how to run his restaurant.
Notes: Anne, not part of the episode's story, interviews Helen Parrish at the intermission.

Ford Theatre — *"The Tryst"* (NBC, June 17, 1954)

Writer: Ivan Turgenev. *Cast*: Edward Arnold, Anne Francis, William Lundigan, Vera Miles.

Plot: An innocent relationship and a death turn into a small-town scandal.

Lux Video Theatre — *"Perished Leaves"* (CBS, June 24, 1954)

Director: Richard Goode. *Writers:* Leonard Heideman [Laurence Heath], Emmett Murphy. *Cast*: Anne Francis, Philip Ober, Faith Domergue, Dayton Lummis, Maury Hill, Patrick Miller.

Plot: A client's deathbed wish is granted by a lawyer.

The Perry Como Show (NBC, February 18, 1956)

Host: Perry Como. *Guests*: Henry Fonda, Vera-Ellen, AF, Robby the Robot, The Platters.

Climax! — *"Scream in Silence"* (CBS, January 2, 1958)

Director: Paul Nickell. *Writers:* Eileen Pollock, Robert Pollock. *Host*: William Lundigan. *Cast*: Anne Francis, Skip Homeier, Betty Field, Sidney Blackmer, William Talman, Morris Ankrum.

Plot: Mary Bellason (Anne) suffers a blackout and is convinced that she killed her father (Blackmer).
Notes: One of Anne's best performances during this period. She gives an edgy portrayal as the demoralized, guilt-obsessed daughter of a drunk. This was a role requiring absolutely no glamour, no gloss whatsoever, as Anne depicts a self-contained, pathetically nervous girl who feels responsible not only for her mother's death, but also the murder of her father. The scene where she struggles under narcosynthesis, to truthfully remember how her father was shot, features some of the best acting she ever did. *The Oakland Tribune* called this one a "depresser" that was helped by "believable performances" and "sensitive direction" by Paul Nickell, which added up to "blood-curdling fare."

Studio One — *"Presence of the Enemy"* (CBS, February 10, 1958)

Director: Jack Smight. *Writer*: Tad Mosel. *Cast*: Anne Francis, Tommy Rettig, E.G. Marshall, James Gregory, Bethel Leslie.

Plot: Kristine (Anne) seeks a music career.

Climax! — *"The Deadly Tattoo"* (CBS, May 1, 1958)

Director: Paul Nickell. *Writers:* Ed McBain [Evan Hunter] (story, "The Con Man"), Oliver Crawford (adaptation). *Cast:* Anne Francis, Peter Graves, Henry Silva, Anna May Wong, Olive Deering.

Plot: Detective Steve Baxter's (Graves) mute wife Teddy (Anne) joins him as he canvasses tattoo parlors for a murder clue.

Claudia (pilot) (1958)

Writer: Rose Franken. *Cast:* Anne Francis, Robert Knapp, Doris Kenyon.

Notes: This failed pilot, produced by comedian George Burns and Armand Deutsch, was based on Rose Franken's successful series of novels about the characters of Claudia and David Naughton and their two children. *Claudia* premiered on Broadway in 1941 and inspired two movies starring Dorothy McGuire and Robert Young, *Claudia* (1943) and *Claudia and David* (1946). There was another, earlier, unsuccessful attempt to make it a television series in 1952.

Juke Box Jury (November 7, 1958)

Host: Peter Potter. *Guests:* Anne Francis, Tony Perkins, Marjorie Lord, Rory Calhoun.

Notes: Celebrities were asked to listen to records and judge them by voting "hit" or "miss."

Kaleidoscope — *"The Third Commandment"* *(pilot)* (NBC, February 8, 1959)

Director: Jack Smight. *Writer:* Ben Hecht. *Cast:* Arthur Kennedy, Anne Francis, Fay Spain, Regis Toomey, John Hoyt, Simon Oakland, Jack Weston, Richard Erdman.

Plot: An iconoclastic comedy about a gag writer who becomes a false evangelist and faith healer.

Notes: Ben Hecht's play gives a modern view of one of the Ten Commandments. This was supposed to be the first in a series which would take up each of the Commandments.

"To dispose of the formalities, this Jess Oppenheimer production was excellently produced, directed and acted. It struck one with great emotional impact. But what was Hecht trying to tell us? I, for one, don't know." — Charles Mercer, "On Television," *The North Adams, Massachusetts, Transcript,* February 9, 1959

The David Niven Show — *"The Twist of the Key"* (NBC, May 12, 1959)

Director: Don McDougall. *Writer:* Hank Moonjean. *Host:* David Niven. *Cast:* Anne Francis, Edward Kemmer, John Dehner, Joan Banks.

Plot: A woman's racketeer husband orders a hit on the man she loves.

Notes: A clever mystery (the title has a double meaning), written by Hank Moonjean, a talented and busy assistant director at MGM in the '50s and a producer into the '80s. The acting is strong; Dehner exudes maliciousness as the ruthless husband, while Anne brings a likable wholesomeness to a character that seriously needed audience identification for it to work. Edward Kemmer, best known for the sci-fi TV program *Space Patrol* (1950– 55), is virile, handsome, and likewise appealing as the boyfriend. The ending leaves you hanging, but that's the beauty of it.

Rawhide — *"Incident of the Shambling Man"* (CBS, October 9, 1959)

Director: Andrew V. McLaglen. *Writers:* Charles Larson (story), Fred Freiberger, Charles Larson (teleplay). *Regular Cast*: Eric Fleming, Clint Eastwood, Sheb Wooley. *Guest Cast*: Victor McLaglen, Anne Francis, Gene Nelson, Robert Lowery, Robert Karnes.

Anne on the set of *Rawhide*'s "Incident of the Shambling Man" with King Baudouin of Belgium in 1959.

Plot: The Shambling Man, Harry (McLaglen), a former bare-knuckles fighter, is tormented by his ruthless widowed daughter-in-law Rose Wittman (Anne). By goading Harry into reliving his fighting days, she schemes to make him appear dangerous and declared insane.

Notes: This was McLaglen's final acting role (he died on November 7), directed by his son. Anne has a good role as a former saloon girl who wants a better life and plots to get rid of her loony father-in-law so she can take over her deceased husband's property and money.

On the outside, Rose is sweet, sympathetic and nurturing; on the inside, she is cold, greedy and hard. Anne was perfect for this part as she radiated sweetness, her innocent look ideal for the inwardly evil character, as she twists all the men around her fingers.

Harry is obviously one card short of a full deck; he really doesn't need too much prodding to be violently set off. Rose's comeuppance is a bit sad and avoidable. By all rights, he should have been institutionalized sooner, paving the way for her to have a life of her own, as cold-blooded and deceitful as she was.

Adventures in Paradise — "The Bamboo Curtain" (ABC, December 14, 1959)

Director: Josef Leytes [Joseph Lejtes]. *Writer*: Gene Levitt. *Regular Cast*: Gardner McKay. *Guest Cast*: Anne Francis, David Opatoshu, Patrick Macnee, Anna Sten, Weaver Levy, Philip Ahn.

Plot: Adventurer Adam Troy (McKay) helps Anne Meadow (Anne), an undercover agent posing as a singer, in Hong Kong.

Notes: Anne sings "I Know Why (And So Do You)," written by Mack Gordon and Harry Warren for the 1941 Fox film *Sun Valley Serenade*.

Adventures in Paradise (1959–62) was a popular weekly adventure series centering on handsome Adam Troy, captain of the schooner the *Tiki*, who accepts freelance jobs around the globe. Filming took place on the 20th Century–Fox backlot.

The United States Steel Hour — "Queen of the Orange Bowl" (CBS, January 13, 1960)

Director: Paul Bogart. *Writers:* Roger Squire (story), Robert Van Scoyk (teleplay). *Cast*: Johnny Carson, Anne Francis, Glenda Farrell, Frank McHugh, Elizabeth Wilson, Al Lewis, Nancy Kovack.

Plot: Anne McKenzie (Anne) is a Greenwich Village beatnik who follows her reluctant-to-marry boyfriend Kenneth Rausch (Carson) home for the holidays and alternately clashes with and charms his parents (Farrell and McHugh) and family.

Notes: "This tongue-in-cheek romantic comedy gets by because of the arch manner and knowing ways of Anne Francis, Johnny Carson and Frank McHugh. The obvious little story is a momma's boy-beatnik girl affair that's really too thin even for a spoof, but the light touch of the dialogue and the acting make it fun." — TV-Key, *The Palladium-Times*, Oswego, New York, January 13, 1960

"A good, original comedy.... The script is larded with good gags and situations (most promising: son and father get looped and do a Hawaiian dance in the neighborhood tavern) with old pros like McHugh, Carson and Miss Farrell to get the most out of them." — The TV Scout, *The Post-Standard*, Syracuse, New York, January 13, 1960

Ford Startime — "Jeff McCleod, the Last Reb" (NBC, March 1, 1960)

Director: Paul Nickell. *Writers:* William D. Gordon, Douglas Heyes. *Cast:* Robert Horton, Anne Francis, Ricardo Montalban, Marshall Thompson, Priscilla Gillette, Don Grady, Kathleen Widdoes.

Ricardo Montalban has Anne at knifepoint as a helpless Marshall Thompson looks on in *Ford Startime*'s "Jeff McCleod, the Last Reb."

Plot: Near the end of the Civil War, a wounded Confederate soldier, Jeff McCleod (Horton), hides out at a Missouri farm.

"The men who fought the Civil War were spared few hardships, but at least they didn't have to see, 'Jeff McCleod, the Last Reb' ... [It's] pure potboiler, the sort of story that gives B-movies a bad name.... The cast ... fought hard but had to surrender unconditionally to the devastation of an inferior script."— Fred Danzig, UPI, March 2, 1960

Sunday Showcase — "Our American Heritage: Autocrat and Son" (NBC, March 20, 1960)

Writer: Ernest Kinoy. *Cast*: Christopher Plummer, Ann Harding, Anne Francis, Cedric Hardwicke.

Plot: A drama depicting the life of "The Great Dissenter," Oliver Wendell Holmes Jr. (1841–1935), an associate justice of the United States Supreme Court.

"Cedric Hardwicke and Christopher Plummer play father and son, respectively, and Anne Francis shows up as Jr.'s wife. The drollest remarks are generally direct quotations, and it's a delight to spend an hour devoted to such civilized company."—*Southern Illinoisan*, March 20, 1960

"Last night's play was honest, high-minded and gracefully written. But the viewer felt no surging sense of history. The focus of the story was narrow; it sought to illuminate character, to unfold a brief phase in the life of a man who lived 94 years. In consequence, the story was fragmentary, without conflict or, indeed, any very lively interest.... Another reason that interest in the play was more or less academic can be found in the casting. Now, every member of the company was triumphantly professional. But Sir Cedric Hardwicke and Christopher Plummer do not fit my admittedly Yankee concept of the 'autocrat and son,' as the play was called. Anne Francis gave us a gay, spirited Fanny. Even with the reservations stated above, it was a program that towered over the usual run of TV drama."— Harriet Van Horne, "Van Horne on TV," March 21, 1960

As Fanny, Oliver Wendell Holmes Jr.'s wife, on *Sunday Showcase*'s "Our American Heritage: Autocrat and Son."

The Untouchables — "The Doreen Maney Story" (ABC, March 31, 1960)

Director: Robert Florey. *Writer*: Jerome Ross. *Regular Cast*: Robert Stack, Anthony George, Abel Fernandez, Steve London, Nicholas Georgiade. *Guest Cast*: Anne Francis, Christopher Dark, Richard Rust, Connie Hines, George Mitchell, Robert J. Stevenson.

Plot: Sheik Humphries (Dark), Doreen Maney (Anne) and their gang knock off an armored car. The gang is separated and Doreen is captured after hiding the loot.

Notes: *The Untouchables* (1959–63), narrated by Walter Winchell, was a controversial, violent television program depicting the exploits of Eliot Ness and his group of incorruptible agents. Set in Chicago (and thereabouts) in the 1930s, each episode showed us Ness and his agents at work and sparing no one in the pursuit of law enforcement.

The characters of Sheik and Doreen, known as "The Love Birds," were very loosely based on Bonnie and Clyde. Doreen is described by Eliot Ness (Stack) as "blonde, about 23, pretty, looks a little like Garbo."

Doreen is not a talk-out-of-the-corner-of-her-mouth moll, but a smart cookie who actually seems to be the brains of the gang. She is not unsympathetic. The teleplay gives us a peek at where she comes from, as the gang hides out briefly at her father's Tennessee farm. Mr. Maney (Mitchell) is a Bible-spouting, self-righteous, greedy, abusive man, and we have no trouble relating to Doreen and her early desire to get out of that unpleasant environment. Also key to her character is her loyalty to her younger sister Maybelle (Hines) and her misguided love for Sheik. She clings to the notion that he loves her and will spring her from jail, not realizing that he's using her. "I wonder if that louse has any idea how much you love him," Ness snaps after she tries to seduce him.

In Anne's best scene, her sister comes to see her in jail in hopes of securing the hidden money for Sheik. Doreen goes from impatience at Sheik's lack of action to girlish love for him to the slow comprehension that the man she loves is two-timing her with her own kid sister. The look in Anne's narrowed eyes, the breaking and then deepening of her voice, and finally her calculating mind quickly setting up a plan, is all subtle but very potent.

Also powerful is the conclusion when Doreen's scheme of gunning down Sheik is thwarted by Ness and his men's own hail of bullets. Sheik struggles up and groans, "You double-crossing floozy. You led them right to me. Just to save your own skin." Doreen looks at him steady, straight in the eye, with no emotion, and remarks, "I wouldn't do a thing like that, Sheik. I wanted the pleasure of killing you all to myself."

The Twilight Zone — "The After Hours" (CBS, June 10, 1960)

Director: Douglas Heyes. *Writer — Host*: Rod Serling. *Cast*: Anne Francis, Elizabeth Allen, James Millhollin, John Conwell, Patrick Whyte, Nancy Rennick.

Plot: Marcia White (Anne) goes up to a department store's dark, mysterious ninth floor to buy a thimble. The problem? After she goes to return the item, she is told there is no such floor ... and things are about to get even more bizarre.

Notes: This classic episode is one that Anne said she got the most fan mail for.

The character of Marcia White comes innocently into the department store looking to make a purchase, but is faced with strange happenings. "It was a study of the growth of fear of the complete unknown," Anne told author Stewart T. Stanyard in his book *Dimensions Behind the Twilight Zone.* "I loved [the script]. My first impression was what fun it would be to play that role. The humor in the beginning. The spaciness of each little step that took place, sort of just a little bit off-center until the horror begins for this young woman who has absolutely no memory at all of who she is or why she's on the ninth floor. The progression of the character was a lot of fun."

James Millhollin seems a bit confused over which is the real Anne and which is a mannequin in the classic *Twilight Zone* episode "The After Hours."

Anne admired director Douglas Heyes, his methods and his use of shadows. "He just stepped back and let it happen," she added to Stanyard. "He created wonderful images, the darkness beyond where we were. There was always the feeling of being in another realm when I was doing it. When I was doing the part, there were a few lights and there's darkness beyond. I had to be able to imagine all of these strange things in the darkness that seem to be following her, and her not being able to get down to the root of what all of this was, until the very end."

When Stanyard asked Anne what her favorite moment of the episode was, she replied, "Ah, I think when Doug decided to do that shot of her final desperation — not final desperation, but the impending desperateness behind the rippled glass on that door. I thought that was quite brilliant of him. To see the distortion of her shadow when she said, 'Somebody? Anybody?' And then the final turning event of just crumpling completely, and her fear, and pain."

About Rod Serling, Anne remarked to Tom Weaver that he "was a wonderful man — a brilliant man, with a sense of humor."

Alfred Hitchcock Presents — *"Hooked"* (CBS, September 25, 1960)

Director: Norman Lloyd. *Writers:* Robert Turner (story), Thomas Grant (teleplay). *Host*: Alfred Hitchcock. *Cast*: Anne Francis, Robert Horton, Vivienne Segal, John Holland.

Plot: Ray Marchand (Horton) schemes with his young, college-age girlfriend Nila Foster (Anne) to kill his rich, older wife Gladys (Segal).

Notes: On the surface, this is a conventional story, but the twist ending more than makes up for it. This has one of the better surprise wrap-ups of the series. Anne's character shows her off little; she is basically just there as an object of desire. Robert Turner's short story first appeared in the magazine *Manhunt* in February 1958.

The United States Steel Hour — *"The Yum Yum Girl"* (CBS, November 30, 1960)

Director: Paul Bogart. *Writers:* Latham Toohey (short story), Robert Van Scoyk (teleplay). *Cast*: Anne Francis, Robert Sterling, Leon Janney, William Larsen, Robert Elston, Marilyn Hanold.

Plot: Anne plays Henrietta Harmony, an actress signed by advertising executive Peter Finn (Sterling) to promote a soft drink on a TV commercial.

Notes: "'The Yum-Yum Girl' [is] an amazing piece of theatrics. It is doubtful if there has ever been such a spoof in the history of television. It is not too unusual (said with some reservation) for a play to prick the Madison Avenue game. But when delightful barbs are tossed at the acting game as an added attraction, then you've got something.... Call it madness, call it love, call it kooky. It all wrapped itself into a tidy package of hilarious viewing. The script was bright and bouncy. Some of the lines seemed reminiscent of the old days of the American theater (1930–1945) when the trade abounded with the wittiest of the witty, even at the risk of being corny. The dialogue at some junctures of 'Yum-Yum' even showed real original talent. If these particular lines were lifted, it was from something before my time." — John Miller, *The Lowell Sun*, December 1, 1960

Route 66 — "Play It Glissando" (CBS, January 20, 1961)

Director: Lewis Allen. *Writer*: Stirling Silliphant. *Regular Cast*: Martin Milner, George Maharis. *Guest Cast*: Anne Francis, Jack Lord, Barbara Bostock, Harold J. Stone.

Plot: Insanely jealous Progressive Jazz trumpet player Gabe Johnson (Lord) tries desperately to hold onto his wife Jana (Anne).

Notes: Filmed in Malibu. Tod Stiles (Milner) and Buz Murdock (Maharis) have their hands full trying to protect the harried wife of an admired musician. The title, "Play It Glissando," is translated by Buz here as "cool." Technically, it actually means gliding rapidly through tones.

Not a standard story about domestic violence, Silliphant's teleplay shows both sides of the problem, letting us get a glimpse inside Gabe Johnson's tormented mind, his inability to let go of his wife, his insecurity, fear and remorse. Jana's conflicted feelings for her possessive mate are explored:

> JANA: He put me on a pedestal; put an ivory tower around me.
> BUZ: What's so bad about that?
> JANA: It is when you have to live alone in it and you can't escape. Just a defeated minority of one. The fan who got away.

At the conclusion, there are no easy solutions for the two.

Route 66 (1960–64) was well-known during its run for its hip sensibilities, and this episode is particularly jazz-oriented with its use of slang, atmosphere and music. (Bostock sings "Lover Man" and "A Sunday Kind of Love.") It has been debated that Gabe Johnson is loosely based on jazz great Chet Baker because of Lord's uncanny physical resemblance to the trumpeter, but such assumptions are ungrounded.

Hong Kong — "With Deadly Sorrow" (ABC, February 22, 1961)

Director: Paul Henreid. *Writers*: Robert Blees, Dorothy Robinson. *Regular Cast*: Lloyd Bochner, Rod Taylor. *Guest Cast*: Anne Francis, Lawrence Ung, Mary Murphy, Werner Levy, Paul Kent, Benson Fong, William Berger, Norbert Schiller, Kai J. Kong, Molly Glessing.

Plot: Singer Mary Moore (Anne) is targeted for murder when she tries to leave Hong Kong. Neil Campbell (Bochner), chief of the Hong Kong police, protects her and falls in love.

Notes: Rod Taylor, who starred as Glenn Evans, an American journalist in Hong Kong, is seen only briefly in this episode; this is mainly Bochner's story. Anne sings "S'posin,'" a standard written by Andy Razaf and Paul Denniker.

This was another role giving Anne a chance to run a bit of a gamut; she is seen singing and joking lightheartedly with the suavely handsome Bochner, but turns on the acting chops for an impressive hospital bed scene where she struggles to speak as she writhes in pain, sweating, eyes half-closed, badly beaten. The episode's only sour note is the occasional clumsiness of Paul Henreid's direction.

Route 66 — "A Month of Sundays" (CBS, September 22, 1961)

Director: Arthur Hiller. *Writer*: Stirling Silliphant. *Regular Cast*: Martin Milner, George Maharis. *Guest Cast*: Anne Francis, Conrad Nagel, Betty Garde, Rodney Bell.

Plot: A woman (Anne), doomed by a fatal disease, meets Tod (Milner) and Buz (Maharis) in her aunt's boarding house. Buz falls in love.

Notes: Filmed entirely on location in Butte, Montana. Anne gives one of her best performances as Broadway star Arline Simms who returns home after many years. Secretly, she is dying of lupus, afraid, desperately "leaning on the past" as she seeks out answers. "Father, please help me," Arline pleads with the neighborhood priest (Nagel). "I haven't the strength to fight any more. Nowhere else to turn. I thought maybe the house where I was born; maybe there I'd find something to hold on to. Just as empty as New York. I'm falling; I keep reaching out for something to stop me. I've come home, Father. I've come home to die." That "something to hold on" to turns out to be Buz, who, unaware of her illness, takes to heart what she told him when they first met: "Sundays were always the best days. Sometimes I wonder why we can't live the rest of the week like we do on Sunday." He gives her a month of Sundays before the inevitable happens, restoring her faith; her fatalism turns to happiness as she conquers her fear of death.

This episode walks a fine line, with mawkishness creeping in only occasionally. This is helped by the first-rate performances from the principals, chiefly Anne and Milner. Betty Garde, as Arline's Aunt Lydia, brings some poignancy to her brief scene with Anne; the old pro con-

Top: A candid with Rod Taylor between scenes on *Hong Kong*'s "With Deadly Sorrow." *Left: Route 66*'s "A Month of Sundays" features one of Anne's best performances, as an actress who returns to her hometown to die and ends up finding love with Buz (George Maharis).

veys much with just an expression. Anne works far better with Milner here, although Maharis is her love interest. Her scenes with Milner are infused with some affecting, sincere emotions. Maharis seems slightly stunned, out of his league; when he does get a chance to let loose, it is embarrassing. But, above all, in the acting is Anne, bringing a heartbreaking anxiety and uplifting revitalization to her tragic portrayal.

"Our heroes, Buz and Tod, start their second roving season with a sentimental tale that's almost out of their depth. What saves the boys and the hour is a sensitive performance by guest star Anne Francis, playing a panic-stricken girl they're determined to help. Slow moving and soap-opery though the episode may be, the sincerity of Anne Francis will move you overall." — TV Key Previews, *The Charleston Gazette*, September 23, 1961

Dr. Kildare — *"A Million Dollar Property"* (NBC, October 26, 1961)

Director: Herbert Hirschman. *Writer*: Ernest Kinoy. *Regular Cast*: Richard Chamberlain, Raymond Massey. *Guest Cast*: Anne Francis, Jan Murray, Joby Baker, Tony Monaco, Cathleen Nesbitt, Evelyn Ward.

Plot: Movie star Kathy Stebbins (Anne) disrupts hospital routine with her confidence-draining entourage "The Pride of Lions."

Notes: Dr. Kildare (Chamberlain) learns a lesson in humility as he treats an insecure, troubled movie star he had initially judged indifferently. Her hangers-on undermine her confidence, make her doubt her abilities to perform as a real actress and not just a sex symbol in movies. She falls for the doctor, but soon comes to realize her self-worth. The script is a bit hokey, but the actress' feelings of emptiness and self-doubt are handled with sensitivity by Anne. Chamberlain is likewise affecting as he learns to deal more compassionately with his patients.

Alfred Hitchcock Presents — *"Keep Me Company"* (CBS, November 7, 1961)

Director: Alan Crosland, Jr. *Writer*: Henry Slesar. *Host*: Alfred Hitchcock. *Cast*: Anne Francis, Jack Ging, Edmund Hashim, Sal Ponti, Duke Howard, Hinton Pope, Howard McLeod.

Plot: Young, lonely newlywed Julia Reddy (Anne), unaware of her husband Marco's (Hashim) shady activities, calls in a fake report to the police so that she'll have company while her husband is out. An attractive detective, Joe Parks (Ging), answers the call and gets a surprise.

Notes: Not one of the best *Hitchcock* episodes, although Anne and Ging make a striking, non-romantic couple.

The New Breed — *"Lady Killer"* (ABC, December 12, 1961)

Director: Walter E. Grauman. *Writer*: Alfred Brenner. *Regular Cast*: Leslie Nielsen, John Beradino. *Guest Cast*: Anne Francis, Robert Redford, Martin Balsam, William Swan, Leonard Stone, Rebecca Sand, Ricky Allen. Don Keefer.

Plot: The police are looking for a man who ties up women and steals from them. When his latest victim turns up dead, the police realize they are dealing with a psychopath.

Notes: This police procedural (starring Nielsen as Lt. Price Adams), produced by Quinn Martin, offers very little to a pre-stardom Redford, awkward but handsome as the unstable man Arthur Honniger, and, as one of his victims Phyllis Eberhardt, Anne, who is billed as "Special Guest Star." Anne is earnest and looks great, but the only stretch this role offered her was to look convincing being in love and doing a kissing scene with Martin Balsam, playing her jealous husband Frank. An odd match they were, undoubtedly.

With Gerald S. O'Loughlin in *Going My Way*'s "A Man for Mary."

Going My Way — "A Man for Mary" (ABC, October 31, 1962)

Director: Joseph Pevney. *Regular Cast*: Gene Kelly, Leo G. Carroll, Dick York, Nydia Westman. *Guest Cast:* Anne Francis, Gerald S. O'Loughlin, James Secrest, George Kennedy, Robert Strauss.

Plot: Mary Dunne (Anne), a beautiful, friendly girl, innocently causes trouble among tenants and is evicted by her landlady. Father O'Malley (Kelly) tries to find her a new place, but living in the boarding house he finds are four men — all of whom want to marry her.

Notes: Based on the 1944 movie of the same name starring Bing Crosby, this 1962–63 series told of Father Chuck O'Malley and his parish in a poor New York City neighborhood.

"Guest star Anne Francis is responsible for a very appealing episode which might have been a horrible mishmash if not for her sensitive characterization."— Leonard Hoffman, TV Previews, *Tucson Daily Citizen*, May 22, 1963

The Alfred Hitchcock Hour — "What Really Happened" (CBS, January 11, 1963)

Director: Jack Smight. *Writers:* Marie Belloc Lowndes (novel), Henry Slesar (teleplay). *Host*: Alfred Hitchcock. *Cast*: Anne Francis, Ruth Roman, Gladys Cooper, Steve Dunne, Michael Strong, Tim O'Connor, Gene Lyons.

Plot: When housekeeper Addie Strain (Roman) accidentally kills her wealthy boss Howard Raydon (Lyons), his wife Eve (Anne) is charged with the crime.

Notes: "I never got to meet Alfred Hitchcock," Anne says in the book *The* Alfred Hitchcock Presents *Companion*. "I remember being called in to play whatever role they wanted me to do, good-girl or bad-girl. We had rehearsals in those days, which made work much easier. I later worked with Gladys Cooper in one of those *Hitchcocks* and she and I always broke up numerous times during the shoot. She was just adorable. She ate yogurt and swam each morning, which still amazes me." (Cooper, who played the dead husband's mother in this episode, was at that time in her mid–70s.) See the main biography section for more about this episode.

Alcoa Premiere — "The Glass Palace" (pilot) (ABC, January 17, 1963)

Director: Lawrence Dobkin. *Writer*: Gil Ralston. *Cast*: Ed Nelson, Chester Morris, Joanna Barnes, Anne Francis, Ricardo Montalban, Wallace Ford, Don Hanmer.

Plot: A husband-and-wife skating duo faces trouble before a big show when the husband starts losing his eyesight and his confidence.

Notes: An unsold pilot, produced by Richard Berg, which was to star Ed Nelson and a cranky, boozy-looking Chester Morris. Anne is the wife and ice-skating partner of Montalban. Although a pretty dreadful story, the acting was good; the whole thing was overly dramatic, simplistic and downright stupid. Are we *really* to believe that they would push Ricardo out at the conclusion to ice skate blind just to prove he could do it? Ridiculous.

Existing prints of this episode do not have a title attached, but this story has been referred to as "The Quick and the Dead" in newspapers across the country.

Anne and Ricardo Montalban play a husband-and-wife skating team in the pilot "The Glass Palace."

The Twilight Zone — *"Jess-Belle"* (CBS, February 14, 1963)

Director: Buzz Kulik. *Writer*: Earl Hamner, Jr. *Host*: Rod Serling. *Cast*: Anne Francis, James Best, Laura Devon, Jeanette Nolan, Virginia Gregg, George Mitchell, Helen Kleeb, Jim Boles, Jon Lormer.

   Plot: Backwoods girl Jess-Belle (Anne) sells her soul to a witch (Nolan) for the love of Billy-Ben (Best), who loves another.

Jess-Belle (Anne, right) is prepared to sell her soul to a witch for the love of Billy-Ben (James Best), who's in love with another, Ellwyn (Laura Devon, center), in the classic *Twilight Zone* episode "Jess-Belle."

Notes: Anne is given a terrific opportunity, dramatically, in this *Twilight Zone* episode. She is heartbreaking as she realizes she is cursed to stalk the night as a cat in return for Billy-Ben's love. Jess-Belle is never portrayed as evil, just irrationally in love, and Anne has our sympathies all the way. She and Best have a beautiful scene permeated with a dark air of tragedy, encompassing all that this fine, melancholy Earl Hamner Jr.–written episode is about. She asks the naive Billy-Ben if he knows the meaning of suffering and torment. He replies, "Sure. It's havin' a girl that's your heart's cravin' and have her keep puttin' the weddin' day off," not realizing the true import of the pain deep inside her.

> JESS-BELLE: It's the torment comes from buyin' somethin', findin' out the price is dear.
> BILLY-BEN: Well, what did you buy that cost so dear?
> JESS-BELLE: Somethin' I love.
> BILLY-BEN: You still love it, though the price was high?
> JESS-BELLE: Better than life.
> BILLY-BEN: Better than me?
> JESS-BELLE (*quietly*): Ain't nothin' I love better than you.

The Eleventh Hour — "Hang by One Hand" (NBC, March 27, 1963)

Regular Cast: Jack Ging, Wendell Corey. *Guest Cast*: Anne Francis, James Franciscus, Leslie Denison, Tom Simcox.

Plot: An unstable, selfish, alcoholic wife (Anne) could be the source of her husband Mike Norris' (Franciscus) recurring nightmares.

Notes: *The Eleventh Hour* was a medical drama (1962–64) dealing with psychiatry.

"Some interesting photography saves *The Eleventh Hour* from being an outright bore. The plot involves two not-very-interesting people — James Franciscus as a plodding architect and Anne Francis as his unhappy wife — who are unknowingly torturing each other, while outwardly pretending love. Franciscus' nightmares make this clear to Wendell Corey. It's here that the show's technical excellence is notable — cameraman Dale Deverman has some spectacular effects in the nightmare sequences."—The TV Scout, *San Antonio Express*, March 27, 1963

Ben Casey — "With the Rich and Mighty, Always a Little Patience" (ABC, September 25, 1963)

Director: Paul Wendkos. *Writer*: Norman Katkov. *Regular Cast*: Vince Edwards, Sam Jaffe. *Guest Cast:* Anne Francis, Frederick Beir, David Bond, Henry Corden, Frank Aletter.

Plot: A wealthy, beautiful, pampered patient throws the hospital into chaos while alternately battling and romancing Ben Casey (Edwards).

Notes: The title comes from an old Spanish proverb.

The Alfred Hitchcock Hour — "Blood Bargain" (CBS, October 25, 1963)

Director: Bernard Girard. *Writer*: Henry Slesar. *Host*: Alfred Hitchcock. *Cast*: Anne Francis, Richard Kiley, Richard Long, Barney Martin, Ross Elliott, Anthony Call, Peter Brocco.

Plot: Professional killer Jim Derry (Kiley) falls for Connie (Anne), the paraplegic wife of his intended victim, bookie Eddie Breech (Long).

Notes: This mystery is very complex (and implausible), but the payoff and the direction Anne's character takes at the conclusion make this priceless and entirely worth the trouble. Anne's character is multi-layered; that she is able to elicit sympathy from the audience at the end is a real testament to the actress.

In *The Alfred Hitchcock Hour*'s "Blood Bargain," Anne plays Connie, the paraplegic wife of a bookie (Richard Long) targeted by a hit man.

Arrest and Trial — *"The Witnesses"* (ABC, November 3, 1963)

Director: Alex March. *Writer*: Max Ehrlich. *Regular Cast*: Ben Gazzara, Chuck Connors, John Kerr, John Larch, Joe Higgins, Don Galloway. *Guest Cast*: Anne Francis, Robert Webber, Morgan Jones, Quinn O'Hara, Ed Prentiss, Damian O'Flynn, Douglas Lambert, Teno Pollick.

Plot: Schoolteacher Alice Wellman (Anne) and married man George Morrison (Webber) are having a rendezvous on Mulholland Drive when they witness the murder of a young girl. Alice wants to go to the police, but George persuades her to keep quiet for the sake of their reputations.

Notes: The 90-minute *Arrest and Trial* series (1963–64) was original in that its first half detailed the arrest of the culprits by Det. Sgt. Nick Anderson (Gazzara), while the second half dealt with the subsequent court trial led by attorney John Egan (Connors). Here, the drama centers on Alice Wellman's crisis of conscious. She knows the teenager arrested for the crime is innocent, but she is sweet-talked by her married lover to keep silent.

Anne going over the script with Ben Gazzara during the filming of the *Arrest and Trial* episode "The Witnesses."

Burke's Law — *"Who Killed Wade Walker?"* (ABC, November 15, 1963)

Director: Stanley Z. Cherry. *Writer*: Robert O'Brien. *Regular Cast*: Gene Barry, Gary Conway, Regis Toomey. *Guest Cast:* Rhonda Fleming, Anne Francis, Martha Hyer, Frankie Laine, Nancy Sinatra, Dana Wynter.

Plot: Amos Burke (Barry) must decide which of four women killed millionaire Wade Walker.

Notes: A smooth mystery as only *Burke's Law* could provide back in the '60s. Alas, Anne's part of Suzanne is deliberately superficial, and also quite dull. Suzanne is a model, a former Miss International, hailing from Alabama, who is so vain she has tons of photos of herself around and constantly gazes in the mirror.

Kraft Suspense Theatre — "The Machine That Played God"
(NBC, December 5, 1963)

Director: Paul Wendkos. *Writers:* Robert Guy Barrows, Judith Barrows (story), Robert Guy Barrows (adaptation). *Cast*: Anne Francis, Gary Merrill, Josephine Hutchinson, Malachi Throne, Edmon Ryan, Mary Wickes, Peter Adams, Morgan Mason.

Lawyer Mark Jordan (Gary Merrill) tries to understand why Peggy Merritt (Anne) has guilt feelings about the car accident which killed her husband in *Kraft Suspense Theatre*'s "The Machine That Played God."

Plot: Peggy Merritt (Anne) is tried for negligent homicide after her husband Mike (Adams) is killed in a car accident while she was driving. Even though it was clearly an accident, she fails a lie detector test — the machine that played God. Lawyer Mark Jordan (Merrill) is determined to figure out why the lady has feelings of guilt about the accident.

Notes: This preachy, overlong and complex drama nevertheless features a game cast. (You can really feel Gary Merrill's pain as he tries to sort things out.) It seems rather farfetched that by all accounts the marriage was a happy one and that when the husband's mother immediately accuses the wife of murder and petitions to take their son away, everyone believes the old biddy. This episode could have used a little more common sense and a lot less emotional tumult and guilt. That said, Anne's breakdown on the stand, as she comes to a few realizations about her life and marriage, ones that she has been denying for too long, is exceptionally well-done.

Playing the couple's child is Morgan Mason, the real-life son of actors James Mason and Pamela Mason, and the future husband of singer Belinda Carlisle.

Temple Houston — *"Ten Rounds for Baby"* (NBC, January 30, 1964)

Director: Irving J. Moore. *Writer*: William R. Cox. *Regular Cast*: Jeffrey Hunter, Jack Elam. *Guest Cast*: Anne Francis, Van Williams, Zeme North, Hal Baylor, Dave Willock, William Phipps.

Manager Kate Fitzpatrick (Anne) shows brawler Joey Baker (Van Williams, center) how it's done as Jack Elam helps in *Temple Houston*'s "Ten Rounds for Baby."

Plot: Kate Fitzpatrick (Anne) tries to make a professional boxer out of brawler Joey Baker (Williams).

Notes: Fast-draw Temple Houston (Hunter) was the attorney son of the infamous Sam Houston. He travels around to the circuit courts defending people in the 1880s.

Hunter, who last worked with Anne in *Dreamboat* (1952), was, with William T. Orr and Jack Webb, executive producer of this Western series. He had formed a production company, Apollo Productions, to handle production on the show, but he was not happy with the series. "In the first place, we had no time to prepare for it," he said in 1965. "I was notified on July 17 to be ready to start August 7 for an October air date. It was done so fast the writers never got a chance to know what it was all about. We all wanted to follow the [light comedy] line indicated by the pilot film, which we thought would make a charming series. NBC, however, favored making it serious. Then after 13 episodes, the ratings were rather low and Warners switched to tongue-in-cheek comedy, somewhat on the order of *Maverick*. We wound it up after 26 episodes."

Death Valley Days — *"The Last Stagecoach Robbery"* (Syndicated, March 17, 1964)

Director: Harmon Jones. *Writer*: Stephen Lord. *Host*: Ronald Reagan. *Cast*: Anne Francis, Jesse Pearson.

Plot: Pearl Hart masterminds a stagecoach robbery with her boyfriend Joe.

Notes: One of the fluffier episodes from the long-running (1952 to 1975) Western anthology program. Pearl isn't a ruthless robber, just idolizes outlaws; she merely wants to see if she can get away with the hold-up. Joe, who's in love with her, is reluctant to take part, but goes along. Comic complications ensue. After they succeed, she, to his horror, wants to give the money back. "You don't think I'm a thief, do you?" she asks him incredulously. This is a fun, charming episode, with Anne and Pearson a pleasant, engaging couple, even though the outcome of their questionable actions is a little depressing. This episode is a nice reminder of Anne Francis' light comedy touch.

The Linkletter Show (CBS, May 4, 1964)

Host: Art Linkletter. *Guests*: Anne Francis, Patrice Munsel, Gena Rowlands, Janice Rule.

You Don't Say (NBC, September 21, 1964)

Host: Tom Kennedy. *Guests*: Anne Francis, Barry Sullivan.

Ben Casey — *"A Bird in the Solitude Singing"* (ABC, September 21, 1964)

Director-Writer: John Meredyth Lucas. *Regular Cast*: Vince Edwards, Sam Jaffe, Bettye Ackerman. *Guest Cast*: Anne Francis, Buck Taylor, Stella Stevens, Richard Devon, Patricia Hyland, Virginia Eiler, Sara Taft.

Plot: Ben Casey treats a facially and emotionally scarred woman, Gloria Fowler (Anne), who has been hit by a truck while drunk.

Notes: This is a stunning example of Anne Francis' vast abilities as an actress. Her role as the alcoholic, sarcastic nymphomaniac transformed by love is undoubtedly one of her best.

When we are first introduced to Gloria Fowler, in the pre-credits sequence, she is getting soused at the local bar tended by her friend Harry (Devon). A grubby drunk, seeing a leggy blonde at the bar, comes up from behind her to steal a kiss. As she angrily spins around, we see that the girl has a large scar spread out on the side of her face. Noticing his startled reaction, she lets him have it.

> GLORIA: Whaddya expect in a dump like this ... Princess Grace? This is Wednesday. On Wednesdays I'm Cinderella. And you're no Prince Charming. I wouldn't go to your castle even if your glass slipper did fit.
> DRUNK (*to bartender*): Boy, is this dame stoned.
> GLORIA: By stoned, do you mean like the statue Pygmalion fell in love with or are you alluding to the hardness of my heart because I withhold my beauty from you? Or could you mean, you lousy Skid Row bum, that I'm plastered?
> DRUNK: Who are you calling a bum? Don't you badmouth me.
> GLORIA (*to bartender*): Harry, he's sensitive. He reacts to stimulus. I think, in a subhuman way, he's alive.

Leaving the bar with the livid drunk on her heels, Gloria is hit by a truck. It is quite apparent to the other patients, doctors and nurses at County General Hospital when she is rushed there that Gloria is mean, patronizing, bitter over the way her life has turned out. The imperfection of her face has rendered her cynical. She does admit to Dr. Zorba (Jaffe) that to compensate for her looks, she has built up her mind, but Gloria is not a happy woman.

Into her life comes Eddie Boyd (Taylor), who is in a wheelchair after a fall, paralyzed from the waist down. Having had a similarly hard life, he dropped out of school early to go to work. She begins teaching him poetry and history. She responds to his innocence, his pure faith and unselfishness, and the once-acidic lady begins to change.

What's nice about "A Bird in the Solitude Singing" is that it's not a syrupy piece of fluff, no overwrought emotions on display here, just genuine emotions. Anne is understated, the inner pain just barely contained, her contempt for the world dragging her through life. Gloria's transformation is entirely believable; it is not a sudden change, but one of gradual wonderment on her part, as she finally comes to accept how she looks. Hers is a gorgeous, tender performance, helped immeasurably by the purity of Buck Taylor's unassuming, likable playing. When Eddie reads the poem he has composed for her, it is a lovely moment, a shining example of what really excellent actors can do with simple dialogue.

There are several poetic references in the teleplay; the title of the episode is taken from Lord Byron's *Stanzas to Augusta* from 1816:

> From the wreck of my past, which hath perish'd,
> Thus much I at least may recall,
> It hath taught me that which I most cherish'd
> Deserved to be dearest of all:
> In the desert a fountain is springing,
> In the wide waste there still is a tree,
> And a bird in the solitude singing,
> Which speaks to my spirit of thee.

The Reporter — *"Hideout"* (CBS, October 2, 1964)

Director: Alex March. *Writer*: Ian McLellan Hunter. *Regular Cast*: Harry Guardino, Gary Merrill, George O'Hanlon, Remo Pisani. *Guest Cast*: Richard Conte, Anne Francis, Lloyd Gough, Kurt Kasznar, Martin Priest, Joe Silver.

Notes: See the *Reporter* episode "Rachel's Mother" (below) for more details about this program.

Valentine's Day — "The Fraudulent Female" (ABC, October 9, 1964)

Director: George Marshall. *Writers:* Hal Kanter, Jack Sher. *Regular Cast*: Tony Franciosa, Jack Soo, Janet Waldo, Eddie Quillan, Jerry Hausner, Mimi Dillard. *Guest Cast*: Anne Francis.

Plot: Tony pitches a book about how easy a housewife's day is. To prove him wrong, an acerbic reviewer (Anne) tricks him into taking over his sister's duties at home.

Notes: This fun, short-lived comedy series (1964–65) was created by executive producer Hal Kanter, who explained to columnist Edgar Penton, "In this series we're going to attempt a giant step forward to the 1930s and early 1940s, when comedies were fun... In each of our stories, we want to have at least one comedy routine that will depend as much as possible on physical action. But it will be logically motivated."

Anne is a cool, unruffled book reviewer to Tony Franciosa's book agent on *Valentine's Day*'s "The Fraudulent Female."

This episode was the first filmed but the fourth aired.

The Reporter — "Rachel's Mother" (CBS, October 23, 1964)

Director: Tom Gries. *Writer*: Jerome Weidman. *Regular Cast*: Harry Guardino, Gary Merrill, George O'Hanlon, Remo Pisani. *Guest Cast*: Anne Francis, Walter Pidgeon, Alan Hewitt, Howard St. John, Brenda Vaccaro.

Plot: Crusading reporter Danny Turner (Guardino) goes after a shady combine corporation named "Rachel's Mother," after two children are killed when a faulty tenement railing falls on them.

Notes: This episode was the first filmed for the series, but aired as the fifth.

"Some months ago CBS chief James Aubrey wondered whether it was possible to reconcile truth and fiction so that a reporter would emerge who would be recognizable to the men who ply the craft and at the same time retain the dramatic magnetism with which Hollywood and TV films have invested the fourth estate," wrote TV reporter Robert Musel.

"His executives were dubious," the report continued. "But Aubrey had an idea. He called to one of the most expert and successful authors of the day, Jerome Weidman, and asked him to try to embody his conception into a script. The name of the new one-hour series that flowed from Weidman's gifted pen is *The Reporter*, which will debut on CBS-TV network on Sept. 25.

"Weidman ... said he was just as uncertain as the CBS executives when he first considered Aubrey's suggestion. 'But then Aubrey mentioned that he was thinking of someone like John Garfield [in the lead]. And that brought it right into focus for me. What we wanted was an intestinal character not an intellectual one and the role of the reporter, Danny Taylor, began to build up immediately in my mind.'"

Harry Guardino was cast as Danny and Gary Merrill played his combative city editor on *The New York Globe*, Lou Sheldon. "We're just waiting for some critics to complain about the lack of physical authenticity," continued Weidman to Musel. "We filmed the pilot — with guest stars Walter Pidgeon and Anne Francis — right in the old office of the now defunct *New York Mirror*. Then we had the city room of the tabloid reproduced exactly in the studio. You can't get much more authentic than that."

Hal Humphrey, in his September 1964 syndicated column "TV Comment," wrote about the two episodes of *The Reporter* in which Anne appeared: "An upcoming *Reporter* has Anne cast as a blonde who hangs around a bar. In another episode of the same series she turns gang moll and is very, very tough. 'They were thinking of keeping the blonde in the bar as a regular character,' says Anne, 'but there was a thing in the first one about integration, and somebody at CBS has decided that things about Negroes are out this season — so the idea and the girl were dropped.'"

Anne's no-name blonde is originally from Chicago, but is now a working girl in New York City who "auditions for musicals that never get put on." She hangs around the Press Box, the local bar, drinking, answering trivia questions (don't ask) and playing the piano. Her character had some potential as Guardino's romantic interest (the two had an easygoing chemistry) and as someone he could confide in, but it was dropped immediately. Anne's next episode in this series cast her as a totally different character, a gun moll, and that show aired before this one.

Along the lines of other socially conscious shows of the period, such as *The Defenders* (1961–65) and *East Side/West Side* (1963–64), and later *Judd, for the Defense* (1967–69), *The Reporter* was well-meaning, earnest, and before its time, but also preachy and occasionally pretentious. It boasted good stories, however, and some exciting hand-held camerawork and location shooting. It lasted only four months.

The Man from U.N.C.L.E. — *"The Quadripartite Affair"*
(NBC, October 6, 1964)

Director: Richard Donner. *Writer*: Alan Caillou. *Regular Cast*: Robert Vaughn, David McCallum, Leo G. Carroll. *Guest Cast*: Jill Ireland, Anne Francis, Richard Anderson, John Van Dreelen, Roger C. Carmel, Robert Carricart.

Plot: Napoleon Solo (Vaughn) and Illya Kuryakin (McCallum) break into an underground Yugoslavian fortress to destroy an experimental gas which causes extreme fear.

Notes: Villainous Gervaise Ravel is one of the few out-and-out bad girls Anne ever played, and she's one cool, calculating number. Born in Provance, the thirty-year-old is classified as dangerous and is already a widow, her husband, a shady French minister, having committed suicide a couple of years before. Now she is keeping company with urbane Harold Bufferton (Van Dreelen) who not only has a bankroll but also the same ruthless mindset.

Underneath the calm exterior lies a heart of pure stone and cinder. "Kill him," Gervaise mutters dispassionately. Helping Anne's overall evil look is her dark hair. "Metro studios is giving Anne Francis a big build-up as a fem fatale when she stars in the new series, *The Man From U.N.C.L.E.*," Jack Bradford reported. "To start with, Anne will wear one of the many wigs Liz Taylor uses when she makes movies and that'll be fem fatale enough." Well, unfortunately, she received no *femme fatale* build-up, but she and her suave accomplice did get away at the conclusion to wreck havoc another day.

The Man from U.N.C.L.E. — "The Giuoco Piano Affair"
(NBC, November 10, 1964)

Director: Richard Donner. *Writer*: Alan Caillou. *Regular Cast*: Robert Vaughn, David McCallum, Leo G. Carroll. *Guest Cast*: Jill Ireland, Anne Francis, John Van Dreelen, James Frawley, Gordon Gilbert.

Plot: Having escaped in "The Quadripartite Affair," the devious duo of Gervaise Ravel (Anne) and Harold Bufferton (Van Dreelen) are still up to no good.

Notes: This episode literally starts off with a bang as Gervaise, craftily piloting a helicopter, maneuvers it so Bufferton can blast a U.N.C.L.E. agent, spying on their cliff-top house, with a bazooka.

"The Giuoco Piano Affair" gives Anne a better chance, acting-wise, than her first *U.N.C.L.E.* episode. "She likes power, she has the strength to make use of it and I have the money to buy it for her," Bufferton tells Napoleon Solo (Robert Vaughn). And this strength is best displayed in a honey of a scene between Anne and Vaughn. She and Bufferton have captured Marion Raven (Ireland), and Solo coolly negotiates, over cocktails, with Gervaise. When they start their banter, Gervaise is confident, as is Solo, but as their talk intensifies and he shifts the conversation to chess, we see Gervaise get slightly apprehensive. "Tell me, do you play chess, Madame Ravel?" he asks casually. Gervaise is uneasy. "Right now, no, I would not like to." Solo then gets down to business.

> SOLO: The Giuoco Piano gambit: Bishop to Bishop four, tempting the Queen to rashly move out to Knight three. And the Queen has moved out, hasn't she?
> GERVAISE: But your Queen is threatened. I don't think you'll risk it. I call your bluff.
> SOLO: Oh, it's no bluff. My White Knight has gone to the rescue of my Queen.
> GERVAISE: You don't have a White Knight.
> SOLO: Perhaps your presumption of infallibility is *your* weakness, Gervaise.

"Giuoco Piano" refers to an opening chess move and is Italian for "quiet game."

Jill Ireland's Marion Raven was in the running to become a recurring character, a love interest for Illya Kuryakin (McCallum). In real life, Ireland and McCallum were married at the time.

The Virginian — "All Nice and Legal" (NBC, November 25, 1964)

Director: Don McDougall. *Writer*: Jean Holloway. *Regular Cast*: James Drury, Lee J. Cobb, Doug McClure, Roberta Shore, Clu Gulager. *Guest Cast*: Anne Francis, Harold Gould, Ellen Corby, Judson Pratt, Linda Foster, John Kellogg, Walter Woolf King, Stephen Price, Norman Leavitt, Jeff Cooper, Ollie O'Toole, Robert Gothie.

Plot: Philadelphia lawyer Victoria Greenleigh (Anne) finds opposition when she sets up a practice in Medicine Bow.

Notes: Anne shines in this showcase role, a Jean Holloway–penned feminist story. She is a confident lawyer out to prove herself to a new town and a sexist (but sexy) James Drury. She ends up defending him in court. ("Good luck," he tells her hopefully. "Luck has *nothing* to do with it," she coolly states.) Her cross-examination scene is very nicely played, as with cunning she verbally dances around the witness, finally leading him to where she wants. The story cops out near the end, however; she must choose between love and a career, she can't have both, so Victoria leaves town.

"They used to pay $7500 for guest stars," Anne told Hal Humphrey about her experience

on this episode. "After all, it's a 90-minute show, but the top at Universal is $5000. I don't get it. They've built a big new commissary, but there's no money for the actors. And those tours, migawd! At two-fifty per head, they'll make a million dollars from the tourists." Anne explained that during a break in filming, she was stretched across a couple of chairs in her trailer dressing room, trying to cool off after lugging a wig and a bustle around all morning. "I heard a noise, looked out the window and here was a busload of people pointing cameras at me while the driver was yelling, 'Yes, sir, that's one of the stars taking a break.' I didn't move. There was nothing to do but pretend it wasn't really happening."

Lady lawyer Victoria Greenleigh (Anne) sets up a practice in Medicine Bow in *The Virginian*'s "All Nice and Legal."

"It's a snappy, off-beat episode, which sings the praises of women's rights." — TV Scout, *The Abilene Reporter-News*, November 25, 1964

The Alfred Hitchcock Hour — *"The Trap"* (CBS, February 22, 1965)

Director: John Brahm. *Writers:* Stanley Abbott (story), Lee Kalcheim (teleplay). *Host:* Alfred Hitchcock. *Cast:* Anne Francis, Donnelly Rhodes, Robert Strauss, Patricia Manning.

Anne out on the town with her co-star of *The Alfred Hitchcock Hour*'s "The Trap," handsome Donnelly Rhodes.

Plot: Unhappy wife Peg Beale (Anne) conspires with her hunky boyfriend John Cochran (Rhodes) to murder her husband Ted (Strauss), but things go awry.

Notes: Anne gives a sympathetic showing here as a woman dissatisfied with her life and feeling trapped by her loveless marriage, turning to booze and boys to fill the void. (Nice work, if you can get it.)

The suspense is palpable in this episode, but it is almost ruined by Rhodes' one-note performance and Strauss' wildly fluctuating one. Physically, the darkly gorgeous Rhodes, who was dating Anne at the time, is perfect for the part, and he is convincing in their love scenes, but someone should have coached him on his lines. Ah, the beautiful but the dumb...

Strauss is supposed to be childlike, overly possessive, and just a complete fool. Yet, Strauss' leer and ominous intonations just about give the twist away. And what can you say about the supposedly unsettling twist ending? Sorry, but I laughed.

Burke's Law — *"Who Killed the Jackpot?"* (ABC, April 21, 1965)

Director: Richard Kinon. *Writers:* Gwen Bagni, Paul Dubov. *Regular Cast:* Gene Barry, Gary Conway, Regis Toomey. *Guest Cast:* Anne Francis, John Ericson, Steve Forrest, George Nader, Nancy Gates, Louis Hayward, Jan Sterling.

Plot: Amos Burke and Honey West compete to solve a crime and end up aiding each other while sparring romantically. At the conclusion he broaches the idea of teaming up. "Sorry, Amos, I fly solo," she coolly tells him.

Notes: This served as a pilot for Anne's television show *Honey West*. There were reports that the producers were thinking of adding two more Honey West episodes to *Burke's Law* before going to a new series, but that idea was nixed very quickly. See pages 68–70 for more details about this episode.

Honey West (ABC, 1965–66)

Notes: See pages 228–243 for full episode guide.

You Don't Say (NBC, June 7, 1965)

Host: Tom Kennedy. *Guests*: Anne Francis, Mickey Manners.

The Wonderful World of Disney — "The Further Adventures of Gallegher: The Big Swindle" (NBC, October 3, 1965)

Director: Jeffrey Hayden. *Writer*: Maurice Tombragel. *Host*: Walt Disney. *Cast*: Roger Mobley, Anne Francis, Edmond O'Brien, Harvey Korman, Jon Lormer, John Talbot, Alan Hewitt, Guy Raymond, Arthur Malet.

Plot: A newspaper copyboy from *The Daily Press*, Gallegher (Mobley), teams up with reporter Adeline Jones (Anne) to trap confidence men.

Notes: Richard Harding Davis (1864–1916) introduced the street-smart character of Gallegher in a short story in the late 1800s. In January of 1964, Walt Disney brought the stories to television as a three-part special simply called *Gallegher (Boy Reporter)*. This was followed in September of that same year with another three-parter, *The Further Adventures of Gallegher*. "The Big Swindle" is the second installment. Even though Anne is listed in many sources as being in the first part, "A Case of Murder," she is not.

Anne plays plucky Adeline Jones, the "first lady newspaperman." She and Gallegher go undercover as a wealthy woman and her brother. The light tone makes this one very engaging, and it's a shame this program is not seen as widely as other Disney productions. Mobley is likable and his scenes with Anne have a nice spirit to them. "You're a pretty good fella, for a lady," he tells her. "If I was ten years older, you could be my best gal." It isn't as creepy as it sounds, thanks mostly to the innocent chemistry the two shared.

The Wonderful World of Disney — "The Further Adventures of Gallegher: The Daily Press vs. City Hall" (NBC, October 10, 1965)

Director: Jeffrey Hayden. *Writer*: Maurice Tombragel. *Host*: Walt Disney. *Cast*: Roger Mobley, Anne Francis, Edmond O'Brien, Harvey Korman, Jon Lormer, James Westerfield, Vaughn Taylor, Tom Skerritt, Maudie Prickett, Parley Baer, John Orchard, Edward Platt.

Plot: *The Daily Press* gets sued for libel and it is up to Gallegher (Mobley) and Adeline (Anne) to get proof of corruption in a construction deal involving City Hall.

Notes: More light fun as the copyboy and the lady reporter crash a party to steal some valuable, incriminating documents. Anne dresses up as an Irish maid complete with a wispy

Irish brogue. Disney produced two more *Gallegher* specials, *Gallegher Goes West* (1966) and *The Mystery of Edward Sims* (1968), both without Anne. It's too bad; she was a good foil for Mobley.

The Fugitive — "The One That Got Away" (ABC, January 17, 1967)

Director: Leo Penn. *Writers*: Philip Saltzman, Harry Kronman. *Regular Cast*: David Janssen. *Guest Cast*: Anne Francis, Charles Drake, Charles Bronson, David Renard, Vince Howard, Harlan Warde, Thordis Brandt.

Plot: Undercover agent Ralph Schuyler (Bronson) spies on Felice Greer (Anne) in hopes she will lead him to her embezzler husband Oliver (Drake).

Notes: Lecherous Schuyler poses as the captain of the ship (Richard Kimble [Janssen] is the only other member of the crew) which Felice has hired to take her "sightseeing." Schuyler is sure she'll make contact with her husband eventually.

In the beginning, not much is required of Anne except to be beautiful, charming, look worried and throw off the occasional witty line. She tries (of course) to communicate with the monosyllabic, gloomy Kimble, but he's unresponsive. (That's right, Kimble, *blend* in. Don't make yourself stand out. What a maroon.) She reveals to Kimble that she loves her husband and is "carrying the biggest torch you've ever seen." What she doesn't tell him is that, far from innocent as she initially claims, Oliver Greer not only embezzled the money but she has had it converted into rare coins for safekeeping.

All this is fairly routine — until the end. Sweet, devoted, unsuspecting Felice finds out that her hubby is keeping company in a Mexican hotel with his secretary. The look in her eyes is enough to tear you apart; she's lied and cheated for this man and he's two-timing her. On the verge of tears, clearly dazed and hurting, Felice, one by one, throws the rare coins overboard into the water, as she demands that Oliver tell her about his affair. She allows Kimble to escape and tells the police that Oliver is Kimble. It is a terrific way to wrap up her character.

The Fugitive (1963–67) was a very popular television program about a doctor who is wrongly accused and convicted of murdering his wife. On his way to be executed, he escapes from Lt. Philip Gerard (Barry Morse), beginning his long search to clear his name and to find the one-armed man he saw running away from the crime scene. Week after week, Kimble would travel around, befriending strangers, all of whom were supposed to sense his innate goodness and innocence and allow him to move on to the next town to resume his search. The problem with this is quite apparent herein. Janssen played Kimble as brooding, mumbling, never making eye contact, always giving evasive answers. There was *nothing* attractive or honest about him.

"David was a nice person," Anne told Dann Dulin in 2005. "He loved his booze and would start early in the morning with Scotch. He had a lot of pain in his legs from playing football and that's how he handled it. He *never* showed it."

Dateline: Hollywood (May 2, 1967)

Guests: Anne Francis, Ryan O'Neal, Leigh Taylor-Young.

The Invaders — The Saucer" (ABC, September 12, 1967)

Director: Jesse Hibbs. *Writer*: Dan Ullman. *Regular Cast*: Roy Thinnes. *Guest Cast*: Anne Francis, Charles Drake, Dabney Coleman, Robert Knapp, Kelly Thordsen, Sandy Kenyon, John Ward, Glenn Bradley.

Plot: A spaceship lands, disrupting an elopement and a theft of valuable blueprints.

Notes: This episode was announced under the title "The Shiny Toy." The premise of *The Invaders* (1967–68) was simple: Architect David Vincent (Thinnes) sets to prove the existence of aliens on Earth while also trying to avoid becoming a victim of the malicious extraterrestrials.

As a spaceship lands, it also inadvertently forces down a plane carrying an eloping couple, Robert Morrison (Drake) and Annie Rhodes (Anne). We soon find out that Morrison has stolen more than $200,000 worth of blueprints from his company to satisfy the woman he loves. "Maybe if all your father had left you was a $20 gold piece and a bag full of good wishes, it would mean the same to you," Annie says, by way of an explanation of her greed. Anne has a great delayed, but crafty, reaction when she is asked to choose between the man she's about to marry and the money the blueprints would net. Alas, at the conclusion, the script cheats her. All in all, however, this is a good, fairly exciting episode, as Vincent and his friend John Carter (Coleman) battle the aliens and actually take control of the UFO briefly.

David Vincent (Roy Thinnes) asks for help from Annie Rhodes (Anne) when he finds a deserted flying saucer in *The Invaders'* episode "The Saucer" (1967).

The Joey Bishop Show (May 24, 1968)

Notes: Anne showed movies taken at the May 11–12 Mother Lode Roundup and parade.

The Name of the Game — "Incident in Berlin" (NBC, October 25, 1968)

Director: Seymour Robbie. *Writers:* William Link, Richard Levinson. *Regular Cast*: Gene Barry. *Guest Cast*: Anne Francis, Dane Clark, Geraldine Brooks, Kevin McCarthy, John Van Dreelen.

Plot: In East Berlin, Glenn Howard (Barry) tries to secure the release of his Bureau chief and friend Brian Smith (Clark) who is being used to swap for a spy imprisoned in the U.S.

Notes: *The Name of the Game* (1968–71) was an expensive weekly 90-minute show filmed with the care and sensibilities of feature-length films. There were three rotating

The Name of the Game's "Incident in Berlin" was a suspenseful, taut drama packed with foreign intrigue. Here, publisher Glenn Howard (Gene Barry) and Carol Sherman (Anne) visit a Berlin bar.

stars: Gene Barry as Glenn Howard, the publisher of Howard Publishing, Inc.; Tony Franciosa as correspondent Jeff Dillon; and Robert Stack as FBI agent-turned-editor Dan Farrell.

In the classy "Incident in Berlin," the debonair Barry smoothly moves through dark alleys, banters with spies over a cool game of pool, and plans inventive machinations to free his friend Smith, who is more trouble than Howard initially realizes. He is helped by translator Carol Sherman (Anne), who was in a relationship with married man Smith and is willing to do anything to secure his release. On the surface it seems typical, but chic Anne's role becomes ultimately more complicated — and interesting.

Director Robbie uses the Berlin locations to maximum effect, replete with some uniquely odd footage of German girls wrestling each other on a bar. The acting is good all around, with Barry having some sporting banter with sleek John Van Dreelen, who is running the political swap. The around-the-corner spying, switching cars, and shadows makes "Incident in Berlin" a suspenseful, taut drama.

You Don't Say! (NBC, February 3, 1969)

Host: Tom Kennedy. *Guest Panelists*: Anne Francis, Greg Morris.

The Steve Allen Show (August 20, 1969)

Host: Steve Allen. *Guests*: Anne Francis, Cliff Arquette, Kim Weston, The Cannonball Adderly Sextet.

Mission: Impossible—"*The Double Circle*" (CBS, December 7, 1969)

Director: Barry Crane. *Writer*: Jerrold L. Ludwig. *Regular Cast*: Peter Graves, Leonard Nimoy, Greg Morris, Peter Lupus. *Guest Cast*: Anne Francis, James Patterson, Jason Evers, Albert Sklar, Thom Brann, Robert Ritchie.

Plot: A new fuel formula gets into the wrong hands and the team must recover it.

Notes: Each *Mission: Impossible* (1966–73) began with Jim Phelps (Graves) retrieving an audio tape. The voice on it starts with, "Good morning, Mr. Phelps," followed by details of the mission at hand. The voice then wrapped it up: "As always, should you or any of your IM [Impossible Missions] force be caught or killed, the secretary will disavow any knowledge of your actions. Good luck, Jim. This tape will self-destruct in five seconds." It would then self-combust.

Mission: Impossible had good, if complicated, scripts, and some implausible plans to deceive the bad guys. The budget was high and the guest casts were very impressive.

The Name of the Game—"*The Garden*" (NBC, January 30, 1970)

Director: Seymour Robbie. *Writer*: Charles A. McDaniel. *Regular Cast*: Robert Stack. *Guest Cast*: Richard Kiley, Anne Francis, Arch Johnson, Brenda Scott, John Archer, Burt Brinckerhoff, Anne Barton, Woodrow Parfrey, Madeleine Sherwood, Schell Rasten.

Plot: Howard Publishing's editor Dan Farrell (Stack) matches wits with pop psychiatrist Dr. Judson Strode (Kiley), who runs a retreat called "The Garden" for wealthy clients. Can Farrell prove that the doctor is simply exploiting his patients and has no regard for their health or safety?

Notes: Not the ideal story for *The Name of the Game*'s 90-minute format, "The Garden" grates on one's nerves. There's a lot of fine back-and-forth baiting interplay between Stack and Kiley, but, after awhile, the bickering and mental issues of the patients become just too much.

Anne is Marsha Ryman, an "alcoholic sensualist" who, as she caresses Farrell's lobes, confesses to have a thing for ears. (Not kidding. Even more amazing: The way Anne does it and Stack's reaction to it makes it kinda cute.) One bickering scene, a so-called therapy session in a swimming pool, is the best, as the patients cruelly verbally confront each other under the watchful gaze of Dr. Strode. Mrs. Grace Reeder (Barton) challenges Marsha about some time spent with graying Mr. Reeder (Archer).

MARSHA: You've got to be putting me on! What would I want with him? What would *anyone* want with him?

GRACE: Well, aren't we getting choosy all of a sudden.

MARSHA: I'm choosy enough to know what he's worth. If I had to settle for him, I would turn in my woman card.

GRACE: Who are you trying to kid? You'll chase anything that has two legs and even vaguely smells like a man.

The Movie Game (February 15, 1970)

Host: Sonny Fox. *Guest Panelists*: Army Archerd, Jack Albertson, Kathryn Grayson, AF, Gig Young.

The F.B.I. — *"Deadfall"* (ABC, March 1, 1970)

Director: Don Medford. *Writer*: Robert Heverly. *Regular Cast*: Efrem Zimbalist, Jr., Philip Abbott, William Reynolds. *Guest Cast*: Wayne Rogers, Anne Francis, Robert Drivas, Zohra Lampert, Paul Picerni, Barry Russo, Kelly Thordsen, Rick Adams, Erin Moran.

    Plot: The search is on for Mary (Lampert), the kidnapped wife of Fred Cochella (Picerni), a sports arena cashier.

    Notes: Not-so-ruthless Anne is Shelly, the sympathetic wife of kidnapper Ronald Brimlow (Rogers). Tops is the scene where Shelly confesses to their captive how she and her husband turned to crime ("It was so easy ... and it just got easier..."). The deep-felt desperation and loneliness that Anne brings to this role is quite touching. She's strong when she needs to be — handling a gun with ease, throwing a drink in a gang member's face — but underneath there is a vulnerability, which elevates this role to something more. This is another example of Anne bringing more to her characters than what was in the script.

Insight — *"Bourbon in Suburbia"* (Syndicated, April 15, 1970)

Director-Writer: John Meredyth Lucas. *Cast*: Anne Francis, Fred Beir, Paul Carr, Marie Windsor.

    Plot: Claire (Anne), a housewife, struggles with her alcoholism.

    Notes: The popular, award-winning religious program *Insight* aired from 1960 to 1983. The Rev. Philip P. Bruni, director of radio and television for the diocese of Manchester, told the *Nashua Telegraph* in 1971, "The purpose ... is to dramatize the deep ethical and spiritual conflicts of modern man in a way that suggests a humanistic solution.... Some subjects explored in the upcoming *Insight* series include dishonesty in marriage, college agnosticism, psychology of hate, guilt and death, automation, narcotics, spiritual isolation, racism, hypocrisy, morality of warfare, alcoholism, and community-police relations."

    Father Ellwood E. Keiser, the producer-host, stated that the show was concerned "with the dignity of man in the modern world, caught between the confusing forces of good and evil, between strength and weakness." The series' aim was to create a "God-centered universe into which non-believing viewers will be invited to enter and look around."

    It was produced by Paulist Productions in California, and the well-known actors who appeared regularly on the show, said Keiser, worked without pay. "They welcome the freedom and challenge presented by *Insight* to express ideas often taboo on commercial shows. We can say the unpopular thing and speak the truth without fear of buyer retaliation or a ratings slump."

    "Bourbon in Suburbia" was a real showcase for Anne. One impressed reviewer raved, "The mental anguish, remorse and guilt of the alcoholic is starkly and realistically portrayed by Anne Francis...." It's a remarkable piece of bravado acting, as Anne really lets it all hang out. She makes her "typical housewife" role buzz with a realism and grittiness that is harrowing to experience. The show's low budget and minimalist sets only added to the raw emotions being exposed on screen.

Life with Linkletter (July 19, 1970)

Host: Art Linkletter. *Guests*: Anne Francis, Jerry Della Femina, and Prof. (Montana) K. Toole.

Notes: Anne talks about her single-parent adoption.

The Mike Douglas Show (Syndicated, September 18, 1970)

Hosts: Mike Douglas, Roy Rogers, Dale Evans. *Guests*: Anne Francis, ventriloquist Willie Tyler and Lester, singer David Arlen and writer Jimmy Breslin.

Notes: Roy and Dale were guest-hosting with Mike.

The Men from Shiloh — *"Gun Quest"* (NBC, October 21, 1970)

Director: Harry Harris. *Writer*: Robert Van Scoyk. *Regular Cast*: James Drury. *Guest Cast*: Monte Markham, Anne Francis, Sally Shockley, John Smith, Agnes Moorehead, Brandon De Wilde, Joseph Cotten, Rod Cameron, Neville Brand.

Plot: The Virginian is framed for murder and goes looking for the man who did commit the crime.

Notes: "Gun Quest" had quite a cast. Anne has a small part, but again, she makes the most of it. She plays Myra, a "two-bit saloon girl" (with a room over the saloon) in love with gunfighter Boss Cooper (Markham) who leaves her to get married to a "respectable" woman, Nellie (Shockley). Anne is tough and altogether heartbreaking as someone who laments her love for a notorious gunfighter. "She doesn't wake up to the smell of cheap whiskey in her room," Myra says of the twit Boss marries. (And Sallie Shockley is a definite twit.) The episode's basic premise has The Virginian (Drury) being mistaken for Boss and searching for him to clear his name. The acting is okay, with Cameron, Brand, Markham and Anne coming off best. Anne brings gravity and class-consciousness to her slight role.

The long-running West-

Anne had a vivid role as Myra, a "two-bit saloon girl," in *The Men from Shiloh*'s "Gun Quest." Brandon De Wilde makes sure she doesn't leave to warn the man she loves, Boss Cooper, that he is marked for death.

ern series *The Virginian* (1962–71) was renamed *The Men from Shiloh* in its last season. It's interesting to contrast this episode with the *Virginian* that Anne did in 1964. Where that one was fluffy, this one is dark, touching, but uncompromising.

"Don't mess around with Anne Francis. She can take care of herself— a point she proved on *The Men from Shiloh* set where she taped the segment of the NBC show. Anne, an expert in karate, started horsing around with one of the stunt men, flipped him and sent him flying. I'd hate to see the damage she could do when she's not just kidding around."— Marilyn Beck, *Hollywood Hotline*, May 4, 1971

Anne on the set joking with "The Virginian" (James Drury) in *The Men from Shiloh*'s "Gun Quest."

Love, American Style — "Love and the Visitor" (ABC, October 23, 1970)

Director: Bruce Bilson. *Writers:* Valerie Harper, Richard Schaal. *Guest Cast:* Anne Francis, William Windom, Janos Prohaska.

Plot: Claudia (Anne) returns home after a six-month expedition to her amorous husband Harrison (Windom) ... with an equally amorous gorilla.

Notes: "The second segment, with Anne Francis, William Windom and Janos Prohaska, who plays Andy Williams' bear (tonight he's a gorilla), was written by Valerie Harper, of *The Mary Tyler Moore Show*, and her husband, Richard Schaal. It's a funny idea, but Valerie says what you see is quite different from what they wrote."— TV Scout, *The Transcript*, October 23, 1970

> CLAUDIA: There's nothing to worry about. He [the gorilla] is very gentle, he's curious, that's all. He's only a boy.
> HARRISON: I suppose I was only a little nervous, then. But, ah, getting back to what we were saying, Claudia, where are you going to keep him?
> CLAUDIA: Well, could we keep him here?
> HARRISON (*shouting*): Here! (*whispering*) Here? You mean you want to keep that ape, that gorilla, in our house?
> CLAUDIA: Harrison, please, don't whisper in front of him; it's not polite.

HARRISON: Well, where is he going to s-l-e-e-p?
CLAUDIA: There's a joke about that, isn't there? Any darn place he wants to!

Dan August — *"Murder by Proxy"* (ABC, March 4, 1971)

Director: George McCowan. *Writer*: Robert C. Dennis. *Regular Cast*: Burt Reynolds, Richard Anderson, Norman Fell. *Guest Cast*: Anne Francis, Diana Muldaur, Ned Romero, Roger Perry, Burr De Benning, Ford Rainey, Milton Selzer.

Plot: When a race car driver is killed, Det. Lieutenant Dan August's (Reynolds) high-school sweetheart Elizabeth (Muldaur) is one of the suspects.

Notes: This was the first episode filmed, but the twenty-second aired. Anne plays Nina Porter, another lush, the wife of Hal (Perry). There's much tension in the marriage. Years before, she had an affair with the murder victim, Gabe Redfern (who we never see), a childhood rival of her husband's, a fact she needles him with. The highlight of the episode for Anne is when she takes August on a drunken chase through the streets — he in a police car, she in a race car. This episode was combined with another *Dan August* episode, "The King Is Dead," to make the television movie *The Jealousy Factor*.

My Three Sons — *"Fergus for Sale"* (CBS, September 20, 1971)

Director: Earl Bellamy. *Writer*: George Tibbles. *Regular Cast*: Fred MacMurray, William Demarest, Stanley Livingston, Barry Livingston, Tina Cole, Beverly Garland, Dawn Lyn, Ronne Troup. *Guest Cast*: Anne Francis, Lois January, Judy March, Alan Caillou (voice of Fergus, uncredited).

Plot: Uncle Charley (Demarest) puts an ad in the newspaper looking for a prospective wife for marriage-minded Scottish cousin Fergus (MacMurray, in a dual role), so he can go home to Scotland. Terri Dowling (Anne), a bowling alley waitress well into her 30s, hasn't had "her cargo shifted much," so she answers the ad and piques Fergus' interest.

Notes: At this point in the *My Three Sons* run, the writers were really stretching it, and the show wasn't as fresh as earlier seasons. MacMurray's apparent lack of interest was a factor, especially in his dual role as Cousin Fergus, which is not helped by the poor dubbing of Alan Caillou's burr.

My Three Sons — *"Lady Douglas"* (CBS, September 27, 1971)

Director: Earl Bellamy. *Writer*: George Tibbles. *Regular Cast*: Fred MacMurray, William Demarest, Stanley Livingston, Barry Livingston, Tina Cole, Beverly Garland, Dawn Lyn, Ronne Troup. *Guest Cast*: Anne Francis, Frank De Vol, Charles Lampkin, Janice Carroll, Alan Caillou (voice of Fergus, uncredited).

Plot: Fergus asks Terri to marry him, but she doesn't feel she's good enough to go to Scotland and mingle with royalty, and turns him down. Terri reveals in this episode that she has been married before; her husband was killed overseas in the Korean War.

Notes: A better episode for Anne than the previous "Fergus for Sale." She has a first-rate, heartrending scene where she confesses a few "truths" about herself to Fergus. Mistaking one identical cousin for another, she tells Steve that she's no lady. He had been wary of her as a match for Fergus, but now sees her sincerity. Anne is so likable and sweet, her speech so heartfelt, she infuses this scene with the warmth that so obviously came out of it.

My Three Sons — *"Goodbye, Fergus"* (CBS, October 4, 1971)

Director: Earl Bellamy. *Writer*: George Tibbles. *Regular Cast*: Fred MacMurray, William Demarest, Stanley Livingston, Barry Livingston, Tina Cole, Beverly Garland, Dawn Lyn, Ronne Troup. *Guest Cast*: Anne Francis, John McLiam, Alan Caillou (voice of Fergus, uncredited).

Plot: Wedding day for Fergus and Terri.

Notes: Cousin Fergus gets cold feet, feeling now that *he's* not worthy of Terri — ai, yi, yi, those two crazy kids. Just before the wedding, he confesses that he doesn't have a lot of servants and his castle in Scotland is not grand. This scene would have played better if, perhaps, MacMurray were allowed to use his own voice. The dubbing of his voice by Caillou takes the genuine feeling out of this scene.

Columbo — *"Short Fuse"* (NBC, January 19, 1972)

Director: Edward M. Abroms. *Writers:* Lester Pine, Tina Pine (story), Jackson Gillis (teleplay). *Regular Cast*: Peter Falk. *Guest Cast*: Roddy McDowall, Anne Francis, Ida Lupino, James Gregory, William Windom, Steve Gravers, Rosalind Miles, Lew Brown.

Plot: Unstable Roger Stanford (McDowall) kills his uncle David L. Buckner (Gregory) and plants misleading evidence.

Notes: This is a crafty, twisty episode with a standout performance by McDowall as the deceptively child-like but brilliant young man who devises an ingenious way to kill his uncle. Anne is comparatively underused as Valerie Bishop, the executive secretary Roger uses romantically as a pawn in his murder scheme. This was Anne's first of two episodes of *Columbo*, a series that did not tap into her potential; both of her roles on the show were minor.

Password All-Stars — *"Anne Francis vs. Arte Johnson"* (ABC, February 28, 1972)

Host: Allen Ludden. *Guests:* Anne Francis, Arte Johnson.

Ironside — *"A Man Named Arno"* (NBC, March 9, 1972)

Director: Chris Christenberry. *Writer*: Helen McAvity. *Regular Cast*: Raymond Burr, Don Galloway, Don Mitchell, Elizabeth Baur. *Guest Cast*: Nico Minardos, Anne Francis, Howard Lees, Woodrow Parfrey, Tom Geas, Karen Bouchard.

Plot: Robert Ironside (Burr) is after a major dope pusher. Could this case be related to the disappearance of an old friend?

Notes: Don Weis started this episode as director, but there was a death in his family, so Chris Christenberry stepped in on the second day and finished it.

When a bullet grazed his spine, Robert Ironside, chief of detectives of the San Francisco Police Department, was paralyzed from the waist down and confined to a wheelchair. He becomes a special consultant for the police department, operating his own separate unit. After his star-making hit television show *Perry Mason* (1957–66), Raymond Burr hit the jackpot again with *Ironside* (1967–75).

"Special Guest Star" Anne has another slim role that pays off at the conclusion. She plays elegant Angela Griffin, whose husband Ken (Minardos) is missing. She goes to her old friend Ironside for help. The mystery gets a little involved and very confusing as two cases connect as one. The episode's wrap-up is improbable, but intelligently played by both Burr and Anne.

Wouldn't It Be Great If ... (Syndicated, August 20, 1972)

Notes: Anne discusses her philosophy on success.

Gunsmoke — "Sarah" (CBS, October 16, 1972)

Director: Gunnar Hellstrom. *Writer*: Calvin Clements, Sr. *Regular Cast*: James Arness. *Guest Cast:* Anne Francis, Anthony Caruso, Rex Holman, Jonathan Lippe [Goldsmith], Mike Lane, Alberto Pena, John Orchard, Ronald Manning, Kay E. Kuter, George Keymas, Larry Duran.

Plot: After tracking an outlaw on the trail, Marshal Matt Dillon (Arness) meets old flame Sarah (Anne Francis), who passes him off as her husband.

Notes: Even though the episode is named for Anne's character, it isn't the showcase role it could have been for her. Sarah had known Matt years before, when he was a deputy; now a widow, she makes ends meet by running an middle-of-nowhere saloon where disreputable persons have a drink or two before pushing on.

The story is convoluted; the reasons for Dillon posing as her husband rather lame. Anne gets to emote in two quiet scenes with Arness as their feelings, long buried, come to the surface once more, flickering briefly. Unfortunately, Arness' function in these scenes is to react and he does so in a deadpan fashion. Also, there is just no chemistry between the two.

The map of the past relationship, though, is told on Anne's expressive face and in her voice as she regrets their parting all those years before. Just before riding away at the end, she shrugs, resigned to her fate. "I'll get by. I always have."

Assignment: Vienna — "Queen's Gambit" (ABC, November 9, 1972)

Director: Paul Stanley. *Writer*: D.C. Fontana. *Regular Cast*: Robert Conrad, Charles Cioffi, Anton Diffring. *Guest Cast*: Anne Francis, Robert F. Simon, Arthur Brauss, Péter Vajda, Joby Baker.

Plot: Jake Webster (Conrad) is hired by museum curator Aline Masterson (Anne) to locate the missing Royal Crown of Bosnia.

Notes: The jet-setting *Assignment: Vienna* (1972–73) was shot on location in Vienna. Robert Conrad worked undercover for the government while running Jake's Bar & Grill. This series, along with *The Delphi Bureau* and *Jigsaw*, rotated under the umbrella title *The Men*.

Search — "Countdown to Panic" (NBC, February 7, 1973)

Director: Jerry Jameson. *Writer*: Judy Burns. *Regular Cast*: Hugh O'Brian, Pamela Jones, Tom Hallick, Keith Andes. *Guest Cast*: Howard Duff, Ed Nelson, Anne Francis, Jack Ging, Robert Webber, Fred Downs.

Plot: The team from Probe Division of World Securities searches for a man who has caught a deadly, highly contagious infection on a deep-sea dive.

Notes: The alternate title for this episode was "The Carrier." *Search* was inventive for 1972–73. (Its unique premise was borrowed for the much later *Fortune Hunter*; Anne appeared in that series' pilot.) Agents of a hi-tech international private investigation company carry audio receivers, tiny cameras and telemetry units attached to ties or rings. These gadgets are monitored by fellow agents at headquarters and they supply the field operatives with help and intelligence.

As Beth Parker, the wife of infectious carrier Commander William Parker (Nelson), Anne's part is pathetically underwritten, giving her not much to work with. She's properly sad, loyal and bitter when she thinks her husband's dead, but finally, when he's found alive, she slowly comes to the realization that her hubby is freakin' off his rocker. Her final scene, leaning over a sweaty, delusional, hemorrhaging Nelson, is a good one for both underrated actors.

Columbo — "A Stitch in Crime" (NBC, February 11, 1973)

Director: Hy Averback. *Writer*: Shirl Hendryx. *Regular Cast*: Peter Falk. *Guest Cast*: Leonard Nimoy, Anne Francis, Nita Talbot, Will Geer, Aneta Corsaut, Jared Martin, Victor Millan.

Plot: Dr. Barry Mayfield (Nimoy) is a heart surgeon who devises what he thinks is the perfect surgical murder.

Notes: Anne's role of Nurse Sharon Martin is slight, but she's portrayed as smart enough to figure out the plan right away. Before she can reveal all, however, she is murdered. It's not much of a part. Sharon is a likable character, joking with intended murder victim Dr. Edmund Hidemann (Geer), so her death does come as a surprise.

Barnaby Jones — "Murder in the Doll's House" (CBS, March 25, 1973)

Director: Lawrence Dobkin. *Writer*: Benjamin Masselink. *Regular Cast*: Buddy Ebsen, Lee Meriwether. *Guest Cast*: Anne Francis, Jack Cassidy, Estelle Winwood, Richard Derr, Cathy Lee Crosby, Whit Bissell, Phillip Pine.

Anne helps Robert Conrad search for a stolen royal crown in *Assignment: Vienna*'s "Queen's Gambit."

Plot: Barnaby Jones (Ebsen) is hired by a publisher to find author Harry Doyle (Derr) and the missing last pages of his manuscript.

Notes: Anne plays alcoholic heiress Miriam Woodridge, unhappily married to opportunist Craig (Cassidy), and still haunted by the drowning 25 years before of the love of her life Tom Jordan. At a party hosted by Craig's eccentric great-aunt Anita (Winwood), who lives in a fantasy world where she talks to her dolls, some tense emotions come to the surface between the couple. It's a helluva scene, played softly and sensitively by Anne and Cassidy, and speaks volumes about her character.

> MIRIAM (*taking double Scotch from him*): Did the bar guarantee this to have a bell?
> CRAIG: I don't think anybody can guarantee your bells any more, Mir.
> MIRIAM: I thought maybe the champagne would do it. It isn't really a bell. I don't know what it is. But it does ring ... and then everything is quiet, peaceful, for a little while. You know, I think your Aunt Anita maybe has the right idea. She always seems so happy somehow.
> CRAIG: You call that happy?
> MIRIAM: You know when things went sour? When Tom Jordan drowned.
> CRAIG (*hurt*): Thanks a lot. That's when we got married.
> MIRIAM (*whispering*): Sour. They've never really been sweet since. Have they, darling? (*drains her drink*)

The Wide World of Mystery — *"Night Life"* (ABC, March 28, 1973)

Cast: Anne Francis, Charles Aidman, Joel Fabiani, Tim Matheson, Heather MacRae.

Plot: Paul Ross (Aidman) confronts his faithless wife Midge (Anne) and her lover Tommy (Matheson) at a nightclub.

Notes: These *Wide World of Mystery* episodes were videotaped, aired late at night, and were like feature-length movies. The series was also called *Wide World of Entertainment*.

Insight — *"Happy Birthday, Marvin"* (Syndicated, April 10, 1973)

Director: Hal Cooper. *Writer*: Lan O'Kun. *Cast*: Bob Newhart, Anne Francis, Harold Gould, Clint Howard.

Plot: A man deals with middle age, his self-worth and his belief that his dream of dying on his birthday will come true.

Notes: Bob Newhart's deadpan, seriocomic, slightly hesitant delivery is perfect for this casually paced, thought-provoking gem. His everyman quality as Marvin serves him well as he gets fed up being bullied by his disdainful boss Morris (Gould), who also happens to be his brother-in-law. Anne plays Marvin's wife of sixteen years, Gert, who tries to understand what her husband is going through, and supporting him in the end. Anne plays off both Newhart and pompous Gould equally well, going in two different directions. With Newhart, she is quiet, practical, loving; with the sturdy Gould, she gets down to business, standing her ground, toughly defending her husband, and talking plain to her overwhelmed brother. Again, *Insight* supplied her with a three-dimensional part she could sink her teeth into. For more on *Insight*, see page 192.

35th Annual Las Floristas Headdress Ball (April 22, 1973)

Anne was the color commentator on this April 6 event alongside Bill Burrud.

The Wide World of Mystery — "Chant of Silence"
(ABC, May 9, 1973)

Director: William Graham. *Cast*: Steve Forrest, Anne Francis, Clu Gulager, John McLiam, Rafael Campos.

Plot: A state police officer (Forrest) masquerades as a bishop visiting a New Mexico monastery. He's looking for a fugitive skyjacker who parachuted into the area with $300,000 and is posing as a novice monk.

Notes: "Anne Francis found the odds to her liking when she made 'Chant of Silence,'" reported Bob Martin. "She was the only woman in the cast. 'But now the bad news,' she said. 'The entire show takes place in a monastery.'"

The episode was filmed at a monastery and retreat house in the San Bernardino Mountains. "Several of the monks were hired to join the extras as background atmosphere," continued Martin. "One day, veteran Hollywood extra William Sinclair decided it was time to do what all extras do shortly after noon: check with his agent to see where he would be working the following day.

Charles Aidman (seated) and Anne face off in *The Wide World of Mystery*'s "Night Life" as Joel Fabiani stands by.

Bill, being a nice guy, was willing to check for another extra he had been working with. 'Would you like me to check for you, or do you have a call for tomorrow?' he asked the brown-robed man. 'My friend, I have a call every day for the rest of my life,' replied Brother Robert, one of the real-life monks."

Cannon — "Murder by Proxy" (CBS, October 10, 1973)

Director: Robert Douglas. *Writer*: Robert W. Lenski. *Regular Cast*: William Conrad. *Guest Cast*: Anne Francis, Linden Chiles, Ross Hagen, James Nolan, Nancy Merwan, Charles Seel, Terry Lumley, Jock Gaynor, Nancy McCormick, Marj Dusay.

Plot: Public relations agent Peggy Angel (Anne) is framed for murder and asks her old friend Frank Cannon (Conrad) for help.

Notes: *Cannon* (1971–76) was a popular detective program with an unlikely hero at the fore. William Conrad was not someone you would call a typical action hero — bald, overweight and unable to take part in the usual chases and such. But what he lacked in those areas he made up for in wit and cleverness, and *Cannon* was one of the better cop shows on television.

What's so nice about this episode (which, honestly, doesn't give Anne much to do) is the way she and Conrad work together. They were friends since he directed her in *Brainstorm* (1965); you can see the easy way they interact, the respect they have for each other as performers, the comfortableness they share on camera. At one point he tells her she has a "very sexy voice." She says, confused, "What, Frank?" The good humor they share here is most palpable at the fade as he makes her promise not to argue in public again, since it had gotten her in trouble in

Frank Cannon (William Conrad) talks to Peggy Angel (Anne) about her murder case in *Cannon*'s "Murder by Proxy." The two first worked together when he directed her in the movie *Brainstorm* (1965).

the past. Peggy replies that she will never argue again, period, and, with that, he hands her his bill for PI services rendered. She looks it over and deadpans, "Oh, that's not funny, Frank," as he gurgles with delight. Simple moments like these are gems.

The F.B.I. — "Ransom" (ABC, December 30, 1973)

Director: Earl Bellamy. *Writer*: Ed Waters. *Regular Cast*: Efrem Zimbalist, Jr. Philip Abbott, Shelly Novack, *Guest Cast*: Zalman King, Jerry Houser, Michael Conrad, Anne Francis, Fred Beir, Jo Ann Harris.

Plot: The daughter, Tish (Harris), of a Durham, North Carolina, couple, the Lamaires, is abducted. The girl, who dislikes her stepmother (Anne), sees a chance to get back at her by telling her kidnappers to increase the ransom. She soon regrets that decision.

Notes: Anne is listed as a "Special Guest Star." Her role consists of being the concerned and loving stepmother who is unjustly despised by her angry stepdaughter.

Banacek — "Horse of a Slightly Different Color" (NBC, January 22, 1974)

Director: Herschel Daugherty. *Writers*: Harold Livingston (story), Jimmy Sangster (teleplay). *Regular Cast*: George Peppard, Ralph Manza, Murray Matheson. *Guest Cast*: Anne Francis, Tim O'Connor, Lane Bradbury, Ramon Bieri, John Crawford, Linden Chiles, Harry Carey, Jr., Pamela Hensley.

Plot: A $5 million horse is switched before a big sale.

Notes: Chauvinistic, "irresistible" Polish-American Thomas Banacek (Peppard) solved crimes for insurance companies, commanding high fees and chauffeured around by his own driver.

The series' sexism is especially evident in this episode, as horse owner Katherine Wells (Anne) is derided for her take-charge attitude, not mincing words, being strong and knowing exactly what she wants. "Maybe you're afraid of me," she tells Banacek. "Men *are* afraid of me. I guess it's because I believe in going after what I want." And she's successful at it, is audacious, but is viewed as unpleasant and not a real woman because she plays a man's game — and does it better. Katherine has to be put in her place not only by Banacek, but by the man who loves her, horse trainer Howard James (O'Connor). The "tough little package," as one character calls her, follows *him* at the end, her strong spirit broken by the now-dominant male. Oh, please. Still, while she's allowed to ride roughshod, Anne is authoritative and feisty.

Star George Peppard is also listed as the second-unit director on this episode.

Ironside — "Class of '40" (NBC, February 7, 1974)

Director: Barry Shear. *Writers:* Richard L. Breen, James T. Surtees (story), Richard L. Breen, James T. Surtees, Norman Jolley (teleplay). *Regular Cast*: Raymond Burr, Don Galloway, Don Mitchell,

"Maybe you're afraid of me," horse owner Katherine Wells tells Banacek (George Peppard). "Men *are* afraid of me. I guess it's because I believe in going after what I want." A scene from *Banacek*'s "Horse of a Slightly Different Color."

Elizabeth Baur. *Guest Cast*: Anne Francis, Jason Evers, Marshall Thompson, William Bryant, Jackie Coogan, Leif Erickson, Fay Spain, Alice Backes, Peter Brocco, William Bryant.

Plot: At Robert Ironside's (Burr) high school class reunion, there's murder in the air and past bitterness is exposed.

Notes: A superb episode showing the sentimental side of cankerous Ironside, as he and Officer Fran Belding (Bauer) go back to his hometown, Summerfield, for the reunion.

> IRONSIDE: It's a funny thing about a hometown: You can go years without ever giving it a thought, but you really never forget. The memories are all there, ready to be dredged up. You just don't realize how deep the roots go until you come back again for a visit.
> FRAN: Thomas Wolfe said, "You can't go home again."
> IRONSIDE: He didn't say it wasn't worth a try.

Coming home again is complicated, however, by two murders. And now someone is out to kill Ironside.

Anne has a marvelous role as Karen Gillis. "You're still the prettiest girl in this school," Ironside affectionately tells her. Karen is unhappily married to Dick (Bryant). "I know what used to keep him late for dinner, even keep him out all night sometimes," she tells Ironside by way of an explanation when her husband is late for the class dinner. "Does that shock you? The perfect couple, meant for each other, marriage made in Heaven. I'm afraid those clichés don't fit any more." When her spouse turns up dead, Karen is numb. "Dead. He's really dead. You know, I can't bring up a tear. Not a one. Is that a terrible thing?" Anne is heartbreaking in these scenes, but even more so later when the man she really loves, Howard Stahle (Evers), is briefly suspected of the murder. Her big, teary-eyed monologue about protecting the one you love, grasping for happiness, finally, after all these years, is played splendidly.

There is a nice nostalgic aura to this episode, helped by the intercepting of black-and-white photographs and sound bytes to evoke the past. A first-rate show all the way.

Kung Fu — "Night of the Owls, Day of the Doves" (ABC, February 14, 1974)

Director: John Llewellyn Moxey. *Writers*: Frank Dandridge, Ed Waters (story), Ed Waters (teleplay). *Regular Cast*: David Carradine, Philip Ahn, Radames Pera. *Guest Cast*: Barry Atwater, Ken Swofford, Anne Francis, Rayford Barnes, Arlene Farber, Juno Dawson, Paul Harper.

Plot: A group of prostitutes want to start a new life with land they have inherited from a now-deceased client, but the local cattlemen's association wants the land as well. A group known as OWL is out to drive the women away.

Notes: The group in this episode, OWL (Order of Wisdom and Law), is similar in method and garb to the Ku Klux Klan. Master Kan (Ahn) tells young Caine (Pera) via flashback, "Beware of judgments of others. In this imperfect world in which we live, perfection is an illusion. And so the standards by which we seek to measure it are also, themselves, illusions. If perfection is measured by age, grace, color of skin, color of hair, physical or mental prowess, then we are all lacking. And it is well to remember that the harshest judgments are reserved for ourselves."

Anne's strong-willed character, Ida Quinlan, is the madam of the whorehouse and leader of the girls. She, like the others, sees the land inherence as a way to a better life. All are ready to fight for their right for happiness and to positively change their lives and surroundings ("It's more than a piece of land; it's a future"). In one violent standoff, as they defend themselves as the OWLs attack their house, a bullet strikes Ida's shoe. "Blasted," she laments casually, "I just bought those shoes." Anne's playing is forceful and sturdy, and her accent and general look is ideal for the period setting. The cinematography by Chuck Arnold is extremely effective, especially during the horrific night attacks.

The cult favorite *Kung Fu* (1972–75) was a philosophical Western about orphan Kwai Chang Caine (Carradine), born in the mid–1800s and raised by Buddhist monks. They teach him spirituality, peace, tranquility, the "oneness of all things"—and kung fu. After killing a member of the Chinese royal family, he goes on the run and ends up in America; he is a loner, looking for his long-lost brother, but stopping to help others when he can.

Celebrity Sweepstakes (Syndicated, June 2, 1974)

Host: Jim McKrell. *Guest Panelists*: Anne is one of six celebrities.

The Tonight Show Starring Johnny Carson (NBC, June 7, 1974)

Host: Johnny Carson. *Guests*: Anne Francis, Buddy Greco, Fritzie.

Dinah (Syndicated, December 3, 1974)

Host: Dinah Shore. *Guests*: Anne Francis, Anne Bancroft, B.B. King, Aaron Williams, Freddie the puppet and psychiatric social worker Annette Baron.

Notes: Anne sings "Baby Child" and talks about adoption.

Archer — *"The Vanished Man"* (NBC, March 6, 1975)

Director: Arnold Laven. *Writer*: Harold Livingston. *Regular Cast*: Brian Keith, John P. Ryan. *Guest Cast*: Anne Francis, Don Porter, Jean Rasey, Clifford David, Walter Scott, Victoria Young, Karen Carlson.

Plot: Hit-and-run driver Angela Lawrence (Anne) returns to the scene of the accident and realizes that the body of the man she hit has disappeared. Her husband Robert (Porter) hires Lew Archer (Keith) to solve the mystery.

Notes: Filmed at Marino del Rey and Malibu. *Archer* was based on the Ross Macdonald detective novels about gruff Lew Archer, a former cop. The program only lasted three months in 1975.

Movin' On — *"The Price of Loving"* (NBC, April 2, 1975)

Regular Cast: Claude Akins, Frank Converse, Roosevelt Grier, Art Metrano. *Guest Cast*: Anne Francis, John Schuck, Frank Campanella, Kelly Jean Peters, Christopher Crew, Sean Maley, Chris Valentine, Jay Robertson.

Plot: A trucker (Schuck) has two wives, Betsy (Peters) in San Francisco and Abby (Anne) in Reno. One has four kids, the other is pregnant.

Notes: Running from 1974 to 1976, this program about gypsy truck drivers Sonny Pruitt (Akins) and Will Chandler (Converse) filmed on different locations around the United States every week.

Ellery Queen — "The Adventure of the Lover's Leap" (NBC, September 18, 1975)

Director: Charles S. Dubin. *Writer*: Robert Pirosh. *Regular Cast*: Jim Hutton, David Wayne, John Hillerman. *Guest Cast*: Don Ameche, Anne Francis, Jack Kelly, Ida Lupino, Craig Stevens, Susan Strasberg, Jason Wingreen, James Lydon.

Plot: Ellery Queen (Hutton) and his father, Inspector Richard Queen (Wayne), try to determine if an heiress' fall from her balcony was murder or suicide.

Notes: An engaging, albeit short-lived (1975–76), mystery series, set in the late '40s, *Ellery Queen* was blessed with an ideal father-and-son duo in Jim Hutton and David Wayne, veteran guest stars, and clever, fun teleplays. This one is no exception, an airy whodunit with the proper twists, turns and basic ingredients, all mixed together agreeably.

Regrettably, Anne is the one cast member who gets shut out. Even though one character says, rather prophetically, "There's something about that woman ...," there just isn't anything about Nurse Evelyn Chandler. She's murder victim Stephanie Talbott Kendrick's (Lupino) prim, soft-spoken live-in nurse, that's all. The

Gypsy truck driver Sonny Pruitt (Claude Akins) has to break the news to Abby (Anne) that her trucker husband is a bigamist in *Movin' On*'s "The Price of Loving."

biggest "shock" intended for her character is when Ellery sees her away from the mansion all glammed-up and purdy. Oh, my goodness gracious ... *not*. Oh, well, at least Anne has a good chuckle listening to Abbott & Costello on the radio at the beginning of the episode.

Barnaby Jones — "Theater of Fear" (CBS, September 26, 1975)

Director: Walter Grauman. *Writer*: Robert W. Lenski. *Regular Cast*: Buddy Ebsen, Lee Meriwether, John Carter. *Guest Cast*: Anne Francis, William Smithers, Daniel J. Travanti, Mary Ann Chinn, John S. Ragin, Dorothy Scott, Dawn Lyn, Royce Wallace.

Plot: A former stage star tries to make a comeback, but is terrorized by an unknown person.

Hoofin' it up: Buddy Ebsen and Anne take time out for an impromptu dance on the set of *Barnaby Jones'* "Theater of Fear."

Notes: The episode was titled "Dark Legend" before it was filmed. The role of actress Shirley Evans, trying to make a comeback in the theater, is one that few actresses could resist playing. It's a part requiring absolute hysterics, a real rollercoaster of emotions. Someone is terrorizing Shirley, by calling her up late at night and breaking into her house.

This episode has to be seen to be believed. Amid ringing phones, the wind cascading through billowing curtains, noises in every dark corner, Shirley Evans runs aimlessly around her house, screaming and hyperventilating, ending up crouching, shaking in the closet. It's quite a performance, just for the sheer stamina Anne displays. Her final confrontation with Barnaby Jones (Ebsen), mixing tears, laughter, anger and a little girl's innocence, is brilliant. "You don't know what it's like out there every night. All those faces, studying me, staring at me. *Those stupid faces eating at me.* I'm never gonna do that again. Never! Never!" Whew.

Petrocelli — *"Terror by the Book"* (NBC, December 10, 1975)

Director: Irving J. Moore. *Writer*: Jeff Myrow. *Regular Cast*: Barry Newman, Susan Howard, Albert Salmi. *Guest Cast*: Anne Francis, Dick Butkus, Dewey Martin, Bing Russell, Ned Wilson, S. John Launer, Marj Dusay, Michael Bell.

Plot: A best-selling author is killed.

Notes: *Petrocelli* (1974–76), a legal drama about lawyer Tony Petrocelli (Newman) and his wife Maggie (Howard), was spun-off from the character Newman played in the feature film *The Lawyer* (1970). *Petrocelli* was an okay mystery series, far too cutesy with the husband-and-wife exchanges, but it did employ novel flashbacks wherein we see, as they are accused, innocent witnesses committing the murders. Unfortunately, "Terror by the Book" featured one of the most overused murder motives: an author getting killed because he wrote a book revealing all about the people he knows, usually hometown friends. Anne, as Emily Burke, is the prime suspect here (and as such doesn't have much to do); now a respectable mother, she was once the "high-school swinger."

S. W.A. T. — *"Silent Night, Deadly Night"* (ABC, December 13, 1975)

Director: Bruce Bilson. *Writer*: Herb Bermann. *Regular Cast*: Steve Forrest, Robert Urich, Rod Perry, Mark Shera, James Coleman. *Guest Cast*: Rose Marie, Anne Francis, Michael Callan, Elizabeth Baur, Frank Campanella, Richard Forbes, Jodean Russo [Lawrence], Alan Oppenheimer, Morgan Jones.

Plot: In the hospital for cosmetic surgery over the Christmas holiday, lonely and jaded millionairess Doris Wainwright Bristol (Anne) is in danger after a thief kills her bodyguard in an attempt to steal her expensive jewelry.

Notes: Anne plays a vain woman again, all preoccupied in her own little world, selfish, but soon learning to reach out and care.

HILDA (*looking at Doris' jewelry*): Wow, that's a lot of ice!
DORIS: Yes, yes, I'm, I'm very attached to it. It was a second anniversary present from my third husband. Or was it a third anniversary present from my second husband?
HILDA: Well, it's the thought that counts.

S. W.A. T. (1975–76), which stood for Special Weapons and Tactics, was about a squad who aided the regular police on assignments requiring military action and weaponry.

Mobile One — *"The Listening Ear"* (ABC, December 22, 1975)

Director: George Sherman. *Regular Cast*: Jackie Cooper, Julie Gregg, Mark Wheeler. *Guest Cast*: Anne Francis, Warren Stevens, Whitney Blake, Vito Scotti, Roger Perry, Raynold Gideon, Stuart Nisbet, Joseph Ruskin.

Plot: A mentally disturbed woman calls the TV station and admits to killing her husband. She is threatening to kill again.

Notes: A crime show that ran for four months, *Mobile One* shot around Los Angeles and starred Jackie Cooper as Peter Campbell, a reporter for TV station KONE.

Bert D'Angelo/Superstar — "Scag" (ABC, June 26, 1976)

Director: Virgil W. Vogel. *Writer*: Stephen Kandel. *Regular Cast*: Paul Sorvino, Robert Pine, Dennis Patrick, Allison Giannini. *Guest Cast*: Anne Francis, George Maharis, Van Williams, Paul Kent, George Murdock, Barney Phillips, George Skaff, Susan Sullivan.

Plot: A criminal's bail is arranged by a shady bail bondsman in exchange for the man's million-dollar stash of heroin.

Notes: A New York City cop transferring to San Francisco was the premise for this Quinn Martin–produced cop show, which only lasted seven months.

Wonder Woman — "Beauty on Parade" (ABC, October 13, 1976)

Director: Richard Kinon. *Writer*: Ron Friedman. *Regular Cast*: Lynda Carter, Lyle Waggoner, Richard Eastham, Beatrice Colen. *Guest Cast*: Anne Francis, Dick Van Patten, Bobby Van, William Lanteau, Jennifer Shaw, Lindsay Bloom, Christa Helm, Paulette Breen, Linda Carpenter.

Plot: Diana Prince (Carter) goes undercover at the "Miss GI Dream Girl of 1942" beauty pageant. While investigating the sabotage of radar equipment, she uncovers an assassination attempt.

Notes: Playing the head of the pageant, Anne is all sass, wisecracks and elegance. Her wardrobe alone is carried off with style, particularly the outrageous satin negligee and yellow feathered boa number. In reality, it isn't much of a part, but the line readings of even plain dialogue are fun for Anne watchers. Her best: Breaking up a catfight, a pink turban-wearing Anne reasons, "Look, nobody is going to be Miss Dream Girl with a black eye and a fat lip."

Police Woman — "Broken Angels" (NBC, November 9, 1976)

Director: Corey Allen. *Writer*: Kenneth Peters. *Regular Cast*: Angie Dickinson, Earl Holliman, Charles Dierkop, Ed Bernard. *Guest Cast*: Anne Francis, Robert Walden, Frank Aletter, Chuck McCann, Pat Cranshaw, Tom McDonald, Dale Robinette.

Notes: Anne plays Sergeant Loretta Muldare, an old friend and fellow officer of Pepper's (Dickinson). Loretta is tormented by her job in the child abuse unit, and develops a drinking problem because of the horrors she encounters every day on the job. Anne's inherent likeability serves her well here, especially in the scene where Pepper first sees her drunk at a bar. Before this, Loretta has been cautious, no-nonsense, keeping her problem a relative secret. She has spilled a drink on herself and as she looks up at Pepper, eyes squinted, shy smile on her face, you just feel this poor woman's anguish. It's an amazing performance, one that clearly deserved some type of nomination.

Baa Baa Black Sheep — "The Deadliest Enemy of All: Part 1" (NBC, January 11, 1977)

Director: Barry Shear. *Writer*: Philip DeGuere. *Regular Cast*: Robert Conrad, Simon Oakland, Dana Elcar, James Whitmore, Jr., Dirk Blocker. *Guest Cast*: Anne Francis, Linda Scruggs Bogart, Jason Corbett, Nancy Conrad.

Plot: Major Greg "Pappy" Boyington (Conrad) falls for the nurse, Caroline Holden (Bogart), treating him for burns on his hands.

Notes: This World War II series (1976–78) told of the adventures of Boyington's group of misfit flyers, Squadron 214, in the South Pacific. The show was based initially on Boyington's same-titled book. The famous flyer was also a technical adviser on the series. In late 1977, the series name was changed to *Black Sheep Squadron*.

Unfortunately, Anne does not have the main role here as the nurse who falls in love with Pappy. That "honor" goes to an actress with the unlikely name of Linda Scruggs Bogart, and she's as bad as her name. Instead, Anne plays head nurse Lt. Comdr. Gladys Hope, who initially is interested in Pappy but is ignored by him in favor of the harder-to-get Holden. It isn't much of a role, but Anne plays it efficiently with the proper leadership qualities.

Baa Baa Black Sheep — "The Deadliest Enemy of All: Part 2" (NBC, January 18, 1977)

Police Woman's "Broken Angels" features one of Anne's most vivid performances as Sergeant Loretta Muldare who, tormented by her job in the child abuse unit, develops a drinking problem.

Director: Barry Shear. *Writer*: Philip DeGuere. *Regular Cast*: Robert Conrad, Simon Oakland, Dana Elcar, James Whitmore, Jr., Dirk Blocker. *Guest Cast*: Anne Francis, Linda Scruggs Bogart, Jason Corbett, Nancy Conrad.

Plot: Pappy (Conrad) and Nurse Holden (Bogart) see their relationship progress, but she soon learns that her husband, thought to have been killed in action, has been found and is coming home.

Notes: The real-life "Pappy," Major Gregory Boyington, has a cameo. This episode is a little better for Anne as head nurse Lt. Comdr. Gladys Hope because she has an excellent scene with Nurse Holden, giving her heart-to-heart advice on her relationship with Pappy. But, honestly, why *anyone* thought this overwrought story arc required two parts is beyond comprehension.

Police Woman — "Murder with Pretty People" (NBC, February 22, 1977)

Director: John Newland. *Writer*: Max Hodge. *Regular Cast*: Angie Dickinson, Earl Holliman, Charles Dierkop, Ed Bernard. *Guest Cast*: Dennis Cole, Anne Francis, Liam Sullivan, Julie Adams, Allan Carr, John Crawford, Henry Olek, Geoff Edwards, Morgan Fairchild, Kirsten Baker.

Plot: Pepper (Dickinson) goes undercover as a model to solve the murder of ruthless model agency owner Liz Adams (Anne).

Notes: Although Anne is featured only in the first seven minutes of this episode and then summarily dismissed with a bullet, she really makes her presence felt. Dropping her already deep voice down an octave, she is all hardness, insults and bitchiness, making it easy to believe that *everyone* wants this shrew dead. Complaining about a model who defected to another agency, Liz is furious: "I hope her face breaks out in terminal acne, the little ungrateful snitch." Then, thinking it over with a wicked smile on her face: "On second thought, make that not too bad a case of acne. She'll be back, begging me to sign her again.... When she does come back, I think I'll ignore her for a few days. And then, very reluctantly, I'll agree to handle her again. But only ... only if she loses ten pounds. Let her suffer; let her *not* eat cake."

Also worth noting is the performance by Julie Adams as a model friend of Liz's who comes to the funeral. Adams gives her role an intense, devastating edginess that is striking.

Hawaii Five-O — "*When Does a War End?*"
(CBS, March 16, 1977)

Director: Ernest Pintoff. *Writer*: Arthur Bernard Lewis. *Regular Cast*: Jack Lord, James MacArthur, Kam Fong. *Guest Cast*: Bennett Ohta, David Dukes, Anne Francis, Donna Benz, Tom Fujiwara, Joshua Boyd, Bill Valentine, Claudia Lowndes, Lydia Jade, Barbara Kelly.

Plot: Yuhio Muromoto (Ohta), a Japanese businessman with a secret past, is targeted by Willie (Dukes).

Notes: "I had a wonderful experience. I liked Jack [Lord]," Anne said in 2005. "The fun part ... was sitting on the side of the road with a Japanese-Hawaiian driver and talking philosophy. We had a marvelous time."

"Special Guest Star" Anne has a rather conventional role as Alicia Wade, Muromoto's secretary. But, befitting her billing, the smallness of her part is rewarded at the conclusion. The acting in this one ranges from embarrassing (Benz as the businessman's daughter is just plain awful) to okay (Dukes' performance is uneven) to excellent (Ohta). Anne only really gets to shine at the conclusion, as the hate she has suppressed for years is allowed to reach its full potential. A lot of good it does her.

The Eddie Capra Mysteries — "*How Do I Kill Thee?*"
(NBC, September 29, 1977)

Director: Sigmund Neufeld, Jr. *Writer*: Robert Swanson. *Regular Cast*: Vincent Baggetta, Wendy Phillips. *Guest Cast*: Anne Francis, Edie Adams, Mark Stevens, Robert Loggia, Bruce Kirby, Christopher Stone, Vic Tayback.

Plot: A merciless Hollywood television correspondent (Adams) is killed.

Notes: Anne plays the murder victim's sister who is in love with her sis' ex (Loggia) and stands to inherit all her money. There's not much here for Anne to do, unfortunately.

Flying High — "*Fear of Cheesecake*" (CBS, September 29, 1977)

Director: Peter H. Hunt. *Writer*: Juliet Law Packer. *Regular Cast*: Connie Sellecca, Pat Klous, Kathryn Witt, Howard Platt. *Guest Cast*: Bill Daily, Anne Francis, Eileen Heckart, John Hillerman, Sam Jaffe, Jerry Mathers.

Plot: During a flight, the crew is exposed to food poisoning.

Kathryn Witt, Anne, Pat Klous, Eileen Heckart and Connie Sellecca in *Flying High*'s "Fear of Cheese-cake."

Notes: The series' main characters were Sunwest Airlines stewardesses Marcy (Klous), Lisa (Sellecca) and Pam (Witt).

Vega$— *"Mother Mishkin"* (ABC, October 11, 1977)

Director: Bernard McEveety. *Writer*: Ron Friedman. *Regular Cast*: Robert Urich, Bart Braverman, Phyllis Davis, Judy Landers, Naomi Stevens, Tony Curtis. *Guest Cast*: Molly Picon, Anne Francis, John Durren, Rex Holman, Joe Kapp, Sid Caesar, Ross Martin.

Plot: A former madam (Picon) starts receiving death threats.

Notes: Making something out of nothing is a mark of a true professional. Anne had her share of movie and television roles that were underdeveloped in character or screen time. In a less capable actress' hands, these roles would have fallen flat, lost in the shuffle because of their sheer banality. Anne was, more often than not, able in these instances to add a little something extra to her roles, making them come alive at unexpected moments, no matter the length or shortcomings of the part.

This breezy *Vega$* episode is a prime example. Her character, ex-prostitute Lillian Ross (I kid you not), is just *there* from time to time, not doing much of anything, an overly cheery (so you know *something* is up) friend of marked-for-death madam Mother Mishkin (an irritating and unlikely Picon). Anne does one almost unnoticeable thing early on when Mother reassures detective Dan Tanna (Urich) that Lillian is a happy person. You can *just* see Anne's eyes cloud over; it's brief, but effective, a very nice touch. The best, however, comes in her last scene: Sitting with an unsuspecting Mother, the cheerful Lillian changes before our eyes, her voice dropping ominously, eyes gazing unseeing, scarily, straight ahead at nothing, as she confronts Mother. It's quite a conclusion to her character, but what comes before, alas, does not support the quiet desperation Anne gives here, in her big scene. A damn shame.

Fantasy Island — *"Queen of the Boston Bruisers"* (ABC, October 28, 1977)

Director: Earl Bellamy. *Writers*: John Kind, Frank Dandridge (story), Steve Fisher, Skip Webster (teleplay). *Regular Cast*: Ricardo Montalban, Hervé Villechaize. *Guest Cast*: Anne Francis, Christopher Norris, Mary Jo Catlett, Don DeFore, Joanna Barnes, Jonathan Frakes, Larry Huffman, Sweet Dick Whittington.

Plot: Roller derby queen Drusilla "Rowdy" Roberts (Anne) wants to become a lady for the sake of her daughter Shirley (Norris), who is marrying into society.

Notes: One of the most unusual roles Anne Francis has ever attempted; that she succeeded so admirably is proof of her versatility and overall game attitude toward her craft. Mr. Roarke (Montalban) and Tattoo (Villechaize) discuss the reason she is on the island:

> TATTOO: I know what her fantasy is.
> ROARKE: What?
> TATTOO: She wants to beat up Hooligan Hanreddy without the referee stopping her.
> ROARKE: Hooligan Hanreddy?
> TATTOO: Yeah, she's Rowdy's worst enemy. She's a terrible woman. She skates for the Cleveland Commandos.
> ROARKE: I see. Well, I'm happy to say that Rowdy wants something very different. Her fantasy for the weekend is to be a lady, Tattoo.

The unlikely teacher of these lady-like manners is Tattoo himself. "I got all the grace of a drunken giraffe," she apologizes to Tattoo when she steps on his toes as he's teaching her to dance. It might be a cheap laugh, but the sight of 5'8" Anne and the 3'10" Villechaize works its comedy spell.

The scene showing Rowdy and her much-hated archenemy, Hooligan Hanreddy (a priceless Mary Jo Catlett), talking trash to each other after a roller derby match is hilarious stuff. Both actresses look like they're having a ball playing these outrageous characters and their enjoyment is infectious. Likewise the scene where Hanreddy crashes the daughter's wedding and she and Rowdy go at it in front of the guests.

This is quite an episode.

Charlie's Angels — *"Pom Pom Angels"* (ABC, November 1, 1977)

Director: Cliff Bole. *Writer*: Richard Carr. *Regular Cast*: Kate Jackson, Jaclyn Smith, Cheryl Ladd, David Doyle, John Forsythe. *Guest Cast*: Anne Francis, Lonny Chapman, Stephanie Blackmore, Rick Casorla, Ben Davidson, Fran Ryan, Sandy Ward, Cis Rundle.

Plot: The Angels go undercover as cheerleaders to break up a band of religious fanatics headed by Eddie Cobb (Chapman), who is known as "The Good One," and his right-hand gal Margo (Anne).

Notes: A brief, but marvelously effective villainous role for Anne. "Tonight's ceremony is the mark of your redemption," Margo intones. "As I've told you, The Good One found me and delivered my way out of prostitution. I, too, was served by bread, and wore sack cloths for days on end; it was when my bleach blonde hair was shorn. I accept The Good One." A good episode, with some fun lines:

EDDIE COBB: Silence! ... You will bow your head.

KRIS MUNROE [*angrily*]: I'm not gonna bow my head to you ... or anyone else in this grease pit!

Greatest Heroes of the Bible — "Moses: Part 1" (NBC, November 20, 1977)

Director: James L. Conway. *Writer*: Stephen Lord. *Cast*: Julie Adams, Robert Alda, Lloyd Bochner, Joseph Campanella, Anne Francis, Frank Gorshin, John Marley, Peter Mark Richman.

Plot: God instructs Moses to lead the Israelites out of Egypt.

Notes: In this short-lived series recreating significant events in the Bible, Anne plays Zipporah, the wife of Moses (Marley). Contrary to sources, Anne is not in the next episode, "Moses: Part 2," although her name does appear in its credits.

What Really Happened to the Class of '65? — "The Girl Who Always Said No" (NBC, January 19, 1978)

Director: Seymour Robbie. *Writer*: Robert Blees. *Regular Cast*: Tony Bill, Jack Ging. *Guest Cast*: Anne Francis, Cliff De Young, Linda Purl.

Plot: A senior class beauty, pushed by her mother to marry a wealthy man, instead becomes interested in a forest ranger.

Notes: The original title for this episode was "The Class Beauty."

Quincy M.E. — "Physician, Heal Thyself" (NBC, February 22, 1979)

Director: Corey Allen. *Writers*: Aubrey Solomon, Steve Greenberg. *Regular Cast*: Jack Klugman, Garry Walberg, John S. Ragin, Val Bisoglio, Robert Ito, Joseph Roman. *Guest Cast*: John Dehner, June Lockhart, Milt Kogan, Asher Brauner, Joby Baker, Don Reid, Anne Francis, Lisa Blake Richards, Paul Sorensen, Tara Buckman, Philip Pine, Virginia Vincent, Karen Philipp, James Rosin.

Plot: Quincy (Klugman), medical examiner for the Los Angeles County Coroner's Office, faces a cover-up as he confronts Dr. Ronald Shafer (Dehner) who he believes was drunk when he performed a faulty abortion on a teenager.

Notes: Anne has only two scenes as Elizabeth, the concerned wife of the troubled doctor. In her best scene, sparring with Quincy through a chain-link fence, she refuses to admit that her husband has a drinking problem or that it is interfering with his work. Another notably strong performance is supplied by June Lockhart as Dr. Blair, chief of surgery at Shafer's clinic.

O'Malley (pilot) (NBC, 1980)

Director: Michael O'Herlihy. *Writer*: George Schenck. *Cast*: Mickey Rooney, Anne Francis, Peter Coffield, Tony Devon, Thomas G. Waites, Richard Clarke, Sarah Abrell, Jeffrey DeMunn, Paula

Trueman, Mark Linn–Baker, Robin Mary Paris, Martin Rosenblatt, Bernie McInerney, James Dukas, Cherry Jones.

Notes: How could this miss? The likeably gruff Rooney plays an ex–New York City cop-turned-detective. Tooling around in a 1959 Cadillac, he uses his street smarts to solve his cases. Anne plays his ex-wife in just one scene.

Fantasy Island — *"The Swinger"* (ABC, February 9, 1980)

Director: Cliff Bole. *Writer*: Worley Thorne. *Regular Cast*: Ricardo Montalban, Hervé Villechaize. *Guest Cast*: Anne Francis, Howard Morris, Jack Carter, Judy Landers.

Plot: A recently separated man wants his swinging youth back, but gets jealous when he meets up with his wife, who also seems to be enjoying her newly acquired freedom.

Notes: Anne looks chic (in some disco-era fashions) as Maxine Dodge, wife of Herman (Morris) who is having a mid-life crisis. Seeing him with a younger gal, she wryly retorts, "By the way, are you dating or adopting?" Anne works well with Morris, cramping his style when she shows up unexpectedly during his fantasy.

> HERMAN: Maxine, are you trying to ruin my fantasy?
> MAXINE: Herm, I spent too many years as your wife worrying about your fantasies to worry about them now.

As Herman keeps trying to prove that he's not too old to play the field, a bemused but caring Maxine patiently bides her time as he finally wises up. It's a sweet, slight story, played nicely by the two.

The Littlest Hobo — *"Romiet and Julio"* (CTV, March 20, 1980)

Director: Simon Christopher Dew. Writer: William J. Keenan. *Regular Cast*: London. *Guest Cast*: Leslie Nielsen, Anne Francis, Liz Ramos, Gordon Thomson, Jim Locksley, Jack Creley, Allan Aarons, John Swindells, Tony Moffat-Lynch, Leo Leyden, Barry Baldaro.

Plot: London the dog helps two young people find love and happiness despite their battling parents.

Charlie's Angels — *"Angels of the Deep"* (ABC, December 7, 1980)

Director: Kim Manners. *Writer*: Robert George. *Regular Cast*: Jaclyn Smith, Cheryl Ladd, Tanya Roberts, David Doyle, John Forsythe. *Guest Cast*: Patti D'Arbanville, Antonio Fargas, Gary Lockwood, Sonny Bono, Moe Keale, Bradford Dillman, Anne Francis, Soon-Tek Oh.

Plot: Everyone is after a sunken ship's cargo of "dynamite Maui grass."

Notes: Anne has a good role as Cindy Lee, a no-nonsense buyer for a major drug operation. She and "her people are a major source of marijuana coming into the West Coast."

When two aging, halfwit hippies, Claude (Lockwood) and Marvin (Bono), get the marijuana shipment intended for shady restaurant owner Tony Kramer (Dillman), the two go to Cindy for a buy. The first time we see Cindy is from behind. The two chuckleheads approach, then, upon seeing her face to face, they pause and skeptically look at each other.

> CINDY (*seriously*): What's wrong?
> CLAUDE: Oh, it's nothing. It's just you're not what we thought you'd be. You're different.
> CINDY (*deadpans*): Well, you're not exactly what I expected either. Where's the sample? I haven't got all day.

Anne gives her character a strong authority, able to take on the big boys, a sardonic touch. When Tony tries to outsmart her, she doesn't back down.

TONY: Boy, are you a cold one.
CINDY: My grandchildren don't think so.

Trapper John, M.D. — *"Slim Chance"* (CBS, December 7, 1980)

Director: Seymour Robbie. *Writers:* Judy Merl, Paul Eric Myers. *Regular Cast*: Pernell Roberts, Gregory Harrison, Madge Sinclair, Charles Siebert, Christopher Norris, Brian [Stokes] Mitchell. *Guest Cast*: Pamela Franklin, Steve Franken, John McCook, Tim O'Connor, Anne Francis, Jacque Lynn Colton.

Plot: Is a diet guru ruining a young woman's health?

Notes: Dr. John McIntyre (Roberts), chief of surgery at San Francisco Memorial Hospital, and Dr. George "Gonzo" Gates (Harrison) pose some ethical questions to Dr. Edain (O'Connor), whose diet methods are more than unconventional — they're deadly. His wife Gail (Anne), using alcohol to cope with her guilt feelings, has a strained relationship with him. In a good scene, she confesses that she misses the days of his respectability. "You know, it's just my luck. I married a doctor who keeps people thin. Not sober," she sighs. Unfortunately, Anne's character is relegated to the sidelines by the episode's writers, so the couple's marital issues are not given a proper resolution. The doctor regains his principles, but his wife is nowhere around.

Dallas (CBS)

• *"End of the Road: Part 1"* (January 16, 1981)

Director: Irving J. Moore. *Writer*: Leonard Katzman. *Cast*: Barbara Bel Geddes, Jim Davis, Patrick Duffy, Linda Gray, Larry Hagman, Steve Kanaly, Ken Kercheval, Victoria Principal, Charlene Tilton, Susan Howard, Leigh McCloskey, Joel Fabiani, Audrey Landers, Barbara Babcock, Morgan Woodward, Harry Carey, Jr., Anne Francis, William Smithers.

• *"End of the Road: Part 2"* (January 23, 1981)

Director: Irving J. Moore. *Writer*: Leonard Katzman. *Cast*: Barbara Bel Geddes, Jim Davis, Patrick Duffy, Linda Gray, Larry Hagman, Steve Kanaly, Ken Kercheval, Victoria Principal, Charlene Tilton, Susan Howard, Leigh McCloskey, Joel Fabiani, Audrey Landers, Barbara Babcock, Anne Francis, William Smithers, Monte Markham, Ted Shackelford, Joan Van Ark, Robert Rockwell, Richard Derr.

• *"Making of a President"* (January 30, 1981)

Director: Gunnar Hellstrom. *Writer*: Arthur Bernard Lewis. *Cast*: Barbara Bel Geddes, Jim Davis, Patrick Duffy, Linda Gray, Larry Hagman, Steve Kanaly, Ken Kercheval, Victoria Principal, Charlene Tilton, Susan Howard, Leigh McCloskey, Joel Fabiani, Audrey Landers, Morgan Woodward, Anne Francis, William Smithers, Susan Flannery, Noble Willingham, Monte Markham, Don Starr, Meg Gallagher, Paul Sorensen, Jeff Cooper.

• *"The Quest"* (February 13, 1981)

Director: Gunnar Hellstrom. *Writer*: Robert J. Shaw. *Cast*: Barbara Bel Geddes, Jim Davis, Patrick Duffy, Linda Gray, Larry Hagman, Steve Kanaly, Ken Kercheval, Victoria Principal, Charlene Tilton, Susan Howard, Leigh McCloskey, Joel Fabiani, Audrey Landers, Morgan Woodward, Anne Francis, William Smithers, Susan Flannery, Monte Markham, Don Starr, Meg Gallagher.

Notes: The less said about Anne's four-episode stint on the popular nighttime soap opera *Dallas* (1978–91), the better. She plays Arliss Cooper, the down-to-earth mother of Mitch Cooper (McCloskey), a pre-med student who marries Lucy Ewing (Tilton). Arliss and her other daughter, the devious Afton Cooper (Landers), have come for the wedding in these episodes. Anne is barely given anything to do; she simply stands there. It's an insult to her talents. The character of Mitch Cooper stayed on the series until 1982, but these are Anne's only episodes.

Fantasy Island — "Ole Island Oprey" (ABC, May 16, 1981)

Director: George W. Brooks. *Writer*: Valerie Allen. *Regular Cast*: Ricardo Montalban, Hervé Villechaize. *Guest Cast*: Jimmy Dean, Wendy Schaal, Anne Francis.

Plot: Charlie Rowlands (Dean) wants his daughter Jennie (Schaal) to get a chance to sing at the Oprey ... but does *she*?

Notes: This is one of those episodes that make you just shake your head in disbelief. The idea of wasting a talent, not to mention the name value, of someone like Anne Francis in the small role of bar owner Lottie McFadden is just wrong. She is merely there to pine a little for Charlie, sport a nice Texas accent, and exude some fun-loving energy. This she does ... but it gives her very little to do. Anne has one humorous moment, scarcely perceptible during a big bar brawl. While Charlie is whupping some ass, Lottie is safely out of the action, perched on the bar, eating popcorn and enjoying the show. "Attaboy, Charlie," she laughs. It's brief, but at least it's something.

CHiPs — "In the Best of Families" (NBC, February 21, 1982)

Director: John Florea. *Writer*: Rick Mittleman. *Regular Cast*: Erik Estrada, Larry Wilcox, Robert Pine, Paul Linke. *Guest Cast*: Anne Francis, Michael Morgan, Timothy Patrick Murphy, Lori Sutton, K.C. Winkler.

Plot: A woman plans an armored car robbery with her two sons.

Notes: Who would have guessed that Anne's performance as Susan Wright on *CHiPs* would be one of the best and funniest of her career? Susan controls her two inept, dim-witted sons, Joey (Morgan) and Alex (Murphy), with the appropriate iron hand. Her hubby has been in jail for three years and is soon to be released; he has been taking the rap for them "out of sheer love," Susan tells her boys, as she masterminds a plan to get some needed cash for his homecoming. The plan is an overly complicated hit (involving bees) on an armored car.

It's a total hoot seeing Anne threatening her boys with a raised hand or slapping one for saying the plan is a bad idea (it *is*), as she varies between true motherly concern and really, *really* tough "love." Anne shows authority, but dashes her role with some lightheartedness. The final car chase with the police is amusing, as Susan and her boys wildly drive out of control. On the soundtrack you can hear Anne screaming in the car, "Dumb, dumb, dumb!" and other frustrated statements directed at her confused sons, ending with the cry, "You're just like your father!"

American Playhouse — "Charley's Aunt" (Showtime, February 6, 1983)

Director: William Asher. *Writers:* Brandon Thomas (play), Ron Friedman (adaptation). *Cast*: Charles Grodin, Victor Garber, Joyce Bulifant, Anne Francis, Efrem Zimbalist Jr., Vincent Gardenia, Ilene Graff, Barrie Ingham, Connie Mason, Mews Small, James Widdoes.

Notes: "Charley's Aunt is an old play," wrote Debra Morgenstern Katz in *Video View*. "The story is old. The jokes are old, the twists and turns are old. So why is it still funny?" The play, written by Brandon Thomas, first opened in London in 1890. It was such a success that it was revived on screen and countless times on stage.

In this production recorded live on stage at the La Mirada Civic Theatre in Southern California in 1982, Charles Grodin manically, comically runs amok masquerading as Donna Lucia D'Alvadorez, Charley's (Widdoes) rich widowed aunt from Brazil ("where the nuts come from"). "And in the middle of all this gadding about," explains Katz, "in walks the real aunt of Charley, who is, as played by Anne Francis, as graceful and elegant as any woman who walked the grounds of Yale in 1908."

Anne gives a welcome wry reading to her lines, as she realizes what's going on, but playfully plays along. By contrast, her scenes with Efrem Zimbalist Jr., as an old beau she still has feelings for, are wistful and moving; the two work very well together.

"*Charley's Aunt* is a light, predictable farce, full of idealized romance, hidden identities and slapstick humor. The breezy, witty dialogue and robust performances by all concerned make tonight's *American Playhouse* presentation a thoroughly entertaining TV experience....

Grodin, a wonderful comic actor, throws himself into the title role with engaging enthusiasm. At 52, the actor ably manages to play a college student with conviction and vigor.... As the real Dona Lucia D'Alvadorez, who discovers in Zimbalist a long-lost love, Anne Francis turns in a delightfully smug effort."— Daniel Ruth, *Chicago Sun–Times*, May 11, 1987.

Simon & Simon — "Shadow of Sam Penny" (CBS, November 3, 1983)

Director: Vincent McEveety. *Writer*: Michael Piller. *Regular Cast*: Gerald McRaney, Jameson Parker. *Guest Cast*: Robert Lansing, Anne Francis, Scott Brady, Joan Leslie, Elisha Cook, Jr., Dane Clark, Philip Bruns, Cal Bartlett, Clete Roberts.

Plot: Private detectives Rick Simon (McRaney) and A.J. Simon (Parker) help famous old-time detective Sam Penny (Lansing) solve a thirty-year-old case.

Notes: This episode was meant to be a pilot for the character of Sam

Simon & Simon's "Shadow of Sam Penny" was meant to serve as a pilot for a potential TV starring Robert Lansing. Anne played old flame Angel Barkley, just out of jail after 30 years.

Penny, but it is easy to see why it didn't sell. While the cast of vintage actors is a welcome sight and they are more than competent, the story is overly complicated.

Anne plays the manipulating Angel Barkley, just out of jail after 30 years. The man who put her there, Sam Penny, was in love with her then and is in love with her now. Angel uses this to get him to help her secure missing diamonds from thirty years before. We don't know much about Angel, but Anne makes her likable, frisky and wholly capable of a double-cross, even to Penny. It would have been interesting to see how her character developed if the show went to series.

Elisha Cook Jr., as Dutch Silver, part of Angel's gang in the old days, has a fun scene. Out of jail, now in a nursing home, he talks tough, pointing his finger at some of the other residents of the home, acting like they're back in the Chicago of yore, telling them to stay away from his side of the home. It's a humorous moment, conjuring up a lot of memories of the parts Cook played in the movies of the '30s and '40s.

Trapper John, M.D. — "Fat Chance" (CBS, December 4, 1983)

Director: Susan Oliver. *Writer*: Barry Pollack. *Regular Cast*: Pernell Roberts, Gregory Harrison, Madge Sinclair, Charles Siebert, Christopher Norris, Brian [Stokes] Mitchell, Robin Ignico, Simon Scott, Michael Tucci. *Guest Cast*: Shirley Hemphill, Anne Francis, Sandy Helberg.

Plot: A delicate operation is made even riskier when the patient (Hemphill) doesn't follow the doctor's orders.

Note: "Special Guest Star" Anne is not part of the main story, but is involved with a mix-up concerning a sick dog. Playing Mrs. Havenhurst, whose husband helped build the hospital, she is a chairperson in a Right to Life organization. When she overhears the doctors talking about an operation, she thinks they will be performing an abortion and she becomes concerned — not realizing the patient is a dog in a life-threatening situation.

The director of this episode was Susan Oliver (1932–90), a very busy actress who dabbled in directing near the end of her career.

Riptide

• "Pilot" (NBC, January 3, 1984)

Director: Christian I. Nyby II. *Writer*: Stephen J. Cannell, Frank Lupo. *Regular Cast*: Perry King, Joe Penny, Thom Bray, Anne Francis, Jack Ging. *Guest Cast*: Karen Kopins, Robert Viharo, Patrick Dollaghan, Marla Heasley, Eugene Butler, Lee Patterson, Frank McCarthy, Ray Girardin, Robin Evans, Ingrid Anderson, Patrika Darlo, Greg Lewis, Dave Adams.

Plot: The boys try to clear a woman suspected of being in cahoots with smugglers.

• "Hatchet Job" (NBC, January 31, 1984)

Director: Ron Satlof. *Writer*: Mark Jones. *Regular Cast*: Perry King, Joe Penny, Thom Bray, Anne Francis, Jack Ging. *Guest Cast*: Maylo McCaslin, Beau Starr, Randi Brooks, Deborah Shelton, Mike Genovese, Tom Pletts, Katherine Kelly Lang.

Plot: Trying to bust the Pier 56 burglar, the boys help a girl mixed up in a cold-case murder.

• "The Mean Green Love Machine" (NBC, February 7, 1984)

Director: Guy Magar. *Writer*: Stephen J. Cannell. *Regular Cast*: Perry King, Joe Penny,

Thom Bray, Anne Francis, Jack Ging. *Guest Cast*: Mary-Margaret Humes, Tamara Stafford, James Luisi, Robert Sampson, Sam Scarber, East Ismael Carlo, Bruce Tuthill.

Plot: A girl's father is missing and she enlists the boys' help in finding him.

- **"Diamonds Are for Never"** (NBC, February 21, 1984)

Director: Gloryette Clark. *Writer*: Babs Greyhosky. *Regular Cast*: Perry King, Joe Penny, Thom Bray, Anne Francis. *Guest Cast*: Kathryn Witt, John Anderson, Pepper Martin, Peter Hobbs, Robin Evans, K.C. Winkler.

Plot: A stewardess is framed and the boys set out to clear her name.

Notes: Anne plays Mama Jo, salty captain of the touring boat the *Contessa* and its all-girl crew. She was seen in the pilot and only three regular episodes after that. In fact, after Anne's major contribution to the pilot, it wasn't until the fourth episode that she made another appearance. (She was always listed in the credits.)

It seems, judging by her participation in her episodes, that the writers were at a loss. She was presented as good-hearted but gruff, resembling Tugboat Annie in looks, speech and manner. She wouldn't let Nick (Penny) and Cody (King) go near her girls, threatening to "pound them to the ground" or with a punch to the face.

In the pilot, Mama Jo is referred to as a "den mother with a baseball bat," but she helped the guys whenever she could. In "Hatchet Job," she bails them out of jail and in "The Mean Green Love Machine" she gives them valuable information about one of their clients. But these appearances were fleeting, not enough for us to get to know her tough Mama Jo all that well. Her last episode, "Diamonds Are for Never," shows her only in the last couple of minutes. Her look is different here; they prettied her up and she was no longer the cranky, weather-beaten captain she played so well.

In the next episode, "The Hardcase," it's revealed that the boat was sold and that Mama Max (Marsha Warfield) was now in charge of the all-girl crew. Unlike Mama Jo, however, she let her girls mingle with Nick and Cody.

See pages 116–118 for more about this series.

The Love Boat — "Santa, Santa, Santa" / "Another Dog Gone Christmas" / "Noel's Christmas Carol" (ABC, December 15, 1984)

Director: Richard Kinon. *Writers*: Lan O'Kun, Mike Marmer, Henry Colman, Ben Joelson, Art Baer. *Regular Cast*: Gavin MacLeod, Fred Grandy, Bernie Kopell, Ted Lange, Pat Klous, Ted McGinley, Jill Whelan. *Guest Cast*: Anne Francis, Ray Walston, Howard Morris, Scatman Crothers, Shea Farrell, Justin Gocke, Avery Schreiber, Michelle Johnson, Kim Lankford.

Partners in Crime — "Getting in Shape" (NBC, December 22, 1984)

Director: Kevin Connor. *Writers*: John Stern (story), Larry Brody (teleplay). *Regular Cast*: Lynda Carter, Loni Anderson, Leo Rossi, Walter Olkewicz. *Guest Cast*: Eileen Heckart, Vincent Baggetta, John Calvin, Anne Francis [as Anne Lloyd Francis], Linden Chiles, Clare Peck.

Plot: Blackmail and murder at a health resort.

Notes: This episode came just before the end of this series' four-month run. *Partners in Crime* had an unusual premise: Two women, both once married to the same man, inherit his detective agency and decide to go into the business themselves. It was light fun, bolstered by the playful humor and chemistry of the two leads. It certainly deserved a better fate. Unfortunately, this particular episode doesn't show Anne off to any advantage, nor does it give her much screen time. She plays a health instructor, full of pep, but that's about all.

Murder, She Wrote — "The Murder of Sherlock Holmes" (pilot) (CBS, December 30, 1984)

Director: Corey Allen. *Writers:* Richard Levinson, William Link, Peter S. Fischer (story), Peter S. Fischer (teleplay). *Cast:* Angela Lansbury, Eddie Barth, Jessica Browne, Bert Convy, Herb Edelman, Anne Francis [as Anne Lloyd Francis], Michael Horton, Tricia O'Neil, Dennis Patrick, Raymond St. Jacques, Ned Beatty, Arthur Hill, Brian Keith, Rosanna Huffman, Richard Erdman.

Plot: Jessica Fletcher (Lansbury), a retired schoolteacher living in Cabot Cove, Maine, has just written her first book. When her nephew (Horton) is accused of a murder at a costume party, Jessica begins her first real-life investigation in hopes of clearing his name.

Notes: This was the two-hour pilot (and premiere) for the long-running mystery-comedy series (1984–96), and also Anne's first of three appearances in varying roles. Anne friskily plays the tipsy and wisecracking Louise McCallum who is unhappily married to tycoon Caleb (Keith). ("Don't tell me I look like hell; I feel worse ... and I'm in no mood for a lecture," she grumbles.) It is Caleb, dressed as Sherlock Holmes at a costume party, who is supposedly murdered. "Half the country had reason to kill him," Louise sardonically snaps. "The other half didn't know him."

Crazy Like a Fox — "Premium for Murder" (CBS, January 13, 1985)

Director: Paul Krasny. *Writer:* Stephen Lord. *Regular Cast:* Jack Warden. John Rubinstein, Penny Peyser. *Guest Cast:* Anne Francis [as Anne Lloyd Francis], Gerry Gibson, Robert Pine, Lydia Lei, Peter Hobbs.

Plot: Sister Laura Jennings (Anne) hires Harry Fox (Warden) to find out why a call girl was named in a priest's will.

Notes: Private eye Harry and lawyer Harrison K. Fox (Rubinstein) were a father-and-son team who solved crimes together on *Crazy Like a Fox* (1984–86), a light-hearted crime show. Here, Anne plays an old flame of Harry's, now a nun. "You were always unpredictable," Harry mutters. Anne clearly is having fun as the unconventional Sister. She and Warden, who received a suspended license in the beginning of the episode, have a cute scene as she wildly drives him around, loving every minute of it as he holds on for dear life.

Hardcastle and McCormick — "The Long Ago Girl" (ABC, February 11, 1985)

Director: Richard A. Colla. *Writer:* Stephen J. Cannell. *Regular Cast:* Brian Keith, Daniel Hugh Kelly. *Guest Cast:* Anne Francis [as Anne Lloyd Francis], Russell Arms, Amy Stock, Mike Tully, Lou Felder, Ed Bernard.

Plot: Hardcastle is reunited with an ex-girlfriend when he investigates the death of her husband.

Notes: Anne is the title, '40s movie star Jane Bigelow, who is the lost love of Judge Milton

Harry's (Jack Warden, left) old girlfriend, now Sister Elizabeth (Anne), enlists the help of Harry and his son Harrison (John Rubinstein, right) in clearing the good name of a priest who died in a plane crash in *Crazy Like a Fox*'s "Premium for Murder."

G. Hardcastle (Keith). In 1943, she had stood him up at the train station, where he was prepared to propose to her before he went off to war. When he hears that her husband has died, he goes to her house. He is shot by an intruder, which leads to his reunion with Jane.

Anne's Emmy-caliber performance was definitely one of the best she has ever given. Her first scene with Keith, as he lies in his hospital bed, is gorgeously played by both, the sensitive handling of the dialogue and the teeming emotion they bring to their reunion very potent. They are superb in their quietness, sentimental without being mawkish, making time stand still for just a moment as they remember the past. (Hardcastle puts on one of Jane Bigelow's "old movies," called here *Possessed* from 1943; it is actually a clip of Anne with John Lupton from *Battle Cry*.)

The actress portraying Anne's character in the flashback scenes is Amy Stock, who got her start as a Spokesmodel Champion on TV's *Star Search* (1984–85). Unfortunately, Stock looks nothing like Anne, especially glaring in view of the movie clip showing her as a young actress.

Finder of Lost Loves — *"Connections"* (ABC, April 13, 1985)

Director: Jeffrey Hayes. *Writer*: Chris Manheim. *Regular Cast*: Anthony Franciosa, Deborah Adair, Anne Jeffreys, Richard Kantor. *Guest Cast*: Robin Strand, Peter Mark Richman, Anne Francis [as Anne Lloyd Francis], Claudia Cron, Larry Flash Jenkins, Ed Kenney, Fredric Lehne, Wendy Schaal.

Plot: A successful man wants to reunite with his estranged foster family and young brother.

Notes: Opening with the sappy Burt Bacharach–Carole Bayer Sager theme song, sung by Dionne Warwick, this dud went downhill fast. Fortunately, *Finder of Lost Loves'* meager audience was ensnared in this syrupy drivel for only 23 episodes, this being the last aired.

Anne has very little to do here as Ruth Cunningham except look worried, sweet and teary-eyed, all of which she does reasonably well under the circumstances. Peter Mark Richman, playing her husband Frank, has a better part as the bitter father unwilling to reconcile with his foster son. Anne manages to display some genuine silent emotion at the end, preventing this from being a total loss.

Murder, She Wrote — "Keep the Home Fries Burning"
(CBS, January 19, 1986)

Director: Peter Crane. *Writer*: Philip Gerson. *Regular Cast*: Angela Lansbury, Tom Bosley, William Windom. *Guest Cast*: Norman Alden, Orson Bean, Gary Crosby, William Lucking, John McCook, Henry Polic II, Alan Young, Anne Francis, Sharon Acker, Rosanna Huffman, Marcia Rodd.

Plot: At the Joshua Peabody Inn, Jessica Fletcher (Lansbury) investigates a murder and the illness of several people who ate strawberry preserves.

Notes: Anne portrays the sarcastic, efficient Margo Perry, a State Health Department inspector called to the small town. ("She reminds me of a drill sergeant I had once," Cabot Cove's Dr. Seth Hazlitt shudders.) Anne and Lansbury play off each other well in a few scenes, as the condescending and mocking Margo underestimates Jessica's perception and skill at detecting. "My job is bad food, not murder," she haughtily informs the sleuth. Big city Margo's reactions to the "primitive" small town are priceless. "Do you accept credit cards here in Peyton Place?" she dismissively asks a cashier at a local diner.

True Confessions — "The Decision" (Syndicated, September 8, 1986)

Host: Bill Bixby. *Guest Cast*: Anne Francis, Jeff Corey, Jon Cypher, Terry Moore.

Plot: A woman must decide if she wants to have a mastectomy.

Notes: *True Confessions*, supposedly based on real-life stories torn from the pages of the famous magazine, was a five-days-a-week, half-hour syndicated TV anthology, which ran from September 1986 to January 1987.

Jake and the Fatman — "Fatal Attraction" (CBS, September 29, 1987)

Director: Ron Satlof. *Writer*: Douglas Stefen Borghi. *Regular Cast*: William Conrad, Joe Penny, Alan Campbell. *Guest Cast*: Anne Francis, Karen Austin, Kim Ulrich, James Karen, Eugene I. Peterson, Allan Rich, Rebecca Bush, Bruce Greenwood, James Avery.

Plot: When an old friend (Peterson) of District Attorney Jason McCabe (Conrad) is murdered, he and his partner, special investigator Jake Styles (Penny), suspect the widow (Austin) and her younger stepson (Greenwood).

Notes: This was the pilot for the popular and very entertaining legal-detective series which ran from 1987 to 1992. Conrad plays an unconventional ("Listen, creep, I'm gonna take you apart like a clock!"), take-no-prisoners-in-the-courtroom D.A., and Joe Penny is affable as his investigator (his arrest of a beautiful drug suspect is silky smooth). It isn't clear but, judging by this episode, Anne was to have a recurring role as McCabe's old friend Dixie, a singer at the restaurant he frequents. Anne sings two songs here, "It All Depends on You" and "You Took Advantage of Me," flirts with McCabe, and does a little celebrating with him and Jake at the conclusion. The character, an appealing foil for Conrad, was dropped, however.

"Television has been home to many a 'gruff but lovable' cuss, but McCabe in his disheveled cantankerousness has real dimension — at least as played by the burly and corpulent William Conrad, tearing into the role like Henry VIII demolishing a pheasant.... An impudent note is sounded with Conrad's early appearance as McCabe in court — asleep. He wakes up in time to win a conviction with a hokey burst of hambone theatrics. Love at first snore! And it only gets better; McCabe lives in a wonderfully homey dump, has a slovenly bulldog who's even jowlier than he is, and often repairs to a bar where the beautiful Anne Francis croons balmy ballads warmingly. The murder case on the premiere is better than usual in this kind of show...." — Tom Shales, *The Washington Post*, September 29, 1987

Matlock— *"The Starlet"* (NBC, February 28, 1989)

Director: Harvey S. Laidman. *Writer*: Marvin Kupfer. *Regular Cast*: Andy Griffith, Nancy Stafford, Julie Sommars. *Guest Cast*: Anne Francis, Rebecca Staab, Roddy McDowall, Nia Peeples, Charles Cioffi, Tuesday Knight, Tom Everett, Theresa Hayes, Richard Newton, Steven Anderson, Tonya Lee Williams.

Plot: Benjamin Matlock (Griffith) defends the accused-of-murder daughter (Staab) of his old friend Janet Masters (Anne).

Notes: According to Anne, "Andy was fun to work with, and, of course, he did his Southern accent. I had just finished doing *Steel Magnolias* in Chicago several days before. So after being immersed in this character who had a Southern accent, I was doing it on the *Matlock* set and it drove Andy up the wall. He'd say in a very slow, patient voice, 'Anne, please don't do the Southern accent. I do the Southern accent.' He wasn't really mad."

This was a nice little part for Anne, especially the few scenes she has with Griffith. They have a fun chemistry, an easy familiarity that suits their characters. The scene where they sit and reminisce about the old days, laughing, is a honey. It was preceded by a sweet, nostalgic rendition of "My Buddy" by Griffith.

The Golden Girls— *"Till Death Do We Volley"* (NBC, March 18, 1989)

Director: Terry Hughes. *Writers:* Tracy Gamble, Richard Vaczy. *Regular Cast*: Bea Arthur, Betty White, Rue McClanahan, Estelle Getty. *Guest Cast*: Anne Francis, Robert King.

Plot: When Trudy (Anne) dies after a tennis match, her old friend Dorothy (Arthur) feels responsible.

Notes: This enjoyable episode is a perfect showcase for Anne's wry comedic delivery, as she plays Dorothy's prank-loving, barb-throwing best friend from high school. She and Arthur banter back and forth, insulting each other:

> TRUDY: You're on, you middle-aged cow!
> DOROTHY: I'm looking forward to it, you miserable sack of cellulite!

Murder, She Wrote — "*The Big Show of 1965*" (CBS, February 25, 1990)

Director: Jerry Jameson. *Writer*: Robert Van Scoyk. *Regular Cast*: Angela Lansbury. *Guest Cast*: Michael Cole, Anne Francis, Elaine Joyce, Connie Stevens, Donald O'Connor, Sheldon Leonard, Gavin MacLeod, Don Most, Jeff Yagher, Joy Garrett, Timothy Williams, John Rubinow, Kim Strauss.

Plot: Jessica Fletcher (Lansbury) opens the old murder case of singer Richie King (Strauss), who was killed in 1965. She attends a nostalgic reunion at the television station where King was stabbed decades earlier. There, Jessica meets the singing Haley Sisters (Anne, Joyce, Stevens), all of whom seem to have something to hide.

Notes: This enjoyable episode features Anne, Elaine Joyce and Connie Stevens singing two songs together, "Just One of Those Things" and "You're Gonna Hear from Me." As Lee, the oldest of the three sisters, Anne figures prominently in the mystery. It was an excellent, emotional role for her.

Dark Justice — "*The Doctor Is In*" (CBS, September 14, 1993)

Director: William Malone. *Writer*: Merl Edelman. *Regular Cast*: Bruce Abbott, Clayton Prince, Janet Gunn, Dick O'Neill. *Guest Cast*: Anne Francis, Kavi Raz, James Sloyan.

Plot: A doctor kills a patient but he cannot be prosecuted because the only witness has had a stroke and cannot testify.

Notes: Nicolas Marshall (Abbott) leads a double life on *Dark Justice* (1991–94): By day, he is a respected judge following the law; by night, he employs unconventional methods to bring to justice bad guys who escaped the law. Anne is billed as "Miss Anne Francis" in the credits.

Burke's Law — "*Who Killed Nick Hazard?*" (CBS, January 21, 1994)

Director: Dennis Dugan. *Writer*: Joel J. Feigenbaum. *Regular Cast*: Gene Barry, Peter Barton. *Guest Cast*: Buddy Ebsen, Anne Francis, Edd Byrnes, Martin Kove, Jameson Parker, Tanya Roberts, Robert Sacchi, Kirsten Holmquist.

Plot: A detective is murdered at a private eye convention.

Notes: Gene Barry returned to his old role of Amos Burke in this fleeting 14-episode revival of his earlier *Burke's Law* (1963–66), this time assisted by his son Peter (Barton). Again executive produced by Aaron Spelling, the series lacked the sophistication and smoothness of the original, but Barry, in his mid–70s, still had the stuff and infused his character with the proper stylishness and silkiness that was his hallmark — even though the writing wasn't up to his level.

The "hook" of this episode was the casting of actors who played detectives in past television shows: Anne (*Honey West*), Ebsen (*Barnaby Jones*), Byrnes (*77 Sunset Strip*), Kove (*Cagney & Lacey*), Parker (*Simon & Simon*), and Roberts (*Charlie's Angels*). Anne plays Honey Best, whose ex-husband Nick Hazard (Sacchi) is killed at a convention for private eyes.

It is not true that the producers were unable to use the "West" name for legal reasons. Gloria Fickling, who with her husband Skip created the Honey West character, was never approached for the clearance of rights, but would have been more than happy to do so. In fact, Honey Best bears practically no resemblance, except for her black turtleneck garb and judo, to Honey West.

Of all the guest stars, Anne has the best part. We learn that she and Hazard had an "ugly divorce" and at the divorce proceedings she lost her temper, slugged him and broke his jaw. "Nick did have a way of bringing out the worst in people," she admits. "He could be so infuriating." But, she sighs, "There's still a part of me that loves the poor lug, albeit a very small part." While she does help with the investigating (which includes some playful banter between her and Barry), she is also a suspect, having taken out a million-dollar insurance policy on Hazard three weeks before his murder.

Robert Sacchi, who plays the much-loathed, obnoxious Nick Hazard, has made his career as a Humphrey Bogart lookalike, something that's mentioned in this episode. Anne even does a brief Bogart impersonation.

Fortune Hunter — "The Frostfire Intercept" (Fox, September 4, 1994)

Director: Lewis Teague. *Writer*: Steve Aspis. *Regular Cast*: Mark Frankel, John Robert Hoffman. *Guest Cast*: Anne Francis, Chris Sarandon, Manuel DePina, Dana Wheeler-Nicholson, Hank Stone, Heidi Mark, Antoni Corone, Michael Shamus Wiles, Jeff Moldovan, Lisa Hickey, Judy Clayton, Carla Capps.

Plot: The darkly attractive Frankel plays Carlton Dial, who is on a mission to Morocco to recover a stolen weapons system.

Notes: This was the pilot episode. In two scenes Anne plays Dial's boss at Intercept Corporation, the no-nonsense, commanding Mrs. Brady, "with a wry touch" (*Variety*, September 1, 1994). By the second episode, however, she was replaced by the younger Yvonne (Kim Faze), who gave Dial his assignments via a special video link.

Although never acknowledged as such, this series was a modernized retread of *Search* (1972–73), another show which Anne guested on. At headquarters, John Robert Hoffman played Harry Flack, the "geek" who monitored everything the agent did in the field, giving him instructions and helping him out of tight spots.

The lighthearted show lasted until just October 2, 1994; it merited a better fate. British-born Mark Frankel was only 34 years old when he was killed in a motorcycle accident in 1996.

Wings — "The Lady Vanishes" (NBC, April 23, 1996)

Director: Jeffrey Melman. *Writers*: Ian Gurvitz, Michael Sardo. *Regular Cast*: Tim Daly, Steven Weber, Crystal Bernard, Tony Shalhoub, Amy Yasbeck, Rebecca Schull, David Schramm. *Guest Cast*: Michelle Nicastro, Weston Blakesley, Anne Francis, Ellen Ratner.

Plot: Antonio (Shalhoub) briefly meets a woman who suddenly disappears. He becomes obsessed with finding her, without even a name to go on.

Notes: *Wings* (1990–97) was a popular comedy series set at an airport on the resort island of Nantucket, off the Massachusetts coast. This episode was a homage to the *film noirs* of the 1940s and '50s. Anne's bit as a dame named Vera, well received by the studio audience, is found near the end. The slang-talkin' Vera sashays on and trades corny dialogue with pilot Joe Hackett (Daly). Watching her wiggle away, Joe asserts, "She may have some miles on her, but she's got a walk I can feel in my left pocket."

Home Improvement — "A Funny Valentine" (ABC, February 11, 1997)

Director: Peter Bonerz. *Writer*: Charlie Hauck. *Regular Cast*: Tim Allen, Patricia Richardson, Earl Hindman, Zachery Ty Bryan, Jonathan Taylor Thomas, Taran Noah Smith, Richard Karn, Debbie Dunning. *Guest Cast*: Anne Francis, Janeane Garofalo, Anthony Russell.

Plot: Tim Taylor (Allen) is contacted by singer Liddy Talbot (Anne) who knew his late father many years before; he thinks she once had an affair with him and is scared to meet with her at the Hotel Shipman where she is singing and playing piano.

Notes: Home Improvement (1991–96) starred stand-up comedian Tim Allen as the host of the Detroit-based how-to cable television show *Tool Time*. This Valentine's Day episode has Tim searching for a missing present he bought months earlier for his wife Jill (Richardson), and the angst Tim feels when he briefly meets singer Liddy Talbot, the mother of a girl, Elizabeth, that he knew in high school. She wants to have a talk with him about his father, but Tim fears the worst and doesn't want to hear anything that might tarnish the memory of his dad.

This is a very special episode, containing a warm, lovely performance by Anne. Her heartfelt, misty-eyed speech to Tim about his father is beautiful, delicately played by the actress. Her speaking voice is especially expressive and lyrical during this scene. Another fantastic aspect of this particular show is her poignant rendition of the Rodgers and Hart standard "My Funny Valentine" and her spirited, mirthful and unexpected version of The Monkees' theme song, "Hey, Hey, We're the Monkees."

Conan — *"The Curse of Afka"* (Syndicated, November 21, 1997)

Director: Frank Wayne. *Writers:* Charles Henry Fabian, Dennis Richards. *Regular Cast*: Ralf Moeller, Danny Woodburn, Robert McRay, TJ Storm, Jeremy Kemp. *Guest Cast:* Aly Dunne, Lydie Denier, Anthony DeLongis, Scott Ripley, Anne Francis, Anthony Nacarato, Eduardo Idunate, Angel De La Pena.

Plot: Gypsies steal money from Conan and his friends to buy horses.

Notes: This short-lived (22 episodes) adventure series was based on Robert E. Howard's classic barbarian pulp character. Filmed in Puerto Vallarta, Mexico, the series took more of a tongue-in-cheek approach than the Conan movies starring Arnold Schwarzenegger. German-born former Mr. Universe Ralf Moeller is just as muscular, dense and monosyllabic as Arnold was in the part — making him an ideal Conan. Anne fits right into the campy atmosphere with her silly role of Gagool, a medicine woman. Her line readings are priceless. "Help yourself, milord," she says grandly. "We gypsies have very little to offer, but you are welcome to whatever we have." And she looks fabulous in her gypsy garb, bandana over her head, eyes slightly buggy, as she peers into her crystal ball. The acting by the principals is rather rough and amateurish, so it's nice seeing an old pro at work, having fun with her part and showing the kids how it's done.

Nash Bridges — *"Sacraments"* (CBS, May 15, 1998)

Director: Deran Sarafian. *Writer*: John Wirth. *Regular Cast*: Don Johnson, Cheech Marin, Jaimé P. Gomez, Jodi Lyn O'Keefe, Jeff Perry, James Gammon, Kelly Hu, Angela Dohrmann, Suki Kaiser, Ron Russell. *Guest Cast*: Anne Francis, Cole Stratton, Clay Wilcox, Skip O'Brien, Rainbow Borden, Jill Lover, Adele Uddo.

Plot: Insp. Nash Bridges' (Johnson) father Nick (Gammon) is reunited briefly with his long-lost love Julia Ann Porter (Anne).

Notes: *Nash Bridges* was a popular cop show (1996–2001) about the Special Investigations Unit of the San Francisco Police Department. Anne plays yet another long-lost love from World War II. Why producers were casting her older than she actually was, since she still looked good, is a puzzlement. Here, we are told, she was 17 years old in 1944 when her father disapproved of her love match with Nick. Rough-hewn, gravel-voiced James Gammon was also playing older; he was born in 1940. But, then again, even though he was a good ten years *younger* than Anne, his weather-beaten countenance suggested just the opposite. They were an odd match, truth be told, but their acting together in their reunion is touching, teary and quite emotional. The part gave her some good opportunities to shine, especially one extended, poignant monologue to Nash explaining her back-story with his father.

The Drew Carey Show — "Nicki's Parents" (ABC, February 25, 1998)

Director: Sam Simon. *Writer*: Matilda Hokinson. *Regular Cast*: Drew Carey, Diedrich Bader, Kathy Kinney, Christa Miller, Ryan Stiles. *Guest Cast*: Anne Francis, Barry Corbin, Larry Brandenburg, Meagen Fay.

Plot: Drew meets Nicki's (Kate Walsh, not in episode) parents, Charlene and Chuck Fifer (Anne and Corbin), for the first time, but without Nicki, who has been detained because of snow. During dinner, Drew inadvertently causes the couple to fight and Charlene demands a divorce.

Notes: Drew Carey's successful sitcom (1995–2004) found him playing an assistant personnel director of a Cleveland department store. Anne has only one scene, at dinner with Corbin and Carey, but gets some good insults in, including hilariously calling Drew "fat boy." It wasn't much of a part, but it was good exposure on a hit television show.

The Drew Carey Show — "Nicki's Wedding" (ABC, November 4, 1998)

Director: Gerry Cohen. *Writers:* Diane Burroughs, Joey Gutierrez. *Regular Cast*: Drew Carey, Diedrich Bader, Christa Miller, Craig Ferguson, Kathy Kinney, Kate Walsh, Ryan Stiles. *Guest Cast*: Anne Francis, Barry Corbin, Brent Jasmer, Jana Marie Hupp.

Plot: Drew goes to Nicki's (Walsh) wedding and makes a fool out of himself.

Notes: In the February 25 episode, Nicki and Drew were engaged; they had broken up since then. In this episode Drew learns that she's marrying another, and he actually attends the wedding to prove to her, himself and everyone else that he's over her. Alas, Anne's role is even smaller here than in the previous *Carey* episode.

Fantasy Island — "Heroes" (ABC, January 23, 1999)

Director: Perry Lang. *Writers:* Chris Weitz, Paul Weitz (story), Ed Zuckerman (teleplay). *Regular Cast*: Malcolm McDowell, Sylvia Sidney, Mädchen Amick, Edward Hibbert, Fyvush Finkel. *Guest Cast*: Anne Francis, Pat Harrington, Jr., John Ashton, Arye Gross, Dwight Schultz.

Plot: Actors Dirk (Harrington, Jr.) and Bobby (Ashton), the past stars of the television show *The Hard Squad*, want to relive their glory days, but find it too difficult. When Cassie (Anne), the actress they both had a crush on years before, is kidnapped, they go back into action to save her.

Notes: This was the last episode of the second incarnation of *Fantasy Island*, which was revived with little interest for five months in 1999. Malcolm McDowell starred as the mysterious Mr. Roarke.

Directed by *Little Vegas'* Perry Lang, "Heroes" was a clever spoofing of cop shows in general and Anne's Honey West image in particular. She's Cassie, the former star of TV's

Police Gal, who joins two former members of TV's *The Hard Squad*, Dirk and Bobby, in "missing the old action" and being sick of retirement. Their wish comes true as they go on a case like the old days. It was a light, funny segment, capped by the three of them tied to chairs, waiting for an explosive to go off. "But being here with you two...," Dirk says, a bit misty-eyed. "The old camaraderie, the good feeling, the gratuitous violence. I feel *alive* again!"

Without a Trace — "*Shadows*" (CBS, April 15, 2004)

Director: Randy Zisk. *Writers:* Jan Nash, Jennifer Levin. *Regular Cast*: Anthony LaPaglia, Poppy Montgomery, Marianne Jean-Baptiste, Eric Close. *Guest Cast*: Martin Landau, Valerie Mahaffey, Megan Henning, Anne Francis, Robert Pine.

Plot: Martin Fitzgerald (Close), of the FBI's Missing Person Squad, is put on the case of his missing Aunt Bonnie (Mahaffey), who has cancer. He and fellow agent Samantha Spade (Montgomery) soon learn her secret: She has been helping terminally ill people end their lives.

Notes: This was Anne Francis' last performance. And, while it is a brief appearance, it is truly a special one, handled with skill and sensitivity by the actress. She plays Rose Atwood, whose husband Wallace (Howard Mann) is suffering from metastatic lung cancer. Martin and Samantha's investigation for the aunt eventually leads to Rose. A year earlier her son had gone to the police and accused his mother of hiring someone to euthanize his father; nothing could be proven and the case was dropped. Bonnie had been his nurse. What the agents find out surprises them, as Rose details the night Bonnie assisted in ending her husband's life:

> MARTIN: So, Bonnie killed your husband.
> ROSE (*tears welling up, but forcibly*):   No, cancer killed my husband. Bonnie just helped end his suffering.

Her scene with Howard Mann as he lies in bed getting ready to die is lovely and heartbreaking, both actors underplaying, giving their roles a deep profundity; you feel a genuine sense of loss. It is criminal that Mann (1923–2008) was not credited for his valuable contribution to this episode.

C. *Honey West* Episode Guide

(ABC-TV, 1965–66) Four Star Productions. *Producer:* Richard Newton. *Executive Producer:* Aaron Spelling. Developed for TV by Gwen Bagni and Paul Dubov. *Regulars:* Anne Francis (Honey West), John Ericson (Sam Bolt), Irene Hervey (Aunt Meg), Bruce (Bruce the Ocelot)

• Episode 1: "*The Swingin' Mrs. Jones*" (September 17, 1965)

Director: Paul Wendkos. *Writers*: Gwen Bagni, Paul Dubov. *Guests*: Ray Danton, Winnie Coffin [Collins], Marvin Brody, Louise Arthur, Than Wyenn, Dan Gazzaniga, David Armstrong, J.P. Burns, Joel Lawrence.

Plot: A blackmail ring, headed by Sonny (Danton) and his mother (Coffin), preys on wealthy married women.

Disguise the Limit: The show starts with Honey disguised as an old lady delivering blackmail money in a back alley. The rest of the episode has Honey in disguise as "Mrs. Jones," a wealthy married woman, at a resort. Sam poses as a ladies man.

Gadgets: Compact radio, radio sunglasses, earring receiver, tear-gas earrings, garter gas mask, transmitter in cocktail olive. "To protect myself," Anne told Kay Gardella, "I grab a garter off my leg which is immediately converted into a gas mask. That's probably the most daring gimmick we use — but it's no 'killer bra.'"

Boy-Girl Moment(s): Honey and Sam pretend to be a romantic twosome. When he flirts with a bevy of beautiful ladies, Honey, across the pool and speaking through her compact radio to his radio sunglasses, cramps his style by teasing him.

Belle of the Brawl(s): In the beginning of the episode, Honey takes on goons in an alley. After flipping one, she has the drop on them with a gun. Then another comes from behind and clobbers her. "I should've known they would have played it cozy," she groans to Sam when he runs up to help.

Commentary — Notes: Anne actually shows her belly button in this episode. On TV's *I Dream of Jeannie* (1965–70), NBC's censors refused to allow Barbara Eden to show hers, insisting she cover up.

The character of Honey West is said to be 25 years old in this episode, the only episode to give her age. Anne was in her mid–30s at the time, but the ever-youthful actress, throughout her career, looked much younger, often able to play characters 10 to 20 years younger than her actual age.

"Miss Francis is a petticoated Bond,

Portrait.

a dish, suffering underdevelopment only in her execution of jiu-jitsu. On the premiere she was tangled up with an inexhaustible but dull assortment of resort bums with huge chests, some of whom were involved in a blackmail racket which she broke up. ABC might make the top ten if they could devise a way so that Honey didn't have to talk." — Jack Gould, *New York Times*, September 20, 1965

• **Episode 2: *"The Owl and the Eye"*** (September 24, 1965)

Director: Paul Wendkos. *Writer:* William Bast. *Guests:* Lloyd Bochner, Richard Loo, William Bramley, John McLiam.

Plot: Art thieves bypass Honey and Sam's security system in an art museum. Their target: a jade owl statuette.

Gadgets: Lipstick transmitter.

Honey Talk: Villain Tog (Richard Loo) menacing Honey: "When my dogs become unmanageable, Miss West, I use this special weapon to tranquilize them. A few hours' rest, I am sure, would be most beneficial for you as well."

Knowing that smooth art collector Gus Patterson (Bochner) is interested in her and might have some information she could use, Honey seductively coos into the phone, accepting a date with him.

> AUNT MEG: Girl, you're in the wrong profession.
> HONEY: Gotta get dressed.
> AUNT MEG: Why bother?

Belle of the Brawl(s): An extended chase and fight on a boat. Honey outwits some Dobermans by spraying fire extinguisher foam on the deck, making them slip and scamper away. She brutally karate chops and kicks the pursuing bad guys.

Commentary—Notes: To show the insurance company that her security system is better than the company's present one, a sleek Anne, complete with her famous cat suit and high boots, effortlessly burglarizes the museum and replaces a priceless jade owl with a fake one.

• Episode 3: *"The Abominable Snowman"* (October 1, 1965)

Director: Paul Wendkos. *Writers:* Gwen Bagni, Paul Dubov. *Guests:* Henry Jones, Barry Kelley, George Keymas.

Plot: Honey and Sam go after narcotic traffickers who smuggle junk in snow globes.

Disguise the Limit: Honey dresses up in black wig, gown and long gloves, affecting a French accent, at a charity ball. Sam's disguise is merely a pair of glasses.

Gadgets: Regular (Sam) and Lorgnette (Honey) radio eyeglasses, and a car phone, which was still novel in the '60s.

Boy-Girl Moment(s): Sam and Honey they bicker constantly in this episode, but Honey tries the "nice" approach after an argument:

> HONEY: Sam, you look very handsome today.
> SAM (*flattered*): Yeah, I do?
> HONEY: It's a certain quality. It's elusive, but it's there.

Belle of the Brawl(s): There's a doozy of a car chase, filmed at some cockeyed angles. Honey violently brawls in an elevator with a gunman. The scene is shot from a cramped, cool-looking position from above.

Commentary—Notes: This episode boasts some interesting camerawork, courtesy of the always-inventive Paul Wendkos.

Bruce is particularly bad-tempered in this episode ("Even Bruce is upset," Honey says to Sam, somewhat explaining). As Anne and Ericson are trying to get through a scene (passing the cat between them at one point), Bruce wildly thrashes around and even swipes at Anne's face. Trying to keep the cat under control, Anne (who never misses a line) attempts to put Bruce over her shoulder. As the scene fades, Bruce bumps heads with Anne. Later, even guest Henry Jones has trouble keeping Bruce steady in his lap. Jones hilariously struggles with an open-mouthed Bruce, who is spitting and going crazy.

Anne has a nice comedic moment: After using a snow globe to bash a criminal over the head, Honey gets white stuff all over her purse. Sam notices that her lipstick is also smeared unaware that it's some of the contents of the snow globe's cocaine. Rubbing it in, her lip gets numb: "My lip feels funny. It feels numb, like a shot of Novocain." The voice Anne does to suggest gradual numbness is priceless.

After beating up the bad guys, Honey goes to the phone to call the police. As she starts talking, one of the guys starts getting up. "Excuse me," she tells the police lieutenant on the phone. Putting the receiver down, she matter-of-factly says to the guy, looking down, "Excuse me," karate chopping him back down to the floor again. She goes back to the phone, smilingly finishing her conversation. Flippant moments like this were Anne's forte on the show.

- **Episode 4: *"A Matter of Wife and Death"*** (October 8, 1965)

Director: John Florea. *Writer:* Tony Barrett. *Guests:* Dianne Foster, James Best, Henry Beckman, Michael Fox, Henry Brandon.

Plot: Honey and Sam tangle with diamond smugglers.

Gadgets: A "shotgun" listening device (also seen in the pilot that aired on *Burke's Law*), miniature TV eye plant, radio sunglasses.

Belle of the Brawl(s): Honey makes short work of a girl on a boat — no contest. Sam fights a scuba diver with a harpoon gun and doesn't fare nearly as well.

- **Episode 5: *"Live a Little ... Kill a Little"*** (October 15, 1965)

Director: Murray Golden. *Writer:* Tony Barrett. *Guests:* Warren Stevens, Harry Millard, Mary Murphy.

Plot: When a girl breaks up with a mobster, Honey must find her before an assassin does.

Disguise the Limit: Honey, cracking her gum and assuming a Brooklyn accent, poses as a dime-a-dance girl.

- **Episode 6: *"Whatever Lola Wants..."*** (October 22, 1965)

Director: John Peyser. *Writer:* William Bast. *Guests:* Audrey Christie, Johnny Haymer, Horst Ebersberg.

Plot: Where has an embezzler stashed his money?

Gadgets: Pen with noxious gas, necklace transmitter, compact transmitter.

Honey Talk: "I like your style, Honey," says the head of a crooked racing syndicate. "It's too bad you're running on the wrong track."

Notes — Commentary: Villainous Lola Getz (Christie), who had been hosting a party, blows up her mansion, destroying her secret operation, evidence — and apparently her whole circle of friends!

- **Episode 7: *"The Princess and the Paupers"*** (October 29, 1965)

Director: Virgil W. Vogel. *Writer:* Leonard Stadd. *Guests:* Bobby Sherman, Michael J. Pollard, Philip Ober, Nino Candido, Stanley Adams.

Plot: Honey and Sam try to find Nicky Vanderhyden (Sherman), the kidnapped rock-'n'roll-singing son of a millionaire (Ober).

Gadgets: Suntan lotion transmitter, face powder chemically treated to be seen under ultraviolet light.

Honey Talk: The name of a song demo: "There Are Footprints on the Ceiling Because I've Been Walking in My Sleep Over You."

Commentary — Notes: Locating a money container in the water, a bikini-clad Honey is spotted by a big, hairy, amorous man (Bern Hoffman). As he playfully reaches for her, Honey, smiling all the way, grabs his outstretched arm and flings him behind her, where he belly flops into the water face first. She continues exiting the water smiling.

"Bobby Sherman, who is more often found on *Shindig*, plays a rock'n'roll singer who arranges his own kidnapping on *Honey West*. It's not much of a mystery, but Anne Francis and John Ericson take on the assignment with incredible conviction and you may like the scene when Honey wire taps the abductors via her powder puff."—*The Morning Herald*, Hagerstown, MD, October 29, 1965

• Episode 8: *"In the Bag"* (November 5, 1965)

Director: Seymour Robbie. *Writers*: Gwen Bagni, Paul Dubov. *Guests*: Everett Sloane, Maureen McCormick, Robert Carricart.

Plot: The obnoxious child (McCormick) Honey is hired to escort between divorced parents is abducted, inadvertently leading to diamond smugglers.

Gadgets: Pen homing device, lipstick receiver.

Boy-Girl Moment(s): When an exhausted and frazzled Honey gets off a plane with the brat, she and Sam matter-of-factly kiss each other hello on the lips.

Honey Talk: "You know, we've never been introduced," Honey says to a man who comes out of nowhere with gun drawn.

While Honey is minding the unruly child on the plane, she gets fed up. "Oh boy, just wait until you grow up and you're in my neighborhood," she growls.

Commentary—Notes: In sharp contrast to the show's usual easygoing, glib humor is the understated, creepy scene where Sloane returns the child. The brat doesn't understand what's happening—he is trading her for the bag Honey and Sam have. Without actually saying anything outright, Sloane implies extreme menace to the child. This episode was his last acting role; he died on August 6, 1965, reportedly a suicide.

A pre-*Brady Bunch* Maureen McCormick plays the obnoxious child Honey is hired to escort between divorced parents in the episode "In the Bag." Everett Sloane, who's about to abduct the child, looks overwhelmed.

- **Episode 9:** *"The Flame and the Pussycat"* (November 12, 1965)

Director: James Goldstone. *Writer:* George Clayton Johnson. *Guests:* Sean McClory, Harry Basch, Ken Lynch, Liam Sullivan.

Plot: Honey and Sam battle an arsonist.

Honey Talk: Honey has a run-in with a condescending investigator, Mr. Canby (Sullivan), at an insurance company after she accidentally allows an arsonist to escape. Later, mad at the insurance company for turning down their help, Annie starts throwing darts at a photo of Mr. Canby in her office.

> SAM: Feel better now?
> HONEY: Not yet. This kind of therapy takes time.

Commentary—Notes: This is one of the funnier episodes of the series. In one scene, a policeman is about to give Honey a parking ticket. Indicating Bruce, who is waiting in the car for her, she smiles, "I'm sorry, officer, he'll never double park again," before speeding off.

Honey, hit over the head, is stuffed into a car trunk, gas exhaust filling her space. In a rather obvious, but kinda ingenious way to get out of her deadly situation, a coughing Honey uses the jack they left in the trunk to pry open her death trap.

- **Episode 10:** *"A Neat Little Package"* (November 19, 1965)

Director: Murray Golden. *Writers:* Gwen Bagni, Paul Dubov. *Guests:* J. Pat O'Malley, Roy Jenson, Val Avery.

Plot: Honey and Sam are hired by an amnesiac to find out why he has $150,000.

Disguise the Limit: Honey dresses up as a dark-haired cigarette girl.

Gadgets: Radio planted in rug, glasses radio, watch camera.

Belle of the Brawl(s): Honey hits a guy with her cigarette tray, and then beats the stuffing outta him. She then takes out three guys in a room. Finally she is captured by two of them. As they are going down some stairs to the outside, Honey kicks one guy down the stairs and flips the other into a nearby pond. Then Anne's stunt double Sharon Lucas really shows her stuff when one of the guys brutally tackles her into the pond, in a spectacular fall. Ultimately, there is a free-for-all in the pond that also involves Sam. After everyone is finally arrested, Sam sighs, "What am I going to do with you?" Honey answers, "Buy me a Polynesian dinner. I'm hungry after all that swimming."

- **Episode 11:** *"A Stitch in Crime"* (November 26, 1965)

Director: John Peyser. *Writers:* Gwen Bagni, Paul Dubov. *Guests:* Charlene Holt, Laurie Main, James B. Sikking, Herbie Faye.

Plot: Honey and Sam, hired to deliver valuable gowns to a fashion show, are hijacked.

Disguise the Limit: Aunt Meg gets into the act by posing as a seamstress at a fashion charity. Honey poses as "Miss Helga from West Germany," a well-known model. Honey (with crazy wig and dark glasses) and a nonsense-poem-spouting Sam (beard, mustache, glasses) pose as beatniks in a coffeehouse. Anne is tops as the emotionless beatnik in the coffeehouse, and her limited German "accent" is a hoot.

Gadgets: Wireless bug on Bruce's "dress collar."

Belle of the Brawl(s): At a diner, Sam takes on the tough guys who had cut him off on the road. Honey helps Sam by splashing hot coffee in one guy's face and tripping him.

Commentary—Notes: The start of a minor running joke involving Bruce: "You won't have any trouble. Bruce hates violence," Honey tells a nervous man she leaves Bruce with.

• Episode 12: *"A Million Bucks in Anybody's Language"* (December 3, 1965)

Director: John Florea. *Writers:* Tony Barrett. *Guests:* Steve Ihnat, Harry Bellaver, Ken Lynch, Sarah Selby, Percy Helton.

Plot: Honey investigates a gang with counterfeit plates.

Disguise the Limit: Honey goes undercover as a waitress (wearing tiger-striped bathing suit, stockings and heels) at the Tiger's Torso drive-in restaurant.

Gadgets: Pen radio, lipstick radio, bugging device.

Boy-Girl Moment(s): Admiring Honey in her bathing suit, Sam whistles, "If you wore that around the office, we could up the fee."

Honey Talk: "Try to keep up, Sam! I'll keep in contact," Honey tells her exasperated partner as she speeds away in her sports car alone.

Belle of the Brawl(s): There's a terrific brawl in a cabin. John Ericson's stunt double does a tremendous leap over a car to knock down a bad guy.

Commentary—Notes: "*Honey West* should be ashamed of itself with its latest potboiler of a mystery. Surely they aren't serious with this plot about counterfeiters and men who arrange their own 'murders.'"—*The Albuquerque Tribune*, December 3, 1965

• Episode 13: *"The Gray Lady"* (December 10, 1965)

Director: Walter Grauman; *Writers:* Richard Levinson, William Link. *Guests:* Cesare Danova, Kevin McCarthy, Nancy Kovack.

Plot: Honey and Sam try to safeguard the Gray Lady jewels owned by a movie star.

Gadgets: Lipstick radio, camera connected to TV, grappling hook.

Honey Talk: Mr. Ivar (McCarthy) to Honey just before their big fight: "All right! Let's play your game, Miss West. We ... are ... going ... to ... have ... a *ball*."

There's a lot of first-rate, cool dialogue in this, one of the best episodes of the series. It was written by Richard Levinson and William Link (later creators of *Columbo* and *Murder, She Wrote*), who won an Edgar for this episode; there is a big difference in tone between this and the other episodes of the series.

The story starts in a hotel room with a sophisticated bang when Honey gets the drop on a charming jewel thief, Abbott (Danova), in action. Near the finale, the thief and the PI meet again, same situation, she with gun on him again:

> ABBOTT: I didn't think you'd expect me here tonight. Ah, that's the trouble with me, over-confidence.
> HONEY: We all have our faults.
> ABBOTT (*darkness spreading over his face*): Curiosity seems to be one of yours. Could get you killed one of these days.

Belle of the Brawl(s): The last fight is undoubtedly the best executed of the series. It starts with Mr. Ivar drop-kicking Honey. Eventually, she rolls into a handstand in front of him. Falling backwards into him, she knocks him down, landing on him in the mount posi-

Honey watches as Mr. Ivar (Kevin McCarthy) shoots to kill in "The Gray Lady." This episode is considered by many to be one of the best of the series. Richard Levinson and William Link, won an Edgar for their teleplay.

tion and administering a series of chops. She finishes him off with a series of vicious (close-up) chops to the neck and then a brutal uppercut. Whew!

Commentary — Notes: Anne's cool, deadpan repartee and chemistry with elegant Danova make Link and Levinson's words come alive with a lighthearted sexiness.

Leaving Mr. Ivar unconscious from their fight, sprawled out on the floor, Honey goes over to the mirror to comb her hair before she casually exits the room. You go, girl!

When Sam says they could go to jail for what they're doing, Honey quips, "Sing Sing swings this time of year." But, with the show set in California, they (of course) wouldn't go to Sing Sing. This was an in-joke (Anne Francis was born in Ossining near Sing Sing, delivered by the Sing Sing doctor). One of Anne's movies, *Dreamboat* (1952), also has a reference to Sing Sing.

> "'The Great Lady' [*sic*] is not heroine Anne Francis, but a movie star of sorts whose jewels are constantly being stolen. Anne and sidekick John Ericson are baffled by the missing baubles in this gaudy little romp which offers less than sparkling performances by guest actors Bert Parks, Nancy Kovack, Pat Collins, Kevin McCarthy and Cesare Danova."—*Syracuse Herald Journal*, December 10, 1965

The above "review" is a classic case of a "reviewer" who didn't watch the episode in question. The Gray Lady is the name of the coveted jewel prized by thieves. In fact, this episode, the first to be filmed for the series but delayed, is probably the best of the entire series, with good performances by all.

• Episode 14: *"Invitation to Limbo"* (December 7, 1965)

Director: Tom Gries; *Writers*: William Link, Richard Levinson. *Guests*: Louise Troy, Wayne Rogers, Peter Leeds, Stacy Harris.

Plot: Honey and Sam are hired to find an information leak in a company.
Disguise the Limit: Top hat-wearing cigarette girl at The Sandbox.
Gadgets: Chewing gum listening device, powder puff radio.
Boy/Girl Moment(s): After warning Honey to stay in her car and wait for the police to arrest the bad guys:

LIEUTENANT: You think she'll stay put?
SAM: Are you kidding? If I know Honey, she's leaving her car now.
(*She is ...*)

Commentary—Notes: This is the only episode to actually very briefly evoke the series of books written by the Ficklings: Leaving a steam room in a hurry to catch the crooks, Honey doffs her towel and slips into a coat. Later, she looks uncomfortable. When Sam asks her what's the matter, she nervously says, "I'm a little chilly; I wonder when that steam bath closes. I forgot something..."

• Episode 15: *"Rockabye the Hard Way"* (December 24, 1965)

Director: Bill Colleran; *Writers*: Gwen Bagni, Paul Dubov. *Guests*: Vincent Beck, Larry D. Mann, Paul Sorensen, Joe Don Baker, Gil Lamb.

Plot: Honey and Sam tangle with spies drugging the drivers who are transporting secret weapons.
Disguise the Limit: Honey goes undercover as a waitress, Sam as a wolfish truck driver.
Honey Talk:

SAM: We could get five years for breaking and entering.
HONEY: Don't be silly, Sam. We're not going to break anything.

Belle of the Brawl(s): Honey beats up the same poor, helpless guy twice in this episode.

First, although he cockily thinks he has her at gunpoint, she throws a suitcase at him, then knees and forearms his face. Later, she and Sam put a strap across the floor in a darkened room, knocking him down. With the man sprawled out on the floor, Sam yields to Honey: "You're closer." Taking the cue, she rushes over and crushingly karate chops the guy's neck.

Commentary — Notes: Anne coolly plays a game of pool in a gown. Her nonchalant reaction to being surprised at gunpoint while she is searching the suitcase is priceless.

• **Episode 16: *"A Nice Little Till to Tap"*** (December 31, 1965)

Director: Jerry Hopper; *Writer:* Tony Barrett. *Guests:* Anthony Eisley, Peter Leeds, Howard McNear, Marvin Brody, Lou Krugman.

> *Plot:* Honey poses as a bank teller to foil a gang of bank robbers.
> *Disguise the Limit:* Throughout, Honey masquerades as the bank teller.
> *Gadgets:* Pen radio.
> *Boy-Girl Moment(s):*
> After Sam rescues Honey from the ice warehouse, she's shivering.

> SAM (*reassuring*): It's all right, it's all right. There's nothing to be afraid of any more.
> HONEY: I'm not afraid — I'm freezing!

Belle of the Brawl(s): Honey doesn't do much fighting in this episode (or much else); it is mostly Sam. The battle in the ice warehouse is a good one, through.

• **Episode 17: *"How Brillig, O, Beamish Boy"*** (January 7, 1966)

Director: Ida Lupino; *Writer:* Don Ingalls. *Guests:* John McGiver, Norman Alden, Howard Dayton, Monte Hale.

> *Plot:* A gang kidnaps Sam to trade his life for a money package in Honey's possession.
> *Gadgets:* Transmitter eyeglasses, lipstick bomb.
> *Honey Talk:* In keeping with the episode's title (based on "'Twas Brillig"), there are references to Lewis Carroll throughout. "If it isn't Malice in Wonderland," remarks Honey, greeting Mr. Brillig (McGiver).
> *Commentary — Notes:* Honey's office is located on 60 West Beverly Hills Drive in Los Angeles. A peek at Sam's ID card notes that he is 38, 6'2", with brown hair and blue eyes, 185 pounds. (While we're at it, Sam's truck and Honey's car's license plates, respectively, are 1406 122 and 1ET 974.)

• **Episode 18: *"King of the Mountain"*** (January 14, 1966)

Director: Thomas Carr; *Writer:* Jay Simms. *Guests:* David Opatoshu, Dennis Patrick, Charles Lane, Richard Kiel.

> *Plot:* Honey poses as a nurse and is hired by reclusive billionaire Kelso King (Opatoshu), who is afflicted with a rare biochemical illness.
> *Disguise the Limit:* Honey impersonates a nurse. ("Florence Nightingale, you old son of a gun," Sam whistles as he sees Honey, in nurse's uniform, put a gun in her handbag.)
> *Gadgets:* Thermometer microphone, camera watch, bag-clasp radio.
> Looking up at the menacing 7'2" Grolago (Kiel) for the first time, Honey nervously smiles, "And whose little boy are *you?*" Later, when she's making tea, Grolago comes in and

gruffly announces, "I'll make the tea, you fix the shots." Forcibly, Honey remarks, "Let's get one thing straight! *You* make the tea; *I'll* fix the shots!"

Belle of the Brawl(s): Honey generally tries to avoid the imposing Grolago, even though he chases her all around the house, throwing things at her. But when he attacks Sam, choking him, Honey takes a 2 × 4 and wraps it across Grolago's back!

Commentary — Notes: "My uncle was in town from Michigan, and he and my grandfather wanted to come out to CBS Studio Center and visit me while I was working. Anne Francis is a dear lady. That particular *Honey West* was being shot on a house set with a big staircase, and she sat on the stairs chatting with my grandfather and uncle. My grandfather knew she was a movie star, and he was quite enchanted with the whole thing."— Richard Kiel to Tom Weaver, *Starlog* #353, March 2007

- **Episode 19: *"It's Earlier Than You Think"*** (January 21, 1966)

Director: James H. Brown; *Writer*: Marc Brandell. *Guests*: James Griffith, Leonid Kinskey, Maurice Dallimore, Ken Lynch.

   Plot: Honey and Sam are after document forgers.
   Gadgets: Necklace microphone.
   Honey Talk: A lab technician gives Honey a long, involved and complicated analysis of paper. "You follow me, Miss West?" Honey's reaction, from happy interest to cluelessness, is fun. "Yeah ... what do you mean?"

- **Episode 20: *"The Perfect Un-Crime"*** (January 28, 1966)

Director: Sidney Miller; *Writer*: Ken Kolb. *Guests*: David Brian, Byron Foulger.

   Plot: Arthur Bird (Foulger) steals money from the department store he works for, then hires Honey and Sam to "perform a burglary in reverse"— return the cash.
   Disguise the Limit: Aunt Meg poses as a dissatisfied customer.
   Belle of the Brawl(s): Mayhem and silliness ensue in the department store as the fight (Honey and Sam vs. some baddies) involves golf balls and other assorted merchandise. Sam has a helluva sword fight with Mr. Rockwell (Brian) with baseball bats. Honey, with much flair, hits Rockwell with a swirl of her cape.

- **Episode 21: *"Like Visions and Omens ... and All That Jazz"***
   (February 4, 1966)

Director: John Florea; *Writer*: Tony Barrett. *Guests*: Nehemiah Persoff, Fred Beir, June Vincent, Mimsy Farmer, Benny Rubin.

   Plot: Honey and Sam confront a blackmailer and phony mystic whose "predictions" always suspiciously come true.
   Boy-Girl Moment(s): Sam meets Honey at the airport. "Get in the truck and stay down!" he warns her. Typically, she ignores him and ends up saving his life.

- **Episode 22: *"Don't Look Now, but Isn't That Me"*** (February 11, 1966)

Director: James H. Brown; *Writers*: Gwen Bagni, Paul Dubov. *Guests*: Alan Reed, Louis Quinn, Jonathan Hole.

In one of the best episodes of the series, "Don't Look Now, but Isn't That Me," Anne played a dual role: Honey West and Brooklynese moll Pandora. Here she relaxes on the set in her jeweled bracelet that doubles as handcuffs.

Plot: Fur thieves use a double of Honey to carry out their crimes.

Disguise the Limit: This episode, one of Anne's best (and my favorite), features her in a dual role — as Honey and as bad guy Chick's (Alan Reed) lookalike dark-haired, gum-chewing Brooklynese moll, Pandora. The moll pretends a couple of times to be Honey and, later, Honey pretends to be the moll. Even when she's Pandora dressed as Honey, Anne makes you believe she's not really Honey — if you know what I mean.

Gadgets: Jeweled bracelet doubles as handcuffs.

Boy-Girl Moment(s): After a typical fight, Sam admits that he was worried about her. Honey says simply, "You're sweet."

Belle of the Brawl(s): In a truly vicious move, Honey takes off her belt and slings it around a thug's neck, following that with a crushing chop across his throat!

Honey Talk: Anne's Pandora character has a broad accent and is unable to correctly say the word "fine." Chick is working on her diction, so she can successfully masquerade as Honey.

> CHICK (*formally*): Good morning, Miss West. How are you?
> PANDORA: Greetin's to you, I'm foin...
> CHICK: No, no! You haven't got it!
> PANDORA: Listen, Rex Harrison you ain't.
> CHICK (*raising fist*): I oughta...
> PANDORA: James Cagney neither, for that matter.

Commentary — Notes: "Heroine Anne Francis, who will masquerade at the drop of a hat, almost outshines herself in 'Don't Look Now, but Isn't That Me?' Honey appears as herself, posing as 'Pandora Fox,' a look-alike who says 'foin' instead of 'fine.' She also doubles as Pandora who is trying her best to act like Honey so she can steal $50,000 worth of fur in this glib and often amusing script, the two goils (or is it girls?) have a knockdown, drag-out fight, thanks to some nifty trick photography."—*Syracuse Herald-Journal*, February 11, 1966

• **Episode 23:** *"Come to Me, My Litigation Baby"* (February 18, 1966)

Director: Thomas Carr; *Writers*: Gwen Bagni, Paul Dubov. *Guests*: Ellen Corby, James Brown, Michael Fox, Army Archerd.

Plot: Little Nellie Peedy (Corby) runs a school of litigation — a gang that stages "accidents" in order to collect damages.

Disguise the Limit: Honey goes undercover as a little ole helpless Southern girl.

Commentary — Notes: In a scene that feels like padding, the "Honey West Walk," a new "dance," is introduced in a nightclub, by Ron Lerner and Kami Stevens. After they dance, an understandably reluctant Honey and Sam are called up. Both hesitate — and who could blame them? The only fun moment here is near the fadeout, when Honey and Sam seem to improvise and use karate chops on each other, etc., in the dance.

"You are soon to be exposed to a *Honey West* dance. It all came about when five-year-old Debbie Rosen, the daughter of Burt Rosen, a vice president of Four Star, which produces the show, was dancing around the Rosen living room. She punctuated her dance with odd arm movements. Her father asked her what she was doing. 'I'm doing the Honey West dance,' Debbie said. Rosen told this to Leo Gutman, Four Star's vice president in charge of promotion, among other things. And the idea bulb clicked on. So Gutman had some dance experts create a *Honey West* dance, a cross between the latest discotheque step and a karate session. An episode of the show will be written to give Anne Francis a chance to do it. And, hopefully, she'll also demonstrate it on *The Hollywood Palace* and such programs. It may help the show. Almost as much as a few good scripts." — Dick Kleiner, "In Hollywood," January 14, 1966

• Episode 24: *"Slay, Gypsy, Slay"* (February 25, 1966)

Director: James H. Brown; *Writer*: Tony Barrett. *Guests*: Michael Pate, Ralph Manza, Arline Anderson, Byron Morrow.

Plot: Honey and Sam get mixed up with a bunch of gypsies.

Disguise the Limit: Honey dresses up as a dark-haired gypsy. Sam is practically unrecognizable as an old prospector, *a la* Gabby Hayes.

Gadgets: Sunglasses radio.

Belle of the Brawl(s): There's an incredible battle in a cave with the gang and a "rampaging" gorilla. Honey goes mano-a-mano with the gorilla in a surprisingly exciting brawl.

• Episode 25: *"The Fun-Fun Killer"* (March 4, 1966)

Director: Murray Golden; *Writer*: Art Weingarten. *Guests*: Marvin Kaplan, Woodrow Parfrey, John Hoyt, Ken Lynch.

Plot: A merger between toy companies is threatened by murderous robots.

Gadgets: Lock-picking gun.

Honey Talk: Honey is sitting on a couch watching television with Bruce. "Bruce, why do we *always* have to watch your show? You see one jungle picture, you've seen them all." When the doorbell rings, Honey asks him, "Are you expecting someone? Don't move; I'll get it myself." Bruce, very irritable in this scene, snarls straight into Anne's face — she doesn't flinch!— and when she gets up to answer the door, it takes a swipe at her.

Belle of the Brawl(s): When the robot attacks Honey, she gets off six (useless) shots (one of the very few times she fired her gun in the series) before it knocks her headfirst into the wall, knocking her cold. (Sharon Lucas takes an incredible head shot against the wall, by the way.)

Notes — Commentary: Looking through the toy laboratory, Honey stops short, noticing a doll that looks exactly like her, equipped with a gun. It's an inside joke; the Honey West doll was in stores at the time (and has remained a highly prized collectors' item).

Honey has a great creeped-out reaction to man stroking a stuffed cat as if it were real.

"It's an agreeable whodunit, with the usual amount of flip dialogue and suspense." — *Syracuse Herald-Journal,* March 4, 1966

- **Episode 26: *"Pop Goes the Easel"*** (March 11, 1966)

Director: James H. Brown; *Writers*: Lila Garrett, Bernie Kahn. *Guests*: George Furth, Robert Strauss, Larry D. Mann.

Plot: A soup can, with a label painted by a sought-after pop artist, is stolen.

Boy-Girl Moment(s): They discuss the case while eating sandwiches and drinking milk. Sam uses her milk to make his points; Honey ends up drinking both glasses.

Honey Talk: A mad art lover boasts of his "magnificent" collection of stolen art treasures by Renoir, Picasso, etc. Honey smiles, "They're very nice, but there's something special about a simple can of soup."

Commentary — Notes: Honey and Sam briefly sing "The Prisoner Song" at the conclusion, then break out laughing at the fade.

- **Episode 27: *"Little Green Robin Hood"*** (March 18, 1966)

Director: Sidney Miller; *Writer*: Ken Kolb. *Guests*: Edd Byrnes, Severn Darden, Allen Jenkins, Eleanor Audley.

Plot: A man thinking he's Robin Hood (Byrnes) steals jewels from the rich.

Gadgets: Ring signal.

Boy-Girl Moment(s): When Sam flirts with the maid who works for their client, Honey is more bemused than jealous. (Sam is cute here, as he winks and smiles at the maid.)

Honey Talk:

SAM: Oh, this is ridiculous. Where would you be if you were Robin Hood?
HONEY: Fighting Basil Rathbone on *The Late Late Show*.

Belle of the Brawl(s): Sam and the pseudo–Robin, re-enacting Little John and Robin Hood's encounter on the log over a creek, have an embarrassing, awkwardly staged "fight." This is made up for later by having a tremendous brawl in a small room — with Honey beating up both a man and a woman. During this big fight, Anne (not her stunt double) gets off a *terrific* right hook to a villain's jaw. (Anne waves her hand afterwards, as if in pain. Was it a real punch?)

- **Episode 28: *"Just the Bear Facts, Ma'am"*** (March 25, 1966)

Director: James H. Brown; *Writers*: Gwen Bagni, Paul Dubov. *Guests*: Richard Carlyle, Frank Wilcox, Mousie Garner, Marvin Brody.

Plot: When a stuntwoman is killed on a movie set, Honey replaces her to find the killer.

Disguise the Limit: Honey poses as a stuntwoman. Sam is an actor in a bear suit. Also, during a dream sequence, Honey envisions herself and Sam as Valentino and Beatrice

Dominguez tangoing in *The Four Horsemen of the Apocalypse* (1921), and herself as a flapper dancing the Charleston and as a *Perils of Pauline* type tied to the train tracks.

Boy-Girl Moment(s): After Sam films a scene as a bear, Honey says, "Sam Bolt, you sure do have talent. No matter what anybody says, you're this honey's bear."

The show ends with Sam in bear suit as they kiss through his costume.

Honey Talk: After Honey beats up a bad guy, she stands over him and drawls, "Another hombre bites the dust." Then, seeing Sam across the Western street, they face each other, hands on hips as though they had holstered guns.

SAM: Whenever you're ready, ma'am.
HONEY (*thinks about it*): I give up (*flopping arms down*).

They walk away, arms around each other.

Commentary — Notes: The fact that Honey is playing a stuntwoman for the star of the movie being made — but Sharon Lucas is doubling *her* — is a little odd, but this episode is a good showcase for Lucas. Anne's dream sequence impersonations unquestionably show her off to good effect.

• Episode 29: *"There's a Long, Long, Fuse A'Burning"* (April 1, 1966)

Director: Thomas Carr; *Writers*: Gwen Bagni, Paul Dubov. *Guests*: Dick Clark, Lennie Bremen, Paul Dubov, John Holland.

Plot: Honey and Sam go after bank robbers with the help of a gone-straight ex-con and his old cronies.

Gadgets: Compact radio, radio eyeglasses, kewpie-doll bomb.

Commentary — Notes: Playing Police Lt. Badger in this episode is Paul Dubov, who co-wrote many of the episodes (including this one) and developed the series with his wife Gwen.

• Episode 30: *"An Eerie, Airy, Thing"* (April 8, 1966)

Director: James H. Brown; *Writers*: Richard Levinson, William Link. *Guests*: Lisa Seagram, Adam Williams, Ken Lynch.

Plot: A man (Williams) on

Honey West in action, unaware of dead body.

a building ledge will only come down if his wife comes and talks to him. Problem? She's dead.

Commentary — Notes: That the criminal thought he could get away with the crime after an autopsy was performed is a little far-fetched.

Anne's speech to the man on the ledge to get him down is, as usual for her, well done and very dramatic. "You have two choices," Honey tells him. "The pavement or the jury. At least with the jury you've got a chance."

"*Honey West*, on ABC, will be coming up soon with an episode about a suicide-bent man on the ledge of a building. My friend with the needlepoint knows that plot very well. Honey, the fearless lady private eye with the high-style clothes, will ultimately climb out on the ledge. We will be treated to frequent dizzy-making shots of the street and traffic far below. Ultimately the distraught character will climb in whimpering or be hauled to safety. With this obvious shortage of basic situations that can be built into rigid time periods, television's continuing attraction obviously must come from other quarters — good writing with some novel twists in the plot's path, better than average acting and interesting production."— Cynthia Lowry, March 25, 1966

This above report, widely circulated, does *Honey*'s last episode an injustice. While undoubtedly the weakest of the shows, the man-on-the-ledge scenario is not as Lowry describes it and is unique to such situations.

Bibliography

Books

Baumann, Marty. *The Astounding B Monster Book.* New York: Dinoship, 2005.

Beck, Ken, and Jim Clark. *The Encyclopedia of TV Pets.* Nashville: Rutledge Hill Press, 2002.

Bruce, Lenny. *How to Talk Dirty and Influence People: An Autobiography.* Chicago: Playboy Press, 1965.

Fickling, G.G. *Blood and Honey.* New York: Pyramid, 1961.

_____. *Bombshell.* New York: Pyramid, 1965.

_____. *Girl on the Loose.* New York: Pyramid, 1958.

_____. *A Gun for Honey.* New York: Pyramid, 1958.

_____. *Honey on Her Tail.* New York: Pyramid, 1971.

_____. *Stiff as a Broad.* New York: Pyramid, 1971.

_____. *This Girl for Hire.* New York: Pyramid, 1957.

Fotre, Vincent. *The Trailmakers.* New York: Berkley Medallion, 1961.

Francis, Anne. *Voices from Home: An Inner Journey.* Millbrae, CA: Celestial Arts, 1982.

Gordon, Bernard. *Hollywood Exile: Or How I Learned to Love the Blacklist.* Austin: The University of Texas Press, 2000.

Grams, Martin J., and Patrik Wikstrom. *The Alfred Hitchcock Presents Companion.* Churchville, MD: OTR Publishing, 2001.

Gregory, Mollie. *Women Who Run the Show: How a Brilliant and Creative New Generation of Women Stormed Hollywood.* New York: St. Martin's, 2002.

Hunter, Evan. *The Blackboard Jungle.* New York: Simon & Schuster, 1954.

LeBell, Gene. *The Godfather of Grappling.* Santa Monica, CA: Gene LeBell, 2005.

Lennart, Isobel. *Funny Girl* (script). 1967.

Millner, Cork. *Santa Barbara Celebrities: Conversations from the American Riviera.* Santa Barbara, CA: Santa Barbara Press, 1986.

Roberts, Kenneth. *Lydia Bailey.* New York: Doubleday, 1947.

Schary, Dore. *Heyday: An Autobiography.* New York: Little, Brown, 1979.

Spada, James. *Streisand: Her Life.* New York: Crown, 1995.

Sperling, Cass Warner, and Cork Millner. *Hollywood Be Thy Name: The Warner Brothers Story.* Lexington: University Press of Kentucky, 1998.

Stanyard, Stewart T. *Dimensions Behind* The Twilight Zone: *A Backstage Tribute to Television's Groundbreaking Series.* Toronto: ECW Press, 2007.

Weaver, Tom. *They Fought in the Creature Features: Interviews with 23 Classic Horror, Science Fiction and Serial Stars.* Jefferson, NC: McFarland, 1995.

Articles

Abbe, James. "Abbe Airs It." *Oakland Tribune,* January 2, 1958.

"Actress Gets Twin Bed in Divorce Settlement." *Sunday Times Signal* (Zanesville, OH), April 17, 1955.

"Actress Reviews Roles from Model to Mother." *The Post-Standard* (Syracuse), February 22, 1978.

"Actress to Tell Her Faith." December 20, 1975.

"Anne Francis An Acting Veteran At Ripe Old Age Of 23." *The Newport News,* January 11, 1954.

"Anne Francis: 'Born Again.'" *Nashua Telegraph,* January 9, 1978.

"Anne Francis Glad She Got It Hard Way." Publication unknown, October 5, 1969.

"Anne Francis Shows Her Versatility." *The Oakland Tribune,* February 14, 1965.

"Army General's Film from Experience." *Idaho State Journal,* March 3, 1972.

Banner, Glen. "A Touch of Nostalgia." *Kokomo Tribune,* January 12, 1975.

"Barbra's Co-Star." *Wisconsin State Journal,* June 11, 1967.

Barron, Mark. "Broadway: Sidewalks Serve As Film Studio." *Mansfield News-Journal* (Ohio), April 2, 1950.

Beck, Marilyn. "Marlo Thomas to Take Vacation." *Burlington Times-News* (North Carolina), December 19, 1970.

_____. "Hollywood Hotline." *Pasadena Star-News,* May 4, 1971.

Beckerman, Jim. "Press Agent Leo Pillot, 85; Did 'Plugola' for Top Stars." *The Record* (Bergen County, NJ), April 5, 1995.

Berg, Louis. "Palomino Blonde." *Los Angeles Times*, June 29, 1952.

Berk, Ed. "'Riptide' Ratings: A Lot for a Little." *Daily Intelligencer/Montgomery County Record*, January 17, 1984.

Blass, Terry. "One Honey of an Anne Francis Interview." http://templeofschlock.blogspot.com/2010/06/one-honey-of-anne-francis-interview.html.

Bobbin, Jay. "TV Q&A." *Frederick News-Post* (Maryland), February 7, 1998.

Bradford, Jack. "TV Week." *Independent Star-News*, August 16, 1964.

Bradley, Matthew R. "Altair Ego: An Out-of-This-World Interview with Anne Francis." *Filmfax*, May 2000.

Byers, Bill. "She's Honey West, a Private Eye-Full." *The Abilene Reporter-News*, October 7, 1965.

Carroll, Harrison. "Hollywood." *The Evening Independent*, June 22, 1956.

Champlin, Charles. "Video Stars Pack Exposure Power." *Los Angeles Times*, September 30, 1966.

Church of Religion Science ad. *Independent Press-Telegram*, February 7, 1976.

Crosby, Joan. "The Optimistic Anne Francis." *Corpus Christi Caller-Times*, November 21, 1971.

Crowther, Bosley. "THE SCREEN IN REVIEW; *So Young, So Bad*, Produced by the Danzigers, Bows at the Criterion." *The New York Times*, July 24, 1950.

"Despite the Pace Bob Hope Still has Life." *The Daily News* (Pennsylvania), December 12, 1985.

Dulin, Dann. "Down to Earth." *A&U: America's AIDS Magazine*, November 2005. http://www.aumag.org/features/AnneFrancisNov05.html.

Duncan, David. "Hollywood Heroine." *Film & TV*, August 11, 1997.

Fidler, Jimmy. "Fidler in Hollywood." Publication unknown, February 9, 1952.

_____. "Hollywood Roundup." *The Evening Standard* (Pennsylvania), July 21, 1954.

"Film Actress Wed to UCLA Student." *Los Angeles Times*, May 18, 1952.

Foster, Bob. "TV Screenings: '*Honey West* Preview Clicks.'" *The Times* (San Mateo, CA), April 22, 1965.

"'Funny Girl' Role for TV: Anne Francis Raps Rush-Through Scene." *Kingsport Times*, July 5, 1967.

Gardella, Kay. "TV Creates New Image: Soft, Warm Females Passé." *Pasadena Star-News*, August 4, 1965.

Gould, Jack. "New Television Programs Range from Refreshing to "a Little Sick."" *Des Moines Register*, September 20, 1965.

Graham, Sheilah. "Hollywood Today." *San Antonio Express*, May 27, 1953.

_____. "Inside Hollywood with Sheilah Graham." Publication unknown, February 4, 1968.

Hanauer, Joan. "Television in Review: Three Hours of 'thwack-bonk.'" *The Valley Independent*, September 2, 1978.

Handler, David. "NBC's New *Riptide* May Make Waves." *The Post* (Frederick, MD), February 15, 1984.

Handsaker, Gene. "Anne Francis Started Work Early in Life." *Paris News*, August 16, 1951.

_____. "Hollywood." *The Hammond Times*, December 7, 1951.

Harris, Eleanor. "Cover Girl." *Radio Mirror*, March 1946.

Harris, Elliott. "HOLY COW A moooving experience for Cincinnati." *Chicago Sun-Times*, April 2, 2002.

Henniger, Paul. "Is Keegans' CBS' 'Rich Man'?" *Journal-News* (Ohio), May 1, 1976.

Hoffman, Leonard. "TV Previews." *Tucson Daily Citizen*, May 22, 1963.

"Honey West Is TV's Swingingest Gal." *Express and News*, November 7, 1965.

Hopper, Hedda. "Drama: Three Stars Selected for Harding Original." *Los Angeles Times*, June 26, 1951.

_____. [untitled]. *Los Angeles Times*, March 19, 1952.

_____. "British Space Travel Movie Set for Duff." *Los Angeles Times*, October 21, 1952.

_____. "1965 All New Year for Anne Francis." *Los Angeles Times*, January 1, 1966.

Humphrey, Hal. "A Female Private Eye-ful." *Los Angeles Times*, August 22, 1965.

_____. "Good Loser with Winning Ways." *Los Angeles Times*, May 26, 1966.

_____. "TV Comment." *The Daily Review Sunday Previewer*, September 27, 1964.

_____. "Viewing TV: Too Well Adjusted?" *Waterloo Daily Courier* (Iowa), June 3, 1960.

Hunt, Mrs. W. West. "They Cast Off Darkness." *Los Angeles Times*, October 12, 1959.

"Impressive List of Actors Cast in Loew's Film." *The Post-Standard* (Syracuse), February 22, 1955.

"Independent Producer Goes On Nerve, Ideas." *Cumberland Sunday Times*, November 17, 1974.

"*Insight* Series to Begin Jan. 24." *Nashua Telegraph*, January 2, 1971.

James, Liza. "An Emotional Ringer." *Tucson Daily Citizen*, November 5, 1960.

J.E.V. "Capsule Comment: Honey West." November 7, 1965.

Johnson, Erskine. "In Hollywood." *The Portsmouth Herald*, March 28, 1955.

Katz, Debra Morgenstern. "On the Cable: *Charley*: Still Crazy After All These Years." *Video View*, February 7, 1983.

Kaufman, Millard. "A Vehicle for Tracy: The Road to Black Rock." *The Hopkins Review*, vol. 1, no. 1, Winter 2008.

Kilgallen, Dorothy. "The Voice of Broadway." *The Pottstown News*, May 10, 1952.

_____. "The Voice of Broadway." *New Castle News* (Pennsylvania), February 9, 1965.

Kleiner, Dick. "Anne Francis Is Victim of *Riptide*." *The Post* (Frederick, MD), March 21, 1984.

_____. "Anne Francis May Change Name." *Waterloo Daily Courier* (Iowa), August 3, 1970.

_____. "For Don Knotts ... Sex Rears Comic Head." Publication unknown, December 4, 1968.

_____. "In Hollywood." *Austin Herald* (Minneapolis), January 14, 1966.

_____. "Lowcost *Survival*: Dream or Nightmare?" *Playground Daily News,* January 20, 1970.

Larsh, Richard H. "Movie Review: *Elopement* Rumble Along In Dull Auto Ride, Lacks Luster." *Pacific Stars & Stripes*, January 2, 1952.

Lowry, Cynthia. "*Honey West* Is Not Just an Average Girl." *Burlington Daily Times-News* (North Carolina), August 12, 1965.

_____. "Monotonous TV Plots Memorized By Viewer." *Cumberland Evening Times*, March 25, 1966.

_____. "So You Thought *Flipper* Was Perfect for the Kids!" *The Cedar Rapids Gazette*, January 27, 1966.

"LWV Bids New Voters to Party at City Hall Rotunda Today." *Los Angeles Times*, September 4, 1952.

Manners, Dorothy. "Hollywood." *Anderson Daily Bulletin*, August 24, 1967.

Martin, Bob. "Reruns Battle for the No. 1 Spot." *Press-Telegram*, May 9, 1973.

_____. "TV's Original Lady Detective Turns Madam in New Movie." *The Independent-Press-Telegram and the Evening News*, October 13, 1974.

McLellan, Dennis. "Honey's Back in Town: The Book Is Not Yet Closed on 'Sexiest Private Eye' Ever to Grace a Cover." *Los Angeles Times*, December 17, 1986.

McReynolds, Bill. "Movie Racks Newman Up." *Armadillo Globe-Times*, December 12, 1956.

Mercer, Charles. "On Television: Third Commandment' Has Great Emotion Impact; Lacks Motivation." *The North Adams, Massachusetts, Transcript*, February 9, 1959.

Miller, John. "The TV Critic: 'Yum-Yum Girl' Yummy." *The Lowell Sun*, December 1, 1960.

Misurell, Ed. "TV Cameos: Anne Francis, A Realist in a Make-Believe World." *The Titusville Herald* (Pennsylvania), October 26, 1965.

"Mitzi Gaynor Wins Poll as Best Bet for Stardom." *Los Angeles Times*, October 10, 1951.

Morris, Frank. "Here, There and Hollywood." *Winnipeg Free Press*, December 19, 1951.

"Movie Life." *The Lowell Sun*, August 30, 1963.

"Movie Star Falls Off Horse and Hurts Leg." *The Hammond Times*, May 7, 1952.

Muir, Florabel. "Looking at Hollywood: She Makes a Romeo of Don Knotts." *The Abilene Reporter*, December 22, 1968.

Musel, Robert. "On the Air: 'Reporter' to Portray Real Newsman." *Anderson Daily Bulletin*, August 8, 1964.

"Mystery Woman Hunt On." *Oakland Tribune*, May 13, 1956.

"New Dramatic Series Debuts on Channel 4." *The Valley Independent*, May 1, 1971.

O'Dell, Cary. "Anne Francis' Radio and TV Days." *Nostalgia Digest*, October–November 1996.

"*One-Way Ticket to Hell*" (review). *The New York Times*, December 8, 1955.

"Pair Gets Roles in Video Film." *The Fresno Bee*, January 5, 1969.

Pappas, Leona. "On the Air with Leona Pappas." *Express-News*, October 18, 1970.

Parke, Joanne, and Paula Dranov. "The Watergate Women: Colsons 'Closer.'" *Chronicle-Telegram*, March 1, 1978.

Parsons, Louella. "Deal Is Off for RKO's *Shrike*." *The Cedar Rapids Gazette*, December 2, 1952.

_____. *The Lowell Sun*, May 6, 1954.

_____. "Louella Parsons in Hollywood: Kim Going to Cannes for *Picnic*." *The Daily Review*, March 9, 1955.

_____. "Louella's Movie-Go-'Round." *Albuquerque Journal*, September 20, 1955.

_____. "Louella's Movie-Go-'Round." *Albuquerque Journal,* December 24, 1956.

Pearlman, Cindy. "Witherspoon Finds 'Honey' of a Project." *Chicago Sun-Times*, July 16, 2001.

Penton, Edgar. "New Comedy Draws from the Era of Pratfalls." *PC*, July 18, 1964.

"People, etc." *Tucson Daily Citizen*, March 2, 1968.

"People in the News." *Independent* (Long Beach, CA), December 15, 1964.

Rae, Norman. "Call for Love" (review of *Girl of the Night*). *The Sunday Gleaner*, July 30, 1961.

"Record Co. Must Pay Songstress." *Independent* (Long Beach, CA), February 20, 1959.

Rice, Dan. "Jaclyn Smith Goes Sleuthing with Corbin Bernsen's Ghost." *The Ironwood Daily Globe*, December 11, 1992.

Rich, Allen. *TV Week* Interview, March 6, 1966.

"Robert Taylor Stars in State's Detective Drama *Rogue Cop*." *The Calverton News*, October 24, 1954.

Robinson, J. Dennis. "NH Film: *The Whistle at Eaton Falls*." http://www.seacoastnh.com/louis/whistle2.html. 1997.

Russell, Fred. "Passing Show: Inside Briefs About the Movies." *The Bridgeport Post*, September 12, 1960.

Sar, Ali. "Contrived Madness Figures in 'Perfect

Crime' Design of *Brainstorm* Thriller." *The News* (Van Nuys, CA), May 27, 1965.

Sasso, Joey. "Through Channels." Publication unknown, March 9, 1979.

Schallert, Edwin. "Drama: *Abdullah* on Program for Flynn, Addams; Anne Francis Gets Top Break." *Los Angeles Times*, November 25, 1953.

_____. "Drama: Kirk Douglas-Garland Costarring Indicated; Evans to Do Super Heavy." *Los Angeles Times*, July 10, 1951.

_____. "She's Anne of the 1000 Misfortunes: Newcomer's Movie Debut Marked by Series of Accidents." *Los Angeles Times*, June 24, 1951.

Scott, Vernon. "Actress Anne Francis Finds Little at End of Rainbow." *The Fresno Bee*, November 30, 1959.

_____. "Anne Hits Hit Spot After Low." *The Cedar Rapids Gazette*, August 24, 1967.

_____. "Anne Is One Lovely Who Is Still a Star." *The Cedar Rapids Gazette*, February 1, 1972.

_____. "*Hello, Dolly!*: Milliner in Cast, Miss McAndrew, Is Classic Beauty." *Lebanon Daily News* (Pennsylvania), January 21, 1970.

_____. "In the Role of Female Detective Sultry Beauty Learns Judo." *Times Recorder* (Zanesville, OH), March 9, 1965.

_____. "Social System Isolates Hollywood's Show Folks." *Chronicle-Telegram* (Ohio), November 5, 1958.

"Shapely Anne Francis Proves Zanuck Wrong." *The Florence Morning News* (South Carolina), May 30, 1954.

"Show Beat." *The Logansport Press* (Indiana), June 9, 1964.

"*So Young So Bad*" (review). *The Evening Capital* (Annapolis, MD), September 26, 1950.

Stanley, John. "Anne Francis: What a Honey." *San Francisco Chronicle*, May 14, 2006.

Stern, Harold. "Actor in *Honey West* Sees Emphasis Different." *The Record* (Troy, NY), November 6, 1965.

Talcove, Rick. "'Asylum' Exposes Lives of Jet Set Members." *The News* (Van Nuys, CA), December 6, 1970.

Thomas, Bob. "Low Cost Film Stresses Truth." *Newport Daily News*, February 27, 1970.

"Times-Standard TV Log." *The Times-Standard*, October 26, 1974.

T.N.T. "*So Young So Bad*" (review). *The Post-Standard* (Syracuse), October 12, 1950.

"TV Female Sporting New Look." *The Daily Review* (Hayward, CA), November 3, 1965.

"TV Forecast: *Mongo's Back in Town*." *Tucson Daily Citizen*, December 4, 1971.

"TV-Key." *The Oswego Palladium-Times* (NY), January 13, 1960.

"TV Key Previews." *The Charleston Gazette*, September 22, 1961.

"TV Previews." *Edwardsville Intelligencer*, February 13, 1974.

"TV Scout." *The Abilene Reporter-News*, November 25, 1964.

"TV Scout." *The Albuquerque Tribune*, December 3, 1965.

"TV Scout." *The Morning Herald* (Hagerstown, MD), October 29, 1965.

"TV Scout." *The Post-Standard* (Syracuse), January 13, 1960.

"TV Scout." *The Transcript*, October 23, 1970.

"TV Scout." *The Transcript*, April 26, 1976.

"TV Tonight." *Syracuse Herald-Journal*, April 7, 1965.

"TV Tonight." *Syracuse Herald-Journal*, December 10, 1965.

"TV Tonight." *Syracuse Herald-Journal*, February 11, 1966.

"TV Tonight." *Syracuse Herald-Journal*, March 4, 1966.

Untitled. *Cumberland Times* (Maryland), June 23, 1946.

Vadeboncoeur, Joan E. "Finale Is Tops for *Satan Bug*." *Herald-Journal*, April 29, 1965.

_____. "TV's Most Lethal Lady." *Syracuse Herald-American*, October 3, 1965.

Vale, Virginia. "Star Dust." *The Soda Springs Sun* (Idaho), May 16, 1946.

Vasche, Mark. "Anne Francis, Still a 'Honey,' Looks to Better Film Days." *The Modesto Bee*, May 16, 1971.

Voedisch, Lynn. "Anne Francis Feels Kinship to Character in 'Magnolias.'" *Chicago Sun–Times*, November 6, 1988.

_____. "Constance Towers Adds Tension to *Steel Magnolias*." *Chicago Sun–Times*, March 6, 1989.

_____. "Steel Magnolias' Is a Treasure." *Chicago Sun–Times*, November 6, 1988.

"Washington's Cane Is Anne's Walking Aid." *The Star*, November 14, 1952.

Werts, Diane. "Drawing a Bead on Honey West's Private (Eye) Life." *Newsday*, April 24, 1999.

"When a Girl Grows Up." *Radio Mirror*, March 1947.

Wilson, Earl. "Earl Wilson Says." *Delaware County Daily Times*, September 15, 1960.

_____. "It Happened Last Night." *Press-Telegram* (Long Beach, CA), February 1, 1955.

Wylder, Robert C. "Star-Filled 'Remote Asylum' Remains Remote, Obscure." *Independent Press-Telegram*, December 7, 1970.

Websites

www.afi.com
www.annefrancis.net
www.imdb.com

INDEX

Numbers in **_bold italics_** indicate photographs.

The A-Team 116
Aalberg, John 132
Abandon Ship 109
Abbott, Bruce 224
Abbott & Costello 205
Abeloff, Dr. Robert 57, 62–63, 64, 67
The Abilene Reporter-News 186
"The Abominable Snowman" (*Honey West*) 83, 230–231
About Schmidt 121
Adams, Edie 210
Adams, Julie 210
"Adventure of the Lover's Leap" (*Ellery Queen*) 205
Adventures in Paradise 13, 162
"The After Hours" (*The Twilight Zone*) 64, 165–167, *166*
Agar, John 25, *25*
Ah, Wilderness! 124
Ahn, Philip 203
Aidman, Charles 199, *200*
Akins, Claude 204, *205*
The Albuquerque Tribune 234
Alcoa Premiere 172, *173*
The Alfred Hitchcock Hour 50, 56, 64, *64*, 172, 175–176, *176*, 186
Alfred Hitchcock Presents 64, 167, 170
The Alfred Hitchcock Presents Companion 172
"All Nice and Legal" (*The Virginian*) 185–186, *185*, 194
All the King's Men 24
Allen, Tim 109, 225–226
Ameche, Don *115*, 153
American Magazine 34
American Playhouse 216–217
Anderson, Jack 60
Andrews, Dana 56, 66, *68*
Angeli, Pier 19, 49
"Angels of the Deep" (*Charlie's Angels*) 214–215
"Anne Francis vs. Arte Johnson" (*Password All-Stars*) 196
Anne of the Indies 14
Ann-Margret 88
Ant, Adam 156
Apollo Productions 180
Archer 204
Archer, John 191
Arness, James 197
Arnold, Chuck 204

Arrest & Trial 64, 177, *177*
Arthur, Bea 154, 223
Ashton, John 227–228
Asner, Ed 106
Assignment: Vienna 197, *198*
Astaire, Fred 153
Astounding B Monster Book 5
The Atlantic Monthly 158
Aubrey, James 182, 183
Aunt Jenny's True Life Stories 5
Austin, Karen 222
The Avengers 79, 83

Baa Baa Black Sheep 98, 208–209
Baby Doll 41
Bacharach, Burt 222
Bad Day at Black Rock 3, 34–37, *35*, *36*, 50, 81, 108, 132, *134*
Bad Day at Honda see *Bad Day at Black Rock*
"Bad Time at Honda" 34, 36
Bagni, Gwen 69, 242
Baker, Chet 168
Baker, Joe Don 104
Ball, Lucille *84*, 95, 122
Balsam, Martin 171
"The Bamboo Curtain" (*Adventures in Paradise*) 162
Banacek 98, 201–202, *202*
Banjo Hackett: Roamin' Free 13, 109–110, 149–150
Bankhead, Tallulah 18
Barnaby Jones 13, 98, 198–199, 205–207, *206*, 224
Barrios, Richard 9
Barry, Gene 68, 69, 85, 177, 189–190, *190*, 224–225
Barry, Harold 157
Barrymore, Ethel 7
Barton, Anne 191
Barton, Peter 224
Basehart, Richard 65
Bassler, Richard 20
The Bastard 112
Batman 82
Battle Cry 30–31, *31*, 132–134, 221
Baudouin, King *161*
Baumann, Marty 5, 6, 26
Baur, Elizabeth 203
Baxter, Anne 20
"Beauty on Parade" (*Wonder Woman*) 1, 208
Beck, Ken 81

Beck, Marilyn 194
Beggarman, Thief 112, 151
Believe It or Not 11, 158
Ben Casey 3, 64, 175, 180–181
Ben-Hur 38
Benchley, Nathaniel 139
Benchley, Peter 139
Benchley, Robert 139
Benedict, Richard 144
Benton, Suzanne 97
Benz, Donna 210
Bergen, Polly 19, 67
Berk, Ed 116
Berkman, Ted 60
Berlin, Pamela 118
Bernsen, Corbin 120
Bert D'Angelo/Superstar 208
Best, James 174–175, *174*
Bethune, Zena 121
"The Big Show of 1965" (*Murder, She Wrote*) 224
Big Town 5
The Big Valley 81, 83
Bill Haley and the Comets 38
Binyon, Claude 18
"A Bird in the Solitude Singing" (*Ben Casey*) 180–181
Bishop, Joey 92
Bitabit, Bruce 81, 228–243
Black, Lisa Hartman 120
"Black Sheep" (*Kraft Television Theatre*) 158
Black Sheep Squadron see *Baa Baa Black Sheep*
Blackboard Jungle 3, 37–41, *37*, *39*, 134–135
Blackman, Honor 79
Blacula 128
Blankfort, Michael 14
Blass, Terry 40
Blau, Raphael 60
Blood and Honey 70, 71, 72
"Blood Bargain" (*The Alfred Hitchcock Hour*) 175–176, *176*
Blowen, Michael 153
Bob & Carol & Ted & Alice 96
Bobbin, Jay 120
Bochner, Lloyd 168
Bogart, Humphrey 225
Bogart, Linda Scruggs 208–209
Bombshell 70, 72, 75–76
Bono, Sonny 214
Booth, Phillip 6

Borgnine, Ernest 126, 139
Born Again 110–112, *111*, 112, 151
Bosley, Tom 112
Bostock, Barbara 168
The Boston Globe 153
"Bourbon in Suburbia" (*Insight*) 192
Boyington, Major Greg "Pappy"
    208–209
The Boys in the Band 100
Bradford, Jack 184
Bradley, Matthew R. 7, 11, 24, 36,
    41, 55
Brainstorm 3, 66–67, *68*, 69, *69*,
    141–142, *141*, 201
Brand, Neville 193
Bray, Thorn 116, 117
Bregman, Buddy 53
Brenneman, Amy 121
Breslin, Howard 34, 36
Brice, Fanny 87, 88
The Brick Foxhole 34
Bridges, Lloyd 12, 95, 106, 143
The Bright Promise 20
Brinkley, William 139
"Broken Angels" (*Police Woman*)
    208, *209*
Bronson, Charles 188
Brooks, Richard 34–35, 38, 41
Brothers, Joyce 156
Brown, Harry 55
Bruce, Lenny 26
Bruni, Rev. Philip P. 192
Bryant, William 203
Burke's Law 64, 68–70, 78, 80, 81,
    177, 186–187, 224, 231
Burke's Law (1994) 85, 224–225
Burns, George 160
Burr, Raymond 196, 203
Burrud, Bill 199
Byers, Bill 6
Byrnes, Edd 85, 224
Byron, Lord 181

Cabin B-13 20
Cabot, Susan 19
Caged 8–10
Cagney, James 5, *23*, 24–25, 28
Cagney & Lacey 224
Cagney Productions, Inc. 24
Caillou, Alan 195, 196
Calhoun, Rory 51, *52*, 139
Calhoun-Orsatti Enterprises, Inc.
    see Rorvic Productions
The Call Girl 58
Calvert, Corinne 20
Cameron, Rod 193
Campos, Rafael 135
Campus, Michael 97–98
Cannell, Stephen J. 116
Cannon 98, 200–201, *201*
Cannon, Dyan 96
Carey, Drew 227
Carey, Macdonald 20
Carlisle, Belinda 179
Carpenter, Carleton 12, 13, *13*, 126
Carr, Richard 99
Carradine, David 204
"The Carrier" see "Countdown to
    Panic"

Carroll, Harrison 33
Carroll, Lewis 237
Carson, Johnny 92, 162
Carter, Dixie 121
Carter, Lynda 208
Cassidy, Jack 199
Cat on a Hot Tin Roof 55
The Catered Affair 51
Cates, Gil 154
Cates, Joseph 60
Catlett, Mary Jo 212
Celebrity Sweepstakes 204
Chamberlain, Richard 170
Champion, Marge 19
Chandler, Raymond 118, 153
"Chant of Silence" (*The Wide
    World of Mystery*) 200
Chaplin, Sydney 87
Chapman, Lonny 212–213
The Charleston Gazette 170
"Charley's Aunt" (*American Play-
    house*) 216–217
Charlie's Angels 1, 85, 110, 114, 212–
    213, 214–215, 224
Chayefsky, Paddy 51
The Chicago Sun-Times 118, 122,
    153, 217
CHiPs 114, 216
Christenberry, Chris 196
Christmas Bells 6
Clark, Dane 189
Clark, Jim 81
Clark, Superior Judge John Gee
    53–54
"The Class Beauty" see "The Girl
    Who Always Said No"
"Class of '40" (*Ironside*) 202–203
Claudelle Inglish 62
Claudia (film) 160
Claudia (TV) 160
Claudia and David 160
Climax! 159, 150
Close, Eric 228
Clouser, Suzanne 109
Coast to Coast on a Bus 5
Coleman, Dabney 189
Collins, Pat 236
Colson, Charles 110–112
Colson, Patty 110–112
Columbo 98, 105, 196, 198, 234
"Come to Me, My Litigation
    Baby" (*Honey West*) 239–240
Comes a Day 55
Conan 120, 226
"Connections" (*Finders of Lost
    Loves*) 221–222
Connolly, Maureen 110, 150
Connolly, Mike 55
Connors, Chuck 107, 109, 177
Conrad, Robert 197, *198*, 208, 209
Conrad, William 66–67, 200–201,
    201, 222–223
Converse, Frank 204
Cook, Elisha, Jr. 218
Cooper, Gladys 64, 172
Cooper, Jackie 208
Corbin, Barry 227
Corey, Jeff 109
Corey, Wendell 138, 175

Cornell, Don 131
Cotten, Joseph 8
"Countdown to Panic" (*Search*)
    197–198
Crawford, Broderick 24
Crazy Like a Fox 114, 220, *221*
Crenna, Richard 109
Criss Cross 13
Cronyn, Hume 158
Crosby, Bing 172
Crosby, Joan 100, 102
Crossfire 34
The Crowded Sky 56–57, *57*, *58*,
    139–140
Crowley, Mart 100
Crowther, Bosley 8–9, 128, 132
The Cry of the Laughing Owls see
    Johnny Tiger
Cry Panic 108, 148
Cummins, Peggy 20
"The Curse of Afka" (*Conan*) 226

Dailey, Dan 131
The Daily Globe 120
The Daily Review 80
Daily Variety 117
The Daily Word 113
Dallas 114, 215–216
Daly, Tim 225
Daly, Tyne 121
Dan August 96, 195
Danova, Cesare 234–236
Danzig, Fred 164
Danziger, Edward J. 10
Danziger, Harry Lee 10
Dark, Christopher 165
Dark Justice 224
"Dark Legend" see "Theater of
    Fear"
The Dark Mirror 13
Darnell, Linda 14
Dateline: Hollywood 188
The David Niven Show 160
Davis, Bette 3, 122
Davis, Richard Harding 187
"Deadfall" (*The F.B.I.*) 192
"The Deadliest Enemy of All: Part
    1" (*Baa Baa Black Sheep*) 208–
    209
"The Deadliest Enemy of All: Part
    2" (*Baa Baa Black Sheep*) 209
"The Deadly Tattoo" (*Climax!*)
    160
Dean, Jimmy 216
Death Dance at Madelia see *The
    Intruders*
Death Valley Days 180
"The Decision" (*True Confessions*)
    222
Decoy 79
Deer, Susan 109
The Defenders 183
De Haven, Gloria 109
Dehner, John 160, 213
The Delphi Bureau 197
Demarest, William 195
Denison, Anthony John 118
Denniker, Paul 168
De Rochemont, Louis 12

Derr, Richard 199
Detour to Terror 114, **114**, 152
Deutsch, Armand 160
Deverman, Dale 175
DeVito, Danny 85
Devon, Laura **174**
Devon, Richard 181
De Wilde, Brandon **193**
Dexter, Brad 50
"Diamonds Are for Never" (*Riptide*) 219
The Dick Powell Show 68
Dickinson, Angie 208, 210
Dieterle, William 8
Dietrich, Marlene 20, 129
Dig a Dead Doll 70
Dillman, Bradford 214
Dimensions Behind the Twilight Zone 166
Dinah 204
Dinan, Patsy 51
Disney, Walt 62, 187
Dix, Robert 33
"The Doctor Is In" (*Dark Justice*) 224
Dr. Kildare 64, 170
"Dr. Violet" (*Suspense*) 158
Dominguez, Beatrice 242
Don't Go Near the Water 51, 53, **54**, 139
"Don't Look Now, but Isn't That Me" (*Honey West*) 238–239, **239**
"Don't Rain on My Parade" 89
"The Doreen Maney Story" (*The Untouchables*) 165
"The Double Circle" (*Mission: Impossible*) 191
The Double O Kid 120, 155
Douglas, Diana 12
Douglas, Robert 41
Doversola, Gordon 78
Drake, Charles 188, 189
Dreamboat 18–19, **19–20**, 29, 128–129, 180, 236
The Drew Carey Show 120, 227
Drury, James 96, 185, 193–194, **194**
Dubov, Paul 69, 242
Duggan, Andrew 104
Dukes, David 210
Dulin, Dann 122, 188
Duncan, David D. 41, 55, 84, 95
Dungeons and Dragons see *Mazes and Monsters*
Dunne, Philip 14
Durant, Don 134
Durante, Jimmy 7
Dynasty 80

East Side/West Side 183
Ebsen, Buddy 85, 199, **206**, 207, 224
The Eddie Capra Mysteries 210
Eden, Barbara 229
Edwards, Vince 175
"An Eerie, Airy, Thing" (*Honey West*) 242–243
Eighth and Elm 20

Elam, Jack **179**
The Eleventh Hour 175
Elg, Taina 33
Ellery Queen 5, 205
Elopement 17–18, **18**, 19, 126–128, **127**
The Encyclopedia of TV Pets 81
"End of the Road Part 1" (*Dallas*) 215
"End of the Road Part 2" (*Dallas*) 215
Ephron, Henry 129
Ephron, Phoebe 129
Ericson, John **35**, 67, 69, **70**, 80, 81, 82, 228–243
Escape If You Can see *So Young So Bad*
The Evening Capital 124
Evers, Jason 203
"Ev'ry Other Day" 13, 126
Ewell, Tom 50, **50**

Fabiani, Joel **200**
The Facts of Life 20
"The Faithful Heart" (*Lights Out*) 158
Falk, Peter 105
Fancher, Hampton 98
Fantasy Island 110, 114, 212, 214, 216
Fantasy Island (1999) 120, 227–228
Farah, Jameel see Farr, Jamie
Farr, Jamie 40, 135
Farrell, Glenda 26, 162
"Fat Chance" (*Trapper John, M.D.*) 218
"Fatal Attraction" (*Jake and the Fatman*) 222–223
Father's Little Leaguer see *The Great American Pastime*
Fayed, Dodi 85
Faylen, Frank 142
The F.B.I. 98, 192, 201
F.B.I. Story: The F.B.I. Versus Alvin Karpis, Public Enemy Number One 108–109, 148
"Fear of Cheesecake" (*Flying High*) 210–211, **211**
"Fergus for Sale" (*My Three Sons*) 195
Fickling, G.G. 70, 75, 78, 236
Fickling, Gloria 70, 75, 78, 82, 83, 85, 224, 236
Fickling, Forrest "Skip" 70, 75, 76, 78, 224, 236
Fidler, Jimmy 19, 129
Field, Sally 104
Filmfax 11, 30, 43, 49, 67, 96
Finders of Lost Loves 114, 221–222
A Fire in the Sky see *The Intruders*
Fireball Forward 105, 147
Fisher, Steve 131
"The Flame and the Pussycat" (*Honey West*) 233
Flying High 210–211, **211**
Forbidden Planet 1, 2, 3, 4, 42–47, **43, 44, 45, 46, 47**, 61, 122, 135–136, **136**, **137**
Ford, Glenn 37, **37**, 38, **39**, **40**, **54**

Ford Startime 163–164, **163**
Ford Theatre 159
Forever Amber 20
The Forgotten Man 103, **104**, 146–147
Forrest, Steve 33, 200
Forsythe, John 108
Fortune Hunter 197, 225
Foster, Bob 78
Fotre, Vincent 99
The Four Horsemen of the Apocalypse 242
Foxworthy, Robert 108
Franciosa, Tony **182**, 190
Francis, Arlene 22, 62
Francis, Edith 5, 6
Francis, Phillip 5, 6
Franciscus, James 175
Frankel, Mark 225
Franken, Rose 160
"The Fraudulent Female" (*Valentine's Day*) 63, 182, **182**
Freeman, Mona 30
From Hell to Borneo 62
"The Frostfire Intercept" (*Fortune Hunter*) 225
The Fugitive 95, 188
"The Fun-Fun Killer" (*Honey West*) 240–241
Funny Girl (stage) 87
Funny Girl (film) 86, 87–92, **89**, **90**, **93**, 94, **94**, 142
"A Funny Valentine" (*Home Improvement*) 225–226
"The Further Adventures of Gallegher: The Big Swindle" (*The Wonderful World of Disney*) 187
"The Further Adventures of Gallegher: A Case of Murder" (*The Wonderful World of Disney*) 187
"The Further Adventures of Gallegher: The Daily Press vs. City Hall" (*The Wonderful World of Disney*) 187

Gabor, Eva 53, **54**
Gallegher (Boy Reporter) 187
Gallegher Goes West 188
Gallo, Lillian 106–107
Gammon, James 226–227
Garde, Betty 169
Gardella, Kay 79, 229
"The Garden" (*The Name of the Game*) 191
Gardner, Ava 21–22
Garfield, John 183
Garland, Beverly 79
Gaynor, Mitzi 19
Gazzara, Ben 105, 177, **177**
Geer, Will 198
Gemini Rising 95, 103
Gentlemen Prefer Blondes 129
"Getting in Shape" (*Partners in Crime*) 219–220
Gillette, Priscilla 129
Gilligan's Island 95
Ging, Jack 116, 170
Girl in the Dark see *Girl of the Night*

Girl in the Night see *Girl of the Night*
A *Girl Named Sooner* 109, 149
Girl of the Night 3, 13, 58–62, **59**, **61**, **62**, 97, 140, **140**
Girl on the Loose 70, 72
Girl on the Prowl 70
"The Girl Who Always Said No" (*What Really Happened to the Class of '65?*) 213
Gish, Dorothy 12
"The Giuoco Piano Affair" (*The Man from U.N.C.L.E.*) 184
Givot, George 157
"The Glass Palace" (*Alcoa Premiere*) 172, **173**
The Globe-Times 49
The Godfather of Grappling 78
Going My Way (film) 172
Going My Way (TV) 64, **171**, 172
Golden Bullet see *Impasse*
The Golden Girls 114, 223
Goldstein, Samuel 25
Goldstone, James 108
"Good Housekeeping" (*Kraft Television Theatre*) 158
"Goodbye, Fergus" (*My Three Sons*) 196
Gordon, Bernard 107–108
Gordon, Clarke 145
Gordon, Mack 162
Gorshin, Frank **115**
Gottlieb, Alex 131
Gould, Harold 156, 199
Gould, Jack 229
Graham, Sheilah 23, 92
Granger, Stewart 41, 135
Grant, Cary 131
Graves, Peter 160, 191
"The Gray Lady" (*Honey West*) 234–236, **235**
The Great American Pastime 50, **50**, 138–139
The Great Gabbo 157
The Greatest Heroes of the Bible 213
Greenspun, Roger 143
Greenwald, Dr. Harold 58, 60
Greenwood, Bruce 222
Gregory, James 196
Gregory, Mollie 106
Griffin, Merv 6
Griffith, Andy 223
Grodin, Charles 217
Guardino, Harry 182–183
A *Gun for Honey* 70, 75
"Gun Quest" (*The Men from Shiloh*) 193–194, **193**, **194**
Gunsmoke 98, 197
Gutman, Leo 240

Hackett, Buddy 26
Hackett, Joan 64, 141
Hale, Alan, Jr. 32
Hale, Barbara 24, 129
Hale, Edward Everett 158
The Hallelujah Trail 65
Hamlin, Harry 118
The Hammond Times 128
Hamner, Earl, Jr. 175

Handler, David 116
Handsaker, Gene 128
"Hang by One Hand" (*The Eleventh Hour*) 175
"Happy Birthday, Marvin" (*Insight*) 199
"The Hardcase" (*Riptide*) 219
Hardcastle and McCormick 3, 220–221
Hardwicke, Cedric 164
Harling, Robert 118
Harper, Valerie 194
Harrington, Pat, Jr. 227–228
Harris, Eleanor 7
Harris, Jo Ann 201
Harrison, Gregory 215
Hartford, Dee 98
Hashim, Edmund 170
"Hatchet Job" (*Riptide*) 218, 219
Haunts of the Very Rich 105–107, 147
Have You Seen My Son 120, 156
Hawaii Five-O 98, 210
Hawk of the Desert 20
Hayes, Gabby 240
Hayward, Susan 14, 20
Hecht, Ben 157, 160
Heckart, Eileen 108, **211**
Helfer, Ralph 81
Hell of Borneo see *From Hell to Borneo*
Hello, Dolly! 92
Hemingway, Ernest 20
Hemphill, Shirley 218
Henley, Jack 26
Henniger, Paul 110
Henreid, Paul 8, 9–11, **9**, **126**, 168
Hepburn, Katharine 3, 92, 142
The Herald-Journal 65, 78
"Heroes" (*Fantasy Island*) 227–228
Hervey, Irene 67, 81, 83, 228–243
Heston, Charlton 141, 158
"Hey, Hey, We're the Monkees" 226
Heyes, Douglas 167
"Hideout" (*The Reporter*) 181–182
Higgins, John C. 144
Hines, Connie 165
The Hired Gun 50–51, **52**, **53**, 139
Hitchcock, Alfred 18, 172
Hoffman, Herman 50
Hoffman, John Robert 225
Hoffman, Leonard 172
"Hold My Hand" 131
Holden, Joyce 19
Holland, Dr. Jack 113
Holliman, Earl 51, 108
Holloway, Jean 185
Hollywood Exile or How I Learned to Love the Blacklist 107
The Hollywood Palace 240
The Hollywood Reporter 26, 80, 81, 91, 117
Holmes, Bill 50
Holmes, Oliver Wendell, Jr. 164
Home Improvement 13, 109, 225–226
Home Improvements 109
Honey in the Flesh 70

Honey on Her Tail 70, 76
Honey West (TV) 1–2, 3, 4, 67–86, **70**, **71**, **73**, 87, 94, 99, 110, 120, 121, 187, 224, 227 228–243, **232**, **239**, **242**
Honey West (book series) 70–78, 82, 83, 236
"Honey West Walk" 240
Hong Kong 13, 168, **169**
Hook, Line and Sinker 95–96, **97**, 144
"Hooked" (*Alfred Hitchcock Presents*) 167
Hoover, J. Edgar 108
Hope, Bob **115**, 153
Hopper, Hedda 20, 22, 67
"Horse of a Slightly Different Color" (*Banacek*) 201–202, **202**
Horton, Michael 220
Horton, Robert 167
Hostile Guns see *The Hired Gun*
House on Haunted Hill 11
"How Brillig, O, Beamish Boy" (*Honey West*) 237
"How Do I Kill Thee?" (*The Eddie Capra Mysteries*) 210
Howard, Robert E. 226
Howard, Susan 207
Hume, Cyril 42
Humphrey, Hal 7, 52, 56, 69, 83, 183, 185
Hunter, Evan 37, 38
Hunter, Jeffrey 18, 19, **20**, 66, 67, **141**, 142, 180
Hunter, Tab 30, 31
Huston, Walter 7
Hutton, Jim 205

I Dream of Jeannie 229
"I Know Why (And So Do You)" 162
"I Like It Here" (*Kraft Television Theatre*) 159
Impasse 96, **98**, 144–145
"In Love with Love" (*Kraft Television Theatre*) 158
"In the Bag" (*Honey West*) 81, 232, **232**
"In the Best of Families" (*CHiPs*) 216
"Incident in Berlin" (*The Name of the Game*) 189–190, **190**
"Incident of the Shambling Man" (*Rawhide*) 161–162
Insight 192, 199
The Intruders 86–87, **86**, 146
The Invaders 95, 188–189, **189**
"Invitation to Limbo" (*Honey West*) 236
Ireland, Jill 184
Ironside 98, 196, 202–203
"It All Depends on You" 223
"It's Earlier Than You Think" (*Honey West*) 238
Ives, Burl 6

"Jack and the Beanstalk" 6
Jackson, Anne 8, 124
Jaffe, Sam 181

Jake and the Fatman 13, 114, 222–223

Jakes, John 112

James, Liza 60

Janssen, David 188

The Jealousy Factor 195

"Jeff McCleod, the Last Reb" (*Ford Startime*) 163–164, *163*

"Jess-Belle" (*The Twilight Zone*) 64, 174–175, *174*

Jigsaw (film) 10

Jigsaw (TV) 197

The Joey Bishop Show 189

Johnny Tiger 62

Johnson, Don *112*, 226–227

Johnson, Emile Richard 103, 105

Johnson, Erskine 22, 33

Johnson, Van 7

Jones, Allan 81

Jones, Dean 110, *111*

Jones, Jack 81

Jones, Jennifer 8

Jones, L.Q. 134

Journal of Fear 33

Joy, Nicholas 138

Joyce, Elaine 224

Judd, for the Defense 183

Juke Box Jury 54, 160

Jurado, Katy *39*

"Just One of Those Things" 224

"Just the Bear Facts, Ma'am" (*Honey West*) 241–242

Justice see *The Rocket Man*

Justice Brown see *The Rocket Man*

Kaleidoscope 160

Kanakeredes, Melina 121

Kanter, Hal 182

Kashfi, Anna 139

Katz, Debra Morgenstern 217

Kaufman, Millard 34, 36, 37, 41, 132

Kazan, Elia 41

"Keep Me Company" (*Alfred Hitchcock Presents*) 170

"Keep the Home Fries Burning" (*Murder, She Wrote*) 222

Kefauver, Senator Estes 40

Keiser, Father Ellwood E. 192

Keith, Brian 204, 220, 221

Kelley, Clarence M. 108

Kelly, Gene 172

Kelly, Jack 43, *44*

Kelly, Nancy 100

Kelvaney see *Rogue Cop*

Kemmer, Edward 160

Kerr, John 33, 56, *57*, 58, *59*, 60, *140*

The Kid from Outer Space see *The Rocket Man*

Kiel, Richard 237–238

Kiley, Richard 176, 191

Kilgallen, Dorothy 16, 67

The Killers 13

King, Henry 21

King, Perry 116, 117, *117*, 219

"The King Is Dead" (*Dan August*) 195

King of the Khyber Rifles 20

"King of the Mountain" (*Honey West*) 81, 237–238

Kirby, Michael 7

Kiss for a Killer 70

Kleiner, Dick 92, 97, 98, 114, 116–117, 240

Klous, Pat 211, *211*

Klugman, Jack 213

Knotts, Don 96–97, *99*, *145*

Knudsen, Harold 134

Kohlmar, Fred 128

Korvin, Charles 15

Koster, Henry 18, 42, 128

Kovack, Nancy 236

Kove, Martin 224

Kraft Suspense Theatre 64, 178–179, *178*

Kraft Television Theatre 11, 158

Kung Fu 98, 203–204

Ladd, Cheryl 110

"Lady Douglas" (*My Three Sons*) 195

Lady in the Dark 6

"Lady Killer" (*The New Breed*) 170–171

"The Lady Vanishes" (*Wings*) 225

Laguna Heat 118, *119*, 153

Lamkin, Marguerite 55

Lamkin, Speed 55

Lampert, Zohra 192

Landers, Audrey 216

Lang, Perry 118, 227

Langley, Adria Locke 24

Lansbury, Angela 220, 222, 224

Lansing, Robert 217–218, *217*

Larsh, Richard H. 17–18

"The Last Stagecoach Robbery" (*Death Valley Days*) 180

The Last Survivors 109, 149

Laurie, Piper 55

Laven, Arnold 49

Lawrence, Gertrude 6

Lawrence, Jack 131

The Lawyer 207

Leachman, Cloris 106, 109

Learned, Michael 110

LeBell, Gene 78–79

Legally Blonde 85

Leigh, Janet 31, 132

Lennart, Isobel 87, 92

Leonard, Elmore 118, 153

Lerner, Ron 240

Let's Pretend 5

Levinson, Richard 234–236

Lewis, Jarma 33

Lewis, Jerry 95–96, 97, *97*

Lewis, Monica 19

Liberty Magazine 157

Life with Linkletter 193

Lifeboat 18

Lights Out 11, 158

"Like Visions and Omens ... and All That Jazz" (*Honey West*) 238

Lindfors, Viveca 67

Link, William 234–236

The Linkletter Show 180

The Lion in Winter 92, 142

A Lion Is in the Streets 1, *23*, 24–25, 30, 129, *130*

"The Listening Ear" (*Mobile One*) 207–208

"Little Green Robin Hood" (*Honey West*) 241

Little Leaguer see *The Great American Pastime*

Little Mo 110, 150

Little Vegas 118–119, 155, 227

The Littlest Hobo 214

"Live a Little, Kill a Little" (*Honey West*) 231

Lockhart, June 213

Lockwood, Gary 214

Loew, Lieutenant Jimmy 50

Loggia, Robert 210

London, Julie 71

Long, Huey 24

Long, Richard 176, *176*

Loomis, Dr. Evarts 113

Lopez, Perry 134

Lord, Jack 168

The Los Angeles Times 25, 60, 70, 78, 82, 83, 84, 109, 156

Lost Boundaries 12

Lost Flight 95, *95*, 142–143

Love, American Style 98, 194–195

"Love and the Visitor" (*Love, American Style*) 194–195

The Love Boat 114, 219

Love Can Be Murder 120, 155

The Love God? 96–97, *99*, 145–146, *145*

Love Me, Love Me Not 20

"Lover Man" 168

Lover's Knot 120, 156

The Lowell Sun 167

Lowry, Cynthia 80, 243

Lucas, Sharon 79, 233, 242

Lukas, Paul 157–158

Lumet, Sidney 142

Lundigan, William 17, *18*, 20, *127*, 128

Lupino, Ida 95, 205

Lupton, John 30, *31*, 221

Lux Video Theatre 159

Lydia Bailey 14–17, *15–16*, 19, 20, 23, 128

Lyons, Gene 172

Macdonald, Ross 204

"The Machine That Played God" (*Kraft Suspense Theatre*) 178–179, *178*

MacLaine, Shirley 152

MacMurray, Fred 195–196

Mahaffey, Valerie 228

Maharis, George 64, 65, *66*, 168, 169–170, *169*

Main, Marjorie 116

"Making of a President" (*Dallas*) 215

Malone, Dorothy 30

"A Man for Mary" (*Going My Way*) *171*, 172

The Man from U.N.C.L.E. 64, 183–184

"A Man Named Arno" (*Ironside*) 196

"The Man Without a Country" (*Believe It or Not*) 158
Manhunt 167
Mann, Delbert 109
Mann, Howard 228
Manners, Dorothy 88
The March of Time 12
Marcus, Lawrence B. 67
Markham, Monte 193
Marks, Barbara 33
Marley, John 213
Marshall, George 96
Marshall, William 16, 128
Martell, Kurt 33
Martin, Bob 107, 200
Martin, Eugenio 107
Martin, Quinn 109, 171, 208
Marty 109
Marvin, Lee 36
The Mary Tyler Moore Show 194
Mason, James 179
Mason, Marsha 120
Mason, Morgan 179
Mason, Pamela 179
Massey, Raymond 30
A Masterpiece of Murder 114, **115**, 153
Matheson, Tim 199
Matlock 114, 223
"A Matter of Wife and Death" (*Honey West*) 231
Maverick 180
Maxwell, Marilyn 100
Mazes and Monsters 114, 152
Mazursky, Paul 40
McAndrew, Marianne 92
McBain, Diane 62
McCallum, David 184
McCann, Chuck 97, 98
McCarthy, Frank 20, 105
McCarthy, Kevin 234–236, **235**
McCay, Peggy 138
McCloskey, Leigh 216
McClure, Doug 112
McCormick, Maureen 232, **232**
McCrea, Joel 34
McDermott, Tom 80
McDowall, Roddy 196
McDowell, Malcolm 227
McGivern, William P. 31
McGuire, Dorothy 160
McHugh, Frank 162
McLaglen, Victor 162
McLellan, Dennis 70–71
McLeod, Catherine 10
McQueen, Justus E. see Jones, L.Q.
McRaney, Gerald 217
Meadows, Jayne **115**
"The Mean Green Love Machine" (*Riptide*) 218–219
Medford, Kay 90, 92, 142
Meeker, Ralph 95, 108, 143
The Men (TV) 197
The Men from Shiloh 98, 193–194, **193**, **194**
Mercer, Charles 160
Meredith, Don 109–110
Merrill, Bob 87

Merrill, Dina 100
Merrill, Gary 20, **178**, 179, 183
The Mike Douglas Show 193
Miller, Ann 139
Miller, John 167
Miller, Nolan 80
Millhollin, James **166**
"A Million Bucks in Anybody's Language" (*Honey West*) 234
"A Million Dollar Property" (*Dr. Kildare*) 170
Millner, Cork 14, 19, 62
Mills, Donna 106
Milner, Martin 168, 169–170
Minardos, Nico 196
Mission: Impossible 95, 191
Misurell, Ed 79, 82
Mitchell, George 165
Mitchum, Robert 131
Mobile One 207–208
Mobley, Roger 187
The Modesto Bee 23
Moeller, Ralf 226
Mongo's Back in Town 103–105, 147
Monica Productions 10
The Monkees 226
Monroe, Marilyn 30, 51, 63, 71, 78, 129
Montalban, Ricardo 105, **163**, 172, **172**, 212
Montevecchi, Lillian 33
Montgomery, George 62
Montgomery, Poppy 228
"A Month of Sundays" (*Route 66*) 168–170, **169**
Moonjean, Hank 160
Moonlighting 84
Moore, Roger 33
Moore, Terry 30, 55
Moran, Jim 95
More Dead Than Alive 95, **96**, 107, 143–144, **143**
Moreno, Rita 8, 124
Morgan, Michael 216
Morheim, Lou 99
The Morning Herald 232
Morris, Chester 172
Morris, Frank 128
Morris, Howard 214
Morrow, Vic 33, 38, 40, 135
Morse, Barry 188
"Moses: Part 1" (*The Greatest Heroes of the Bible*) 213
"Moses: Part 2" (*The Greatest Heroes of the Bible*) 213
"Mother Mishkin" (*Vega$*) 211–212
The Movie Game 192
Movin' On 204, **205**
Muir, Florabel 95, 97
Mullendore, Joseph 80
"Murder by Proxy" (*Cannon*) 200–201, **201**
"Murder by Proxy" (*Dan August*) 195
"Murder in the Doll's House" (*Barnaby Jones*) 198–199
"The Murder of Sherlock Holmes" (*Murder, She Wrote*) 220

Murder, She Wrote 13, 114, 220, 222, 224, 234
"Murder with Pretty People" (*Police Woman*) 209–210
Murphy, Timothy Patrick 216
Murray, Don 86, **86**, 87, 109
Murray, Jan 109
Musel, Robert 183
My Blood Runs Cold 66
"My Buddy" 223
My First Love 114, 154
"My Funny Valentine" 226
My Sister Eileen 13
"My Sweetheart's the Man in the Moon" 109
My Three Sons 98, 195–196
My Wife's Best Friend 20
Myers, Richard 131
The Mystery of Edward Sims 188
The Mystery of Misty Creek 50
Mystery Scene 70

Nachman, Gerald 91
Nader, George 69
Nagel, Conrad 169
Naish, J. Carrol 159
Nall, Roly P. 40
The Name of the Game 95, 189–190, **190**, 191
Nash Bridges 120, 226–227
The Nashua Telegraph 192
"A Neat Little Package" (*Honey West*) 233
Negulesco, Jean 15
Nelson, Ed 172, 197–198
Ness, Eliot 165
The New Breed 64, 170–171
The New York Mirror 183
The New York Times 8–9, 33, 39–40, 128, 132, 143, 145, 229
Newhart, Bob 199
Newman, Barry 207
Newman, Paul 49–50, **50**, 138, **138**
Newsday 67
"A Nice Little Till to Tap" (*Honey West*) 237
A Nice, Pleasant, Deadly Weekend see *A Masterpiece of Murder*
Nicholson, Jack 121
Nickell, Paul 159
"Nicki's Parents" (*The Drew Carey Show*) 227
"Nicki's Wedding" (*The Drew Carey Show*) 227
Nielsen, Leslie 43, **44**, 46–47, **47**, 110, 135, **136**, **137**, **138**, 170
"Night Life" (*The Wide World of Mystery*) 199, **200**
"Night of the Owls, Day of the Doves" (*Kung Fu*) 203–204
Nimoy, Leonard 198
Nixon, President Richard 110
Nolan, Jeanette 174
Nolan, Lloyd 58, 59, **62**
Norris, Christopher 212
North, Edmund 105
North, Sheree 97
The North Adams, Massachusetts, Transcript 160

Nostalgia Digest 5, 11
The Nurses 121

The Oakland Tribune 60, 159
O'Brian, Hugh 99–100, *102*
O'Brien, Margaret 7
O'Brien, Richard 47
O'Connell, Arthur 100
O'Connor, Glynnis 110
O'Connor, Tim 202, 215
O'Dell, Cary 5, 6
O. Henry's Full House 20
O'Herlihy, Dan 109
Ohmart, Carol 11, *12*, 156
Ohta, Bennett 210
"Ole Island Oprey" (*Fantasy Island*) 216
Oliver, Susan 218
O'Loughlin, Gerald S. *171*
Olson, Nancy 7, 30
O'Malley 213–214
On the Waterfront 11
"The One That Got Away" (*The Fugitive*) 188
One Way Ticket see *One Way Ticket to Hell*
One Way Ticket to Hell 22, 33
Oppenheimer, Jess 160
Orr, William T. 180
Orsatti, Victor M. 139
"Our American Heritage: Autocrat and Son" (*Sunday Showcase*) 164, *164*
Out of Her League 121–122
Outward Bound 106
"The Owl and the Eye" (*Honey West*) 229–230

Pacific Stars and Stripes 17–18
The Palladium-Times 162
Pancho Villa 95, *106*, 107–108, 148
Panoramic Productions 25
Pappas, Leona 100
Parents 78
Parker, Eleanor 8
Parker, Jameson 85, 120, 217, 224
Parkins, Barbara 83
Parks, Bert 236
Parrish, Helen 159
Parsons, Louella 20, 32–33, 50
Partners in Crime 114, 219–220
Password All-Stars 196
Patton 105
Paulist Productions 192
Paulson, Rev. Sig 113
Payne, Alexander 121
Pearson, Jesse 180
Peck, Gregory 20
Penny, Joe 116, 117, *117*, 219, 222–223
Penton, Edgar 182
"People Cry at Stations" 53
Peppard, George 202, *202*
Pera, Radames 203
Perera, Lydia 6
"The Perfect Un-Crime" (*Honey West*) 238
The Perils of Pauline 242

"Perished Leaves" (*Lux Video Theatre*) 159
Perry, Roger 195
The Perry Como Show 159
Perry Mason 196
Peters, Jean 14
Peters, Kelly Jean 204
Peterson, Edgar I. 222
Petrocelli 207
Peyton Place 83
Phantom Lady 13
Phillips, Dorothy 11, *12*, 156
Photoplay 19
"Physician, Heal Thyself" (*Quincy M.E.*) 213
Picerni, Paul 192
Pickens, Slim 109
Picon, Molly 211–212
Pidgeon, Walter 42, 43, *44*, 46, 88, *90*, *136*, *137*, 138, 183
Pillot, Judd 17
Pillot, Leo 17
Platinum High School 132
"Play It Glissando" (*Route 66*) 168
Plummer, Christopher 164
Poitier, Sidney 40, 41
Police Woman 1, 3, 208, *209*, 209–210
"Pom Pom Angels" (*Charlie's Angels*) 1, 110, 212–213
Poor Little Rich Girl: The Barbara Hutton Story 114, 154
"Pop Goes the Easel" (*Honey West*) 241
Porter, Don 204
Portrait of Jennie 7–8, 124
The Post-Standard 124, 162
Potter, Peter 54
Potts, Annie 121
Powell, Dick 26, 27, *28*, 68, 131
Powell, Jane 7
Power, Tyrone *21*, 109, 128
The Power and the Prize 42
Powers, Robert 5
Powers, Stefanie 2
Praeger, Superior Court Judge Arnold 63
Prelle, Micheline 14
"Presence of the Enemy" (*Studio One*) 159
Price, Bamlet Lawrence, Jr. 22–23, 25, 30, 32–33, 50
Price, Vincent 95
"The Price of Loving" (*Movin' On*) 204, *205*
Prince, Jonathan 120–121
Prince of Tides 94
Prince Valiant 19
"The Princess and the Paupers" (*Honey West*) 231–232
Prinz, Rosemary 118
"The Prisoner Song" 241
Prohaska, Janos 194
Pulver, Enid 124

"The Quadripartite Affair" (*The Man from U.N.C.L.E.*) 183–184
"Queen of the Boston Bruisers" (*Fantasy Island*) 110, 212

"Queen of the Orange Bowl" (*The United States Steel Hour*) 162
"Queen's Gambit" (*Assignment: Vienna*) 197, *198*
"The Quest" (*Dallas*) 215
"The Quick and the Dead" 172
Quincy M.E. 213
Quinlan, Kathleen 121
Quintero, Jose 100

"Rachel's Mother" (*The Reporter*) 182–183
The Rack 49–50, *50*, 136–138
"The Rack" (*The United States Steel Hour*) 137–138
Rackin, Marty 84
Radio Mirror 7, 13
Raft, George 31, *32*, *133*
Ralph, Sheryl Lee 156
"Ransom" (*The F.B.I.*) 201
Rapp, Carl *106*
Rawhide 161–162, *161*
Ray, Aldo 30, 31
Razaf, Andy 168
The Rebels 112, *112*, 151
Redford, Robert 171
Reed, Alan 239
Reed, Robert 106
Reese, Allen 122
Remick, Lee 109
Remote Asylum 100
The Reporter 64, 181–183
Return 114, 152–153
Reynolds, Burt 47, 96, *98*, 144–145, 195
Reynolds, Debbie 26–27, 51, *131*
Rhodes, Donnelly 186, *186*
Rice, Dan 120
Rich, Allen 79, 83, 86
Rich Man, Poor Man 112
Richards, Jeff 33, 51
Richardson, Patricia 226
Richman, Peter Mark 222
Riesner, Dean 87
Rigg, Diana 1
Riptide 116–118, *117*, 218–219
"The Rival Dummy" (*Studio One*) 157–158
Robbie, Seymour 190
Roberts, Kenneth 14, 128
Roberts, Pernell 215
Roberts, Tanya 224
Robertson, Cliff 100
Robertson, Dale 15, 16, *16*, 20
Robinson, J. Dennis 12
"Rock Around the Clock" 38
"Rockabye the Hard Way" (*Honey West*) 236–237
The Rocket Man 25–26, *25*, 129–130
The Rocky Horror Picture Show 47
The Rocky Horror Show 47
Rogers, Ginger 19, 129
Rogers, Wayne 192
Rogue Cop 31–32, *32*, 42, 132, 133
Roman, Ruth 172
"Romiet and Julio" (*The Littlest Hobo*) 214
Rooney, Mickey 7, 38, 131, 214

Roosevelt, Eleanor 5–6
Rorvic Productions 139
Rose, Helen 44
Rose, Norman 60
Rosemary 5
Rosen, Burt 240
Rosen, Debbie 240
Route 66 168–170, *169*
Rouverol, Jean 9
Rubin, Mann 67
Rubinstein, John 220, *221*
Rubinstein, Zelda 156
Rudolph, Oscar 26
Rule, Janice 19, 56
Runaway see *So Young So Bad*
Rupe, John 6
Rush, Barbara 19
Ruth, Daniel 118, 153, 217
Ryan, Robert 5, 34, 36

Sacchi, Robert 85, 224, 225
"Sacraments" (*Nash Bridges*) 226–227
Sager, Carole Bayer 222
Saint, Eva Marie 11, 156
The San Antonio Express 175
Sanders, George 41, 46
"Santa, Santa, Santa"/ "Another
   Dog Gone Christmas" / "Noel's
   Christmas Carol" (*The Love
   Boat*) 219
"Sarah" (*Gunsmoke*) 197
Sasso, Joey 112
The Satan Bug 64–65, *66*, 69,
   140–141
"The Saucer" (*The Invaders*) 188–189, *189*
Savalas, Telly *106*, 107, 108
Saxon, John 86
"Scag" (*Bert D'Angelo/Superstar*)
   208
Scala, Gia *54*, 139
The Scarlet Coat 41–42, *41*, *42*, 46,
   135
Schaal, Richard 194
Schaal, Wendy 216
Schary, Dore 38, 40, 45, 48, 49
Schary, Miriam 45
Schenck, Nicholas M. 38
Schnee, Charles 56
Schott, Marge 121–122
Schreiber, Lou 21
Schuck, John 204
Schwarzenegger, Arnold 226
"Science Fiction/Double Feature"
   47
Scott, Vernon 51, 55–56, 57, 87,
   88, 92, 102, 105
Scourby, Alexander 55
"Scream in Silence" (*Climax!*) 159
Search 197–198, 225
Searls, Hank 56
Segal, Alex 137
Segal, Vivienne 167
Sellecca, Connie 211, *211*
Selznick, David O. 7
Serling, Rod 49, 56, 137, 167
Seven, Johnny *145*
77 Sunset Strip 224

"Shadow of Sam Penny" (*Simon &
   Simon*) 217–218, *217*
"Shadows" (*Without a Trace*) 122,
   228
Shakespeare, William 43
Shales, Tom 223
Shalhoub, Tony 225
Sharaff, Irene 88
Sharif, Omar 90
Shatner, William 100
Shaw, Irwin 112
Sheen, Martin 109
Shepherd, Cybill 84
Sherman, Bobby 232
Shindig 232
"The Shiny Toy" see "The Saucer"
Shockley, Sallie 193
"Short Fuse" (*Columbo*) 196
Side Show 67
Sidney, George 34
"Silent Night, Deadly Night"
   (*S.W.A.T.*) 207
Silliphant, Stirling 168
Silver Street 103
Simmons, Jean 14
Simon & Simon 114, 217–218, *217*,
   224
Simpson, O.J. *114*
Sinclair, William 200
Siodmak, Robert 12, 13
Sitting Pretty 129
"Slay, Gypsy, Slay" (*Honey West*)
   240
"Slim Chance" (*Trapper John,
   M.D.*) 215
Sloane, Everett 232, *232*
Smidge see Smidgeon, Walter
Smidgeon, Walter 50, *51*, 56, *58*,
   64
Smith, Jaclyn 120
Smith, Kevin Burton 70
The Snatching of Little Freddie see
   The Young Runaways
The Snows of Kilimanjaro 20–22
So Young So Bad 8–11, *9*, *11*, 13,
   124, *126*
Sommer, Elke 78
The Sound of Hunting 55
South Pacific 60
The Southern Illinoisan 164
Sowards, Jack B. 108
Space Patrol 160
Spada, James 91
Spelling, Aaron 67, 68, 80, 85,
   224
Sperling, Cass Warner 62
The Spiral Staircase 13
"S'posin'" 168
Staab, Rebecca 223
Stack, Robert 165, 190, 191
Stagecoach 84
Stanley, John 3
Stanwyck, Barbara 50, 51, 83, *84*
Stanyard, Stewart T. 166, 167
Stanzas to Augusta 181
Star Search 221
Stark, Ray 87, 88
"The Starlet" (*Matlock*) 223
Starlog 79, 81, 238

Steel Magnolias 118, 223
Steiner, Max 134
Sterling, Robert 167
Stern, Harold 82
The Steve Allen Show 191
Stevens, Connie 224
Stevens, Kami 240
Stevens, Stella *115*
Stevens, Warren *44*
Stiff as a Broad 70, 76, 78
Stinson, Charles 60
"A Stitch in Crime" (*Columbo*) 198
"A Stitch in Crime" (*Honey West*)
   233–234
Stock, Amy 221
Stockwell, Dean 7
Stone, Oliver 80
Strauss, Kim 224
Strauss, Robert 186
Streisand, Barbra 87–92, *90*, 94,
   94, 142
Streisand: Her Life 90
Studio One 11, 157–158, 159
Sturges, John 35, 37, 41, 65, 132
Styne, Jule 87
The Subterraneans 56
Sullivan, Barry 97
Sullivan, Liam 50, 233
Summer Holiday 7, 123–124
Sun Valley Serenade 162
"A Sunday Kind of Love" 168
Sunday Showcase 164, *164*
Survival 97–98, 149
Susan Slept Here 26–27, *26–28*,
   28, 130–132, *131*
The Suspect 13
Suspense 11, 158
S.W.A.T. 207
Swerling, Jo 116
"The Swinger" (*Fantasy Island*)
   214
"The Swingin' Mrs. Jones" (*Honey
   West*) 80, 228–229
Swink, Robert 92
Syracuse Herald Journal 236, 239,
   241

*Tab Hunter Confidential: The Mak-
   ing of a Movie Star* 31
Take Care of My Little Girl 19
Talcove, Rick 100
Tamblyn, Russ 33
Tashlin, Frank 26
Taylor, Buck 181
Taylor, Don 33, 100
Taylor, Elizabeth 7, 30, 55, 184
Taylor, Robert 31, 32, 38, 42, 50,
   62, *133*, 135
Taylor, Rod 168, *169*
Teenage Devil Dolls see *One Way
   Ticket to Hell*
The Tempest 43
Temple Houston 64, 179–180, *179*
"Ten Rounds for Baby" (*Temple
   Houston*) 179–180, *179*
The Tender Trap 96
"Terror by the Book" (*Petrocelli*)
   207
Than, Joseph 9

"Theater of Fear" (*Barnaby Jones*) 205–207, **206**
"There's a Long, Long, Fuse A'Burning" (*Honey West*) 242
Theron, Charlize 85
The Thin Man (TV) 50
Thinnes, Roy 189, **189**
"The Third Commandment" (*Kaleidoscope*) 160
35th Annual Las Floristas Headdress Ball 199
This Girl for Hire 70, 72
This Time for Keeps 7, 123, 124
Thomas, Bob 98
Thomas, Brandon 217
Thomas, Frankie, Jr. 158
Thomas, Kevin 156
Thompson, Howard 145
Thompson, Marshall 137, **163**
Tierney, Gene 20
"Till Death Do We Volley" (*The Golden Girls*) 223
Tilton, Charlene 216
The Today Show 116, 204
Tomb Raider 85
Tourneur, Jacques 14
Toussaint, Lorraine 121
Towers, Constance 118
Tracy, Spencer 34, 35, 36, 132, **134**
The Trailmakers 99
The Transcript 109, 194
"The Trap" (*The Alfred Hitchcock Hour*) 186
Trapper John, M.D. 114, 215, 218
Travilla, William 21
Trevey, Ken 110
True Confessions 222
"The Tryst" (*Ford Theatre*) 159
Tucker, Madge 5, 6
Tucson Daily Citizen 60, 92, 103, 172
Turner, Lana 122
Turner, Robert 167
TV Guide 20, 33, 78
TV Week 79, 80, 81
The Twilight Zone 3, 53, 55, 56, 64, 165–167, **166**, 174–175, **174**
"The Twist of the Key" (*The David Niven Show*) 160
Two on a Guillotine 66

The United States Steel Hour 137, 162, 167
The Untouchables 165
Urich, Robert 212
Uris, Leon 30

Vadeboncoeur, Joan E. 65, 80
Valentino, Rudolph 241
Van Dreelen, John 184, 190
Van Dyke, Dick 96
Van Horn, Buddy 79
Van Horne, Harriet 164
"The Vanished Man" (*Archer*) 204

Van Nuys News 100
Variety 24, 49, 60, 225
Vasche, Mark 103
Vaughn, Robert 184
Vega$ 98, 211–212
Vendetta see *Pancho Villa*
Versatile Varieties 11–12, **12**, 156–157, **157**
Video View 217
Villechaize, Hervé 212
The Virginian 64, 185–186, **185**, 193–194
Voedisch, Lynn 60, 118
Voices from Home: An Inner Journey 5, 6, 8, 10, 13, 15, 16, 22, 57, 99, 113, 116
Von Stroheim, Erich 157
Vorhaus, Bernard 8, 9, 10
Voyage to the Bottom of the Sea 65

"Waiting for Onorio" (*Lux Video Theatre*) 159
Walker, Clint 95, **96**, **106**, 107–108, **143**
Wallace, Chris 116
Walsh, Kate 227
Walsh, Raoul 24, 30
Ward, Sela 121
Warden, Jack 220, **221**
Warfield, Marsha 219
Warner, Jack 62
Warren, Harry 162
Warren, Jennifer 109
Warwick, Dionne 222
The Washington Post 223
Wayne, David 205
Weaver, Dennis 103
Weaver, Tom 2, 7, 20, 34, 36, 42, 43, 44, 45, 46, 47, 53, 64, 65, 66, 79, 81, 83, 91, 116, 167, 238
Webb, Clifton 17, 18–19, 29, **127**, 128, 129
Webb, Jack 180
Webber, Robert 110, 177
Webster, Ferris 37, 65
Weidman, Jerome 183
Weis, Don 196
Welch, Raquel 85, 88
Wendkos, Paul 230
Werts, Diane 67–68
"What Really Happened" (*The Alfred Hitchcock Hour*) 64, **64**, 172
What Really Happened to the Class of '65? 213
"Whatever Lola Wants ..." (*Honey West*) 231
When a Girl Marries 6, 7
"When Does a War End?" (*Hawaii Five-O*) 210
The Whistle at Eaton Falls 12–13, **13**, 125–126
Whitmore, James 30
"Who Killed Nick Hazard?" (*Burke's Law*) 85, 224–225

"Who Killed the Jackpot?" (*Burke's Law*) 69–70, 78, 80, 186–187, 231
"Who Killed Wade Walker?" (*Burke's Law*) 69, 177
Widdoes, James 217
Wide World of Entertainment see *The Wide World of Mystery*
The Wide World of Mystery 199, 200, **200**
Widmark, Richard 20
The Wild Wild West 81
Wild Women 99–100, **102**, 146
Wilde, Cornel 41, **41**, 42, **42**, 135
Wilder Days 120
Wilding, Michael 41–42, **42**, 135
Williams, Andy 194
Williams, Esther 7
Williams, Tennessee 41, 55
Williams, Van **179**, 180
Willis, Bruce 84
Winchell, Walter 165
Windom, William 194
Windsor, Marie 100
Wings 120, 225
Winnipeg Free Press 128
Winslow, George 26
Winwood, Estelle 199
"With Deadly Sorrow" (*Hong Kong*) 168, **169**
"With the Rich and Mighty, Always a Little Patience" (*Ben Casey*) 175
Witherspoon, Reese 85
Without a Trace 122, 228
"The Witnesses" (*Arrest & Trial*) 177, **177**
Witt, Kathryn 211, **211**
Woman's World 20
Women Who Run the Show 106
Wonder Woman 1, 98, 208
The Wonderful World of Disney 62, 110, 187
Wood, Natalie 7
Wouldn't It Be Great If... 197
Wylder, Robert C. 100
Wyler, William 87, 91, 92, 142
Wyman, Jane 6
Wynter, Dana 55

Yordan, Philip 107, 108
You Don't Say 180, 187, 190
"You Took Advantage of Me" 223
Young, Otis 98
Young, Robert 160
The Young Runaways 110, 150
"You're Gonna Hear from Me" 224
"The Yum Yum Girl" (*The United States Steel Hour*) 167

Zanuck, Darryl F. 13, 14, 21, 30
Zimbalist, Efrem, Jr. 217
Zimet, Julian 107